Editorial Manager	Chester Fisher
Senior Editor	Lynne Sabel
Editor	John Rowlstone
Assistant Editor	Bridget Daly
Series Designers	QED (Alastair Campbell and Edward Kinsey)
Designers	Jim Marks Nigel Osborne
Series Consultant	Keith Lye
Consultant	Peter Clayton
Production	Penny Kitchenham
Picture Research	Jenny de Gex

First published 1978
Reprinted 1979
Macdonald Educational Ltd.
Holywell House
Worship Street
London EC2A 2EN

2081/3200
ISBN 0 356 05762 3

Designed and created in
Great Britain

Printed and bound by
New Interlitho, Italy

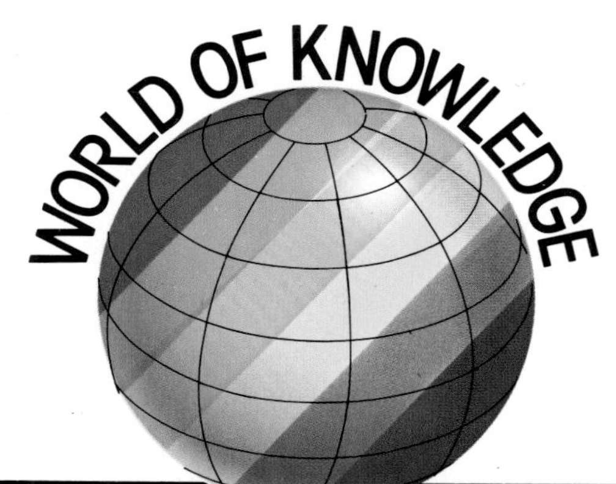

The Coming of Civilization

Ron Carter

Macdonald

Contents

Early Civilizations

The Spread of Civilization

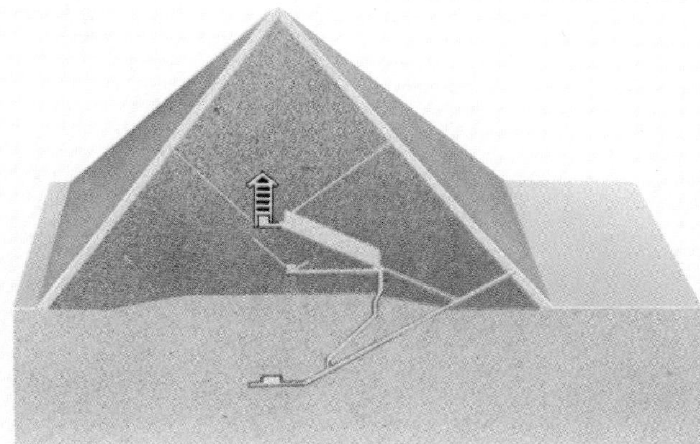

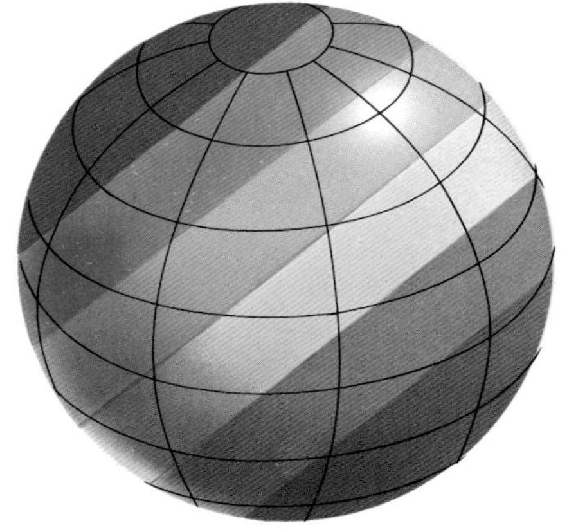

World of Knowledge

This book breaks new ground in the method it uses to present information to the reader. The unique page design combines narrative with an alphabetical reference section and it uses colourful photographs, diagrams and illustrations to provide an instant and detailed understanding of the book's theme. The main body of information is presented in a series of chapters that cover, in depth, the subject of this book. At the bottom of each page is a reference section which gives, in alphabetical order, concise articles which define, or enlarge on, the topics discussed in the chapter. Throughout the book, the use of SMALL CAPITALS in the text directs the reader to further information that is printed in the reference section. The same method is used to cross-reference entries within each reference section. Finally, there is a comprehensive index at the end of the book that will help the reader find information in the text, illustrations and reference sections. The quality of the text, and the originality of its presentation, ensure that this book can be read both for enjoyment and for the most up-to-date information on the subject.

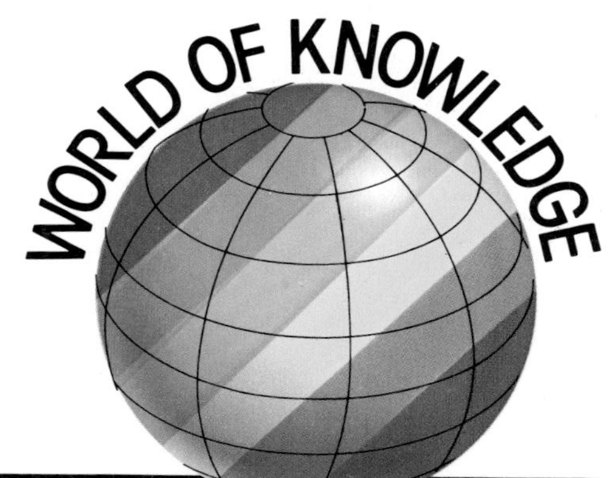

Early Civilizations

Ron Carter

Introduction

Early Civilizations covers a broad timespan of human history, from the emergence of early man to the creation of great civilizations in Mesopotamia, around the Mediterranean Sea and, farther afield, in eastern Asia. Early history involves dramatic accounts of the rise and fall of warring nations led by powerful kings and brilliant generals, and also of tremendous breakthroughs in science and technology, art and architecture, and philosophy and religion. But, of equal importance, there is the story of how ordinary people lived, worked and worshipped and how they were affected by new ideas and inventions. One of the most exciting aspects involved in the study of ancient history is that archaeologists are forever digging up new evidence about the distant past and **Early Civilizations** reflects the latest knowledge and the most recent theories about the origins of our cultural heritage.

No-one can say exactly what constitutes a civilization, nor can one say exactly when a civilization emerged or declined. Here, the historical pattern of 32 peoples shows the already complex world that had evolved by AD 1600.

Timechart

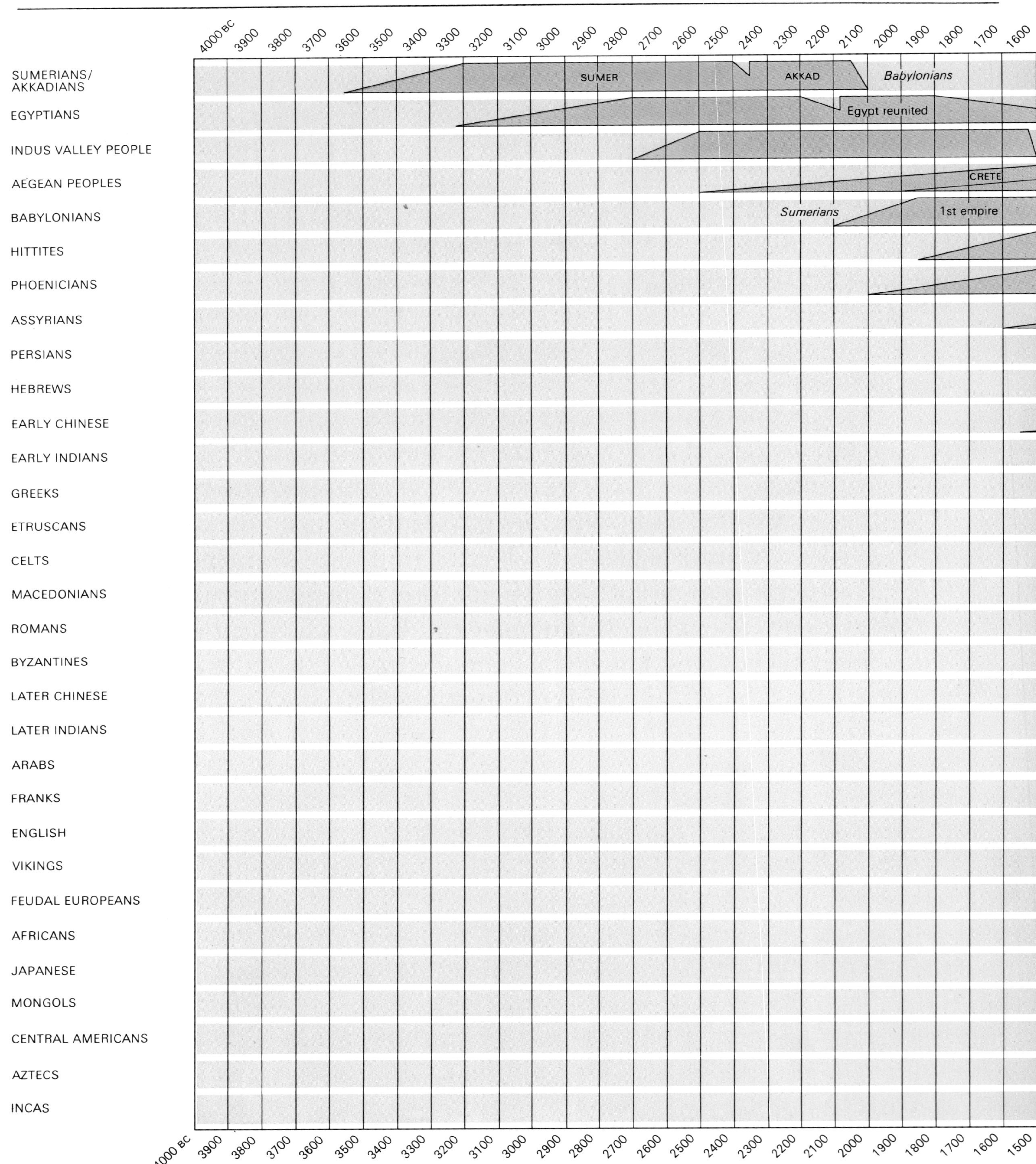

Below: This chart shows when the world's civilizations emerged, flourished and declined. All of them developed over a long period before reaching their peaks and each civilization was unique. Some declined and disappeared slowly, like the Aegean and the Byzantine. Others, like the Assyrian and the Aztec, ended abruptly following military disaster. Some civilizations owed much to earlier, barely-known predecessors. For example, the Maya owed much to the Olmecs and the Babylonians inherited their civilization from the Sumerians. Some civilizations flourished again after long decline. These included the Egyptian, Babylonian, Chinese and Indian, which all survived foreign domination. Some early civilizations, including the Hebrew, Arab, French and Japanese have, in different ways, continued into present times. The Hebrew civilization was tiny; the Mongol vast. Persia, Han China and Rome were roughly comparable. The Inca civilization lasted 2 generations; the Egyptian, over 100. (Italics are used to show connections with earlier or later civilizations.)

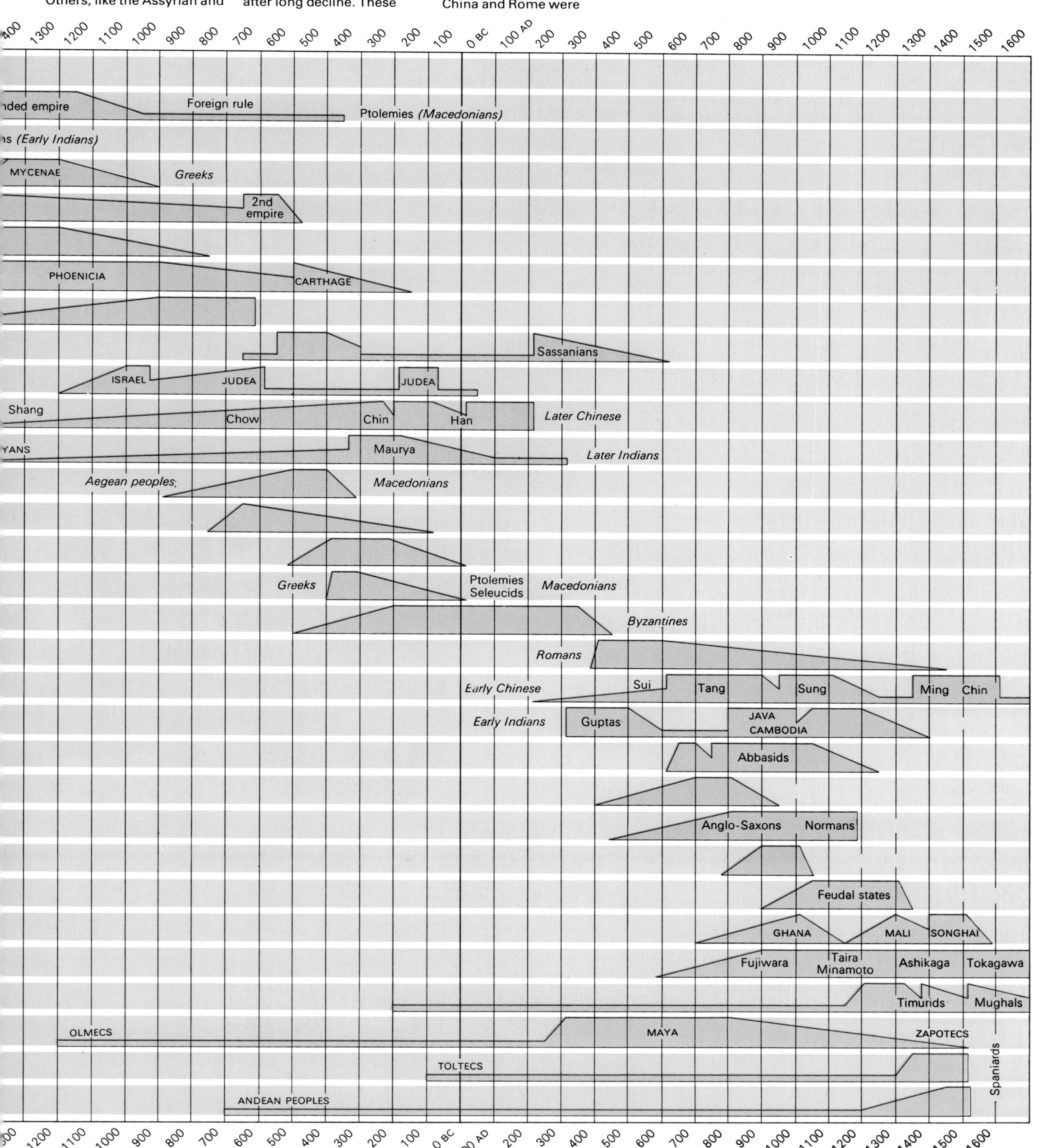

Our knowledge of the life-style and technology of early man has been pieced together by the work of archaeologists and anthropologists. New discoveries are being made all the time, filling in more pieces of the jigsaw puzzle.

Early Man

No one knows when the first true men appeared on earth. A remote ancestor of man *(Ramapithecus)* who lived in India some 14 million years ago, used sticks and stones as simple weapons. About five million years ago, man-like ape, known as AUSTRALOPITHECUS, lived in south and east Africa.

Early men

Between two and three million years ago, two types of upright, walking men, *1470 man* and *Ethiopian man,* lived in EAST AFRICA and had more advanced brains than those of any known previous species. They chipped flakes off stones to make sharp cutting edges and the Stone Age culture that they began, dominated the world until a few thousand years ago. Some scientists think they may have been our direct ancestors, but we have no certain knowledge of who our ancestors were, and we cannot be sure that all present-day men are descended from common ancestors.

Several other kinds of men lived nearer our own times. *Homo erectus* (Upright man) used fire and hunted animals over large areas of Africa, Europe and Asia perhaps 500,000 years ago. Physically, he probably had the power of speech, but we can never know to what extent he used it. *Homo sapiens* (Wise man), who lived in Denmark, Germany and England about 250,000 years ago, had a skull similar to ours in shape. One of several varieties of *Homo sapiens,* NEANDERTHAL MAN, dominated Europe 30,000 to 70,000 years ago (between the last two Ice Ages).

About 35,000 years ago, *Homo sapiens sapiens* (our own sub-species), had firmly established himself. One of his groups, CRO-MAGNON man, migrated from south-eastern Asia into France, Italy and north Africa, where he survived until 10,000 years ago. We do not know whether these early peoples mated outside their own sub-species or groups. Nor do we know why they did not survive. Climatic change, conflict between rival groups, or changes in the available food supply may all in turn have contributed to their doom.

Through evolution, our own sub-species seems to have divided into three main 'RACES': Caucasoids, Mongoloids and Negroids. Examples from each group are: Europeans and Indians; Chinese and Japanese; and Africans. However, most of the world's peoples are mixtures of these 'races'.

Below: Stone Age man survived by adapting to his environment and making use of the materials to hand. *Left,* a boy helps his father to chip flints into tools. *Centre,* 2 men shape tree branches into spears. *Right,* 3 men take to the water on a raft. *Right,* a man prepares antlers and tusks for future use. Expertly-made axes lie in front of him. Simple tents give protection against the cold night.

Reference

A **Aborigines of Australia** provide an interesting example of Stone Age people observed by man in the AD 1800s. They probably migrated from south-eastern Asia into Australia over 30,000 years ago, before the sea covered the land bridging New Guinea to Australia. When the British landed in Australia in 1788, the Aborigines numbered about 300,000. Yet they comprised more than 5,000 tribes speaking 300 different languages. Men used spears, harpoons, hooks, traps, nets, clubs and boomerangs to hunt animals and catch fish. They also smoked out animals and, like the ancient Americans, caught fish by drugging them with the juices of certain leaves and roots. Women and children collected roots, fruits, edible insects and honey. The Aborigines used stone and plant and animal materials skilfully. They carried fire-sticks and other tools in *dilly bags* woven from human hair, grasses and bark fibres. In hunting, they often disguised themselves or covered their bodies with mud to hide their smell from their prey. They wrapped babies in tree bark for warmth, and rubbed their own bodies with animal fats against the cold. Their art portrayed myths and legends and geometrical designs. Stylized dances imitated the movements of a tribe's totem animal or bird. Their musical instruments included DIDGERIDOOS AND BULL-ROARERS. Their religion included the belief in a DREAMTIME. The Aborigines' religion involved complex rituals, ceremonies and magic. Their witch doctors treated physical and mental illnesses skilfully.

Spanish cave paintings

Animals of importance to men 15,000 years ago included reindeer, mammoths, horses and bison. CRO-MAGNON men drew pictures of mammoths on the walls of caves in France.

Art may have begun when men scratched or painted over shadows on cave walls. The first artists then found that they could represent 3-dimensional animals and objects 2-dimensionally. This new ability gave scope to record ideas or preserve pictorially what they saw. Some of the earliest-known animal pictures were en-

Basic necessities of life

Early men gathered fruits, nuts, berries and other edible plant products. They also trapped fish and animals, devising increasingly cunning ways of doing so. They made simple WEAPONS and developed tactics to outwit their prey. About 400,000 years ago they found, probably by accident, that fire, if controlled, could be used to cook meat and other food. Control of fire gave man an even greater advantage over hostile animals.

Early man frequently migrated in the hope of finding suitable land, but whatever the conditions, he always needed to protect himself against bad weather, contrasting temperatures between day and night, and seasonal extremes. CLOTHES and shelter became increasingly complex, where holes in the ground or caves were not always available or suitable. Where possible, men made simple tents from branches and skins, or more durable structures of wood or stone. Walls or

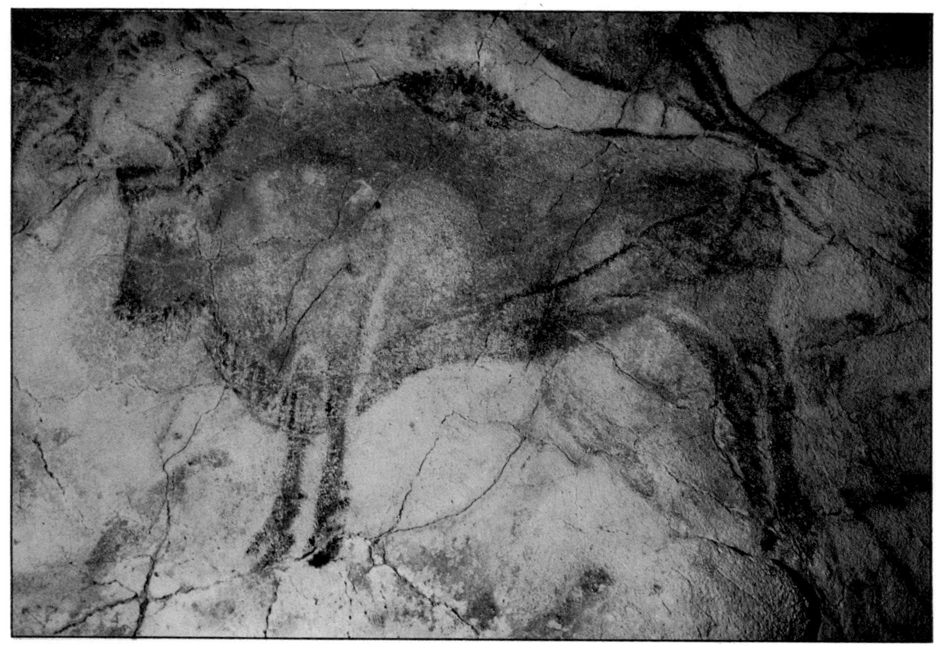

Above: Altamira cave paintings of the Magdalenian people show the advanced stage of art in Spain before 1200 BC.

graved about 27,000 years ago on rock in the Lascaux caves, France. Magic may have inspired art. Possibly artists believed that food-supplying animals would increase if depicted on cave walls.

Australopithecus (southern ape) lived about 4–5 million years ago. He walked upright and probably used bones and stones for immediate purposes before discarding and forgetting them. His remains have been found as far afield as Africa, China, Java and the Middle East.

B

Bones provided an easily-worked material. The earliest known Chinese characters are written on skull bones preserved in the National Museum, Taiwan.

Aborigine with a boomerang

Boomerangs, curved, slightly L-shaped sticks made by some ABORIGINES OF AUSTRALIA, proved effective weapons in hunting and war. There were 3 kinds. *Returning boomerangs* were used in contests of skill and for deflecting birds in flight so that they swooped down, to be scooped into a net. *Non-returning boomerangs,* when thrown accurately, killed or maimed human enemies, animals, reptiles, birds and fish. *Ritual boomerangs,* decorated with secret symbols, were used in dance-mime-song performances and ceremonies. The ancient Egyptians and Hopi 'Indians' of north America also used boomerangs.

C

Civilization is a word that man, throughout his history, has tried to define. In the broadest sense it can be taken to mean a group of people living together, socially and technically in advance of simple hunters. If, in some great world clock true man arrived 24 hours ago, civilization began within the last 5 minutes. An 80-year-old person of today has already lived through one-eightieth of the entire span of civilization.

Clans, social groups composed of several families, supposedly descended from a common ancestor. Several clans may form a *tribe.* An intermediate group is called a *phratry.*

Clothes of early man became increasingly sophisticated. Skins were sewn together with needles of bone and thread from sinews of animals and teeth or shells sometimes decorated the

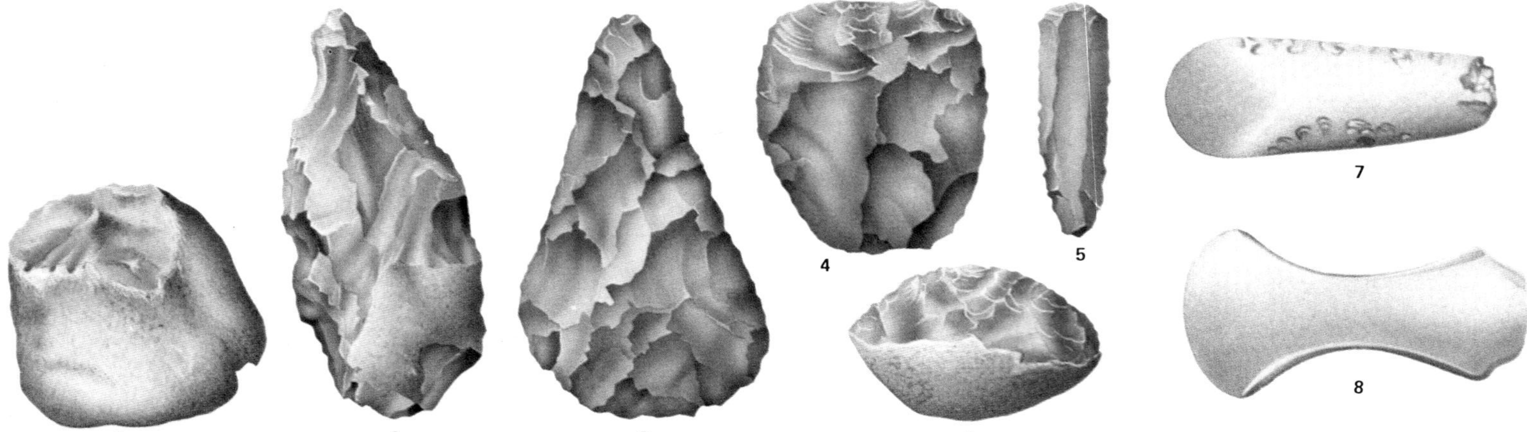

Above: The varied tools of Stone Age man included: **1** pebble chopper (Olduvai Gorge, Tanzania); **2** primitive pointed hand axe with unrefined zig-zag flaking along edge (Fardwick, Kent, U.K.); **3** pointed hand axe (Swanscombe, Kent, U.K.); **4** flaking tool with carefully trimmed edge (Northfleet, Kent, U.K.); **5** knife chopper (Dordogne, France): **6** scraping tool (Dordogne, France); **7** polished axe of the New Stone Age (Mildenhall, Suffolk, U.K.); **8** stone battle axe of the early Bronze Age (Battersea, London, U.K.).

fences supplemented or replaced fire as defences against human or animal marauders.

Perhaps the most important step in man's advance to CIVILIZATION came when he learned to farm. That is, when he sowed seeds to raise crops and domesticated farm ANIMALS. This probably happened in the Middle East about 11,000 years ago, when the taming of the horse is thought to have occurred.

Beginnings of technology

Men's first vehicles were probably the floating logs they clung to, to escape being washed away. Later, they scooped out logs to make early canoes and controlled them with crude paddles. Wooden rollers and levers were used to move heavy stones into position, and large rafts were built to float them downstream. The Sumerians of Mesopotamia used sledges to transport people and materials. With the invention of wheels, animals trained to carry goods could be harnessed to carts.

Man found his earliest materials easily enough. Wood, rushes or earth lay all around him. Dead animals provided furs, skins, BONES, horns and ivory. The need to slice meat and cut and shape materials encouraged men to make the first tools, the earliest being easily-made wooden or bone types. Then men chipped stones into crude knives, axes, hammers and weapons. Flint made the best tools: it could be easily worked into shape and so these were probably the most precious possessions of early people. The first New Stone Age men appeared less than 10,000 years ago in the Middle East. Their improved tools included polished stone axes and flint sickles which were attached to lower jawbones taken from suitable animals. About 8,500 years ago, people in present-day Turkey and Iran began working copper, but the first bronzesmiths did not appear until civilization had been established in Mesopotamia for 1,000 years.

Social groups

The family pre-dated man: animals had grouped themselves into families long before he emerged. Human families probably comprised three generations, although grandparents would be fortunate to survive beyond their mid-30s. Despite enmities and rivalries, relatives had great incentives to stay together in bands. Large families constituted strong defence units, provided that they did not outstrip available food supplies.

Like animal groups, each tribe looked upon a certain area as its own territory, to be exploited for water, food, shelter and materials. As the human population grew by MIGRATION or natural increase, tribes had to defend their territories against invaders. Inflexible 'laws' governed relationships between members of different tribes and even more rigid rules dictated relationships within each tribe. Certain kinds of behaviour were *taboo,* meaning that they violated a tribe's rules and were therefore banned.

Development of religious ideas

When a tribe numbered several hundred people, the *idea* of it as a social group, rather than as a number of individuals, became difficult to comprehend. To solve this problem, some tribes chose symbols to represent them, for example one group became perhaps the Bear tribe, clearly

---

hems and cuffs of skin garments. Necklaces and bracelets of teeth, shells, mother-of-pearl, and fishbone were carved with intricate patterns.

Counting probably began with the body, which provided a 'ready reckoner'. People noticed that they had 1 nose, 2 hands, 4 limbs, 5 fingers on each hand, and 20 fingers and toes. It was no accident that the system of numbers given to the world by the Indian mathematicians was based on 10, or that the Central Americans used a *vigesimal* system of numbering, based on 20s.

Cro-Magnon. Some of the earliest remains of modern man, *Homo sapiens sapiens* were found at Cro-Magnon, in the Dordogne area of south-western France. Cro-Magnon man survived until 10,000 years ago.

D

Dancing and singing gave outlets for people's emotional needs probably before speech developed. So perhaps did the drum, which may have been the first musical instrument.

Didgeridoos and bullroarers, musical instruments made and played by the ABORIGINES OF AUSTRALIA give an insight into Stone Age music. Didgeridoos are drone pipes made from hollowed wood and painted with secret, sacred designs. By using his lips and tongue, a player created animal or bird-like noises. He maintained a continual sound by breathing in through the nose, while at the same time he breathed out through the mouth. Bullroarers are thin, flat pieces of wood attached to cords. Whirled around the head they make a whirring noise, supposedly the voice of an ancestral spirit. Strict religious rules governed the use of both these instruments.

Dreamtime, in translation, is the Australian Aborigine's term for the beginning, when all things were created. They believe that spirits of the unborn come from the Dreamtime and return there at death.

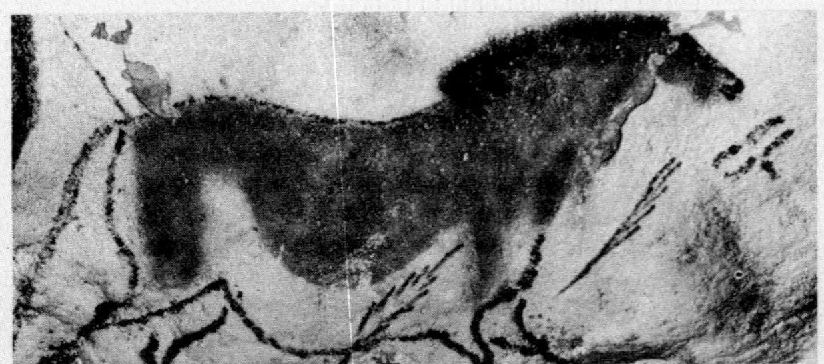

Lascaux Caves painting, Dordogne, France

Left: This stone monument is the Dolmen de Kercadoret in Brittany, France. 'Dolmen' is the term used for a type of prehistoric structure that was built as a burial chamber in the Neolithic period. There are many fine examples in Britain and France.

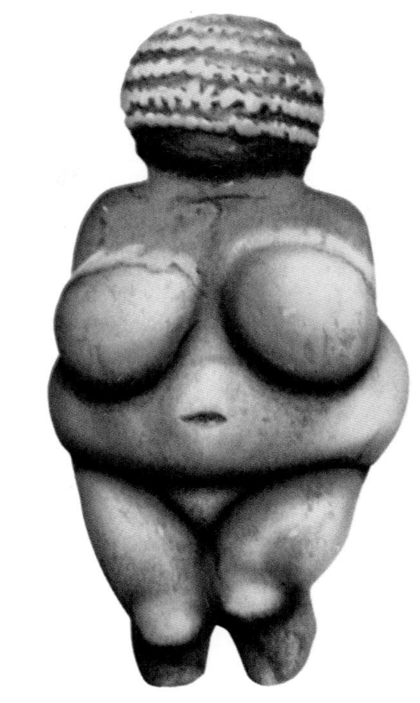

Right: The 'Venus of Willendorf' (Austria) is one of the earliest known works of art. It is a limestone figure, 10 cm high carved perhaps 25,000 years ago to symbolize fertility.

distinguished from the neighbouring Crow people. The images of bear and crow would be the *totems,* or emblems, of the two tribes. Much later, the 'Red Indians' of North America and the Polynesians in New Zealand erected poles with their totems at the top.

Certain natural features within the tribal territory or on the horizon came to be regarded with awe. Natural phenomena such as volcanic eruptions, thunder, lightning, rain, sun, moon and stars, seemed to possess overwhelming power in their own right. Aware of their comparative inferiority, men worshipped them as super-beings, or deities. One deity in particular, the Storm god in the storm-swept Hittite empire, became the chief god. Dead, or even living, leaders became gods in their own right.

Witch doctors emerged, to become the keepers, enforcers and interpreters of tribal behaviour, tradition and magic. Their activities combined simple science with law and superstition. They slew people to gain the gods' favour, but also saved lives by dispensing beneficial herbs or performing simple surgery. Eating a certain animal might be taboo because it possibly either carried disease or, so it was thought, the soul of a dead ancestor.

The universal custom of burying or burning the dead was partly a matter of hygiene, but with burial went the belief in an after-life. People buried their dead with food and a few possessions to comfort them in the next world. Many people believed that the soul of the dead would remain with the tribe.

Man's early method of COUNTING was probably based on the body, when someone noticed

Right: A tomb or *long barrow* built about 4,500 years ago at West Kennett, Wiltshire, U.K., held the bodies of 45 or more people buried at different times. The dead, possibly chieftains, were buried with arrowheads, beads and earthen vessels to comfort them in the after-life. The roof was formed of 50 tonne stone slabs.

E **East Africa** is believed to have been the home of man's earliest-known ancestors. *1470 man* (named from the catalogue number in the Kenya National Museum) was discovered in 1972. Remains of *Ethiopian man* were unearthed in 1974. Both these early men walked erect and made simple tools.

G **Grain** of the prehistoric world was mainly wheat, barley, oats and (in the Americas) maize. Other basic crops included lentils, peas and beans.

L **Levers** were probably first invented by the Magdalenian people of France-Spain some 12,000 to 17,000 years ago. These people also produced the outstanding murals at the Altamira caves, in Spain.

Leisure. Stone Age people probably did not work very hard when the environment became more favourable. They possibly laboured about half the number of hours now worked by people in modern industrial societies. Story-telling would have occupied much of their time after dark. Then as now, children would have played games, imitating their parents' work: hunting, cooking and so on. Games seem to have been popular and adults probably invented them to occupy the family's spare time and energies. The ancient Central Americans played a ball game before the height of their civilization. Sumer appears always to have had 'table games', suggesting that early forms of them predated its civilization.

M **Migration.** Primitive men, like animals, could not live where the climate became too cold, too hot, too wet or too dry. Man's early migrations were almost certainly movements towards more moderate climates and better sources of food supply. One of the greatest migrations of all time began about 30,000 years ago when men walked from Asia into the Americas, over what is now the Bering Strait. About the same time, another people migrated from south-eastern Asia through New Guinea into Australia to form the Aborigines of that country. Arabia, and Central Asia-Mongolia, are believed to have been the starting points of many migrations.

Aborigine with didgeridoo

how many limbs he had. Some observant people detected a constant pattern in the movements of the sun and moon, while some unknown genius linked the idea of number to the rhythm of heavenly movements and so evolved the concept of time. Someone else linked this to the pattern of weather, a first step to an understanding of the seasons. Much later, these ideas were connected to an annual cycle of agriculture.

Man the freebooter

Trade preceded civilization. Barter in salt and gold between peoples who never spoke or even met, was common in Africa until a few hundred years ago. But not all people traded to satisfy their wants. Some turned to robbery or piracy. Tribal law laid down permissible patterns of behaviour with standardized PUNISHMENT for those judged guilty of breaking it.

An early tax collector was the tribal chief who first thought of exacting payment in kind for travellers to drink at his spring or pass through his territory. Inevitably, not all people accepted the rules and people sometimes revolted against their chief or tribal elders.

Man the organizer

Man had learned much, but knowledge was unevenly spread. Here and there, knowledgeable men lived in favourable environments. About 6,500 years ago, such settlements stood poised for the great leap forward into civilization. Unknown men with new talents began to gather together their strands of knowledge and to persuade their fellows to put learning to practical use. The Sumerians were first off the mark. They established settled agriculture, permanent buildings, and an organized economy, and so they pioneered the first recognizable civilization before 4000 BC.

Above: Stonehenge ('hung-up stones'), built on Salisbury Plain, U.K., about 3,800 years ago, may have been an early observatory, or a temple for sun-worshippers. Its builders constructed Stonehenge with a precision based on accurate knowledge of the sun's movements.

Above right: The men who erected the 28-tonne upright stones first dug an incline to a prepared hole, then they dragged a stone to fall into it. While the hoisters balanced the stone vertically, other workmen packed the giant stone firm

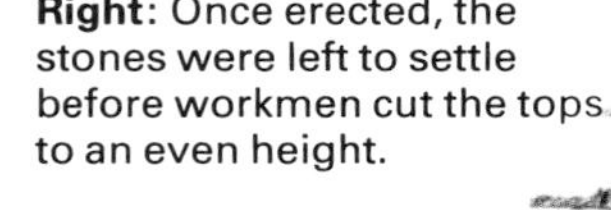

Right: Once erected, the stones were left to settle before workmen cut the tops to an even height.

Right: Horizontal stones were then erected on wooden scaffolding and a lever system used to lay them across the upright pillars.

N **Neanderthal man,** whose brain slightly exceeded our own in size, made spearheads and scrapers from pieces of flint. He practised rituals and buried his dead, but there is no evidence that he produced art. The first of several Neanderthal skeletons was found at Neanderthal, near Düsseldorf, Germany, in 1856 and the earliest remains date from between 400,000 and 200,000 years ago.

P **Punishment** at its simplest was one man's revenge against another. In the case of murder, the dead person's clan or tribe often sought to kill the murderer or another of his group, so starting a blood feud. As social groups grew bigger and more advanced, punishment was used less for revenge, and more to deter others from breaking the 'laws'. It became a mechanism through which rulers enforced obedience to tribal customs. The breaking of a certain taboo brought a specific punishment known in advance of the crime. Law helped to maintain the safe existence of the tribe.

R **Races** in present times include Caucasoids, Mongoloids and Negroids, to which nearly all the world's peoples belong. However, some groups do not fit easily into these categories or combinations of them. Such groups include the Aborigines of Australia, and the Hottentots, Bushmen and Pygmies of Africa. Many scientists believe that the 3 main races at least, descended from common ancestors. Their marked physical differences are thought to have come about through natural selection and adaptation to different environments.

S **Spear-throwers** are notched holders from the end of which spears can be hurled. They increase the force of a throw by giving additional length to the thrower's arm. Australian Aborigines still use spear-throwers.

Cerne Abbas giant, England

W **Weapons** of Stone Age hunters and fishermen included bows and arrows with heads of wood, bone or flint; slings for stones; barbed prongs; and harpoons. Australian Aborigines used BOOMERANGS and SPEAR-THROWERS (perhaps the world's earliest 'machines').

The Sumerians established the first settled civilization, based on agriculture and trade. They built the first cities, invented wheeled vehicles, and laid claim to the first usage of a written language.

The Sumerians

About 6,000 years ago, successive waves of people were migrating into the flat coastal clay and marshlands of what is now Iran and southern Iraq. They called themselves the 'black-headed people', and were probably nomadic shepherds. We know them as the Sumerians and the land in which they settled as the land of Sumer.

The Sumerians established the first recognizable civilization with a workable system of government, and their other achievements include the invention of WHEELED VEHICLES and the use of written language. They developed the scientific practice of agriculture and, on the arts side, evolved a distinctive style of architecture and a complex religion which is reflected in their literature.

The pioneers of civilization

The Sumerians probably conquered and intermixed with an earlier people who had migrated from the Arabian desert and by about 3500 BC, they had established several cities which included ERECH (Uruk), KISH, LAGASH, LARSA, NIPPUR and UR (the best known of the Sumerian cities). These cities were built on land deposited by the life-giving 'twin rivers', the TIGRIS and EUPHRATES, which entered what is now called the Persian Gulf as one waterway, the SHATT-AL-ARAB. The land between the twin rivers was called MESOPOTAMIA, and Sumer lay at its southernmost end. Ur (the ruins of which are now over 160 kilometres inland) may once have stood on the coast.

Above: The map shows Mesopotamia as it may have been in Sumerian times although the present-day Persian (or Arab) Gulf probably extended farther north. Akkad is believed to have been on the Euphrates, near to Kish.

Although the whole of Sumer shared a common culture, the Sumerian city-states (independent cities with their own kings) seldom united and often fought wars against one another. This sometimes resulted in the formation of small empires that rose and fell as the balance of power shifted from one city-state to the next.

However, Sumer lasted well over 1,000 years before it fell to a Semite warrior people from the north, the AKKADIANS, and even then, Sumerian culture continued to dominate the new empire. Many legends surround the person of the Akkadian leader, Sargon I (c.2637-2582 BC), who was once cup-bearer to the king of Kish, including one story which tells that he was found as a baby floating on the river in a basket made of reeds. (This was supposed to have happened

Left: The Standard of Ur depicts the city-state's king celebrating a victory.

Right: The bronze head is probably that of Sargon of Akkad.

Reference

A **Akkadians,** under Sargon I, their humbly-born leader, spread from their capital of Akkad, near KISH on the EUPHRATES, to conquer the whole of MESOPOTAMIA and founded the Akkadian empire which lasted from about 2371-2159 BC.The exact dates are uncertain.
Amorites, a Semitic people from the great desert north-west of Sumer, began to attack and destroy the Akkadian empire from about 2200 BC. About 300 years later, an Amorite prince established himself in Babylon, which became the centre of the Babylonian empire.

B **Burial chamber** of Queen Pu-Abi (or Shub-ad) was the most interesting of 16 royal graves at UR excavated in the 1920s by Sir Leonard Woolley, a British archaeologist. The sacrifice of human beings at the burial of a royal person such as Pu-Abi was once widespread. Later, effigies were substituted for human attendants.

C **Clay tablets,** inscribed in CUNEIFORM with a sharpened reed, were the usual form of letters and documents in Sumer and were often encased in clay envelopes. Many thousands of these tablets are stored in the British Museum.
Cuneiform (wedge-shaped writing) was developed from pictorial writing by the Sumerians, who may have invented the world's first written language. It was much easier to inscribe cuneiform than pictures on clay, and cuneiform was more precise in meaning.

D **Dumuzi** was the Sumerian name of the god of vegetation known to the Babylonians as Tammuz. Vegetation gods symbolized the course of the seasons: the apparent death of vegetation in winter and its 're-birth' in spring.

A Sumerian god

E **Elam,** a country at the head of the PERSIAN GULF, lay east of Sumer. Its site is the present-day Iranian province of Khuzestan. The Elamites wrote in cuneiform, which remains undeciphered to this day. Elam's capital, Susa, flourished from 1200 BC, but was destroyed by the Assyrians in 645 BC. Little is known about the early Elamites, except that Sargon's grandson,

approximately 1,000 years before an account was written of Moses having been found in similar circumstances.)

The city of Ur

A fairly typical example of a Sumerian city was Ur, whose inhabitants believed that it belonged to NANNA, the moon god. He lived, they thought, in the north-western corner of the city which stood higher than the rest and was surrounded by a wall. In this sacred area—a city within a city—the citizens of Ur built many temples for Nanna and also a ZIGGURAT (a square-sided tower), at the top of which Nanna was supposed to live with his wife Nin-Gal. People came to the sacred area not only to visit the temples but also to pay their rents and taxes to the god and to receive justice from him. Although they dealt with officials, the citizens regarded them as mere agents of Nanna, and the priest-king who ruled over the city-state was called his steward.

The ziggurat stood solid like a mountain on the flat plain so that far outside the safety of the city, farmers and herdsmen could see Nanna's abode and take comfort that he was watching over them and protecting them.

The oval-shaped inner city of Ur was a maze of narrow streets, alleys and bazaars. The outer city, five times as big, covered only five square kilometres yet housed about 350,000 people, most of whom were reasonably prosperous and traded in locally-produced or imported goods.

Houses were of clay bricks, either sun-dried or kiln-baked, built round a central courtyard to give privacy. In the courtyard there was a drain to catch the rain-water from the sloping roofs. Houses with an upper floor had a wooden balcony connecting the rooms from the outside of the house, but this was only for the rich as Sumer was built on clay and trees were scarce, though stone was even more rare and costly.

Death and the after-life

Each house had a shrine dedicated to the family's own special deity, who guarded its interests. Wealthy people had statues made of themselves, which they stood in the temples to act as their representatives before the gods whom they would pray to and appease while their owners were about their daily business.

Sumer had many deities and myths. DUMUZI,

Right: Sumer's clay-brick cities were not built to last long. Lacking building stone, the Sumerians had to be continually rebuilding. The ruined mounds, or *tells*, can still be found in the Mesopotamian desert. Bricks were either sun-dried or kiln-baked. Other civilizations, including Egypt, may have borrowed architectural ideas from Sumer, the world's first known civilization.

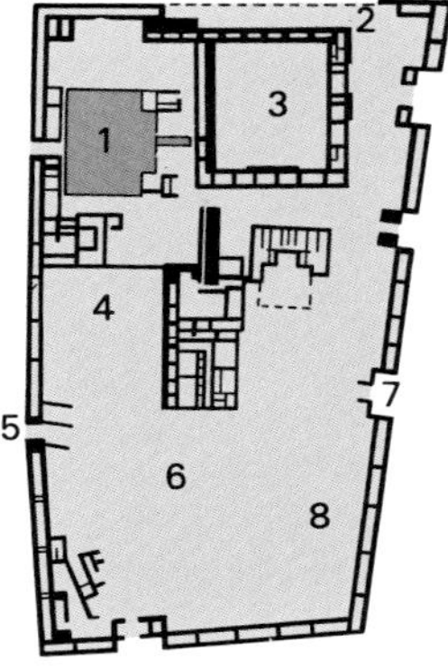

Right: A plan of the city of Ur.
1. Ziggurat
2. Wall of Nebuchadnezzar
3. Courtyard of the Temple of Nanna
4. Site of the early Temple of Nin-gal
5. Houses from the time of Abraham
6. Site of Palace of Ur-Nammu
7. The Cyrus Gate
8. The Early Cemetery

Below: The 'ram caught in a thicket', made of gold, shell and lapis lazuli, is typical of Sumerian art. The 'thicket' may represent the 'tree of life' from Sumerian religion.

NARAM-SIN, made a treaty with Elam as an equal.

Enki, god of wisdom, was, with NANNA and ENLIL, one of the 3 highest gods of Mesopotamia. He is credited with directing plough teams, canals, ditches and buildings and generally promoting agriculture.

Enlil (or Bel) was the god said to have brought the universe into being and to have separated heaven from earth by air. Enlil was a busy god, looking after crops, cattle, agricultural tools, and generally promoting civilization.

Epic of Gilgamesh, the greatest surviving work of Sumerian literature dating from about 2500 BC, was found in the library of an Assyrian king. The story predates the Bible but contains passages similar to the Bible story of Noah and the Great Flood.

Erech (or Uruk), a Sumerian city-state near the Euphrates, north-west of Ur, had a ZIGGURAT and well-stocked libraries, and is mentioned in the Bible.

Euphrates, a river rising in eastern Turkey, flows over 3,500 km south-east into Mesopotamia to unite with the Tigris in the SHATT-AL-ARAB, where it forms marshes. With the Tigris, it made Sumer's existence possible.

King Gilgamesh of Erech

K Kish, a ruined city-state on the Euphrates, lies 20 km from the later ruins of Babylon, and was the site of a temple built by Sargon of Akkad. Kish later flourished under the King NEBUCHADNEZZAR *(see page 37)*.

L Lagash (or Shirpurla), a Sumerian city-state, flourished under the wise rule of Gudea in the 2100s BC. Archaeological excavation, begun in 1877, revealed 30,000 clay tablets there.

Larsa (or Ellasar) was a city-state only 20 km south-east of Erech. Larsa's king is believed to have invaded Canaan in the time of ABRAHAM, 'father' of the Jews *(see page 53)*.

M Mesopotamia (the land between the two rivers) was the Greek name for the area between the Tigris and Euphrates rivers, and the location of 3 great civilizations: Sumerian, Babylonian and Assyrian.

god of vegetation, was believed to die in winter and to be reborn each spring. ENLIL, whose shrine stood in the city-state of Nippur, supposedly separated heaven from earth. He had many other jobs and the Sumerians believed that he created lesser gods to help him in his tasks. ENKI, a practical god who brought order out of chaos, organized agriculture and engineering.

Although the Sumerians believed in an afterlife, their idea of the next world was not attractive. In it, people sat in darkness eating dust and clay, clothed in feathers like birds. Rich and powerful people took great care to enter the next world in the proper way. When Queen Pu-Abi died over 4,500 years ago, her body was dressed in finery and jewellery and taken to a special BURIAL CHAMBER accompanied by two personal attendants, musicians, courtiers, soldiers and servants. Oxen and donkeys walked down the ramp pulling brightly-decorated carts and were guided by their drivers and grooms into position in the tomb, where the whole company took up their proper positions and then drank a drug that made them unconscious. When all was still, workmen killed the animals and walled up the chamber, entombing the living with the dead. Queen Pu-Abi had entered the next world in the style demanded by her rank.

Language, literature and crafts

The Sumerians developed the earliest-known written language. Beginning with PICTOGRAPHS (picture writing), they gradually changed to CUNEIFORM (wedge-shaped writing) that could be quickly inscribed on damp clay tablets with a sharp-ended reed, clay and reeds being the two materials that Sumer abounded in. Thousands of these tablets still survive. The Sumerians also

Above: A silver vase depicting the goddess Ningal, wife of Nanna.

Above: Objects recovered from the royal cemetery at Ur include the decorated dagger and the gold beaker shown. The beaker is from the grave of Queen Pu-Abi of Ur, whose burial chamber is the best-preserved of all the royal graves.

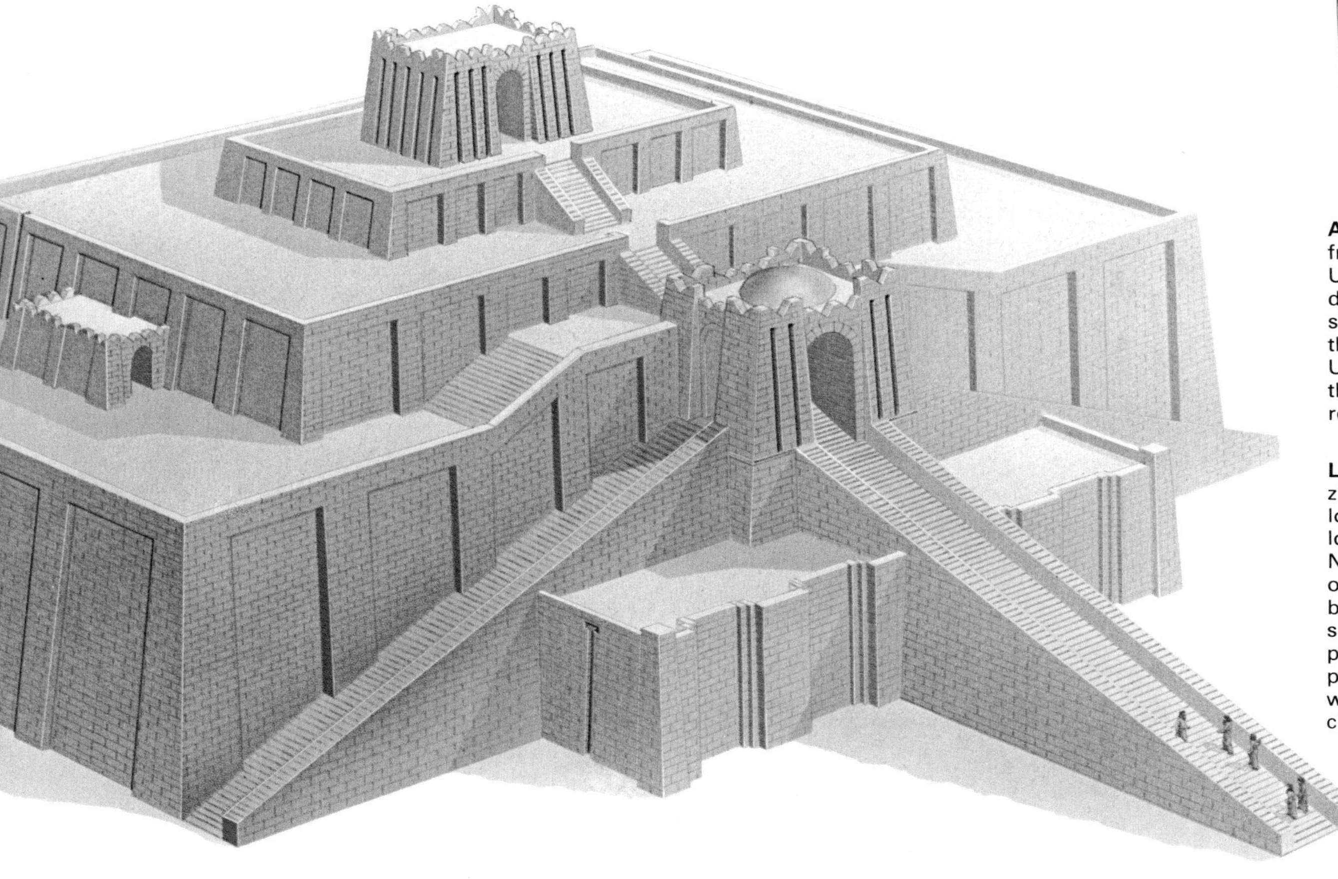

Left: The drawing shows the ziggurat at Ur as it may have looked. In hill-less Ur, it loomed like a mountain. Nanna, god and supposed owner of the city-state, was believed to live at its summit. From that vantage point he watched over and protected from evil, those who worked outside the city's walls.

The name was in use until about AD 1920.

Myths are traditional stories often told to explain ideas that are too complex to understand easily. They are found in religion and literature and often involve gods, semi-divine humans and heroes such as ENKI, Utnapishtim and Gilgamesh. Most peoples have devised myths to explain the existence of the sun, moon and stars, the creation of the world, the coming of men and animals, and the development of agriculture and engineering.

N

Nanna (or Sin), the moon god, was also the god of Ur, to whom the city-state was believed to belong. Nanna was also the chief star god. Sumerians believed he rode across the night sky in a quffah (circular boat) accompanied by stars and planets.

Clay tablet from Lagash

Naram-Sin, grandson of Sargon, expanded the Akkadian empire in the 2200s BC, and reigned for 37 years. After his death, the empire disintegrated, mainly under attacks from the Gutians.

Nippur, which lies 145 km south-east of Babylon, was the leading Sumerian holy city. For this reason it never became a city-state, but the king of the current ruling city-state of Sumeria traditionally claimed it as his own and made a pilgrimage there to receive the blessing of its god, ENLIL.

P

Persian Gulf, known to some countries as the Arab Gulf, is a deep inlet of the Arabian Sea, separating Iran from Arabia. Near its northernmost point it receives the waters of the SHATT-AL-ARAB, which deposit silt, from its swampy delta. Some scholars believe that the silt deposits have moved the Mesopotamian coast much further south than in Sumerian times, and that the site of Ur, now over 160 km inland, may have originally been on the coast.

Pictographs (picture writing) were used to convey messages and meanings before alphabetic languages evolved. Simple pictographs represented concepts such as man, woman, sun, moon and water. In most civilizations, pictographs were replaced by symbols to indicate letters of an alphabet. Nearly all languages, other than Chinese and Japanese, have developed in this way.

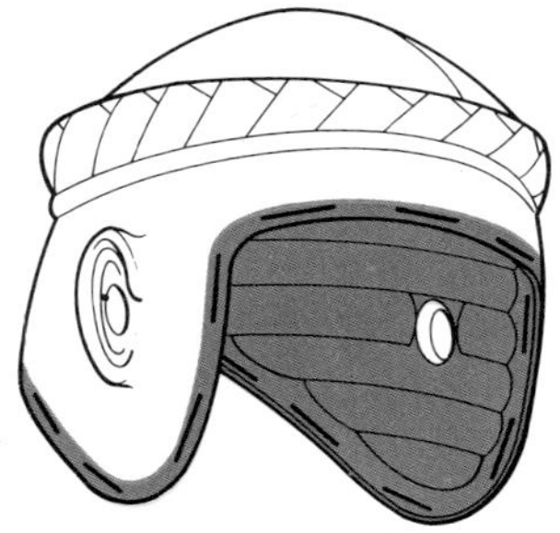

Above and right: The ceremonial helmet *(right)* belonged to King Mes-kalam-du of Ur, and was buried with him. An inner quilting *(above)* was laced into the helmet through the holes in its rim.

Left: Naram-Sin of Akkad is shown on this stele in triumph over an Iraqi king.

Below: The grimmer side of the Standard of Ur shows the city-state at war. It 'reads' from the bottom row upwards. Chariots advance, trampling defeated enemies underfoot. Light infantry armed with axes and spears butcher their naked opponents. Copper-helmeted heavy infantry in cloaks advance ominously. Finally, the king (taller than other figures), confronts the bound prisoners brought before him for judgement. A dwarf holds the reins of the asses which pull the king's war chariot. The pictures show that Sumer was a well-armed military power.

made use of cylinder SEALS for official or business documents which, when rolled over a tablet, left an impression of the pictograph or cuneiform on the seal.

SUMERIAN LITERATURE included the EPIC OF GILGAMESH (legendary king of Erech), in which Gilgamesh mourns the death of his friend Enkidu, who had been created by the gods. Determined to find out how to become immortal, Gilgamesh travels to the Ocean of Death, beyond which he meets Utnapishtim, a semi-divine immortal, who tells him how the gods created a great flood to destroy mankind because they were too noisy. But one god, Ea, warned Utnapishtim of the coming disaster and he escaped by building a boat.

Although the gods were angry at this, Ea persuaded them to grant Utnapishtim immortality. Utnapishtim tells Gilgamesh that the gift of immortality lies in a certain plant. Gilgamesh finds this plant only to be robbed of it by a snake. In despair, he realizes that the gods will not grant immortality to men and that all must age and die.

SUMERIAN ART had a livelier style than that of some other early civilizations, and some splendid examples of it remain. Amongst these is a well-preserved box known as the STANDARD OF UR, which shows the city-state in peace on one side, and at war on the grimmer reverse side.

Other relics of Sumerian art include some magnificent musical instruments such as lyres and harps and some exquisite jewellery made of gold, pearls, cornelian and lapis lazuli, a brilliant blue stone.

S

Seals were used to 'print' marks of ownership or identification in Sumer. They were cylindrical in shape, and carved so that pictographs or later CUNEIFORM imprints were left on clay tablets when the seal was rolled across them. The seals reveal much about Sumerian thought and way of life. For example, the earliest-known script has 31 pictographs for sheep and goats. This strengthens the theory that the Sumerians were originally herdsmen.

Semites, or Semitic-speaking people, include ancient peoples such as Akkadians, Amorites, Assyrians, Hebrews and Phoenicians, and present-day peoples such as Arabs and Jews.

Shatt-al-Arab, a river formed by the confluence of the Tigris and Euphrates rivers, flows about 200 km through marshes into the Persian (or Arab) Gulf.

Standard of Ur, a mosaic work of art in the British Museum, London, shows the Sumerian army at war on one side, and the king of Ur celebrating a victory banquet on the reverse. It is made of white shell, pink limestone and lapis lazuli set in bitumen and mounted on wood. It is the most informative Sumerian object.

Sumerian art includes sculptures of fired clay, soapstone, limestone, marble, diorite and copper. Among the many fine statues discovered are several of Gudea, king of Lagash, animal figures (especially the ram caught in a thicket), and a bronze head, possibly of Sargon of Akkad. Other art forms included jewellery, decorated daggers, beakers, bowls and vases. Two-dimensional art, seen on seals, friezes, tablets, plaques and gaming boards, is lifelike in style and informative. Artists' materials included gold, copper and lapis lazuli (blue stone).

Sargon of Akkad's seal

Sumerian literature includes the *King List* – an account of both mythical and actual reigns, and the *Sargon Chronicle*. Many works were poems, such as

Left: The jewels on this model head were once worn by a Sumerian lady. The leaves, flowers and earrings are of beaten gold. The necklace is of cornelian, pearls, and lapis lazuli.

Below: This ivory gaming board has 14 counters, but no one now knows how the game was played. The Sumerians seem to have valued their leisure, for several games and musical instruments have been found.

Above: A golden bull's head found buried at Ur once adorned a lyre. Experts rebuilt the instrument as it was.

Agriculture and science

The Sumerians may have been the first people to understand the principles of scientific agriculture—the relationship between seeds, soil, water, and the annual cycle of the weather. Barley, their chief crop, was used as a form of money, and they also cultivated flax, lentils, peas, wheat and vetch (a kind of bean), and possibly olives, grapes and other fruits.

To improve agriculture, Sumerian engineers constructed dams and canals, which were also used for water transport. Silt from the river fertilized the land which yielded two crops a year. The Sumerians kept sheep and goats and some pigs—animals considered to be unclean and eaten only by the poor.

The Sumerians took a great interest in mathematics, possibly out of the necessity to survey land. They based their number systems on units of 60 and passed on to present times the 60-minute hour and the 360° circle.

Akkad takes over Sumer

About 1,000 years after civilization began in Sumer, Sargon of Akkad conquered the warring city-states and set up the Akkadian empire which lasted for about 200 years (2371-c.2159 BC). Sargon's first triumph was to make himself king of the city of Akkad, after which he added Kish to his domains. Many battles later, he defeated Erech, broke its walls, and took its king in chains to Nippur. His campaigns took him far and wide, from the backward land of Assyria to the north, to Lebanon (known as the 'land of the cedars' as it supplied so much timber) and to the Mediterranean Sea. He also claimed the conquest of ELAM, a country to the east.

Sargon's main aim in fighting these bloody and exhausting wars seems to have been the sheer glory of conquest, though he was also motivated by the need to gain raw materials such as wood, stone and metals, and to expand his foreign trade on favourable terms. He was history's first great empire builder and his reign lasted for about 56 years, after which he was followed by his grandson, NARAM-SIN (reigned c. 2260-2223 BC), who extended the empire. On the death of Naram-Sin the empire began to decline and break up. Erech rebelled and seized much of the old land of Sumer; the AMORITES attacked from the north-west; but the most powerful attack came from the fair-skinned, barbarian Gutians, who pushed in from the Zagros mountains. The Sumerians called them the 'Mountain dragons' and by about 2160 BC they ruled much of Mesopotamia.

Opposition to the Gutians came from the city-state of Lagash, whose priest-king, Gudea, (reigned c. 2143-2124 BC), halted the Gutian advance. Gudea kept his city-state at peace, preferring prosperity to conquest, but after his death, Sumer came under the leadership of the king of Erech, who finally drove out the Gutians. The Sumerian-Akkadian territories became increasingly unstable politically, and by 2000 BC the Amorites were taking over the city-states.

Despite political and military upheaval, Sumerian civilization did not die. It was absorbed by Babylonia, and later by Assyria, and its influence was felt as far afield as Egypt.

Above; Sumerian seals, when rolled across documents, left a pictographic or cuneiform impression.

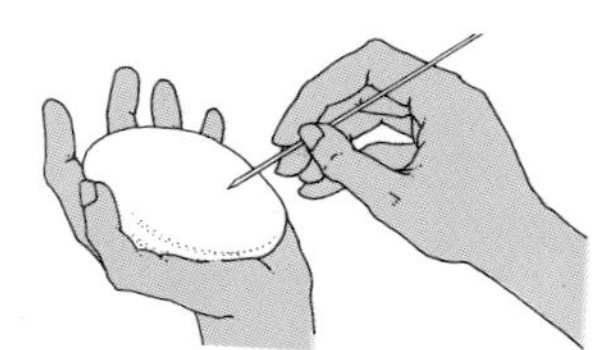

Above: Sumerians wrote on clay with a sharp reed. The pictographs gradually developed into cuneiform.

The Curse of Agade (Akkad), which may have been sung to the music of the lyre. The greatest work of Sumerian literature is the EPIC OF GILGAMESH.

T **Tigris,** a river rising in eastern Turkey, flows over1,800 km south-east into Mesopotamia to unite with the Euphrates and form the Shatt-al-Arab.

U **Ur,** the best known of the Sumerian cities and traditionally the original home of Abraham, 'father' of the Jews, was excavated by Sir Leonard Woolley in the 1920s. Its many important finds included the royal burial chambers.

Gudea, priest-king of Lagash

Uruk, see ERECH.

W **Wheeled vehicles** were probably first invented in Sumer, where they took over from sleds and were in use by about 3250 BC. They were made from 3 pieces of wood and were bound together with wooden battens and leather.

Sumerian toy on wheels

Z **Ziggurats,** square brick pyramids with steps leading upwards, dominated most Sumerian cities. In the hill-less plain of Sumer, the complex structure of the ziggurat looked like an artificial mountain, and was believed to be the dwelling place of the city-state god.

The majesty of the pyramids at Giza is just one of the many wonders left behind by the Egyptian dynasties. The chance discovery of Tutankhamun's priceless treasures has re-awakened our interest in this fascinating era.

The Egyptians

The Egyptians depended upon the Nile River for life even more than the Sumerians relied upon the twin rivers, the Tigris and the Euphrates. The Nile Valley *was* Egypt – a thin ribbon of fertile land hemmed in by sandy desert. The Egyptians became master builders, competent agriculturalists and mathematicians and they established the world's first nation-state. Much of their achievements derived from their obsessive concern with life after death.

The isolated nation-state

HAMITIC PEOPLE began farming along the valley and delta of the Nile about 6,000 years ago. By about 3100 BC, when they had established several small estates, King Menes united the south and the north in one long narrow kingdom extending about 900 kilometres along the Nile. MEMPHIS became the capital soon after 3000 BC.

Egypt regarded its king, or PHARAOH, as a GOD-KING, not as the representative of a god like the Sumerian priest-kings, but as a god in his own right. To govern effectively, the pharaohs divided Egypt into *nomes* (districts), each under a governor.

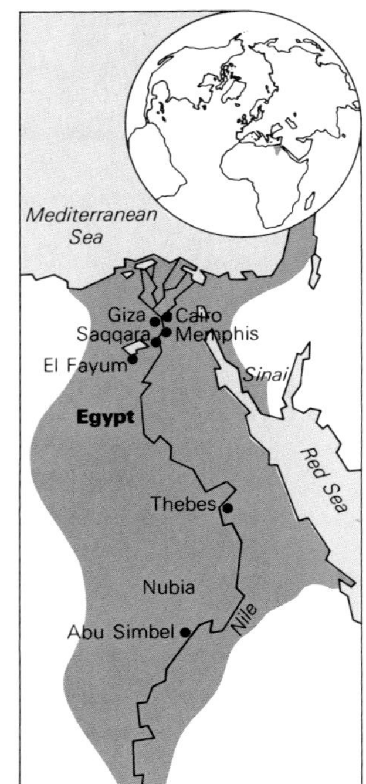

Above: The map shows that the towns of Egypt lay near the Nile. Egypt lies at the cross-roads of 3 continents.

Surrounded by deserts and seas, Egypt was sheltered from raids and invasions for 1,400 years, and its isolated civilization remained almost unchanged for twice that long. Historians have divided Egypt's history between 3100 and 332 BC into 31 royal periods, or DYNASTIES.

The pyramids

The best known feature of ancient Egypt is its pyramids, the earliest of which was built for King Zoser (Djoser) of the 3rd dynasty by IMHOTEP, the first architect named in history. This was a step pyramid located at SAQQARA, near the Nile, south of present-day Cairo, and represented the world's first stone monument. Around the Saqqara pyramid, Imhotep built several courts and temples. Although stone was used for royal and official buildings, such as the pyramids, ordinary Egyptians lived in simple mud-brick houses.

The great pyramids built during the 4th dynasty were located at Giza, now a suburb of Cairo. The two largest were built in the 2500s BC for King KHUFU (Cheops) and his son King KHAEFRE (Chephren). The mysterious sphinx

Below: Stone masons found plenty of suitable material along the Nile Valley.

Below: Levelling the site according to the surveyor's instructions was the first job in building monuments.

Reference

A **Alexander the Great,** king of Macedonia, mastered Greece and took Egypt in 332 BC. After his death, one of his generals, Ptolemy, became pharaoh, and Ptolemaic Egypt lasted from 304 to 31 BC.

Animals played a leading role in the mythology of Egypt. Several important deities took the form of animals or had animal heads, and antelopes, asses, boars, crocodiles, hippopotamuses and scorpions were believed to belong to the god SETH.

Anubis was the jackal-headed god. His role was to weigh human souls in the balance against the feather of Truth. He was also believed to preside over funeral rites, the dead, and open the roads to the next world.

Asia Minor was the name used in ancient times to describe the area now roughly covered by Turkey. The Hittite civilization developed there about 1900 BC.

Illustration on papyrus of animals

C **Carter,** Howard (1874–1939), a British Egyptologist employed by Lord Carnarvon, discovered the tomb of King TUTANKHAMUN in November 1922. It took Carter 10 years to clear the tomb which was packed full with precious objects.

D **Double crown** of Egypt was worn by kings and pharaohs from the time of Menes (reigned c.3100 BC). Pharaohs had a choice of 4 crowns. The conical-shaped white crown represented Upper Egypt; the serpent crown represented Lower Egypt. These 2 were combined into 1 and worn as the double crown, denoting the unity of the country. The fourth was the blue war crown.

Dynasties of Egypt, with approximate dates, were as follows (all BC):

1st	3100–2890
2nd	2890–2686
3rd	2686–2613
4th	2613–2494
5th	2494–2345

Left: The sphinx has a lion's body but a human face, said to be that of Khufu, pyramid builder of the 4th Dynasty. The monument is about 4,500 years old.

Right: The pyramids at Giza were built as royal tombs. Three of them are much larger than the others. The 'Great Pyramid' of Khufu is probably the largest building ever constructed. Next to it is Khaefre's pyramid. Next to that (smaller) is Menkare's pyramid behind the 3 small pyramids of queens in the foreground.

built by Khaefre is believed to have his likeness. These monuments are among man's greatest but most useless achievements. Built as tombs for the pharaohs, the massive pyramids wasted the energies of the nation. To construct Khufu's tomb-pyramid, 100,000 slaves laboured for 20 years, shaping and moving into position about 2,300,000 blocks of stone weighing about two-and-a-half tonnes each. The base of the pyramid is large enough to enclose six football fields. It is a true square to within 15 millimetres accuracy – a tribute to Egyptian skill in mathematics and surveying.

The Egyptian hierarchy

Below the pharaoh, enforcing his will, were the nobles, priests and officials. Chief among the officials, the vizier enforced the law and imposed social and economic order. A vast army of conscientious scribes, or clerks, assisted the officials in controlling agriculture, industry and trade.

Below: Inside the Great Pyramid, burial chambers **(1)** and **(2)** were never completed. The real funeral chamber **(3)**, past the grand gallery **(4)**, was ventilated by shafts **(5)** and **(6)**. After burial, the corridor **(7)** was sealed from within by lowering stone 'plugs' *(right)*. The workmen then escaped through the shaft **(8)** and the corridor **(9)**.

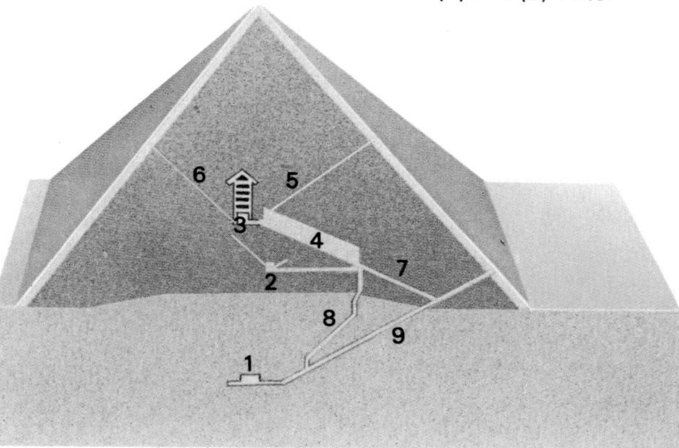

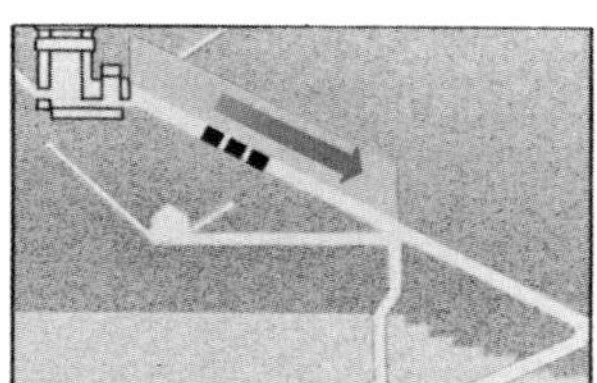

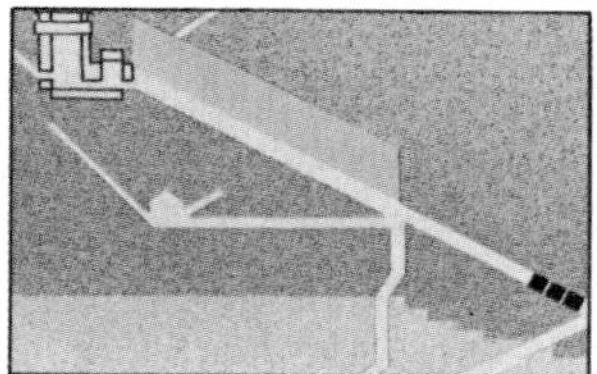

Below: Earth ramps may have been built around the stone pyramids, forming (as in Sumerian ziggurats) sloping paths along which the stones could be dragged to the top.

Below: Moving the massive blocks of stone made heavy demands on human muscle power. Rollers probably eased the burden but pyramid builders did not have pulleys.

Dynasty	Dates
6th	2345–2181
7th–10th	2181–2042
11th	2133–1991
12th	1991–1786
13th–14th	1786–1633
15th–16th	(Hyksos) 1674–1567
17th	1650–1567
18th	1567–1320
19th	1320–1200
20th	1200–1085
21st	1085–935
22nd–23rd	(Libyans) 935–730
24th	730–709
25th	(Nubians/ Ethiopians) 750–656
26th	(Assyrians) 664–525
27th	(Persians) 525–404
28th–29th	404–378
30th	380–343
31st	(Persians) 343–335
Alexander the Great from	332

Egyptian art. The 2-dimensional art of Egypt was often very detailed, and many pictures require close study, especially in the case of religious pictures. These often tell a complex story, and sometimes have HIEROGLYPHICS incorporated into them to explain what is happening. Sculpture, though stiff, is often expressive and always distinctive. Early

Tomb of Nakht

Egyptian buildings were made of solid stone blocks accurately positioned, as in the pyramids. Later buildings had massive lintels supported on tall columns, like those at KARNAK and Luxor. Tomb architecture was intricate, and was more akin to engineering than to art. A great variety of delightful artistic craftwork can be seen in the contents of TUTANKHAMUN'S tomb.

Egyptian literature varies from poems and narratives written for pleasure to the *Book of the Dead*, which was written on papyrus and buried with the dead. It was regarded as a magic charm that would protect them against danger on their journey to the next world. Many

Book of the Dead

Above: Farming, the chief occupation of the Egyptians, was almost entirely carried out along the fertile banks and the delta of the Nile. Many crops were cultivated, including grains, fruits and vegetables. Wine and beer were produced. Scribes forecast the quality of the harvest by measuring the level of the Nile's water. The volume of water largely determined the harvest.

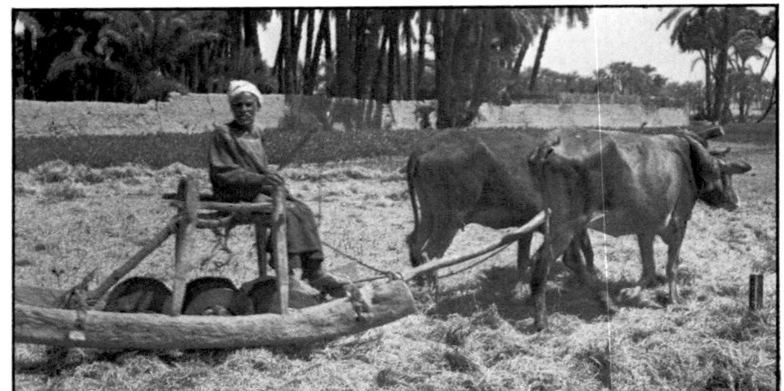

Right: A fellah (Egyptian farmer of present times) ploughs his land with an ox team, using methods unchanged for thousands of years. About 6 out of every 10 Egyptian workers still till the soil or raise animals. Agriculture produces 30 per cent of the gross national product. A pharaoh looking at a present-day field might think (but for the change in dress) he was in his own time.

Below: Irrigation canals flow between plots of cultivated land along the Nile Valley. In Egypt the source of all life is still the Nile. Rainfall is almost non-existent. Many times in their history the Egyptians have dammed the Nile. This has expanded the volume of water for irrigation, so increasing the crop yield.

Taxation and trade

In the almost rainless country, agriculture depended upon the volume of the Nile's waters. NILOMETERS were installed to measure the rise of the river, and so enable the size of the coming harvest to be predicted. The scribes then estimated the likely tax yield, and from this sum, they alloted funds to various government departments to finance new development projects. Scribes also set up check points on the Nile, which was by far the most important trade route, and searched the boats like modern customs men, exacting taxes for the pharaoh.

Apart from stone, Egypt relied heavily upon imported raw materials. Up the Nile from the Mediterranean came timber from Lebanon; semi-precious stones such as malachite and turquoise came from Sinai; copper from Cyprus; and tin, iron, gold and wine from ASIA MINOR and the LEVANT. Down the Nile from Nubia came amethyst and gold; and from east Africa, animals and animal products.

Agriculture

Most Egyptians toiled on the land. They seldom went hungry and their food was varied, but even those who were not actually slaves were often

Right: The shaduf, a simple but effective device for irrigation, has been used in Egypt for 3,500 years. Water is drawn from the Nile or one of its canals into a bucket attached to a weighted pole. The weight lifts the full bucket, which can then be easily emptied into a tank built at a higher level. From the tank, water is channelled through small 'canals' to irrigate land some distance from the river. The canals slope downwards, using the power of gravity.

Egyptian tales, most of them incorporating myths and legends, have been published in English.

El Fayum, west of the Nile, is a low-lying oasis with a lake fed by a canal from the Nile. It was considered to have an ideal climate for crop-growing. Pharaohs of the 12th dynasty irrigated the area and developed it into the garden of Egypt.

Engineers in Egypt first developed technology from the need to control the water of the Nile. They constructed dykes, dams and canals to curb harmful flooding and to provide irrigation, and their skills were also needed in the construction of the country's complex buildings.

Ethiopians, a darker, Hamite people, joined with

Howard Carter

the Nubians to conquer Egypt about 750 BC. Their leader, Piankhi, (c.751–716 BC), took Thebes, which had become semi-independent, before pushing on to Memphis where he founded the 25th dynasty. This is sometimes called the Kushite (Cushite) dynasty after the region of Kush in Nubia-Ethiopia.

F Forced labour was drawn from several classes apart from slaves. Prisoners of war, especially from Nubia and south-western Asia, and even freemen were conscripted for special projects like flood-control or the construction of pyramids and canals. Slaves could be bought and sold, but were allowed to own property and rent land, though serfs were bound to a particular estate and usually sold with it. Generally, Egyptians were not conscripted for the army, which relied mainly on mercenaries, who were mostly Nubians, Libyans and Sherden (an Aegean people).

G God-king. A pharaoh was believed to be the falcon god Horus, son of OSIRIS, master of the sky, whose rebirth he symbolized. To the Egyptians, the sky was a huge falcon with

Pharaoh (right) of Egypt

Right: Surveyors measure a field with their ropes. Accurate land surveying was regarded as highly important by Egypt's rulers. Apart from planning development projects, officials wanted to know the exact size of plots of land in order to tax them justly. Some plots held by smallholders were about 5 hectares. Others plots were 25% or 50% of that area.

Right: A plough team cuts a furrow. The plough came into use in Egypt about 4,500 years ago (when the pyramids were built). At first it was little more than a 2-handled hoe with a shaft added. It took another 1,000 years before the plough had a metal share. Handles were then strengthened by the addition of more cross pieces. Speedier ploughing released men for new trades.

pressed into FORCED LABOUR for the pharaoh. Canals, pyramids, palaces, tombs and temples had to be built and maintained. An unknown scribe recorded the grievances of ancient Egypt's peasants, deploring especially the taxes they had to pay.

Barley, wheat, fruit and vegetables were staple crops. Dates, figs, leeks, onions, garlic, cucumbers, radishes, beans and lettuces were grown and eaten even by the poor. Wine was produced from the plentiful vineyards and beer made from barley. As Egypt increased in prosperity, many peasants' sons became artisans, and contemporary friezes show the work of bakers, brewers, butchers, carpenters, metal workers as well as many others.

The quest for agricultural efficiency turned Egypt's priests and officials into competent scientists and ENGINEERS. They studied mathematics to become accurate surveyors, correctly interpreted the seasons and the annual growth cycle, and calculated that the year had 365 days. They built dykes and dams and IRRIGATION canals, especially at EL FAYUM.

Egypt's architects built on a grand scale. About 1,000 years after the pyramid builders, they constructed mighty temples and tombs at

Above: Ancient Egyptian fishermen on the Nile land a good catch. Fish (which cost nothing) was eaten gladly by poor people, even though it was sacred.

Left: Present-day Egyptians search for fish offshore. Using little equipment they seek free food as the price of their labour. Their ancestors did the same in Pharaonic times.

the sun and the moon for eyes. They believed that Horus's judgement was infallible and that he was 'served by the dwellers of heaven', according to an ancient poem. They also believed that justice was 'what Pharaoh loves', and injustice 'what Pharaoh hates'. To encourage the people to worship them, the pharaohs of the New Kingdom (18th–20th dynasties) had huge statues erected to themselves.

H

Hamitic people lived in the Hamitic language belt which extends across northern Africa from Morocco to the Indian Ocean. Their languages include Berber, Kushitic, Somali and Hausa, which are all closely related to Semitic languages, such as Arabic.

Hathor, Egyptian sky goddess, is often represented as having a cow's head, or a woman's head with cow's ears or horns. She was the protectress of women and the dead, and goddess of love, joy and fun. On New Year's Day priestesses dragged Hathor's image from the temple into the first light of dawn to symbolize that the day of celebration and merriment could begin.

Hieroglyphics were a form of ancient writing which was

Rosetta Stone hieroglyphics

common in Egypt before 3000 BC, and also used by other races including the Indus Valley people, the Hittites, Aegeans, Mayas and Aztecs. Hieroglyphics developed from pictographs, where things were represented by their images. When papyrus was introduced as a writing material in conjunction with an ink made of gum or soot, hieroglyphics became more cursive, or flowing. It was possible to write faster, and to describe more complex things, with signs representing different syllables. *Demotic* hieroglyphics (from democratic – available to all) were the most advanced form developed by the Egyptians. Simpler and quicker for ordinary people to understand, they continued them even after they had designed an alphabet of 24 letters.

Horus, see GOD-KING.

Hyksos, people from south-western Asia, are said to have migrated from Syria, into Egypt. There they seized power in about 1674 BC and ruled from Memphis, until they were expelled in 1567 BC. They were also called the 'Shepherd Kings', and

THEBES, a royal city and burial ground which lay nearly 700 kilometres south of the pyramids.

Ancient Thebes covered some 16 square kilometres. On the east bank of the Nile stood the city of the living, including the great temple of KARNAK, which began to be built during the 12th dynasty (1900s BC) and was still being added to 1,600 years later. The smaller Luxor temple was built about 1400 BC.

City of the dead

Across the Nile on the west bank at Thebes (modern Luxor), lay the 'CITY OF THE DEAD'. Most burials and cemeteries in ancient Egypt were made on the west bank of the Nile in the desert so as not to waste valuable agricultural land and because the Egyptian equivalent of heaven was thought to be in the west with the setting sun. One of the titles of Osiris, the god of the dead, was 'Lord of the Westerners'. At Thebes nobles had brightly decorated tomb-chapels cut into the hillside; the burial chamber with the mummy was deep below them. In the 18th dynasty the pharaohs began to be buried in a remote valley in the Theban Hills now known as the VALLEY OF THE KINGS. The first pharaoh buried there was Thothmes I in c.1512 BC, and most of the pharaohs of the next two dynasties were also buried there. Each tomb is now numbered and the last one found, number 62, is that of TUTANKHAMUN.

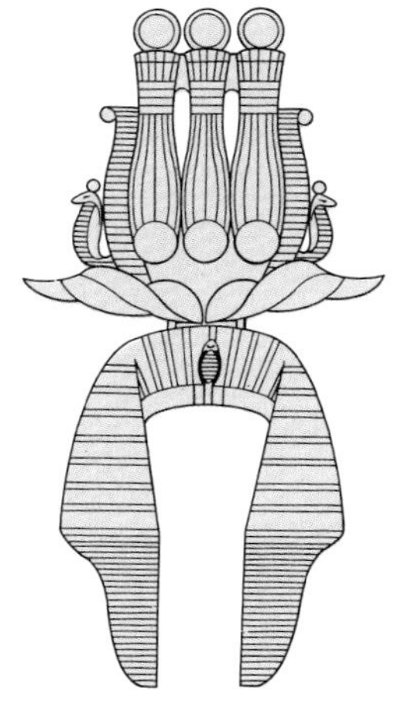

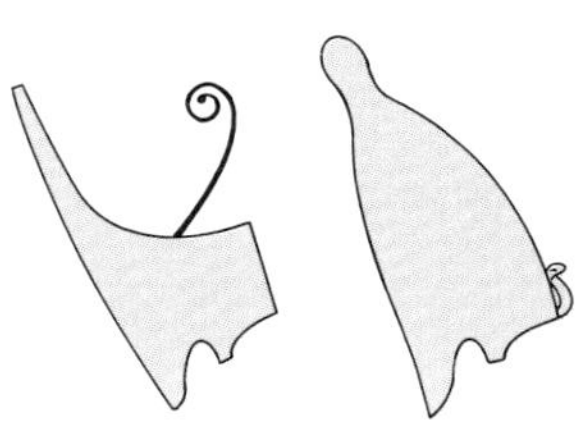

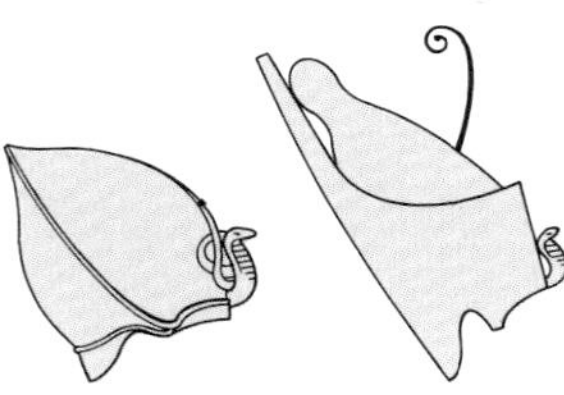

Left: Pharaohs had a choice of the ceremonial crown *(top)*; the white crown of Upper Egypt (*centre right*); the red crown of Lower Egypt (*centre left*); the double crown (*bottom right*); or the blue war crown (*bottom left*).

Above: A solid gold mask covered the head of King Tutankhamun's mummy. The false beard, snake and vulture are royal symbols.

The hall of the Egyptian gods

Isis, the wife of Osiris

Ra, the sun god

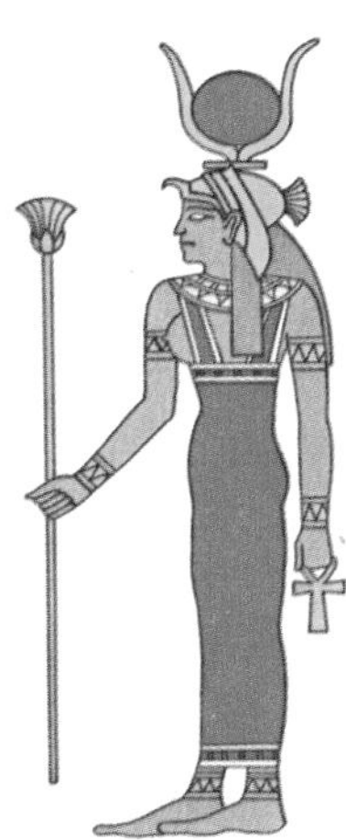

Anubis, the guide of human souls

Hathor, the sky goddess

Seth, the god of all animals

Thoth, messenger of the gods

founded the 15th and 16th dynasties.

Imhotep, counsellor of King Zoser, was a priest, a doctor and an architect, and the people also regarded him as a magician. Together, Zoser and Imhotep constructed the world's oldest-known stone building, the step-pyramid at SAQQARA. It dates from c.2670 BC and was surrounded by temples and courts.

Irrigation in Egypt was largely carried out using the 'basin system'. The cultivated ground was divided into huge areas made into basins by the construction of solid enclosing walls, and when the Nile was in flood, water was diverted into the basins by canals. From each basin (which might cover up to 17,000 hectares) water was channelled into outlying areas. In gardens and orchards, water was hand lifted until the invention of the *shaduf* – a bucket swung on a counter-weighted pail.

Temple of Hatshepsut

Isis, wife and sister of OSIRIS, was the mother of Horus. She collected the pieces of her murdered husband and reassembled him.

Karnak, on the east bank of the Nile, the northernmost point of THEBES, was the site of 3 temples, much of which still stands, including the temple complex of Amun-Re (the sun god), one of the largest in the world. Its construction began during the 12th dynasty. The arch was not used in Egypt, and the roof was

Colossi of Memnon

Most of the royal tombs were robbed of their rich contents centuries ago. Several of them stood open in classical times and Greek and Roman tourist have left their names and comments scribbled on some of the walls.

In the tombs of the nobles the walls are decorated with colourful and lively scenes of everyday life, work in the fields and such-like. The bright paintings in the tombs of the kings are only concerned with scenes of the king in the company of the gods, and extracts from various religious books such as the *Book of that which is in the Underworld.*

It is a curious fact that modern scholars have learnt much of what we know of the daily life of the ancient Egyptians from their way of death; from the detailed painted and carved scenes on the walls and from the many objects placed in the tombs for their owners use in the afterworld. They sincerely believed that they were going to a far better world.

Left: Four giant statues of Ramses II were carved from the rock at Abu Simbel. 3 of the 4 (one lost its head) stared across the Nile for 3,200 years. Then they were cut from the rock and lifted by mechanical means in AD 1964. To save them from flooding caused by the construction of the Aswan High Dam, they were resited nearby.

Above: The throne of King Tutankhamun, made of wood and decorated with gold, shows the king sitting at leisure attended by his wife. They are blessed by the sun's rays.

Religion and mythology

Religion played an important part in Egyptian society. Some of its many deities were believed to control birth and death, while others were responsible for various aspects of daily life: surveying, language, numbers, harvesting and so on. Egypt had two supreme gods, RA (Re) and OSIRIS. In Egyptian mythology, the good god Osiris was killed by his twin brother SETH, who cut his body into pieces. ISIS, wife of Osiris, put his body back together again, so the god was resurrected. Osiris, Isis and their son HORUS, a falcon god, formed a trinity at the top of the pantheon. Their chief helpers included ANUBIS, jackal-headed god of the dead; THOTH; the ibis-headed scribe; and HATHOR, the cow goddess. The role of Anubis was to weigh the heart of each dead person against a feather (symbolizing Truth) on the scales. Monsters devoured those

Nepthys, protective goddess

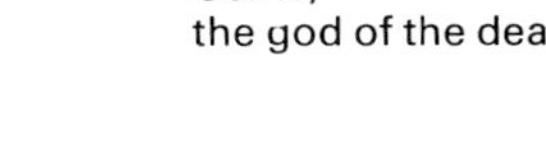

Horus, the sky god

Osiris, the god of the dead

Ptah, the god of Memphis

Sobek, the god of crocodiles

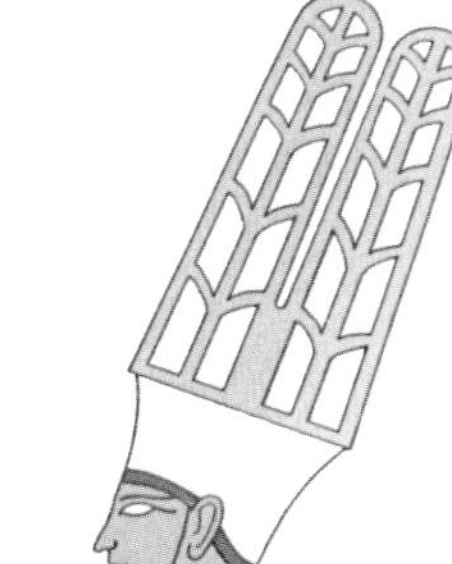

Amon, Lord of the Thrones of the Two Lands

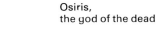

supported by massive lintels on top of giant columns. The great *hypostyle* (pillar-supported) hall was a floor 118 x 52 metres with 134 columns arranged in 16 rows.

Khaefre (reigned c.2560 BC), 4th king of the 4th dynasty, built the 2nd largest pyramid at Giza, and probably also constructed the sphinx.

Khufu (or Cheops, reigned c.2540 BC), 2nd king of the 4th dynasty, erected the largest of the Giza pyramids nearly 5,000 years ago.

Kingdom. Ancient Egyptian history is divided into the following kingdoms:

Period	*Dynasties*
Archaic	1st-2nd
Old Kingdom	3rd-6th
1st Intermediate	7th-10th
Middle Kingdom	11th-12th
2nd Intermediate	13th-17th
New Kingdom	18th-20th
Late	21st onwards

L

Levant is the name used to describe the area from the coast of the eastern Mediterranean, inland to the Nile, Tigris and Euphrates. It has no precise boundaries.

Libyans. Berber tribes from Libya began to attack Egypt during the 19th dynasty, and settled in the delta area west of MEMPHIS. When they were expelled in the 20th dynasty, many returned to become mercenaries in the Egyptian army.

Ram-headed sphinxes

Lower Egypt covers the small delta area between Cairo-Giza and the Mediterranean.

M

Macedon (or Macedonia), the northern part of Greece, dominated Greece by 338 BC, and in 332 BC ALEXANDER THE GREAT set out to conquer Egypt, where one of his generals founded the Ptolemaic dynasty in 304 BC.

Mathematics, geometry and trigonometry were developed by Egyptian priests and officials for use in surveying, irrigation and building. Because the Egyptians were only interested in the applied sciences, it was left to the Mesopotamians to develop them further.

Obelisk, Luxor

Above: Many animals were considered sacred in ancient Egypt. The falcon was one of the highest divinities and represented the idea of 'god' in pictograms.

Below: The Egyptians believed that a man needed his body in the after-life so they preserved the dead by the complex procedure of embalming and mummification.

found to have unjust hearts, whereas good-hearted people were allowed to enter into the after-life.

The traditional religion was disturbed by King Amenophis IV (reigned c.1375-1358 BC), of the 18th dynasty, who changed his name to Akhenaton to symbolize the beginning of a new religion based on the worship of one god only: Aton, the sun. But priests forced his next-but-one successor, Tutankhamun, to restore the old religion within 20 years.

Mummies

A strange custom practised by the Egyptians was mummification, the preservation of dead bodies. The brain and internal organs, excluding the heart, were first removed from the body. Then the body, excluding the head, was steeped in a solution of salt or natron for several weeks. The body was then washed, covered with preservatives and swathed in bandages. The whole process took 70 days.

The art of mummification reached its height during the 21st and 22nd dynasties, and its purpose was to try to preserve as much as possible of a person's identity after death. The idea of a person disappearing into nothing horrified the Egyptians, who even mummified some animals.

Egyptian writing

The waterplant papyrus grew freely in Egypt, providing material for sandals, mats and sailcloth. Above all, it provided a useful writing material similar to paper. A sharpened rush made a pen, and gum and soot were used as ink. Having papyrus instead of clay, the Egyptians had no need to use cuneiform. Instead they developed pictographs into clearer HIEROGLYPHICS.

Early hieroglyphics were pictographs, which later became more abstracted so that they could be written more quickly. Hieroglyphics were carved on the temples and monuments of Egypt, where they can still be read. By about AD 500 they had been forgotten and were regarded only as magical signs through which evil could be communicated. But in the 1820s Jean Champollion, a Frenchman, deciphered them using the ROSETTA STONE.

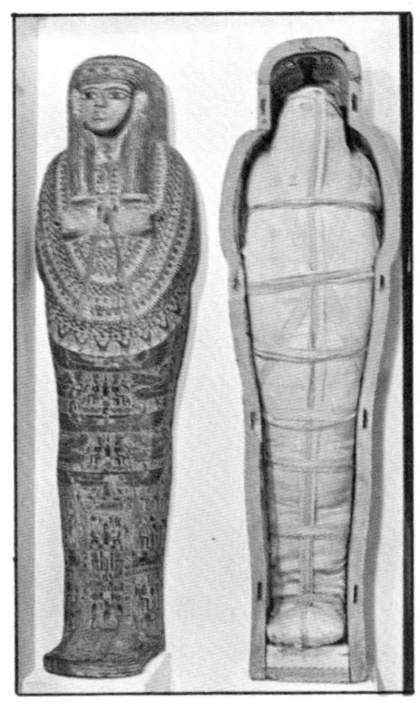

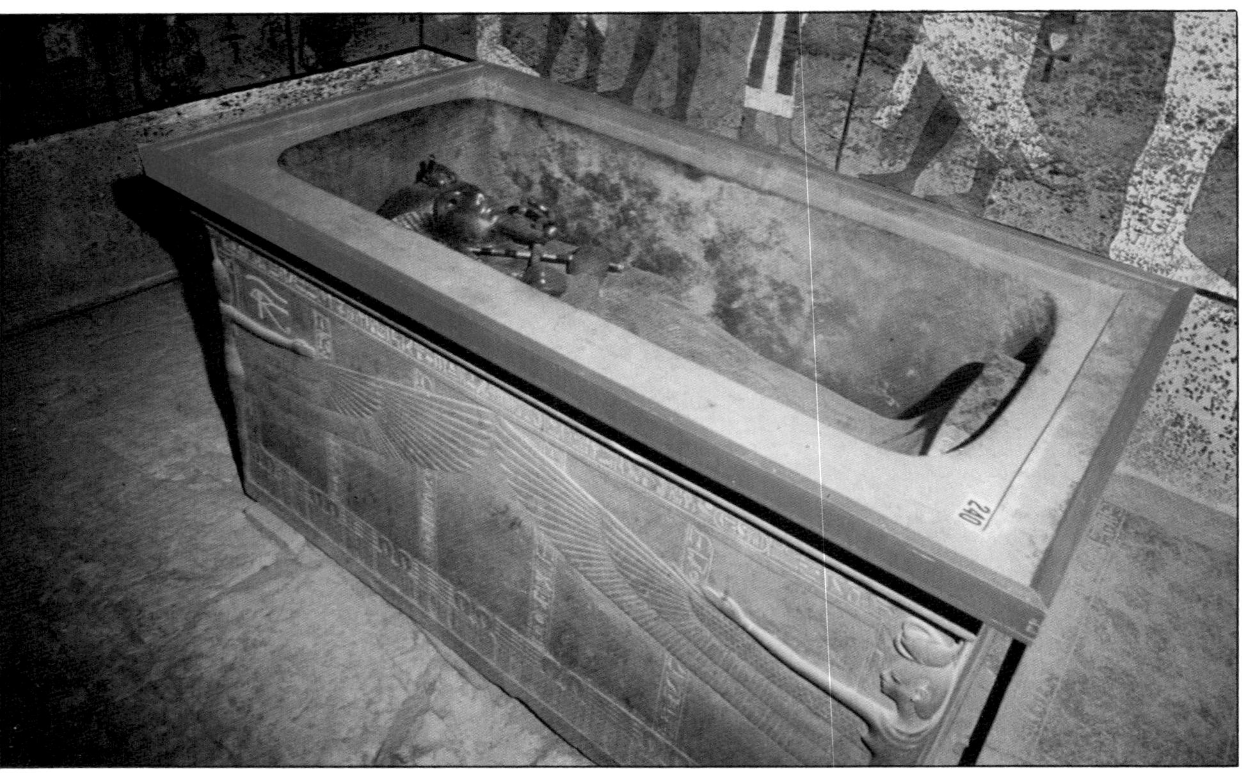

Right: Archaeologists discovered the tomb of King Tutankhamun, dating from 1352 BC, remarkably undamaged by time and robbers.

Memphis, earliest capital of Egypt, is believed to have been founded by Menes, first king of the united country of Lower and Upper Egypt, c.3100 BC.

N

Nilometers, sited at intervals along the banks of the Nile, were stones cut with gradations to measure the water level. Readings helped officials to estimate the volume of water and the consequent likely harvest.

O

Osiris, greatest god of Egypt, represented good. He was slain by his evil brother SETH, but was resurrected with the aid of his wife, ISIS.

Ancient nilometer at Aswan

P

Pharaoh. Although the kings of Egypt were generally referred to as 'pharaohs', the name was not used until the 18th dynasty. *See also* GOD-KING.

R

Ra (or Re), falcon-headed sun god, was the supreme deity of Egypt for 1,000 years. Then it is said that he destroyed most of mankind and his place was taken by OSIRIS.

Ramses (Rameses) II, 3rd pharaoh of the 19th dynasty, reigned 67 years (1304-1237 BC). He built many monuments, including Abu Simbel and statues of himself. His long war with the Hittites speeded Egypt's decline.

Rosetta Stone, a slab of black basalt, found by one of Napoleon's officers near Rosetta, Egypt, in 1799, enabled HIEROGLYPHICS to be deciphered after having been forgotten for many centuries. On it is inscribed a royal decree written in 3 scripts – hieroglyphics, demotic and Greek. Jean Champollion, a French scholar, worked back from the Greek and discovered the meaning of the hieroglyphics. The Rosetta Stone was surrendered to Britain in 1801 and is now in London.

S

Saqqara near Giza and Cairo, is the site of many of Egypt's earliest monuments, including the step-pyramid of Zoser.

Seth, was the evil brother of the god OSIRIS whom he killed and chopped into pieces. Osiris's son Horus then became Seth's eternal enemy, and eventually overthrew him.

T

Thebes, once a cluster of villages, rose to im-

Arts of Egypt

Ancient EGYPTIAN LITERATURE includes mythological or historical romances, poems, essays on morality, school texts, and political propaganda. A popular work, *The Story of the Shipwrecked Sailor,* tells how a sailor became a castaway on an island in the Red Sea, and was given shelter by a strange serpent. *The Tale of the Two Brothers* seems to be connected with the myth of OSIRIS and SETH. In the *Tale of Sinuhe,* a fugitive from Egypt settles in Palestine among the desert nomads. In old age, he is pardoned and allowed to go home.

EGYPTIAN ART forms were varied. However, one rather rigid but fascinating style predominated. Pyramid and temple architecture still stands solid and visual arts can be seen in the many statues, especially those of Pharaoh RAMESES II, and papyrus paintings, which are usually religious in theme. The Egyptians were also fine jewellers, and a wonderful collection of artistic craftwork was found in 1923 when the British Egyptologist Howard CARTER opened the tomb of the teenage pharaoh, Tutankhamun of the 18th dynasty.

History

The kingdom ruled by Menes about 3100 BC comprised UPPER EGYPT and LOWER EGYPT, and to symbolize the unity of the two countries the pharaohs wore a DOUBLE CROWN. The most famous of all the pharaohs is perhaps Rameses II of the 19th dynasty. The Egyptian dynasties ruled for about 1,400 years, after which the Semitic HYKSOS people trickled into Egypt from Syria about 1674 BC and eventually seized the royal power.

The Hyksos lasted 100 years and then the Egyptians ruled until the LIBYANS, who were employed as soldiers by Egypt, seized power to form the 22nd dynasty. This began a long series of disastrous invasions, and the Nubians and ETHIOPIANS ruled Egypt as the 25th dynasty. They were followed by the Assyrians who invaded Egypt and set up the 26th dynasty. The Assyrians were defeated by the Persians, who founded the 27th dynasty. The 31st and final Persian dynasty fell to ALEXANDER THE GREAT of MACEDON in 332 BC. Nevertheless, this was not the end of the Egyptian civilization, which lived on under its new conqueror.

Below: This necklace represents the scarab-god rolling the ball of the sun into the other world, just as the scarab-beetle pushes a ball of dung. He symbolized the renewal of life and the idea of eternity.

Left: This gilded wood statue of Tutankhamun as a harpooner is one of many statues symbolizing the king's after-life.

portance when a Theban family established the 11th dynasty. Later it became the royal residence of pharaohs of the 18th, 19th and 20th dynasties. When Thebes was the capital of the 25th dynasty, it was sacked by the Assyrians and fell into decline. It is the site of the Luxor and Karnak temples and the royal tombs.

Step pyramid, Saqqara

Thoth, divine vizier of OSIRIS and later of Horus, was a god with many functions. He was inventor of all sciences and arts, messenger of the gods, moon god, and keeper of the divine records. Usually shown with the head of an ibis, Thoth is also sometimes represented as a dog-headed ape.

Tutankhamun was one of the last kings of the 18th dynasty. A boy king, he died at the age of 18. His tomb was discovered in 1922 in the Valley of the Kings near Luxor by Howard CARTER.

U

Upper Egypt is the 1,500 km strip of the Nile Valley between Cairo and Egypt's border with Sudan.

V

Valley of the Kings was the area of ancient Thebes lying on the west bank of the Nile. Fearful that tomb robbers would take away their comforts in the after-life, the pharaohs had their tombs constructed underground with a maze of shafts and passages designed specially to conceal the tomb entrance and mislead the robbers. The tomb of Queen Hatshepsut (reigned 1503-1482 BC), for example, is over 200 metres from the entrance and nearly 100 metres below ground. Certain nobles were also entombed in the Valley of the Kings.

The Indus Valley was a rich, fertile land that bore a wealth of agricultural produce. The civilization which grew up there thrived for 1,000 years before mysteriously disappearing without trace.

The Indus Valley People

Above: This statuette of a bearded man — possibly a priest-king — found at Mohenjo daro, is one of the few remaining sculptures from the Indus Valley civilization.

One of the three great 'river civilizations' developed along the valley of the INDUS RIVER in what is now Pakistan. It began about 4,500 years ago and covered a vast area of over a million square kilometres. Some 60 to a 100 separate settlements grew up, centred around HARAPPA to the north and MOHENJO DARO to the south. These two cities each had a perimeter of about five kilometres.

In those days the Indus Valley was much more fertile than it is today. Some scholars believe this is due to a change of climate and that heavy rain once fell in areas now arid. Others think that it is the soil that has deteriorated because the inhabitants felled too many trees and overgrazed sheep and goats. Like the Sumerians and Egyptians, the Indus Valley settlers depended upon yearly silt-bearing floods to irrigate the land. These came in March when snow and glaciers melted in the mountains to the north.

Harappa and Mohenjo daro, of which more

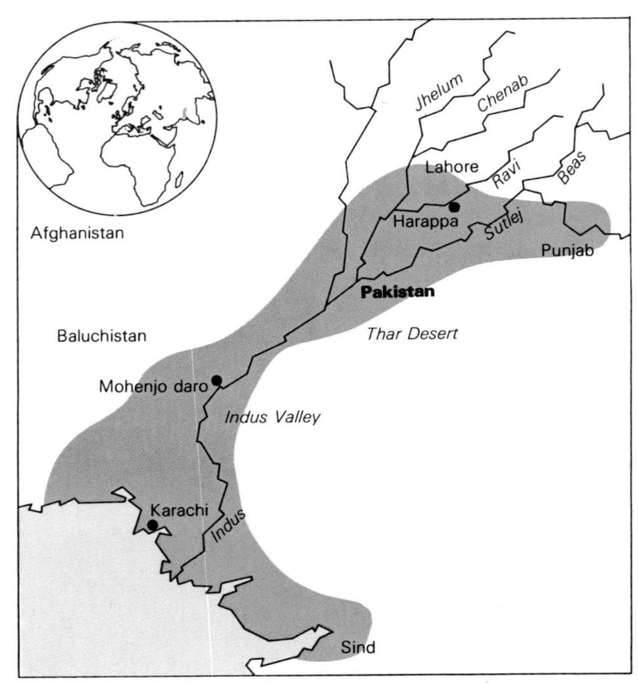

Above: The map shows that the Indus Valley people lived in the region made fertile by the 5 rivers of the Punjab feeding the Indus. Place names refer to present times except for Harappa and Mohenjo daro.

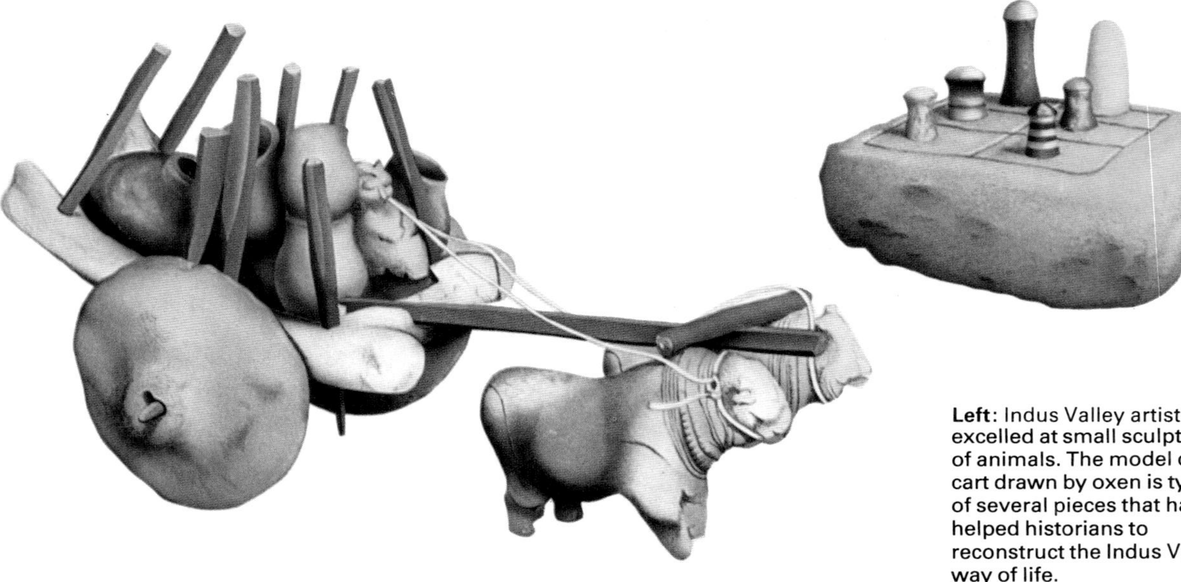

Left: Indus Valley artists excelled at small sculptures of animals. The model of a cart drawn by oxen is typical of several pieces that have helped historians to reconstruct the Indus Valley way of life.

Left: Gaming 'boards' made of solid stone entertained those who had time for leisure in the Indus Valley. Players probably moved the pieces (*shown*) across the 'board' to play a game similar to draughts. This gaming board is much less refined than those found in Sumer.

Reference

A **Amulets** were popular in most ancient civilizations. They were small objects worn as charms to ward off evil.

Aryan people probably began migrating from central Asia about 2000 BC. One branch pushed westwards into Europe, while another moved into the Indus Valley, whose civilization had probably been weakened by natural causes before they destroyed it by war about 1500 BC. The story of how the lighter-skinned Aryans conquered the darker-skinned native population is told in Indian literature. Most Indians, Iranians and Europeans are largely descended from these Aryan (or Aryan-speaking) people.

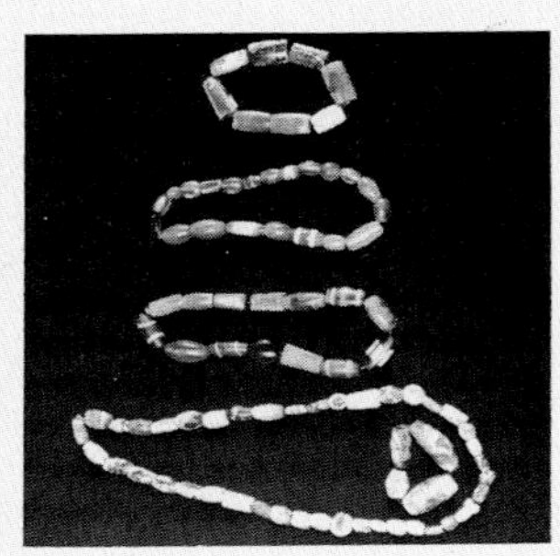

Beads from Mohenjo daro

C **Cotton,** grown widely in the Indus Valley, was spun and woven into cloth for clothes. The methods used changed little until the present century. It is possible that the Indus Valley people were the first to produce cotton cloth. The Egyptians of the same period wore linen.

G **Granaries** were of great importance in the ancient civilizations, where wheat and barley often served as currency. No coins have been found in the Indus Valley, where it is likely that definite weights of wheat grain were used instead of money. The granaries were therefore the 'treasuries', grain playing the part of gold and silver in later civilizations.

H **Harappa,** one of the two main cities of the Indus Valley civilization, stands on the old bed of the Ravi River (south of the present course), about 600 km north-east of Mohenjo daro. The city had a strongly fortified citadel with watch-towers, and was laid out on a grid system. Harappa was thickly populated and workmen lived in lines of barrack-like houses. A dominating building in the city was the granary, covering nearly 3,000 square metres. The ruins of Harappa were largely demolished in 1865, when John and William Brunton, 2 British engineers, used bricks from the ancient city as ballast for the railway they were building from Lahore to Karachi.

Below: The artist's reconstruction of the now-ruined 'great bath' of Mohenjo daro suggests similarities with the huge tanks found in later Hindu temples. The 12 x 7 metres bath was waterproofed with bitumen and fitted with a good drainage system. Bathers entered it at each end, down wide brick stairs with wooden treads.

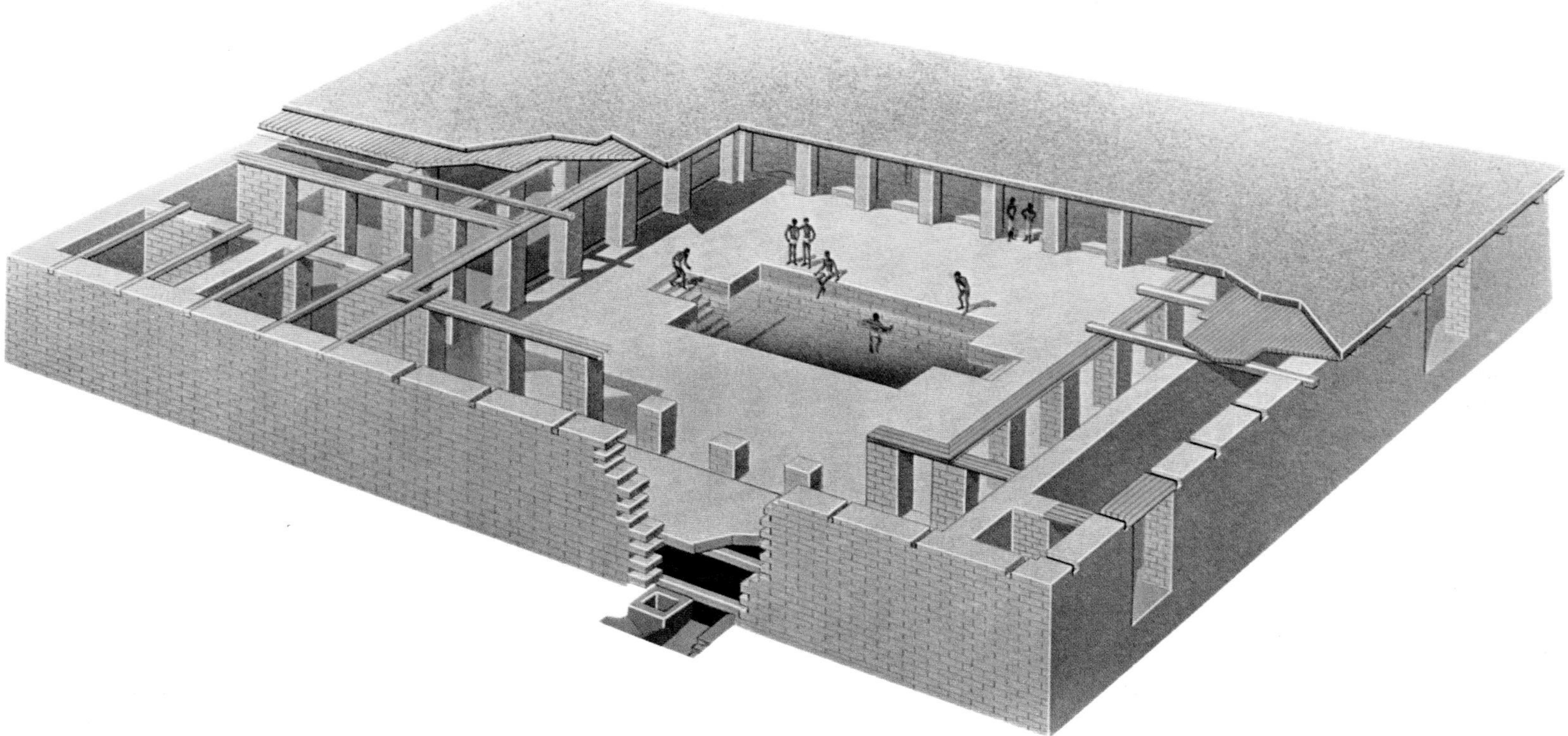

has survived, were both highly-planned cities with wide roads and houses of fired brick. The Indus Valley people excelled at drainage and sanitation. Their houses had private bathrooms drained by earthenware pipes running to main drains under the streets and into huge sump pits. A great public bath has been uncovered at Mohenjo daro and there were many wells.

Mohenjo daro and other Indus Valley cities were planned on a grid system and laid out with precision. No previous civilization had taken town planning so seriously. Houses mostly had at least two floors and were of plain brick without decoration. Roads were wide — often nine metres across and sidewalks were unpaved and dusty. TEMPLE ARCHITECTURE was unimpressive compared with that of Egypt and Sumer.

Government and trade

Little is known about the form that government took in the Indus Valley, although the standardized pattern of town planning suggests that Indus Valley settlements had a strong central government like Egypt. Harappa and Mohenjo daro were quite possibly both capital cities.

WEIGHTS and measures were also standardized, according to archaeologists, and this gives us a fuller picture of the economic life of the people. On a local scale, farmers probably transported their surplus crops to towns in ox-carts to exchange them for such wares as pottery, copper or bronze axes, fish hooks, razors and weapons.

The Indus Valley was fertile but possessed few raw materials, so the people imported certain goods. Imports were paid for by exporting surplus food. Single-masted sailing boats with oars brought copper from what is now the Persian Gulf. Camel and donkey caravans would have brought bitumen and steatite from

Above: The elaborate drainage system of Mohenjo daro provides evidence of town planning by a central authority imposing high standards of hygiene. Drains had manholes at intervals, allowing workmen to clear them of rubbish.

I **Indus River** rises at an altitude of over 5,000 metres in the Kailas range in Tibet, north of the Himalayas. Its length is about 2,700 km. It flows north-west for about 1,000 km, passes through the Himalayas, and then through Punjab and Sind in Pakistan. After flowing through the Thar Desert it is fed by the waters of the '5 rivers of the Punjab': the Jhelum, Chenab, Ravi, Beas and Sutlej.

Indus Valley settlers. Skeletons found in a cemetery at Harappa suggest that 2 basic races of Indus Valley men existed. Most were tall (about 1·75 metres) and Caucasoid in appearance. Others were smaller with finer features and 'Mediterranean' looks. One Mongoloid skeleton was also found in the cemetery.

M **Mohenjo daro** lay about 600 km south-east of Harappa, but unlike the latter, Mohenjo daro escaped vandalism. The site has been only partly excavated. The city had a fortified citadel like the one at Harappa, which it resembled in several ways.

R **Rajasthan,** now a state of India covering roughly the old state of Rajputana, borders present-day Pakistan. It lay about 150 km from the main Indus Valley cities.

Ritual bathing, which now dominates the life of the Indian city of Benares (Varanasi), was practised just as fervently in the Indus Valley settlements. Apart from its hygienic value, bathing is a purification ceremony. It is as essential to Hinduism as it was to the religion of the Indus Valley people.

The ruins of Harappa

S **Script** in the Indus Valley was pictographic and not alphabetical. About 400 signs have been found, and some have only recently been deciphered. The script ran in lines that probably read from right to left, below that left to right, then right to

Sign	Object	Meaning
		possession
		'star', Mars
		black
	2 previous signs combined	black star
		lord
		woman, female

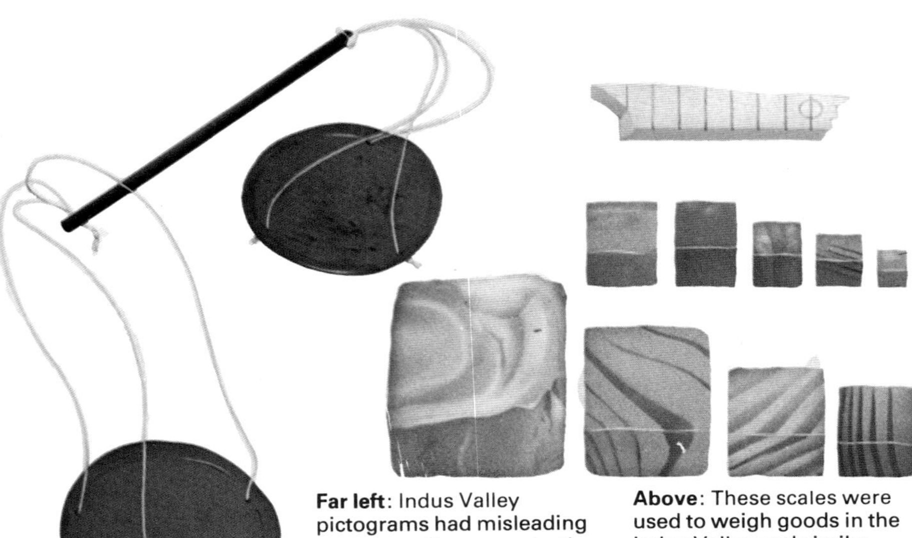

Far left: Indus Valley pictograms had misleading meanings. For example, the pictogram *roof* in the Dravidian language of the Indus Valley had the name *mey*, but it also served to mean *mai*, which, translated, meant *black*.

Above: These scales were used to weigh goods in the Indus Valley and similar ones can be found today. Weights were based on the bright red seed of the gunja plant, conventionally fixed at 0·118 grammes. Officials strictly controlled weights.

Baluchistan, silver from Afghanistan, and lead from RAJASTHAN. Indus Valley people almost certainly traded with the Sumerians, and the two cultures may have been related because pictures have been discovered which show that they wore quite similar clothing and hairstyles.

Language, arts and religion

The Indus Valley people used a pictographic SCRIPT which remains undeciphered to this day. It can still be seen on SEALS, pottery and amulets. The art of the Indus Valley was not outstanding, though some STATUETTES do have a certain graceful style. Jewellery was produced from gold, silver, lapis lazuli and precious stones such as amethysts.

Religion

Religion links the Indus Valley civilization to later periods in Indian history. The god SIVA was worshipped, bulls were sacred, and RITUAL BATHING was almost an obsession. On some seals Siva is shown as a three-headed god, lord of all the beasts.

Agriculture

Indus Valley farmers grew wheat, barley, rice, mustard, sesame, dates, melons and cotton, and they raised cattle, water buffaloes, sheep and pigs. Elephants, camels and horses may have been used as beasts of burden, while cats and dogs were kept both as pets and as working animals. Each city had a huge granary which stocked grain, just as later treasuries hoarded gold.

Decline and fall

The Indus Valley civilization lasted about 1,000 years before it declined and vanished. No one knows for certain why it fell; perhaps the land became infertile or the population outstripped its food supply. It is believed that the coastal areas rose in relation to the sea, so causing flooding inland. A combination of these factors would have weakened the Indus Valley people, leaving them an easy prey for invaders. ARYAN PEOPLE from the north-west probably destroyed the civilization by war about 1500 BC. Only its religion survived.

Above: The lively copper statuette of a dancing girl found at Mohenjo daro displays the vitality characteristic of later Indian sculpture. It is 10 cm high.

left, and so on. There is no indication that the pictographs were developed into cursive or CUNEIFORM writing, *(see page 11)* as in Mesopotamia.

Seals were common in the Indus Valley and many have survived. The motif is often an animal and occasionally a god in a square design. About 4 to 8 pictographs usually appeared above the symbol.

Siva, most important of the Hindu gods, was worshipped in the pre-Hindu Indus Valley settlements. The god is shown on some surviving seals in the form of Pasupati, lord of beasts. Several animals attend him. He has 3 faces, possibly symbolizing that he combines the roles of creator, preserver and destroyer. He sits on a low stool and wears a large horned headdress, which probably signifies his close association with the sacred bull. (Nandi, Siva's bull, is among the most worshipped of idols in present-day India.)

Statuettes found in the Indus Valley sites are among the best pieces of the civilization's art. Most impressive of all is the bronze figurine of a dancing girl.

Temple architecture so far excavated in the Indus Valley is small in scale. Religious buildings seem to have been small shrines rather than massive structures like those that dominated Sumerian and Egyptian cities. The religious buildings discovered by archaeologists differ little from ordinary houses.

Granaries at Harappa

War does not seem to have been a dominant feature of the Indus Valley civilization and few weapons have been found. This fact alone would explain why foreign invaders might have made an easy conquest.

Weights were standardized throughout all the Indus settlements and few fraudulent ones have been found, suggesting that strict control of trading was enforced. Weighing followed a binary system, the ratio being: 1, 2, 4, 8, 16, 32, 64. Weights were usually made of polished stone such as alabaster, limestone and jasper.

The Aegeans founded the fabulous Greek civilization which gave the world its treasury of mythology, art and legends, such as the story of the Minotaur, the topless towers of Ilium and the lost city of Atlantis.

The Aegean Peoples

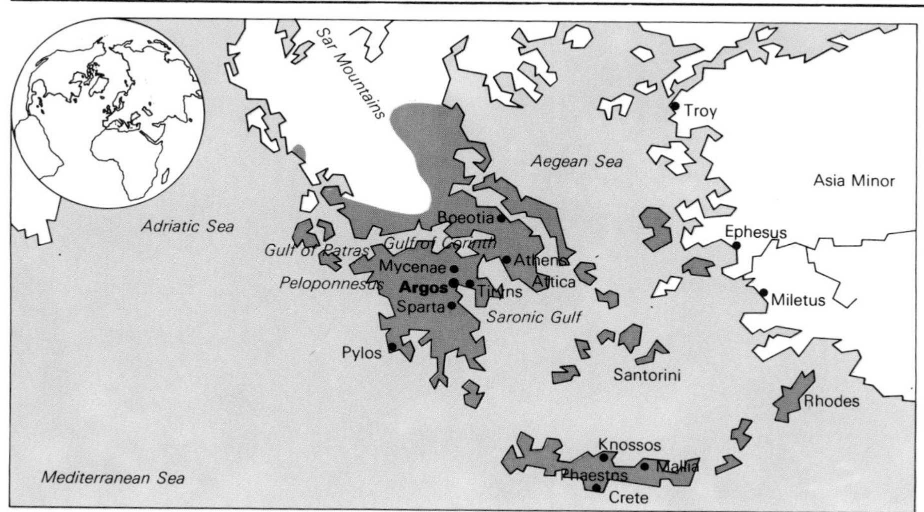

Above: The map shows that the Aegean civilization centred round the Peloponnesus and adjacent parts of Greece, and spread into the Aegean.

The AEGEAN CIVILIZATION of the eastern Mediterranean has two centres: the island of Crete and MYCENAE in the south-east area of the Greek mainland. Scholars differ in their opinions as to whether we should think of the Aegean as one civilization or two. No one knows where the early Cretans came from, but they may have been related to the HITTITES who lived in what is now Turkey. The Cretans were among the earliest peoples to make BRONZE tools and weapons (about 3000 BC). They were also called Minoans, after MINOS, their legendary king.

Beginnings

While the Cretans were establishing a civilization around their capital city of KNOSSOS, several tribes were moving southwards across Greece and by 2000 BC, a Greek mainland civilization was in being at Mycenae.

The Aegean lands had dry, hot summers and wet, mild winters. Mountains dominated both centres and only 20 per cent of the land was fit for cultivation. This limited the population and encouraged the Aegeans to look to the sea. The Cretans came to dominate the sea routes of the eastern Mediterranean and the Mycenaeans gained a reputation for piracy.

The Cretans founded the first civilization in Europe – the ancestor of the present Western civilization. Our knowledge of the Aegean civilization, though scanty, owes much to the work of two archaeologists: Heinrich SCHLIEMANN, who began to excavate Mycenae in 1876; and Sir Arthur EVANS, who began digging at Knossos in 1900.

Language

The solution to several mysteries about Crete may lie in its language. Archaeologists found two scripts in Crete, both inscribed on tablets of clay and written in syllabic scripts. Scholars called the oldest script LINEAR A and the other LINEAR B. Linear A has never been deciphered, but Linear B, deciphered in 1951, is the language of Mycenae. The Mycenaeans may have destroyed the Cretans in war and replaced the Linear A script with their own Linear B. But some scholars believe that Linear B was used in Crete long before Knossos was destroyed in 1400 BC.

Religion

Although the religions of Crete and Mycenae differ, their mythologies have several points of contact and both are part of the great mythology of the Greek world. A gold signet ring from Crete shows a woman praying by a pillar as a god descends from the sky. Cretan deities appeared in human form and dress, and people burnt sacrifices to them from hilltop shrines. Generally little is known about the religion of either Crete or Mycenae, though it is certain that the deities of Mycenae included the chief god, ZEUS, and his sea-god brother, POSEIDON. It is likely that the Mycenaean religion was an early form of the religion practised later by the Greeks.

Reference

A

Achaeans were among the earliest fair-skinned people to enter Greece (about 2000 BC). Sometimes the Greeks referred to themselves generally as Achaeans, though for the Hittites, the Achaeans were the people of a small kingdom on or near Rhodes.

Acrobats, or dancers of both sexes are shown somersaulting over huge bulls in pictures from Crete. The first bull acrobats were of the royal family; later, slaves performed the ceremony. Possibly it was a ritual designed to appease the 'earth bull' believed to be responsible for earthquakes.

Aegean civilization centred around the Aegean Sea — especially Crete and the Greek mainland settlements of Mycenae. It began in Crete about 3000 BC. When Cretan cities were destroyed about 1400 BC, Mycenae became the strongest Aegean power. Dorian Greeks conquered Mycenae and the Aegean civilization ended about 1000 BC.

Arcadians, one of the first fair-skinned people to invade Greece (about 2000 BC), settled in the north-central Peloponnesus. Hundreds of years later they led the resistance to warlike Sparta.

Minoan gold jewellery

Argos, 10 km south of Mycenae, was a Mycenaean citadel set on 2 hills. It had no warrior-nobles of its own.

Artistic craftsmen of Crete were famed throughout the eastern Mediterranean for their gold jewellery, marble vases, and beads of *faience* (a form of glazed earthenware).

Athens was already a place of some importance when Mycenae was at the height of its power and it already had a citadel on top of its acropolis. In mythology, THESEUS left from Athens to slay the Minotaur.

Atlantis is mentioned in the works of the Greek philosopher Plato as the 'lost continent'. In mythology, when the gods shared out the Earth, POSEIDON received a paradise called Atlantis, but its people became corrupt and threatened to dominate the whole world, so ZEUS planned their downfall. One night the sea swallowed up Atlantis in an earthquake. Possibly the real Atlantis was the island of Santorini (Thera), north of Crete.

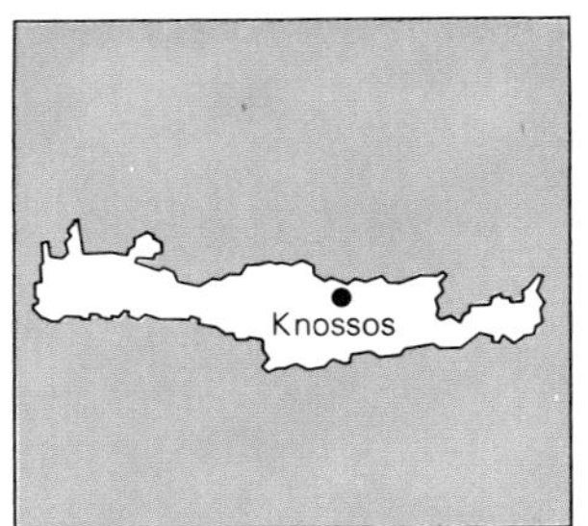

Left: The location map shows that Knossos lay close to the centre of the northern coast of the island of Crete.

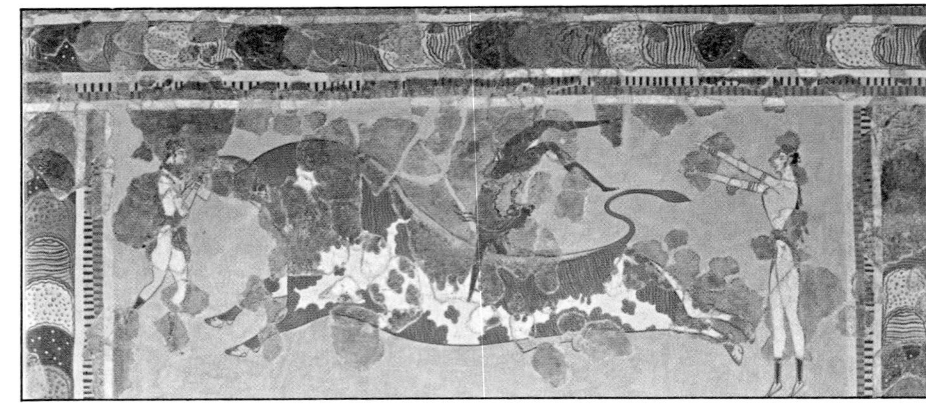

Above: A fresco from Knossos shows highly-skilled acrobats somersaulting dangerosly over a bull. Bull cults were common in early civilizations from Crete to Assyria.

The Cretans built four great palaces: the largest at KNOSSOS, the others at MALLIA, PHAESTOS and Kato Zakro. The palace at Knossos (covering 20,000 square metres) was a maze of halls, stairways, courts and chambers, each designed for a special purpose. There were bathrooms and water closets, and a system of drainage through terra-cotta pipes. Life at court is described in pictures that have survived from Knossos. Some of the most interesting frescoes from the Knossos palace show ACROBATS somersaulting over the horns of giant bulls in some dangerous sport ritual. Royal families seem to have enjoyed a leisurely life and their palaces were unfortified. Court dicing tables inlaid with gold and ivory were among the impressive works of Crete's ARTISTIC CRAFTSMEN.

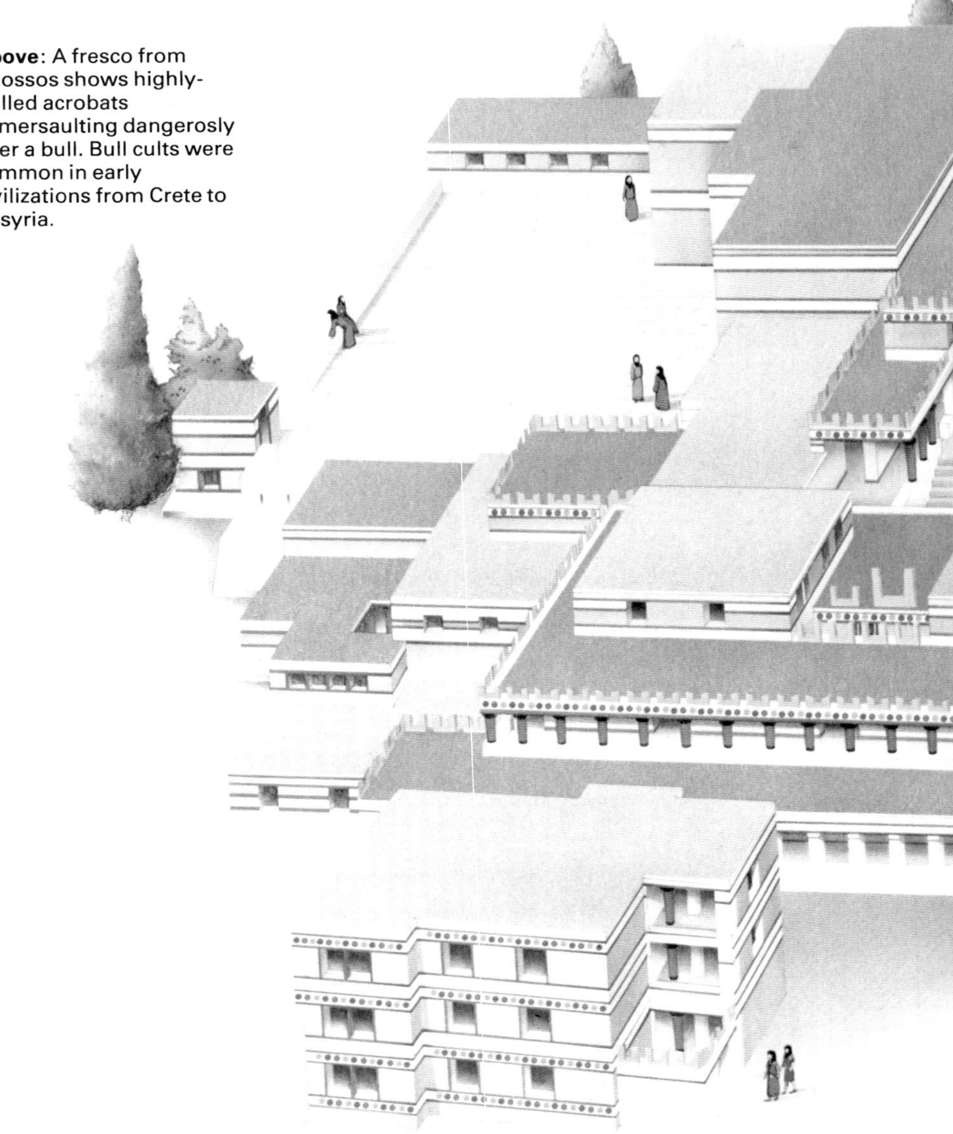

Mythology of Crete

The mythology of the Cretans suggests that they were in close contact with the Greek mainland. Minos, legendary king of Crete, was believed to be the son of Zeus and the goddess EUROPA. He became king of Crete when, in answer to his prayer, Poseidon sent him a sacrificial bull from the sea. (Bulls figure prominently in Cretan mythology and were probably sacred in its religion.) The wife of Minos gave birth to a Minotaur — a bull-headed man who was imprisoned in a maze called the LABYRINTH. To punish the Greeks of ATHENS for murdering one of his sons, Minos decreed that every ninth year (some say every year) they must provide seven youths and seven girls to feed the Minotaur. The monster was eventually killed by one of the intended victims, an Athenian hero named THESEUS.

Evidently the bull was a powerful symbol to the Cretans. Some scholars suggest that it signified the terrifying power of destructive earthquakes that perpetually rocked the island.

Attica, in south-eastern Greece, lay north-east of Mycenae and the Peloponnesus. Athens was founded near its southern shore.

B

Boeotians, one of the early fair-skinned invading tribes in Greece, set up the kingdom of Boeotia north-west of Attica. Long after the end of the Aegean civilization, Boeotia became the persistent enemy of Athens.

Bronze, a tough alloy composed of copper and a small quantity of tin, was first worked by the metalsmiths of Mesopotamia about 3000 BC. Knowledge of the new metal spread quickly to Crete, where metalsmiths put it to good use. But Crete was not rich in metals and soon had to import copper from Cyprus and tin from Spain.

D

Dorians began to invade Greece in force about 1150 BC, though they had migrated into Greece before this. They conquered the Peloponnesus, Crete and Rhodes and ended the Mycenaean civilization. They may have introduced iron tools and weapons into Greece.

E

Europa in mythology was the daughter of a king of Phoenicia. ZEUS fell in love with her, appeared in the form of a bull, and carried her out to sea and off to Crete. She married Zeus and gave birth to MINOS.

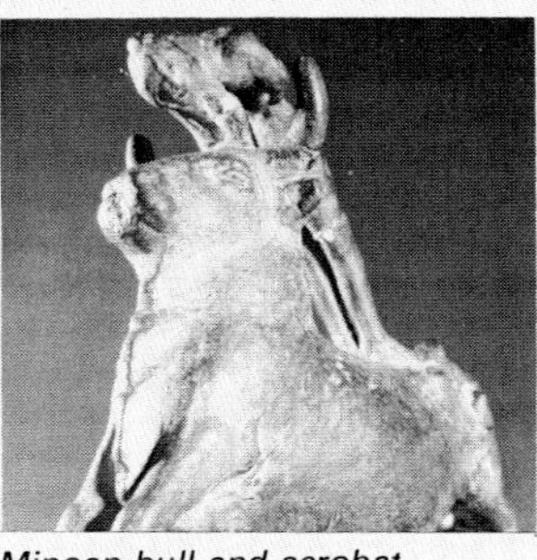

Minoan bull and acrobat

Evans, Sir Arthur (1851–1941) was a British archaeologist who began excavations in Crete in 1893 and at Knossos in 1900. His most noteworthy achievement was the almost total reconstruction of the palace of Knossos — present knowledge of the Cretan civilization comes largely from this work, but later scholars have criticized his methods.

Sir Arthur Evans

H

Hittites, an Indo-Aryan people of Asia Minor, dominated the Middle East for over 700 years between

Below: Knossos, the capital of the legendary King Minos, was one of the greatest cities of the ancient world, with a population in the region of 100,000. As Knossos increased in prosperity, building started on its magnificent and complex palace, in 1900 BC. The discovery of the ruins of the palace by Sir Arthur Evans was one of the most noteworthy events in our century. He found that the palace covered some 20,000 sq. metres and consisted of buildings with 2, 3, 4, and 5 storeys. Thick columns, some painted black, some red and some white supported the various layers and majestic staricases led to the higher levels and roofs. The sacred emblem of Crete, the horns of the bull, topped the roofs. Made of stone and painted gold, they shone brightly in the hot sun. The palace abounded in royal apartments, storage rooms and shrines built around a central paved courtyard.

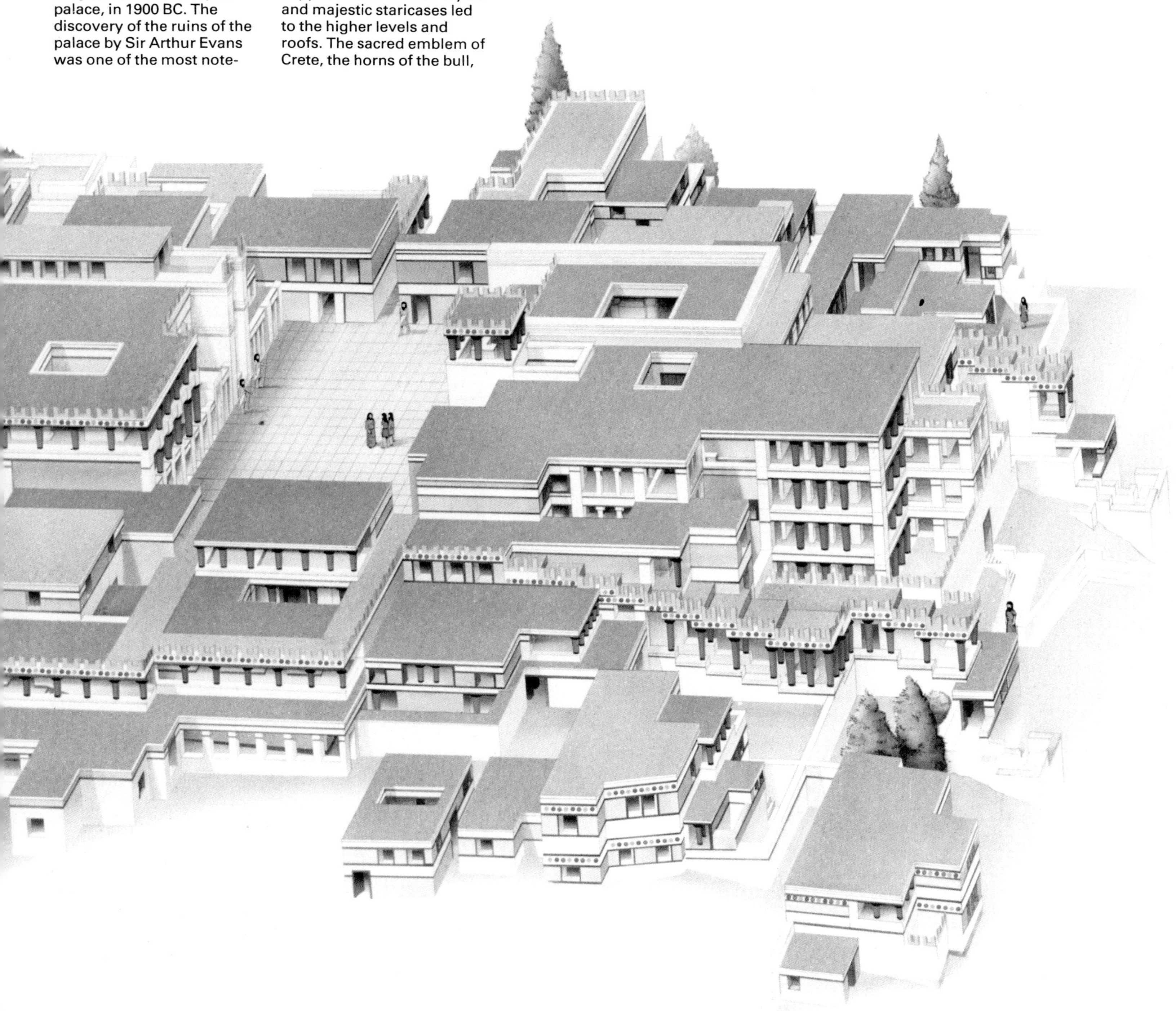

2000 and 1200 BC. *(See page 38.)*

Homer was said to be a blind Greek poet who lived about 800 BC. He is traditionally regarded as the author of the *Iliad* and the *Odyssey*, but some scholars believe that he collected and arranged his 2 epics from earlier material. Others doubt whether there ever was an author named Homer, but if he did exist, he was the first known European writer.

I **Iliad,** one of Homer's 2 great epics, consists of 24 sections which relate a 7-week episode in the Trojan war. The central hero is Achilles, a Greek warrior. When Achilles's commander, King Agamemnon, takes from him a beautiful girl captive, Achilles sulks and refuses to fight, and the Greeks suffer defeats. Eventually, Achilles re-enters the battle and kills Hector, the Trojan leader. Hector was the son of King Priam and was also the brother of Paris, who supposedly caused the war by kidnapping or eloping with Helen, wife of King Menelaus of Sparta.

Illyrians, one of the later invaders of Greece, settled in the western Balkans by about 1000 BC. At one time their power extended from the Danube River to the Adriatic Sea and the Sar Mountains. Later, they occupied the 'heel' of Italy for a while. Some merged with the Macedonians.

Ionians, an invading tribe, settled in central Greece. They later fled from the Dorians into Attica, where some became the ancestors of the Athenians. Others sailed to the coast of Asia Minor and founded 12 towns, including Ephesus and Miletus.

Achilles slaying a Trojan

K **Knossos** was probably founded by the Cretans about 3000 BC. After it developed into a city it was twice destroyed by earthquakes and twice rebuilt. The third (capital) city of Knossos, with its harbour town, may have housed

History of Crete

For about 550 years (1950 to 1400 BC) the Cretans enjoyed a golden age. They needed few soldiers on the island because the sea gave protection from the invasions suffered by most other civilizations. Although earthquakes twice destroyed Knossos, the industrious Cretans rebuilt it, each time better than before. Knossos became the largest European city of its time, with an estimated population of 100,000.

Crete's rulers were probably priest-kings, and there may at one time have been a city-state system rather than a unified central government. The country was self-sufficient in food, providing a diet of fish, meat and various vegetables. Both wine and beer were drunk.

Control of the sea routes was the basis of Cretan power and influence. Several pictures and lead and clay models have survived, showing that Cretan ships were masted and of low freeboard. Cretan seamen brought tin from Spain to supply the island's skilled metalworkers, and gold, pearls and ivory from northern Africa to be fashioned into jewellery. Cretan craftwork was much prized abroad, being superior to that of most neighbouring peoples. Craft products were exported especially to mainland Greece and Egypt, together with olive oil. Cretan sailors established colonies on other islands, including one at RHODES dating from about 1600 BC.

Suddenly, about 1400 BC, the palaces of Crete crashed into ruins. No one knows whether to attribute the destruction to an earthquake or a human enemy like the Myceneans. However, about that time the Cretan-owned island of Santorini (also called Thera, some 125 kilometres north of Crete) exploded in one of the biggest volcanic eruptions known to history. Possibly the resulting tidal wave and ash fallout destroyed Cretan civilization. Some people believe that the sudden disappearance of much of Santorini below the waves may be the real story of the 'lost continent of ATLANTIS'.

If Crete survived the catastrophe of about 1400 BC at all, it was as a much weakened state, fast declining. In art and craft at least, the decline had set in before 1400 BC. The centre of power in the eastern Mediterranean passed to Mycenae and the Cretan civilization perished.

Above: The *labrys*, or double axe was a sacred symbol of the Minoans. It gave its name to the mythical Labyrinth – the complex maze in which the legendary Minotaur lived.

Mycenae

The Mycenaeans were generally a taller and tougher people than the Cretans. Living on the

Right: Snake goddesses were common features of the Cretan and Egyptian civilizations. The priestess of the Cretan snake goddess or earth mother was widely worshipped in caves and hilltop shrines.

Left: These clay tablets show the Cretan script known as Linear A. Sir Arthur Evans was the first to recognize these hieroglyphics, but they remain as yet, undeciphered.

100,000 people. Its splendid palace, covering 20,000 square metres, flourished some 3,500 years ago. Knossos and the other Cretan cities were destroyed mysteriously about 1400 BC.

L

Labyrinth was the complex maze in which the Minotaur lived. When THESEUS entered the Labyrinth to kill the Minotaur he payed out a ball of thread given him by Ariadne, daughter of MINOS. Thus he was able to find his way out after the killing. The legend of the Labyrinth may have been inspired by the maze-like construction of Knossos Palace. The Labyrinth was named after the Cretan double axe (*labrys*).

West Magazines – Knossos

Linear A is the older of 2 scripts discovered in Crete. It was written in syllabic form (each sign representing a syllable) and has not been deciphered.

Linear B is the later of 2 scripts found by archaeologists in Crete. Michael Ventris, a British architect, deciphered it in 1951, and found it to be an early form of Greek.

M

Mallia, one of the chief cities of Crete, had a palace smaller but similar to that of KNOSSOS. Several fine private houses belonging to aristocrats have been excavated there.

Minos, legendary king of Crete, appears prominently in Greek mythology. Several myths surround him, his wife Pasiphae, and his children. Minos is said to have been the first to bring Crete under one ruler. Possibly he was a real person whose awesome power encouraged others to weave stories around his name.

Mycenae has 2 meanings: the city, based on the palace citadel; and the much larger territory controlled by or in alliance with the Mycenaeans. The independently ruled kingdom of PYLOS, for example, is referred to as part of Mycenae.

O

Odyssey, one of Homer's 2 great epics, tells of the adventures of Odysseus (Ulysses) during his return from the Trojan war and the problems he faced on his homecoming.

P

Peloponnesus is the peninsula of Greece south of the gulfs of Patras, Corinth and Saronic. It is linked to Attica by the Isthmus of Corinth. It was the

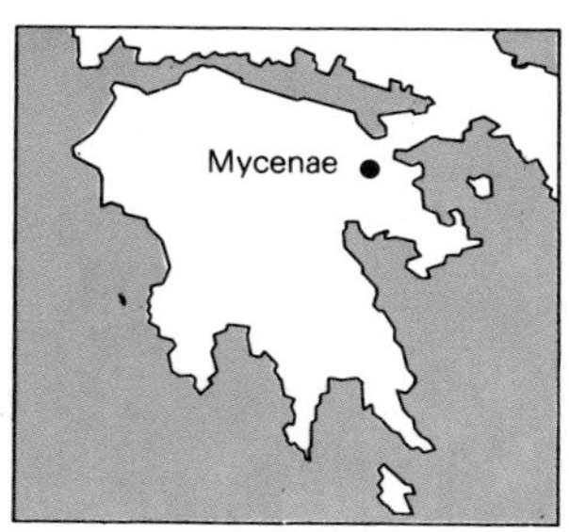

Left: The location map shows that Mycenae lay in the Peloponnesus, near to the land bridge with Attica.

Left: In 1876 the archaeologist Heinrich Schliemann found the gold mask of a Mycenaean of rank who lived 3,500 years ago. He mistakenly believed it to be the mask of Agamemnon. Cretans probably took the idea of mask-making from Egypt.

mainland they had to jostle with other tribes for the limited territory available and with their advanced bronze weapons they easily conquered the stone-age farmers of south-eastern Greece. By 1900 BC they had established fortress towns at MYCENAE, PYLOS, ARGOS, TIRYNS and other sites from which they commanded the land and the nearby sea.

Little is known about the political and social structure of the Mycenaean world, though it may have been organized around city-states. Popula-

Below: The grave circle at Mycenae enclosed 6 royal tombs hewn vertically out of the rock. Archaeologists found 19 skeletons in them.

Disk from Phaestos

heartland of the Aegean civilization on the mainland.

Phaestos, one of the leading Cretan cities, had a palace smaller but similar to the one at KNOSSOS. Some 3,000 seal imprints on clay found at Phaestos have contributed to our knowledge of ancient Crete.

Pylos was one of the chief Mycenaean towns. LINEAR B tablets found at Pylos reveal that a person's status there was measured by amounts of grain. For example, the king was said to be worth 30 units of grain, his minister 10, and so on.

Poseidon, god of the sea and brother of the sky-god ZEUS, was called Neptune by the Romans. He was worshipped by mariners because he was thought to have the power to create storms.

R

Rhodes, an island between Crete and Asia Minor, was colonized by the Cretans about 1600 BC. It was colonized again by Dorians from Argos some time before 1000 BC.

S

Schliemann, Heinrich (1822–90) was a wealthy German businessman who devoted his life to archaeology. Fascinated by Homer's *Iliad,* he began to excavate TROY in 1871 and started on Mycenae in 1876.

Spices and flavourings enlivened the dull, cereal-based diet of the Mycenaeans. They included coriander, sesame, celery, mint and cress.

Schliemann's wife, Sophie

T

Talanton or *talent* was the unit of weight in Crete. It had 2 values: 25.86 kg and 37.80 kg. Volume was measured by the *cup*.

Theseus, an Athenian, was one of the intended victims of the Minotaur. When he landed in Crete, Ariadne (daughter of King MINOS) fell in love with him and helped him to kill the Minotaur. Theseus later abandoned Ariadne on Naxos to the god Dionysos, but became king

Above: The blade of this magnificent Mycenaean dagger inlaid with gold and silver shows nobles attacking 3 powerful lions.

tions were tiny. The kingdom of Pylos had perhaps 200 settlements containing 50,000 people. It was divided into 16 units, each controlled by a governor. Below the Mycenaean court, with its top-ranking nobles and officials, was a class of second-rank, land-holding nobles. Below them were the 'working class' and a class of slaves, most of whom were women, probably seized after their menfolk had been killed in some battle or act of piracy.

Trade, agriculture and crafts

The Mycenaeans (like the Cretans) traded mainly by barter, but barley, and possibly ceremonial axe-heads, passed as a kind of money. The Mycenaeans had a simple number system which, strangely, lacked a symbol for zero. Mycenaean weights were based on the TALANTON, which had two values: 25.86 and 37.80 kilogrammes.

The main crops were barley and, as agricultural methods improved, wheat. SPICES added flavour to the dull diet. Olives, figs and vines were cultivated and bees kept for honey. Small horses, oxen, cattle, pigs, goats and sheep were raised. These provided transport and haulage, food and milk, wool, hides and other products. Specialized tradesmen included coastguards, masons, furniture makers, and an obscure group called 'blue glass paste makers'.

The lion gate palace

Just about the time that Knossos fell (about 1400 BC), the kings of Mycenae rebuilt their hilltop palace-citadel. Impressive entrance gates were built into the walls. One, still standing has a massive lintel topped by a triangular block carved with two lions against a column. Outside the walls, huge beehive-shaped tombs were constructed.

Within the palace the rulers lived comfortably, but less luxuriously than the earlier rulers of Knossos. The Mycenaean court jewellery was superb in quality and may have been Cretan in origin or modelled on Cretan jewellery.

Mythology, legend and history

Mythology, legend and history are intertwined in our knowledge of Mycenae. Much of it comes from two great epics, the ILIAD and the ODYSSEY by the Greek poet HOMER, who wrote 600 years after Mycenaean power had reached its peak.

Historians know that several fair-skinned tribes began to conquer the darker-skinned people of the Greek mainland about 4,000 years ago. The invading tribes included ARCADIANS, ACHAEANS, IONIANS, BOEOTIANS, DORIANS, ILLYRIANS, and THRACIANS. Having subdued much of southern Greece between 1400 and 1200 BC, the Mycenaeans turned to conquests overseas. They attacked TROY in Asia Minor which, according to tradition, fell in 1184 after a ten-year siege. In Homer's epics, the TROJAN WAR was fought because of the love between a Trojan prince and the queen of Sparta. In fact, the Trojan war was probably fought over trade rivalries.

New waves of Dorian Greeks attacked the Mycenaean towns about 1000 BC. The victorious Dorians intermixed with the Mycenaeans, who disappeared from history. The Peloponnesus fell, and only ATTICA kept its freedom. Mainland Europe's first civilization was at an end.

Above: The long Trojan War was finally brought to a close when Ulysses cunningly built a wooden horse, packed it with soldiers, and left it as a gift outside the gates of Troy. He knew the Trojans would take it inside. The Greek soldiers inside the horse came out at night and let their comrades into the city.

of Athens. Many other stories are told about Theseus, including one that he was Poseidon's son.

Thracians, one of the tribes that invaded Greece, settled in an area stretching from north-eastern Greece to the Danube River and the Black Sea. Later, the southern part of this area was called Thrace.

Tiryns was one of the Mycenaean towns. Interesting frescoes and a Hittite figurine have been found there.

Trojan War. According to HOMER, Troy was ruled by King Priam, whose son Paris fell in love with Helen, wife of Menelaus the king of Sparta. Paris either kidnapped or eloped with Helen, and took her to Troy. The whole of Greece was outraged and an alliance of Greek states organized a seaborne invasion of Troy under the leadership of King Menelaus of Sparta, King Agamemnon of Mycenae, Achilles and Ulysses (Odysseus). But after 10 years of siege the walls of Troy still held. Then Ulysses used cunning. He built a wooden horse, packed it with soldiers, and left it outside the Trojan walls. The Greeks then pretended to sail away, accepting defeat. The joyful Trojans came out of their city and dragged the curious 'horse' back inside their walls. That night the Greeks came silently out of the horse, opened the Trojan gates, and let their comrades in. The Greeks then massacred the Trojans, plundered their city and burned it down.

Troy, the city attacked in the Trojan war, lay on the north-eastern coast of Asia Minor, near the entrance to the Dardanelles. SCHLIEMANN began excavations in 1871, which led to the discovery of 9 cities, each built upon the ruins of its predecessors. His belief that Homer's Troy was more than just an imaginary city was finally proved correct.

Bronze miniature of Zeus

Z

Zeus, the sky-god, fathered both gods and men. Well established as chief god in the Aegean civilization, he retained this role among the Greeks of later times. The Romans kept him, but called him Jupiter.

Babylon, with its exotic Hanging Gardens and its ominous Tower of Babel, was the capital of an empire which spanned 1,500 years, situated in a desert where two rivers meet. It was a haven for prophets, astrologers and scientists.

The Babylonians

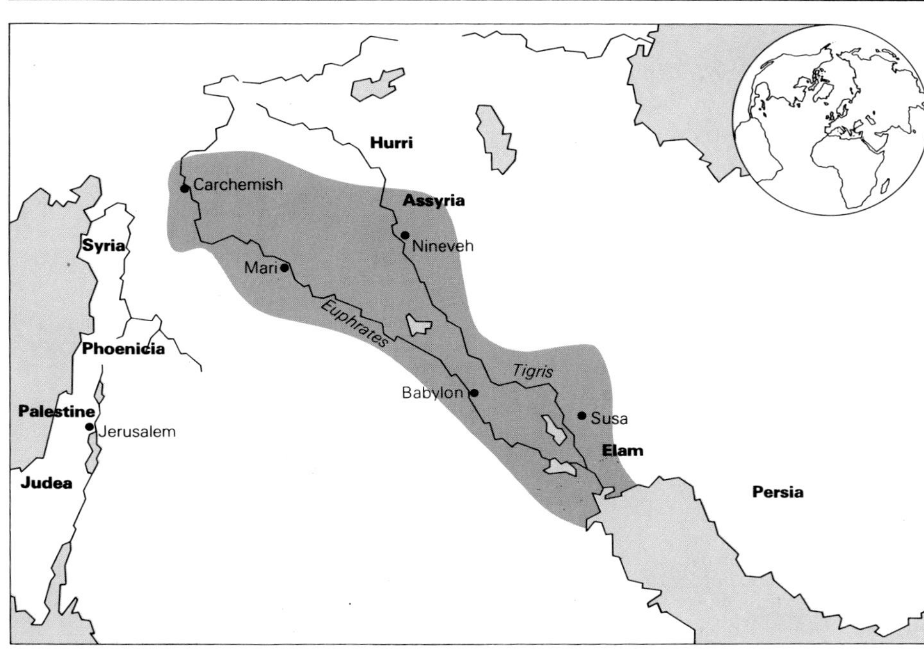

Above: Hammurabi's empire centred on Mesopotamia, the land around the Euphrates and Tigris Rivers. It extended from Sumer into Syria.

The Semitic-speaking Amorites established their civilization around the capital of Babylon about 1900 BC. Unlike the Sumerians, who had to develop civilization from the beginnings, the Amorites inherited the cultural experience of their predecessors. They founded two Babylonian empires separated by 95 years of occupation by their northern neighbours, the Assyrians. Babylonia reached the peak of its influence and expansion under King Hammurabi (reigned 1792–c.1750 BC).

Babylon was a desert city, standing on the life-giving Euphrates River at the point where it curved within 12 kilometres of the Tigris River. A thousand years after Hammurabi, Babylon was famous for its HANGING GARDENS, which became one of the wonders of the ancient world. Babylonian priest-scientists studied ASTROLOGY and continued and extended the number systems of the Sumerians.

Above: Hammurabi, Babylon's lawyer-king, kneels in prayer.

Babylonian society

Below the king, four main classes lived in Babylon: the nobles, the middle class, low-ranking freemen, and slaves. Slaves were allowed to marry free people, and the children of such marriages became free on the death of the slave parent. Yet the status of slaves was far from clear. While one set of laws treated them as people with rights, other laws defined them as no more than possessions of other people.

Babylon and other Amorite cities throbbed with the bustle of workmen and traders. The bricklayers, carpenters, butchers, cooks, brewers, bakers, potters, metalsmiths, masons, spinners and weavers plied their trades as they had done in pre-Amorite times.

Under Amorite kings such as Hammurabi, private enterprise boomed — good reason perhaps for the spate of laws governing contracts and dealings. A vigorous trade developed in slaves, cattle, grain, offices of profit such as priesthoods, loans, deposits, leases, and the hiring of labour and property. Money lenders thrived as the demand for business capital grew. Some of the Babylonian deities were worshipped as gods of commerce who welcomed the use of their temples as trading centres. However, the state also traded through officials called *tamkaru,* who combined the functions of merchants, bankers and government agents generally.

Ordinary people's houses were thick-walled and made of mud, often semi-detached. They were frequently built to suit the site, even at the expense of the inhabitants' needs. Better houses, of baked brick, were of two or more stories built around a central courtyard.

Public buildings in Babylon were much more ambitious architecturally than the private dwellings. During the second Babylonian empire (625-538 BC) Babylon was rebuilt on a vast scale by King NEBUCHADNEZZAR II. The outer wall (24

Reference

A **Anu,** one of the chief gods of Mesopotamia, presided over the sky. He was the city god of ERECH in Sumer (*see page 12*).
Astrolabe is an instrument used for measuring heavenly bodies and checking their patterns and movements. It was essential to astrologers, astronomers and navigators. At sea, the sextant replaced it in the AD 1700s.
Astrology is the pursuit of studying movements of stars and planets in order to foretell events. The CHALDEANS were its greatest exponents. Chaldean priests discarded the sky gods in favour of a system of religion based on astrology and the study of numbers. Priests at first used astrology to predict national events; later, they plotted personal horoscopes. The preoccupation of NABONIDUS (the last king of Babylon) with astrology and numerology (the pseudo-science that claims to tell a person's 'fortune' by studying his name and birth time) caused him to neglect the defence of his empire. Consequently it fell undefended to Persia.

Ivory plaque, c.800s BC

B **Babylonian captivity** came after the Babylonians sacked Jerusalem in 586 BC. The attack was to avenge what the Babylonians considered to be treachery on the part of Judea. Many Jews were exiled to Babylon (traditionally for 70 years, but more probably 53). The Bible mentions 3 deportations.

C **Canal building** was among the most important activities of river civilizations from Egypt to China and Hammurabi's reign was a great canal-building period. Babylon, a desert city dependent upon the river, could expand its population only in proportion to its food supply. Improved

Ibexes in bronze and gold

Above: Mythical animals portrayed on glazed brick once adorned the Ishtar Gate of Babylon's great wall.

metres thick) had a perimeter of 18 kilometres and enclosed a city of 200,000 people. There was a road on top of the wall wide enough for a chariot to turn on. The inner wall had eight impressive gates, each sacred to a different deity. The ISHTAR gate stood over ten metres, with towers twice as high. The gateway was surfaced with glazed blue bricks cemented in bitumen. These were also decorated with magnificent reliefs of bulls, dragons and symbols of the chief god, MARDUK.

The Hanging Gardens overlooked the Ishtar gate. These were probably terraces of earth planted with trees and flowers on a huge step pyramid. Pumps raised water to the terraces through which footpaths led to the top. A road ran from the Ishtar gate to the biggest of all the Mesopotamian ziggurats which another people — the Jews — called the TOWER OF BABEL.

Below: The ziggurat of Babylon rose higher than all its predecessors. The Jews, who helped to build it during the 'Babylonian captivity', thought their taskmasters were trying to reach heaven. Toiling alongside many enslaved peoples speaking different languages, the Jews thought God had confused the workers' tongues so as to make co-operation impossible.

Above and right: Babylon, located on a branch of the Euphrates where it came near to the Tigris, was the hub of the river traffic between the Persian Gulf and the Syrian and Hittite territories to the north.

agriculture depended upon better irrigation. The transference of the centre of civilization in Mesopotamia from the delta region (Sumer) to the plain (Babylon) was a consequence of improved irrigation through the construction of canals.

Carchemish became the eastern capital of the Hittites when they were already in decline. When the Assyrians took Carchemish in 717 BC, Hittite power finally disintegrated.

Chaldeans, a Semitic people, settled in southern Mesopotamia about 1000 BC. Their name became associated with the pursuit of astrology. After an unsuccessful attempt, they eventually seized control of Babylon in 626 BC and founded the second Babylonian empire. This fell to the Persians in 539 BC.

Cyrus the Persian rose from obscurity to found the powerful Persian empire. He overthrew the king of Media (sited in present-day Iran) about the 550s BC and conquered several other kingdoms. Babylon eventually fell to him in 539 BC and he ruled for 10 years.

D

Dreams, now believed to be a key to understanding the unconscious mind, were in ancient times thought to reveal the future.

Clay printing matrix

One of the most famous dreams of all times was that of the pharaoh who dreamed that 7 thin cows ate 7 fat ones. Joseph the Hebrew told him that this meant 7 years of good harvests would be followed by 7 years of famine. In Babylon, *sha'ilu* priests had the special function of interpreting dreams. In theory, the priests took the puzzling dreams to a god who interpreted them for the priests to relate.

E

Ea, Babylonian god of the waters, was also city god of Eridu. He was supposedly the father of MARDUK.

Boxers in clay c. 200s BC

Religion

Civilizations from India to the Aegean (and later to Rome and northern Europe) regularly 'borrowed' gods from one another. According to the Babylonian myth of creation, all things began with the fusion of sweet water with salt water. First came the deities. These included ANU (the powerful) and EA (of great intellect). The goddess TIAMAT personified the sea. Using storms and terrifying winds, the supergod Marduk killed Tiamat, became supreme, and brought order out of chaos. To each subordinate deity Marduk assigned a special role.

Astrology and astronomy

The Babylonians saw the world as a place subject to the whims of the gods. However, it was possible from omens, DREAMS, the movements of animals or unusual births, to foresee what the gods would do. Above all, the key lay in astrology. Priests first used astrology in Babylon to predict affairs of state such as harvests, floods, invasions and the king's life-span. Priestly records tell us: 'If the sun stands in the path of the moon, the king will be secure on the throne,' and 'If in the month of Ab the thunder god casts his mouth, there will be gloom in the land.' The need to be reasonably correct in their predictions must have spurred the priests to the study of more reliable sciences. Only late in Babylon's history did astrologers cast personal HOROSCOPES.

Alongside the astrologers were the astronomers, and from Babylon came the oldest-known astronomical instrument, the ASTROLABE. Astronomers also recorded eclipses of the sun and the moon. There was generally a great interest in numbers. A decimal system coexisted with

F **Fabulous beasts** and monsters were common themes in the world of the ancient Middle East and eastern Mediterranean. Egypt had its sphinx and Crete its minotaur. Genii (who appear in the *Arabian Nights*) were already present in Babylon, as was the dragon, which later made its way to China. Assyria had its human-headed, winged bulls.

G **Ghee** (clarified butter), commonly used in India and nearby countries, was part of the diet of Babylon. Butter is melted or boiled to evaporate the water and to strain or skim off the solid matter. The oil of the butter which remains is the ghee. The Babylonians used it for cooking and also for various medicinal and religious purposes.

Gods were 'borrowed' from other civilizations, although the deity so taken was often given another name. MARDUK, the city god, can be equated with Zeus and Jupiter. ISHTAR, goddess of love, is equivalent to Aphrodite of the Greeks and Venus of the Romans.

H **Hanging Gardens** of Babylon were reputed to be so splendid that they were included among the Greeks' 'Seven Wonders of the World'. Remains of them have been found near the palace. Terraces of deep earth were supported on an arched structure, probably part of a vast step pyramid.

Horoscopes could only be cast when knowledge was available about which planets and stars were visible at the time of a person's birth. Horoscopic astrology therefore had to await the compilation of the zodiac. Although horoscopes were cast in Egypt and Greece, they were almost certainly first cast by the CHALDEANS.

Ea, the god of water, as judge

Hurrians, a little-known people, played an important role in Middle Eastern history during the 1000s BC. They probably came from the Zagros mountains of Persia. They were known to the Sumerians before 2000 BC and probably dominated Assyria during the time of

Left: Hammurabi stands before the sun god to receive the symbols of justice. Below the picture, the king's laws – the most advanced legal code up to that time – were set out in cuneiform writing on the 223-cm high basalt stele. Hammurabi's code gave rough justice with a fine touch of class distinction in its penalties.

Above: On a cylinder seal impression, the sun god Shamesh rises between 2 mountains. Ea, god of the waters, stands to the right facing Ishtar, goddess of love and fertility.

another system based on 60, and its subdivision 12. The Babylonians divided the day into 12 *roms* (each equivalent to two hours). The *rom* was subdivided into minutes, and again into seconds. A cuneiform system of symbols represented numbers up to 59 and these could be added to the symbol that represented 60.

Agriculture

Under Hammurabi a vigorous policy of CANAL BUILDING was undertaken to bring prosperity through increased agricultural yields. The staple diet was barley, which was eaten in the form of unleavened bread and drunk as beer. Other cereals eaten as bread or as a kind of porridge, included millet, wheat, rye and (after about 1000 BC) rice. Cereals were also cooked with honey, milk, GHEE, sesame oil or fruits and made into cakes and biscuits.

Vegetables included onions, beans, peas, lentils, cucumbers, cabbages and LETTUCES; and there were fruits such as apples, apricots, figs, quinces and pomegranates. Above all, there was the date, sometimes made into date wine. Grape wine was also drunk. Added to this fairly varied diet were the products of cows, sheep and goats, whose meat was eaten at festivals.

Holidays

Religious festivals provided the occasion for holidays. These could occupy several days in a month, but there was no weekly day off such as a sabbath. The new year festival lasted from 11 to 15 days. Letters from the second Babylonian empire refer to men complaining about over-work. There is also the hint of a threatened strike: 'The people are not agreeable (to the terms of their task) and will not do the king's work.' However, there was very little democracy in Babylonia.

Language and the arts

The language of Babylonia and its northern neighbour Assyria was Akkadian, and had many forms of local dialect. Akkadian took its system of writing from Sumerian, the world's oldest written language. They were both written in cuneiform on clay tablets. Sumerian works such as the EPIC OF GILGAMESH (*see page 12*) were edited and re-arranged into new forms and Babylonia's own early *Epic of Creation* told how Marduk killed Tiamat and created the world from her body.

Surviving visual arts from Babylonia include a few statues, notably a diorite bearded head,

Below: A boundary stone records the gift of some land in southern Babylonia to Gula-Eves by the local governor. Carved symbols represent the gods invoked to protect the transaction.

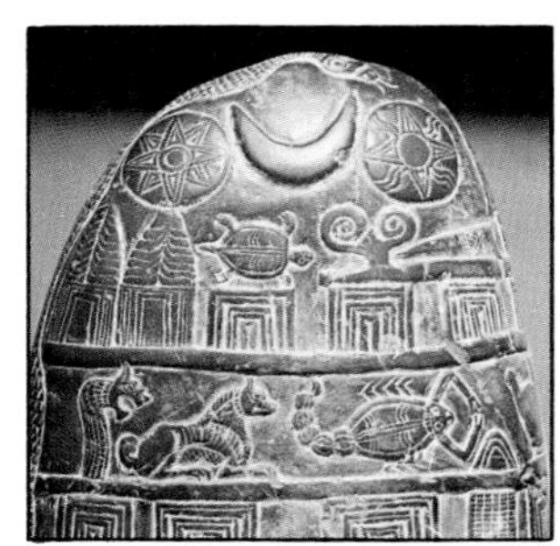

Hammurabi. Their heartland in northern Mesopotamia was called Hurri. They had their own religion but their deities included Teshub (the Hittite storm god) and his wife, Hebat. Some Hittite queens had Hurrian names.

Ishtar (or Astarte) was the Babylonian goddess of love, fertility and nature. In mythology she descended into Hades (hell) to search for and bring back to life her slain lover, Tammuz. This myth is believed to symbolize the re-emergence of plant life in spring, following its 'death' in winter.

Judea, a state in southern Palestine, was named after the tribe of Judah from which came the word *Jew*. Its capital, Jerusalem, was sacked in 586 BC. The state survived until AD 70, when the Romans ended it.

Kassites, probably an Indo-European people, moved westwards from the mountains of Persia. They took Babylon and ruled from there between the 1700s and 1100s BC, when they returned to the Persian mountains. They spoke their own language but did not write it. Their gods were probably related to those of the Persians and Hindus. After their return to Persia they survived as a distinct people for another 1,000 years, but little is known of them.

Lettuces have been cultivated from earliest-known times. They are not found anywhere in the wild state. They were part of the diet of the Babylonians and probably transmitted several waterborne diseases.

Marduk (or Merodach), city god of Babylon, grew in status in step with his city and became supreme god. Hymns composed in his honour are among the noblest pieces in Babylonian literature.

Lion c. 1000s BC

Mursilis I, king of the Hittites, attacked the Kassite rulers of Babylon about 1530 BC. The Hittites claimed that they destroyed Babylon and subdued the HURRIANS, but this is doubtful. Mursilis was assassinated upon his return to the homeland.

Nabonidus (reigned 556- 539 BC), last king of Babylon, may have been a usurper. He was so preoccupied with religious matters that he left the state unde-

probably of Hammurabi, which was found at Susa in Elam. Examples of painting, which tended to follow Sumerian styles, can be found on the walls of Mari on the Euphrates. During the second Babylonian empire, wall motifs such as those on the Ishtar gate were typical and FABULOUS BEASTS and all kinds of monsters abounded.

Law and government

Among Babylon's greatest achievements was Hammurabi's code of laws. This laid down that wrongdoers should be judged and punished by society rather than by the victim or his family. Under the code, a man with a chronically sick wife could remarry if he undertook to continue to support his sick wife. But a debtor could enslave his wife to the man he owed money to for up to three years. If a man divorced his wife without her giving cause, he had to pay her compensation. On the death of a father, all sons inherited equally.

The code dispensed rough justice, but not equally between the classes. For example, if a doctor treated a noble who consequently lost an eye, the doctor's hands were amputated. If the doctor caused the loss of a poor freeman's eye he had to pay 50 SHEKELS of silver as compensation. When a doctor blinded a slave's eye he had to pay half the value of the slave to his or her owner. All killing was punished as murder and courts made no distinction between premeditated murder, manslaughter or accidental death.

If Hammurabi's code was heavy-handed, it was at least every man's right rather than a privilege granted to the few. Courts tried to be fair to the accused, who were allowed up to six months in which to produce witnesses. In Hammurabi the Babylonians had a conscientious king heading an efficient government.

The first Babylonian empire

Under Hammurabi (1792-1750 BC) Babylonia expanded its frontiers to include SYRIA in the west, Assyria in the north, and Elam to the east. Hammurabi deposed local princes and organized the empire into provinces under governors responsible to him. The more Babylonia prospered, the more its desert neighbours envied its wealth.

The frontiers, which had few natural defences, proved difficult to defend and large parts of the empire broke away under Hammurabi's successors. The KASSITES, a hill people from the northwest, took Babylon and ruled the remains of the empire for over 500 years. About 1530 BC, King MURSILIS I of the Hittites raided Babylon in force, beginning a long series of attacks by foreign armies. Another people, the HURRIANS, attacked Babylon from east of the Tigris. Generally, little is known about Babylonia during the thousand years that followed Hammurabi's rule.

Above: The Babylonians used sheep's livers in divination. This clay model shows how they were divided into 55 sections and inscribed with omens and magical formulae.

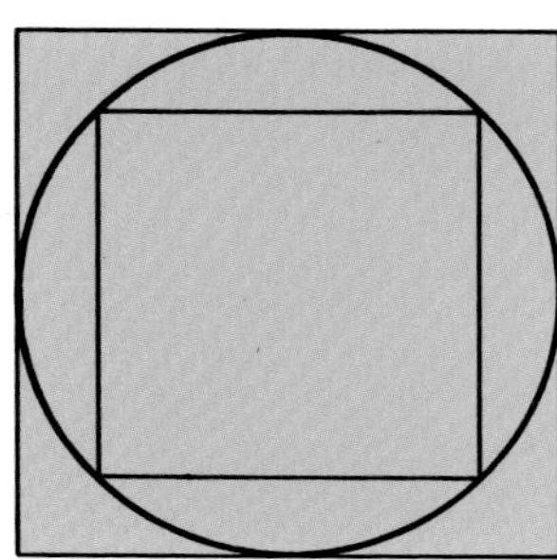

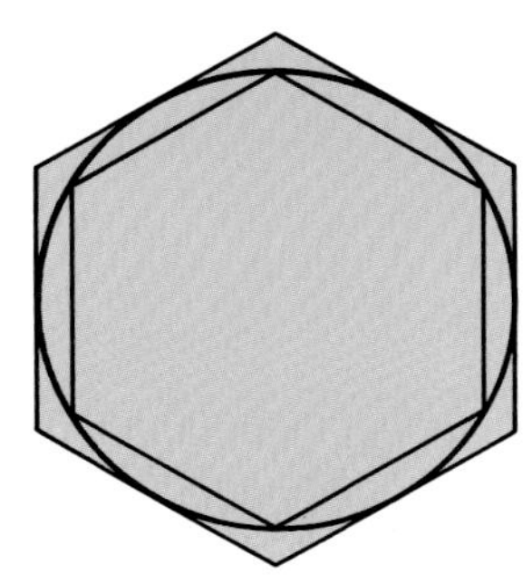

Above: Babylonian mathematicians discovered how to find the approximate area of a circle. They constructed either squares or hexagons to touch inside and outside the circle, then took half the combined areas of the inner and outer figures.

The Assyrian occupation

Nabu-nasir, puppet-king of Babylon ruled without interference from Assyria, because he pursued pro-Assyrian policies. At his death in 734 BC, his kingdom of Babylon had declined into a vassal state of Assyria. South of Babylon, the CHALDEANS (supposedly subject to Babylonia) had controlled the land for about 100 years. They now openly rebelled and seized the throne. The Babylonians then sought the aid of their Assyrian overlords, who drove off the Chaldeans. But the Babylonians paid a heavy price, for in 721 BC the remains of Babylonia passed under Assyrian rule.

The second Babylonian empire

When Assyria's power declined, the Chaldeans at last took Babylon and in 625 BC they set up the second Babylonian empire under King NABOPOLASSAR. The star-studying Chaldeans were to rule Babylonia for 87 brilliant years. Nabopolassar's son, soon to become Nebuchadnezzar II (reigned 605-562 BC) fought the battle of CARCHEMISH in 605 BC. There he defeated the remnant of the Assyrian army together with the army of King NECHO of Egypt, which fled back home in disarray.

Soon, Nebuchadnezzar's empire extended from Elam to the borders of Egypt. It included Syria and PALESTINE. The Jewish kingdom of JUDEA submitted to Nebuchadnezzar, but later unwisely sided with Egypt against him. He sacked their capital of Jerusalem in 586 BC and deported the population to Babylon – a period in their history known as the BABYLONIAN CAPTIVITY. Deliverance came in 539 BC, when CYRUS THE PERSIAN defeated the Babylonian army of King NABONIDUS. Babylonia collapsed and was absorbed into the new Persian empire.

---

fended and he became unpopular both with the priesthood and the people, and his foreign alliances failed.

Nabopolassar, first Chaldean king of Babylon, established the second Babylonian empire in 625 BC. In alliance with the Medes and Persians he destroyed Nineveh, the Assyrian capital, in 612 BC.

Nebuchadnezzar II, king of the second Babylonian empire in 605–562 BC, commanded his father's enemies while he was heir to the throne. He built Babylon into a splendid city and under his rule Babylonia reached its peak.

Necho, Assyria's puppet-pharaoh of Egypt, took advantage of the collapse of Assyria to seize Palestine and Syria. But then he sped north to aid the last stand of the Assyrians. He was beaten by the Babylonians under Nebuchadnezzar and fled back to Egypt.

P

Palestine took its name from *Philistine,* the nationality of Goliath who, according to the Bible, was killed by David. It was also known as Canaan.

S

Shekel was a unit of weight in Babylon, Phoenicia and Palestine. It weighed about 14 grammes.

Syria in ancient times included present-day Syria, Lebanon, Jordan, most of Israel and north Saudi Arabia. It was ruled successively by Amorites, Hittites, Egyptians, Phoenicians, Assyrians, Babylonians and Macedonians.

T

Tower of Babel was probably the ziggurat temple of Babylon. (*Babel* meant 'gate of god' in the language of Babylon.) The Jews thought its purpose was to enable the Babylonians to reach Heaven. They believed that God, angry at its construction, confused people's tongues so that they spoke in different languages. Their inability to co-operate caused the builders to cease work. This, thought the Jews, was the origin of the world's languages. It is likely that the Jews who saw the ziggurat were amazed at its height and overwhelmed by the variety of people they found working on it.

Clay man and dog c. 2000s BC

Tiamat, an early goddess of Babylon, was ousted by MARDUK following a change in the religious pattern of Babylon. In mythology, she represents order.

The Hittites were a warlike tribe about whom very little is known. Their iron swords and strict code of law dominated the Middle East for 300 years.

The Hittites

At about the time of Hammurabi (*see pages 33-37*), the Hittites, an Indo-Aryan people who came from the north, across the Caucasus Mountains, were establishing themselves in ANATOLIA, north-west of Babylonia. Their land had a harsher climate than Mesopotamia — more like that of the Russian steppe. Winter brought biting winds and heavy snow, but the summer sun scorched vegetation. The Hittites settled in the milder river valleys. They unified the isolated city communities of Anatolia and imposed their own system of order on them.

By about 1600 BC the Hittites had set up their capital at HATTUSAS. Soon after, they conquered northern Syria and raided Babylon. Few armies could withstand the Hittite onslaught because they fought with weapons that no one else could match — iron swords. Although the Hittites dominated the Middle East between 1500 and 1200 BC, we know little about them.

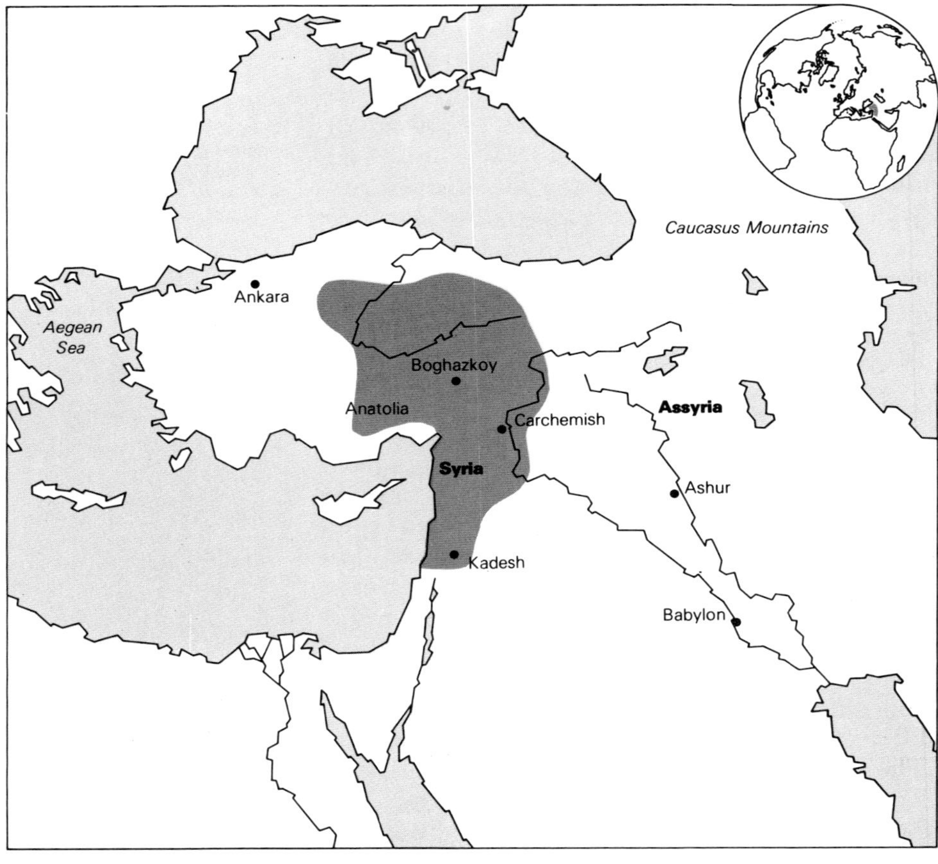

Above: The Hittite empire, centred on Anatolia, flourished from 1500 to 1200 BC with its capital at Hattusas (Boghazkoy). The map shows important places in Hittite times, including Carchemish, the later capital.

Right: The Hittite bas-relief shows a hunting scene. Skilled in war, the Hittites also excelled in hunting.

Social and economic life

The Hittites developed a code of laws similar to Hammurabi's, but it was less harsh, and the death penalty was imposed less frequently. The Hittites paid more attention to putting matters right after an offence and placed less emphasis on punishment.

Hittite kings commanded the army and were chief judges and high priests. After death and CREMATION, they were worshipped as gods. Yet while the early kings had constantly to guard their positions against jealous nobles seeking to usurp the throne, Hittite queens had a degree of power and importance rare in the ancient world. Nobles and officials of the Hittite empire belonged to a small CASTE of people related to the kings. Ordinary people — farmers, craftsmen and the like — probably descended from a native conquered people, the Hattians. The line between freemen and slaves was not clear-cut.

Reference

A **Aegean peoples** who invaded and destroyed the Hittite empire about 1200 BC, were called 'Peoples of the Sea' by the Egyptians. They included especially Mysians and Phrygians. The Phrygians later established an empire in western Anatolia. This was overthrown about 700 BC by the CIMMERIANS.

Anatolia, a mountainous peninsula, forms the Asian part of present-day Turkey. The name came from a Greek word meaning 'sunrise'. Its other name was Asia Minor.

C **Carchemish** was an independent city-state in the 1400s BC which King Suppiluliumas added to the Hittite empire in the 1300s BC. It was the leading city of the weak Hittite states after Hattusas fell, but it was probably controlled by the 'Peoples of the Sea'. It fell to Assyria in 717 BC.

Caste is an hereditary class that no one can leave or enter. The Hittite ruling caste is believed to have descended from relatives of kings.

Cimmerians were first referred to by HOMER *(see page 29)* in the *Odyssey*. He said that they lived in fog and darkness on the edge of the inhabited world. They may have been driven from south-west Russia through the Caucasus Mountains into south-western Asia by the SCYTHIANS. The Cimmerians earned a reputation for plundering.

Hittite goddess

Cremation was the method of disposing of the bodies of dead Hittite kings and queens. Funeral rites lasted about 13 days, although the body was burned by the second day. Women extinguished the fire with beer, wine and *walhi* (a ritual drink). Then they collected the bones, soaked them in fine oil, and laid them on linen on a chair.

Bull rhyton

Religion and the arts

The stormy climate of Anatolia gave rise to the Weather god, who took many forms. In mythology, the Weather god was beaten in combat by an evil dragon. Later, with the help of the goddess Inaras and a human, the Weather god slew his enemy. The Hittites shared with the HURRIANS (*see page 35*) the storm god Teshub, his wife Hebat, and the winged goddess Shaushka.

The *cella* (holiest part of Hittite temples), was approached through two small rooms. The Weather god stood at the end of the dark cella, brilliantly lit by the light of two windows, one either side of him.

The art of the Hittites was less refined than that of their neighbours and featured crudely carved stone lions. Hattusas contained cuneiform writing in several LANGUAGES. The Hittites also used HIEROGLYPHICS.

Iron in peace and war

Hittite farmers had the advantage of iron ploughshares in tilling their thin but fertile soil. Staple crops included barley and EMMER WHEAT, vines and olives. Although bronze was by far the most common metal, the Hittites became the great ironmasters, capable of defeating most enemies. Their standing army probably included foreign mercenaries and units supplied by vassals of the king. The speedy Hittite horse-drawn war chariots carried three soldiers, while the Egyptians carried two.

History

The Hittites arrived in Anatolia about 2000 BC. They conquered the Hattians, absorbed the Hurrians, and spread throughout Anatolia and northern Syria. About 1530 BC, King MURSILIS I (*see page 36*) sacked Babylon. In 1285 BC, King MUTWATALLIS fought the indecisive battle of Kadesh against Pharaoh RAMESES II (*see page 22*). Soon after this, danger flared in the western empire. Vassal kingdoms revolted and AEGEAN PEOPLES (fleeing from the rising power of the Greeks) invaded by land and sea. About 1200 BC they burned Hattusas and Hittite power waned. CARCHEMISH became the eastern capital of a federation of weak Hittite states that survived for another 500 years. In 717 BC, Carchemish fell to new warlords, the Assyrians. Soon, the Hittites disappeared as a distinct people.

Below right: The Hittites, a warlike people from the harsher climate of the north, imposed their own rule on the small city-states of Anatolia. A Hittite soldier stands guard with his iron-tipped spear as a mounted officer approaches.

E

Emmer wheat, an inferior but hardy cereal, was grown by the Hittites to produce flour and a form of beer.

H

Hattusas, the Hittite capital, stood near modern Boghazköy (east of Ankara). Annitas, an early Hittite king, destroyed an earlier settlement there and put the Weather god's curse on anyone who should try to rebuild it. But another king rebuilt it about 1800 BC. About 1200 BC, the 'Peoples of the Sea', the AEGEAN PEOPLES, set it afire.

Hieroglyphics were used by the later Hittites and the inscriptions that have survived were carved on rock or stone monuments. A number of seals and 7 letters written on rolls of lead have also been excavated in Ashur (the old Assyrian capital). Hittite hieroglyphics were deciphered only in AD 1947.

L

Languages of the Hittites numbered 8. Hittite and Akkadian were official languages. Hurrian was also used in some documents. Hattian, Luwian and Palaic were sometimes used by priests. Sumerian was studied as a dead language and the Mitannian language was used occasionally. The Hittites also used hieroglyphics.

Hittite hieroglyphics

M

Mitanni, a Hurrian people, became for a time the dominant people of western Asia. They drove the Egyptians out of northern Syria during the time of Pharaoh Amenophis II (reigned 1450–1425 BC). King Suppiluliumas of the Hittites (reigned 1380–1340 BC) conquered them.

Mutwatallis (King) fought Rameses II at Kadesh in 1285 BC. While fighting in Syria he gave his brother, Hattusilis, large territories to govern. Later, Hattusilis became powerful enough to depose Mutwatallis's son and seize the throne.

S

Scythians, a central Asian people, moved into southern Russia about 700 BC and formed a little-known empire. They probably retreated from central Asia because of Chinese pressure on the Hsiung-nu, nomadic Mongols who raided China. The Chinese pressurized the Hsiung-nu, who pushed the Scythians against the CIMMERIANS.

The Phoenicians, called the 'blood-red men' by those who feared them, were the greatest mariners of their time. Their cunning made them excellent pirates, mercenaries and merchants, and their intelligence shaped our present-day alphabet.

The Phoenicians

Sometime after 3000 BC a people known in the Bible as the CANAANITES moved into the narrow coastal strip between Anatolia and PALESTINE. More than any other people they were merchants and sea-going traders. We know them by their Greek name, Phoenicians. Their land was fertile but tiny, and great powers blocked territorial expansion. But the sea was rich in fish, and the Phoenicians first put to sea to feed an expanding population. Their prosperity lay in the waters that surrounded their lands.

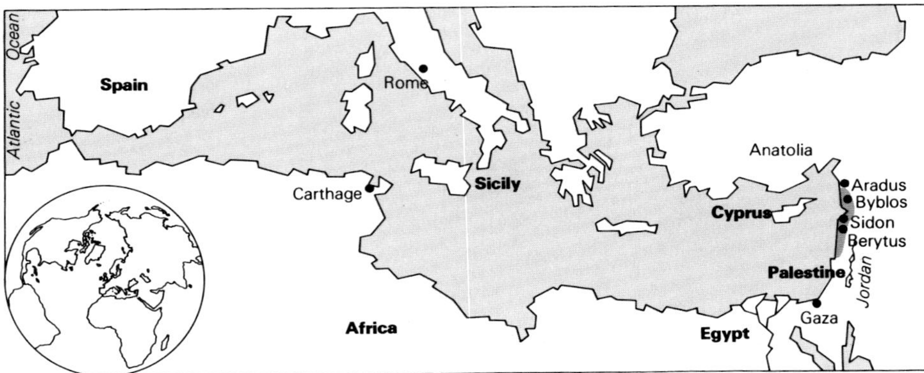

Above: Although their own land was small, Phoenician seamen and colonizers dominated the Mediterranean sea routes. Their ships sailed as far north as Britain and south to Africa, opening up new trade routes and establishing colonies along the Mediterranean coast. Settlements were founded in Carthage, Cadiz, Ibiza, Cyprus and Rhodes.

Above: The cedars of Lebanon, now few in number, once supplied timber for the navies and merchant fleets of the great powers of the Middle East. According to the Bible, 80,000 men took several years to cut and shape cedar wood for King Solomon's temple.

Reference

A **Africa's** boundaries were not clearly defined and no people in ancient times knew the full extent of the continent. To the Romans, Africa was that north-western part of the continent under the control of Carthage which later became a Roman province of Africa.

Alphabet was first developed in the Middle East about 1600 BC. The earliest known alphabet is called the North Semitic and several peoples contributed to its invention. Two other alphabets stemmed from it: the Aramaic, and the Canaanite which was developed by the Phoenicians. Almost all present-day alphabets are derived from the Phoenician. The Greeks added vowels to the all-consonant letters of the Phoenician alphabet, while the Romans gave it the form used in this book. Hebrew and Arabic derive from the Aramaic system.

B **Ba'alat,** the 'Lady of Byblos', had cow horns like the Egyptian goddess Hathor. The integration of these 2 goddesses indicated the close relationship between Byblos and Egypt.

Phoenician ivory (Syrian style)

Baal Hammon and the goddess Tanit were the chief deities of Carthage. Baal Hammon, 'lord of the altars of incense', was the Carthaginian form of the god EL. Tanit, the Carthaginian 'earth mother', became even more important than Baal Hammon by the 400s BC. This was probably because Carthage had by then an agricultural hinterland and needed a goddess of fertility.

Britain was probably visited in the 1100s BC by Phoenician traders in search of tin. They were able to make such a voyage because they navigated by the Pole star, which is still called the 'Phoenician star' by the Greeks.

Byblos, one of the world's oldest inhabited towns, was

Phoenician ship

The Phoenicians were the greatest mariners of their time and their ships visited every part of the Mediterranean coast and probably sailed north into the Atlantic as far as the 'tin isles' of BRITAIN, and south to the western coast of AFRICA. The Phoenician homeland possessed good natural harbours, which they developed into fortified city-state ports. Their leading bases were SIDON and TYRE, and other ports included BYBLOS, Berytus (Beirut) and Aradus (Ruad).

The name PHOENICIA may have come from the Greek word *phoinos* (blood red). The Greeks would have had two good reasons for calling the Canaanite sailors 'red men'. One was their ruddy, seafaring complexions. The other was that the clothing and skin of the seamen often bore traces of the red-purple dye known as 'Tyrian purple'. This dye — highly prized by the rich throughout the ancient world — was obtained from a shell fish called *murex* and produced by secret processes in Sidon and Tyre. The murex secreted the dye only when dead and decaying, so the smell from Sidon and Tyre must have been sickening.

The free enterprise society

Phoenicia never unified. It was a group of allied but independent city-states ruled by merchant-kings who avoided war on land but pursued piracy at sea. If trade declined because of war, Phoenician sailors hired themselves out as shippers or MERCENARIES. No warrior king or heavy-handed central government oppressed the Phoenicians and freebooting and free enterprise were the life blood of their culture, their prime exports being cedar and pinewood.

None rivalled the Phoenicians at business; many envied them. They developed a speedy alphabetical script to keep business records and accounts and designed their cities as fortified business centres instead of trying to rival the splendours of Egypt and Babylonia.

Left: Phoenician 'roundships' lie beached while dockers of the time unload jars, sacks, timber and other exports. Pack mules, once loaded, will carry special goods direct to the importer. The Phoenicians thrived on trade; they exported purple cloth, glassware, and a whole range of goods manufactured from imported materials. Above all, they shipped their 'cedars from the Lebanon' impartially to all those who could afford to pay for them, whether for peaceful or warlike purposes.

a leading trading centre of Phoenicia. Egyptian papyrus was exported to the Greeks through the port of Byblos, so papyrus became known as *byblos*. The name *Bible (Byblos book* or *papyrus book)* comes from Byblos.

C **Canaan** probably meant 'Land of the Purple' (the Tyrian purple). It originally comprised only the coastal strip north of present-day Haifa, but in time its borders changed. In the Old Testament and to the Egyptians, it covered all Palestine including Gaza and the eastern bank of Jordan. **Canaanites** included Phoenicians and, loosely, other peoples occupying the land known as Palestine. The southern Canaanites were conquered by the Hebrews, Aramaeans and PHILISTINES.

D **Dido** is said to have gained the site of Carthage by a trick – only to be expected of the daughter of a Phoenician merchant-king. She bought a piece of hillside 'as big as an ox-hide could cover', and then, cunningly, she cut the hide into thin strips and joined them end to end to form a circle around the base of the hill. Then she claimed the hill as her territory under the terms of the bargain.

E **El,** the great god of Canaan, was believed to make the rivers flow into the seas and so ensure the fertility of the earth. He was 'father of the gods' — especially of Baal.

G **Glass** was in use in the Middle East from about 2500 BC. The earliest known glass objects are a green rod from Babylon and some beads from Egypt. About 1500 BC, the Phoenicians were famed as makers of glass vessels and they probably invented the technique of glassblowing between 300 and 100 BC.

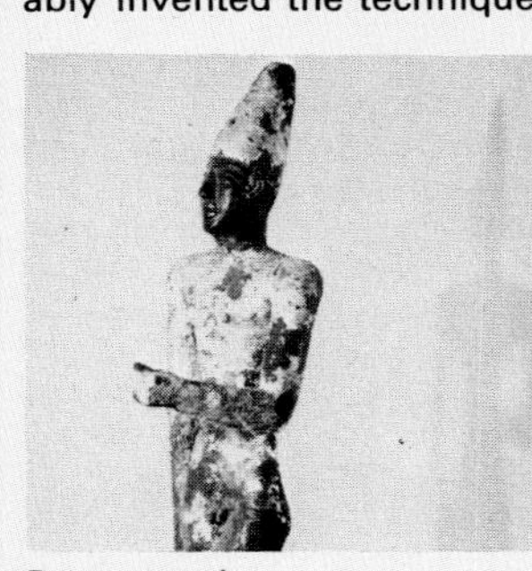

Bronze warrior

M **Mercenaries,** soldiers (and occasionally sailors) who fought for money irrespective of national loyalties, were common in the ancient times. David, who in the Old Testament slew Goliath and eventually became king of Israel, was probably a mercenary.

P **Palestine** (Philistia, land of the Philistines) was the name given by the Greeks about 500-400 BC to

Religion

Phoenician deities were closely connected with those of neighbouring countries. Many were nature gods. BA'ALAT, the 'Lady of Byblos', resembled the Egyptian goddess Hathor. Another deity of Byblos, RA, was akin to his Egyptian namesake. EL, the great god of all Canaan, ensured the fertility of the land although he lived by the sea. His rival was an even greater god, Baal. The word *Baal* in Semitic languages had a generalized meaning and there were as many Baals as there were religious centres. Baal worship was especially repugnant to the Hebrews who settled in southern CANAAN (the 'Land of the Purple').

Language and artistic craftwork

About 1600 BC the Phoenicians realized that all languages used no more than about 30 sounds. For each of 22 sounds they drew a symbol or letter. These 22 letters formed the first ALPHABET. Since then, most of the world (excluding China and Japan) has developed alphabetic languages derived from the Phoenician.

Below left: Fertility goddesses figured prominently in the religion of the Phoenicians and their neighbours. Taken to Carthage, the Phoenician religion became barbarously bloodthirsty.

Above: The shekel, originally a piece of gold or silver weighing about 14 g that circulated as money, later became a coin. A shekel of late Phoenician times shows (*left*) an owl in the stereotyped Egyptian style and (*right*) a dolphin together with the murex from which came the 'Tyrian purple' dye.

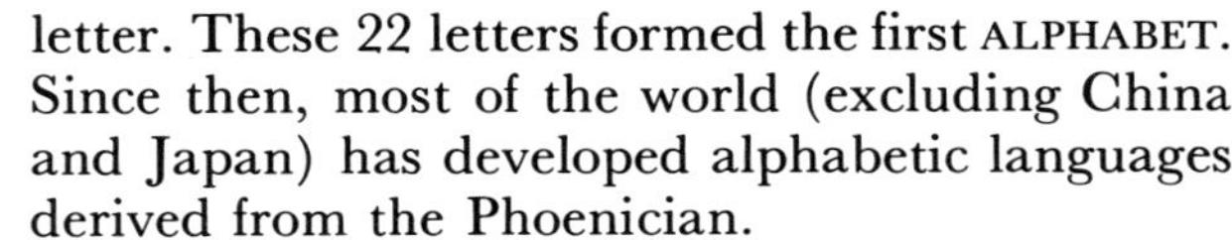

The arts and crafts of Phoenicia had a commercial base. Imported ivory, gold, silver, ebony, silk and precious stones were deftly worked into luxuries for export. Phoenician manufactured exports included jewellery, Tyrian purple cloth, fine linen, furniture, embroideries, metalwork, faience and GLASS. The Phoenicians were possibly the main inventors of glass and the technique of glassblowing.

History of Phoenicia

The Phoenicians developed their city-states over a long period of time (2900–1500 BC). They stood at the crossroads of several great powers and usually had to acknowledge the overlordship of one or more of them. The struggles between the Hittites and the Egyptians especially threatened their welfare and by the 1300s BC, the Phoenician cities found it expedient to divide their loyalties between the two great powers.

When Egypt's power waned (about 920 BC) the Phoenician cities began a period of real independence lasting about two generations, but in 868 BC a new military power, Assyria, advanced into the Mediterranean and forced the Phoenicians to pay tribute. When Assyria fell in 612 BC, Phoenicia became a pawn in a power

---

the coastal regions between Sinai in Egypt and northern Syria.

Philistines were natives of Philistia (Palestine). They used iron tools and weapons which made them more powerful than the CANAANITES and Hebrews. The clash between the Israelites (northern Hebrews) and the Philistines is symbolized in the Bible by the fight between David and Goliath.

Phoenicia covered roughly the area of modern Lebanon and adjacent areas of Syria and Israel. It is not known what name the Phoenicians gave to themselves and their country. Possibly they used the terms Canaanites and Canaan. The name Phoenician probably came from the Egyptian *Fenkhw,* meaning an Asian. This became *Phoinikes* in Greek, which could also mean 'red men'.

Punic Wars were fought from 264-241, 218-201, and 149-146 BC. In each war Rome defeated Carthage. Hamilcar Barca commanded the Carthaginians in Sicily in the first war and his son, Hannibal, commanded all Carthaginian forces in the second war. In the third and final war, Rome showed no mercy. The few citizens of Carthage who survived were sold into slavery and Carthage was totally destroyed.

'Mona Lisa' of Nimrud

The Punic Wars are an important stage in the history of Rome.

R

Ra of Foreign Lands, and Ra who is on Pharaoh's Lake, were 2 Phoenician forms of the great god Ra, borrowed from Egypt.

Rome rose to supremacy in Mediterranean Europe after the decline of Greece and Macedonia. For more than 200 years its great rival was Carthage, which it finally destroyed in 146 BC.

S

Sacrifice of human beings to the gods was an annual event in Carthage. Evidence suggests that sacrifices of boys from leading families were made to BAAL HAMMON and to Tanit. Such sacrifices had once been usual among the Phoenicians and the Israelites. The peoples of Canaan generally thought that the 'first fruits' (including the first-born children) should be offered to the gods. Carthaginian human sacrifice was particularly abhorrent because it continued long after others had abandoned it. The practice of sacrificing animals was still carried on by most

struggle between Chaldean Babylonia and Egypt. In 538 BC, Phoenicia passed under the control of Persia, but again the Phoenicians bought survival by redirecting their loyalties to the new overlords.

Above: Phoenician *biremes* – warships having 2 banks of oars and a single square sail – were built for speed and manoeuvrability. *Round ships* (*right*) were built for trade.

Carthage, the African stronghold

Assyria's bureaucratic rule was irksome to the enterprising Phoenicians and it encouraged more of them to settle in colonies abroad. According to Phoenician tradition, DIDO, a princess of Tyre, led a migration to north-west Africa in 814 BC. There, near modern Tunis, she founded New Capital, now known as Carthage. She is said to have gained the land by a trick.

As time passed, Carthage grew stronger than the homeland had ever been. The Carthaginians built an outer harbour to shelter their commercial ships and an inner harbour as a base for their warships. A tall naval tower was built on an island in the inner harbour and from its heights lookouts kept a constant watch against the approach of enemy vessels or spy ships. All ships entered the fortified harbour through a 22 metres wide gap that could be securely closed by heavy chains.

The city's 80 square kilometres was enclosed by a massive towered WALL along its 35 kilometre perimeter. The defence forces included 300 elephants, 4,000 cavalrymen with horses, and 20,000 infantrymen.

Above: This amphora-shaped sand-core glass bottle dating from the 300s BC illustrates the great skill of Phoenician glassmakers, renowned throughout the Middle East. The Phoenicians probably invented glassblowing between 300 and 100 BC.

The Carthaginian way of life

By 500 BC the city held some 200,000 people. Its African hinterland spread to take in 50,000 square kilometres and another half million people. Like their forebears, the Carthaginians continued to excel as manufacturers, traders, shippers, pirates and colonists and they added SICILY and much of SPAIN to their empire.

In changing times, the bloodthirsty Carthaginian religion was despised by other Mediterranean peoples. Uncaring, the Carthaginians continued to SACRIFICE the children of nobles to appease their horned sky god, BAAL HAMMON. Worshippers sought his favours by practising self-mutilation before him. Other Mediterranean peoples had long abandoned such practices.

The end of Carthage

The chief rivals at sea for the Phoenicians had been the Greeks. From them, the Carthaginians had little to fear. But by 348 BC a more formidable power was rising across the Mediterranean — ROME. In that year, Carthage concluded an advantageous treaty with Rome. The uneasy peace lasted for 84 years until war came between the two powers over a dispute in Sicily. The Romans fought three PUNIC WARS (Carthaginian Wars): 264-241, 218-201, and 149-146 BC. Rome's final triumph was absolute and Carthage disappeared from history and became the Roman province of Africa.

---

peoples in Carthaginian times.

Sicily was a Phoenician colony before it was infiltrated by Greek colonists. In 409 BC, a struggle for Sicily began between Greeks and Carthaginians. Later, the Carthaginians battled with the Romans for the island and by 210 BC, Rome controlled the whole of Sicily, which became its granary.

Ivory of cow suckling calf

Sidon, founded before 2000 BC, developed into a prosperous city over the following 1,000 years. Although the PHILISTINES burned it in the 1100s BC, it recovered. Sidon colonized several places in the eastern Mediterranean, including Cyprus. The city's prosperity continued under the successive rule of Assyrians, Egyptians, Persians, Macedonians and Romans.

Spain was visited by Phoenician traders and colonists from about 600 BC. Later the Greeks founded settlements there and by 520 BC, Carthage held much of southern Spain. Carthaginian-Roman rivalry in Spain led to the second PUNIC WAR and when Carthage finally lost, Spain came under Roman influence.

T **Tyre** probably began as a colony of Sidon. It came under Egyptian control in the 1400s BC and by the 1100s BC it outmatched Sidon in importance. In 814 BC, colonists from Tyre founded Carthage. By then Tyre was caught up in the turbulent affairs of the Assyrian empire. It fell to Babylon in 573 BC, and to Persia in 538 BC. Tyre suffered terrible destruction by ALEXANDER THE GREAT *(see page 16)*.

W **Wall** of Carthage stood over 12 metres high and 9 metres thick. Four-storeyed towers rose high above the wall every 60 or so metres and built into it were lower stables for elephants, higher stables for horses, and barracks for 24,000 soldiers.

Punic tombstone

The all-conquering Assyrians were the supreme masters of war and the most cruel race of their time. Yet their interest in culture was profound and it is largely due to them that we know so much about the ancient world today.

The Assyrians

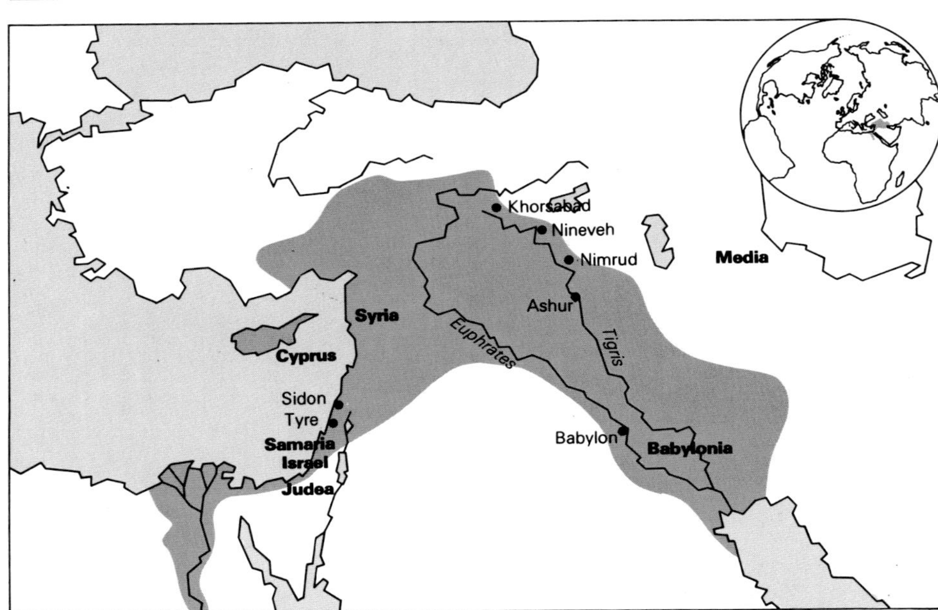

One of the great Mesopotamian civilizations, Assyria was centred on the Tigris River north of Babylon. At first its capital was ASHUR, later NINEVEH. The Assyrians had less fertile land than the Sumerians and Babylonians and consequently there was pressure on them to expand their territory as their population increased. But whenever they tried to push back their borders they were repulsed by powerful neighbours, such as the Hittites and Babylonians.

The warrior state

The Assyrians had to become a warrior people to survive, and all men were conscripted into the army. They attacked, defeated and often annexed neighbouring countries, so creating a vast empire, in the process becoming the supreme masters of the art and science of war. They excelled at siegecraft and their special techniques

Above: The map shows the empire of Assyria, which absorbed all its neighbours between about 880 and 626 BC. The Assyrians 'fell like a wolf on the fold' before they in turn finally succumbed to the Medes and Persians.

Right: Ashurnasirpal II believed that he had a divine right to hunt wild animals and employed hunting dogs to aid in these lavish pursuits.

Reference

Aramaeans occupied Aram, a region of northern Syria, in 1100-700 BC, and seized areas eastwards into Mesopotamia. Assyria fought several wars against them. Tiglath-Pileser I (reigned 1115-1077 BC) claimed to have undertaken 28 campaigns against the Aramaeans and their allies the Ahlamu. Little is known of these people, but King Ashur-resh-ishi (reigned 1133-1116) described himself as 'the one who crushes the widespread forces of the Ahlamu'.

Aramaic became the international language of the Middle East by about 1700 BC. It dominated the area for about 1,300 years, and was even the official language of the Persian empire. It was very likely the language of Jesus. Arabic replaced it after AD 622 and few Aramaic documents have survived because they were written on parchment, and were less durable than writings on clay or stone.

Ashur (or Assur), a warrior god, was the chief deity of Assyria. In the Assyrian version of the Babylonian myth of creation, Ashur replaced Marduk, the chief Babylonian god. Ashur's symbol was a winged circle, often enclosing a male figure wearing a 3 horned headpiece. This man (or god) sometimes held a bow. Ashur's symbol was also used by the kings of Assyria.

Ivory goat

Ashur (or Assur), capital city of early Assyria, was occupied before 2000 BC. It was a small city, the importance of which dwindled as NINEVEH, NIMRUD and KHORSABAD rose in importance. It was finally destroyed by the Babylonians in 614 BC.

Ashurbanipal succeeded his father, ESARHADDON, to the throne of Assyria in 668 BC. According to Esarhaddon's wishes, Ashurbanipal's brother (Shamush-Shum-ukin) became his co-equal as

Ashurnasirpal II

included the use of speedy CHARIOTS from which archers shot arrows with deadly accuracy. Like the Hittites, they had weapons of iron, not bronze. The Assyrians have left us a permanent record of their battles carved in stone on the walls of their splendid palaces.

The Assyrians gained a reputation for CRUELTY. It was said that they skinned their victims alive, impaled or burned them to death. Possibly they themselves exaggerated the extent of their cruelty to discourage resistance, or their enemies overstated the case for propaganda purposes.

Libraries

The Assyrians were not just soldiers and they had a great respect for the culture of the peoples they conquered. When they seized a city they preserved its LIBRARY and their scribes translated the information they found there into the ASSYRIAN LANGUAGE (when necessary), so that it could be put to practical use. The library of King ASHURBANIPAL at Nineveh was particularly impressive, being arranged into sections such as mathematics, astronomy, medicine, religion and history.

Social structure and economic problems

In Assyria, all land was the king's in theory, and to a large extent in fact too. Much of it was given by him to government officials and veteran soldiers as a reward for loyal service. But landholders had to pay TAXES. They paid a 25 per cent tax on grain, ten per cent on straw, and an unknown amount on livestock. They also had to give money to the temples and pay water transport tolls. They could buy themselves out of militia service.

Economic problems motivated some of Assyria's wars. The ARAMAEANS, a group of freebooting nomadic tribes who occupied northern Syria between 1100 and 700 BC, raided and seized large areas of Mesopotamia. When they cut the vital trade links with the Mediterranean coast, the Assyrians pushed them back and brought the whole area westwards to the Mediterranean under their control. Sidon, Tyre and other Phoenician cities became part of the Assyrian empire. Unlike the easy-going Babylonians, the Assyrians brought most of the economy of the

Above: Assyrian astronomers used a circular clay instrument in making calculations. It was inscribed with forecasts derived from their observations of the moon.

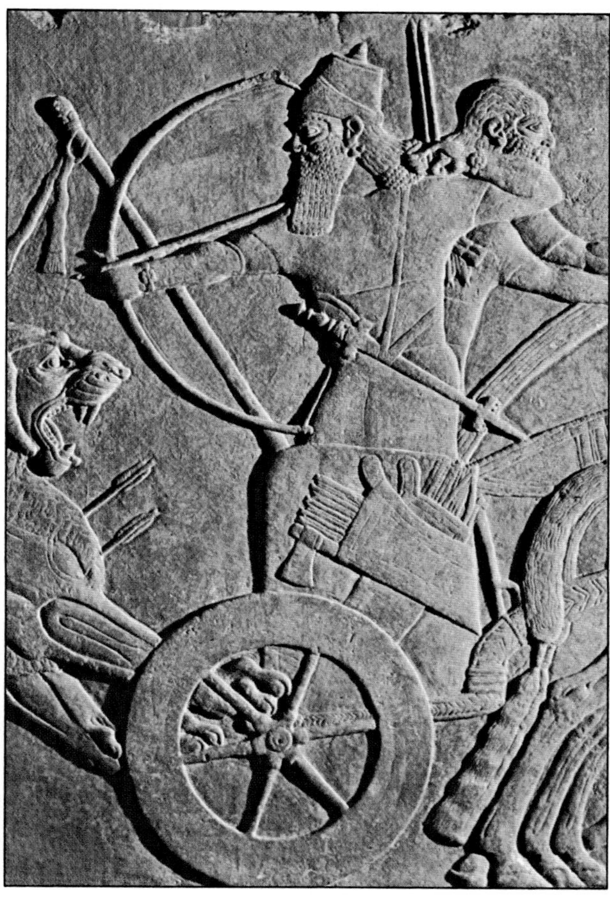

Right: King Ashurnasirpal II, who began Assyria's conquests, relaxes from war by hunting lions. This bas-relief from Nimrud is one of many now in museums, on which the Assyrians recorded in detail their vigorous activities in war and peace. The king aims his bow carefully at a wounded lion while the charioteer whips the horses into a gallop.

Below: Deer run headlong into a trap.

---

crown prince of Babylon. Ashurbanipal was noted for his passionate interest in Nineveh's library.

Ashurnasirpal II kept Ashur as Assyria's religious capital but for strategic purposes moved the secular capital to Nimrud (Calah). Nimrud seems to have been replaced as the capital soon afterwards by the more ancient city of Nineveh.

Assyrian language was at first a dialect of Akkadian. From about the time of TIGLATH-PILESER III it was replaced by Aramaic. This was written on parchment and used to supplement the cuneiform script still used on clay and stone.

C

Chariots, the chief vehicles of the ancient world, were in use in Babylon about 2000 BC, drawn by asses. The Hyksos invaders of Egypt introduced horse chariots into that country about 1700 BC. The Assyrians fitted limb-cutting scythes to the wheels of their chariots which were drawn by 3 horses and carried 1 driver and an archer trained to shoot with deadly accuracy.

Cruelty in warfare and torture after defeat were usual in the ancient world and of all the nations, Assyria's image is worst. However, the Assyrians never staged public spectacles of calculated cruelty such as the Romans delighted in. They seem to have practised cruelty more to deter resistance to their authority. One of the main complainants against Assyria was the kingdom of Judea. Its chief resentment was not Assyria's inhumanity but its commercial success and the alleged practice of witchcraft. Despite the enmity between them, Ahaz, a king of Judea, successfully sought Assyrian aid against Israel and Syria.

Cyaxares is believed to have reigned over Media for about 40 years (c.625-c.585 BC). Little is known about him except what is told by Herodotus. This ancient Greek historian wrote that in his youth Cyaxares was de-

Relief from the Palace of Sennacherib

Below: Having decided to resist rather than surrender, those besieged by the Assyrians usually defended their city desperately, believing that defeat would bring indiscriminate and painful deaths such as flaying or impalement for the leaders, and enslavement and deportation for the survivors. However, not all vanquished enemies were badly treated, and the Assyrians often left a conquered king or governor to rule his city as before, subject to his working for Assyrian interests.

empire under state control and Phoenician resistance to the levying of taxes was finally put down by Assyrian troops.

Religion

The gods and religious festivals of Assyria were closely allied to those of Sumeria and Babylonia. Most Assyrian myths, too, paralleled those of Babylon. ASHUR, the city-god of the capital Ashur, became the national god of the Assyrian empire. Probably to promote loyalty from conquered peoples, Assyrian priests identified him with earlier Mesopotamian gods such as Enlil. In the time of SARGON II, Ashur became identified with Anshar, the celestial world and parent of other gods. Under SENNACHERIB, Ashur became the counterpart of MARDUK (*see page 36*).

Ashur was the religious equivalent of the Assyrian state. As god of the most warlike power in the Middle East he was given detailed written reports by the kings, outlining their military campaigns.

Above: An Assyrian siege tower approaches the wall of the besieged city. Assyrian engineers devised several kinds of assault machines, including battering rams.

Right: Assyrian archers shoot their deadly arrows at the defenders from behind an improvised wickerwork shield.

feated by a Scythian army when he laid siege to Nineveh. Cyaxares took Ashur in 614 BC and, with Nabopolassar, destroyed Nineveh in 612 BC.

Cyprus, because of its position between several great powers, early on became an important trading centre. Mycenaean traders visited the island about 1400 BC. About 800 BC it came under Phoenician rule, and in 709 BC the several kings of Cyprus submitted to SARGON II. It remained part of the Assyrian empire for about 40 years. From about 669 BC Cyprus had over 100 years of independence before its conquest by Egypt.

E **Esarhaddon** succeeded to the throne in 680 BC after his brothers murdered his father, SENNACHERIB. The main Assyrian army prepared to oppose Esarhaddon and the army that he commanded. However, Esarhaddon's enemies became divided among themselves when they heard that the goddess Ishtar favoured him and the main army then acclaimed him. Under his brilliant generalship the Assyrian empire expanded to its greatest extent.

Esarhaddon and captives

K **Khorsabad** was excavated in AD 1842 and 1851. Statues of SARGON II and winged bulls were found and taken to the Louvre, Paris. In 1932, archaeologists found hundreds of clay tablets at the site bearing cuneiform writings in Elamite. These included a list of kings supposed to have reigned from about 2200 to 730 BC.

L **Library** of ASHURBANIPAL at Nineveh was one of the world's greatest collections of recorded knowledge. Present-day information about Mesopotamian science and literature comes largely from material salvaged from the ruins of the library. Records show that the Assyrians continued the scholastic work of the Sumerians and Babylonians. Alongside the scientific documents are extensive pseudo-scientific works such as the study of omens.

M **Media** lay in what is now north-western Iran. Its first known mention

When Ashur became Assyria's capital (about 1350 BC), a great period of ziggurat and temple building began. This continued until the fall of Assyria. Great monuments were built at Nineveh, NIMRUD and KHORSABAD. Like the Babylonians, the Assyrians built splendid palaces with entrances flanked by human-headed WINGED BULLS.

Assyrian art generally followed the pattern of Sumeria and Babylon and was secular rather than religious. But the reliefs that covered the walls of the palaces were essentially Assyrian and depicted lifelike details of dress and weapons, horses and chariots. The Assyrians themselves are pictured as stocky, determined and woolly-bearded and the reliefs confirm their inhumanity.

Administration of the empire

The Assyrian people represented only a fraction of the population of the empire and they had to rely heavily on foreign manpower. A high proportion of their army and their workforce was therefore non-Assyrian. Labour in the homeland was scarce considering the immense amount of building construction that was undertaken and tens of thousands of prisoners of war and exiled peoples were taken in as forced labourers. From Samaria (the capital of Israel) alone, 27,000 people were sent to Assyria as forced labourers.

Payments of tax and TRIBUTE from conquered peoples went mainly to the upkeep of the army and to the cost of building. But Assyrian rule was not without benefits. The new order brought peace and prosperity in place of the perpetual petty wars of smaller states.

Speedy communication between the chief Assyrian cities and the provinces was vital to the existence of the empire. To achieve this, the Assyrians constructed an imperial ROAD SYSTEM with relay stations and guard posts.

The status given to conquered provinces depended largely upon the degree of co-operation they gave to Assyria. Some kept their own rulers but paid tribute to Assyria. Others, although

Above: Men impaled on stakes confirm Assyrian cruelty following the capture of Lachish, near Jerusalem in Judea, about 700 BC.

Below: The heavy, metal-fitted chariots of the Assyrians carried 3 men, like the Hittite chariots. The horses were vulnerable, however, and a startled horse could overturn a chariot, causing chaos on the battlefield.

is in Assyrian documents of the 800s BC. The Median capital, Ecbatana, was on the site of present-day Hamadan. The Median tribes probably remained disunited until about 625 BC when CYAXARES set up a single kingdom of Media.

N **Nimrud** was the military capital of Assyria under ASHURNASIRPAL II. This king celebrated the official opening of the city by giving a 10-day banquet for nearly 70,000 people.

Nineveh was made the capital of Assyria by SENNACHERIB, who transformed it into a magnificent city. It was excavated by the British archaeologist A.H.Layard in AD 1845-51. With great difficulty he removed to the British Museum, London, a remarkable collection of bas-reliefs portraying mostly war or hunting scenes. With them went thousands of clay tablets from Ashurbanipal's library.

Ivory furniture, Nimrud

R **Road systems** in Assyria were established by TIGLATH-PILESER III. Posting stages were organized across the empire so that messages could pass quickly between the king and his provincial governors. Exit roads, surfaced with cobblestones, led out from Assyrian cities to allow for the efficient passage of the armies. Sennacherib decreed that anyone encroaching upon the 'royal road' out of Nineveh would be impaled.

S **Sargon II** founded the last Assyrian dynasty following a military coup. His dynasty included:

Sargon II (r.721–705 BC)
Sennacherib (r.704–681 BC)
Esarhaddon (r.680–669 BC)
Ashurbanipal (r.668–626 BC)
Ashur-etillu-ili (r.c.625–623 BC)
Sin-shar-Ishkun (r.622–c.612 BC)

Sennacherib, son of Sargon II, rebuilt Nineveh and made it the capital. Exasperated by persistent op-

Sargon II and an official

Above: Winged bulls with human heads guarded the gates of King Sargon II's palace at Khorsabad. The bulls had 5 legs, so that 4 could be seen from the side, 2 from the front.

Left: Flushed with success following the storming of a city that long defied them, Assyrian soldiers present the heads of captives taken after its final fall.

allowed to keep their own ruler, had an Assyrian 'adviser' at court. Some had an Assyrian governor who ruled with absolute power.

The Assyrians were the contemporaries of the Babylonians and Hittites, but their period of power began only in the 800s BC. ASHURNASIRPAL II (reigned 883-858 BC) chased the Aramaeans westwards to the Mediterranean and took the Phoenician cities. TIGLATH-PILESER III (a usurper who reigned 745-727 BC) extended the empire from the old Sumerian cities into Asia Minor. He incorporated Palestine and Syria and his armies threatened the borders of Egypt. Babylonia was left to the rule of its own kings so long as they followed Assyria's policies. When the Chaldeans tried to seize control of Babylonia, Tiglath-Pileser III finally annexed it directly to Assyria.

The Sargonid dynasty

In 721 BC, a military revolt placed Sargon II on the throne and his dynasty, too, fought perpetual wars of expansion conquering the Greek cities on CYPRUS. Sargon's son, Sennacherib (reigned 705-681 BC), defeated an alliance of Elamites, Babylonians and Chaldeans and quelled an Egyptian-inspired revolt in Judea.

Exasperated at Babylon's persistent opposition, Sennacherib devastated the splendid city, turning it into a wasteland. Even the city god Marduk was taken into captivity to Ashur. Sennacherib's sons murdered him, possibly because of his destruction of Babylon. One of them, ESARHADDON, (reigned 681-669 BC), rebuilt the city and restored Marduk to his temple.

Esarhaddon's son, Ashurbanipal (reigned 669-626 BC), was a scholar, but nevertheless, he and the two sons who followed him had to fight the same dreary cycle of wars. At this time Assyria's strength was beginning to wane and about 621 BC it came close to civil war. Nabopolassar, the Chaldean who seized the throne of Babylon in 625 BC, allied Babylon with MEDIA. Soon after, Nabopolassar and CYAXARES (the Median king) jointly attacked Assyria. Not all Assyria's vassal states wanted it to fall. They feared that if Assyria collapsed the Scythians, Cimmerians and other nomads would sweep into the Middle East and destroy civilization. But Assyria's allies could not save it and in 612 BC the Babylonians and Medes destroyed Nineveh. It was never rebuilt. In 609 BC, Assyria ceased to exist.

position which he had to face from his vassal, the king of Babylon, Sennacherib destroyed that city. He was subsequently murdered by his sons, possibly because of this.

Taxes were collected by the 'lord of the city' – an agent of the Assyrian government who was often the original ruler of a conquered place. The 'lord' had a small garrison to enforce his orders. Conquered peoples often objected to paying taxes to the Assyrian government. The Assyrians taxed the merchants of conquered Sidon and Tyre on timber from the mountains that entered their warehouses. In protest, the outraged Phoenicians rioted and killed a tax collector before an Assyrian army quelled them. Inspectors enforced the payment of taxes on boats, fisheries, cattle, clipped wool, and even divorces and burials. *Tithes* (10% of the value of certain items, paid to the temple) were charged on date crops, fish catches, cattle, cornland and rents (paid in kind).

Tiglath-Pileser III came to the throne in 745 BC following a revolt in Nimrud (then the capital) where the old royal family was murdered.

Warriors with round shields

He took over when the Assyrian empire was in a state of political anarchy and near to military and economic collapse. The king's brilliant administration and military successes restored Assyrian power.

Tribute was a regular (sometimes annual) sum of money or amount of goods paid by the ruler of a subordinate state to the ruler of a more powerful one. The king paying tribute accepted the other king as his overlord or *suzerain* (usually unwillingly). In theory, payment of tribute also bought peace and protection.

Winged bulls with human heads guarded the entrances of SARGON II'S palace at KHORSABAD. They wore the horned headdress of divinity and probably represented benevolent genii. Being designed to stand against walls, these massive structures had only 2 sculptured surfaces, front and side. A curious feature of the bulls is that they have 5 legs. They were so designed that, when viewed side-on, 4 legs would be visible. The bulls are now at the British Museum.

The Persians were the first race to acknowledge one invisible God and the first to spread the use of money as currency. Under their rule the Middle East enjoyed peace, prosperity and religious tolerance.

The Persians

Most civilizations come to maturity after a long period of cultural and military development, but Persia entered world history with dramatic suddenness about 547 BC. In that year CYRUS II, king of the small Iranian state of Anshan, reached the climax of his career. After 13 years of war he united the several Iranian (Aryan) kingdoms of Media and PERSIA under his leadership so that his domains extended from Asia Minor and the Black Sea to the Gulf of Oman.

The ACHAEMENID DYNASTY that Cyrus founded was to last only two centuries, but it came to rule the largest empire that the world had known up to that time. The old territories of the Sumerians, Egyptians, Indus Valley peoples, Babylonians, Hittites, Phoenicians and Assyrians, were all absorbed into the Persian empire by about 400 BC. Parts of ETHIOPIA, the Balkans and central Asia also came under Persian rule. At its height, the Persian empire was as big as present-day Europe without Russia.

The Persians originated very little; mostly they built upon the achievements of their predecessors and improved them. But the Persian peace that they imposed brought a new stability and prosperity.

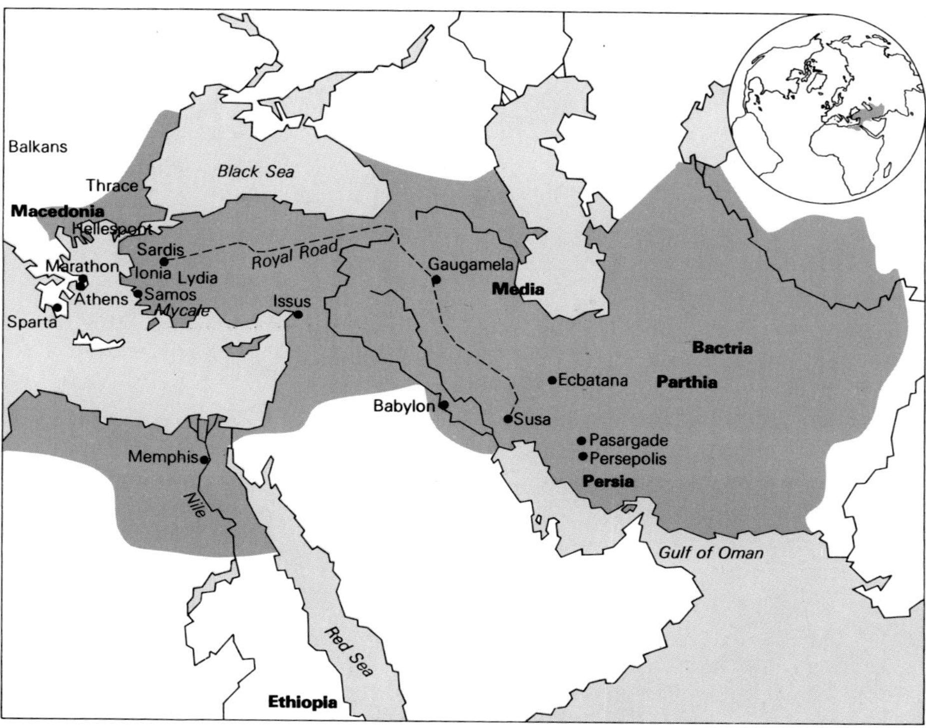

Above: The Persian empire burst suddenly into history to swallow up the territories of all previous civilizations west of China. No other empire equalled its size until Han China and Rome appeared. It fell suddenly to Alexander the Great in 334–331 BC.

Persian government

Although the Persian kings were ruthless in extending their conquests, they were not cruel by comparison with their neighbours and predecessors. Toleration rather than intimidation was the keynote of their imperial policy and the Achaemenid kings sought to assimilate conquered peoples into the empire on favourable terms. Persian rule was less rigid than Assyrian, and so less objectionable. Babylon submitted to Cyrus without a fight and many Babylonians preferred his rule to that of Nabonidus, the last Chaldean king. Instead of destroying Babylon as Sennacherib had done, Cyrus honoured it by making the city one of his several capitals.

The Persian empire was organized into SATRAPIES (provinces) by DARIUS I (reigned 521-486 BC), the third king of Persia. Each satrapy had its *satrap* (governor). But Darius I, mindful perhaps of Cyrus's career, was suspicious of satraps who might grow too powerful and alongside each satrap was a general and also a secretary of state. With power divided between them, the three officials had to report direct to the king. His personal inspectors visited them regularly, accompanied by a troop of soldiers.

The Persians took over and extended the Assyrian road system. The Royal Road, built by Darius, ran 2,500 kilometres from SARDIS to SUSA and was used by traders as well as soldiers.

Reference

A **Achaemenid dynasty** had 11 kings, including: (dates BC)

Cyrus II (the Great)	559–530
Cambyses II	530–522
Darius I (the Great)	522–486
Xerxes I	486–465
Artaxerxes III	358–c.337
Darius III	336–c.330

Ahura-Mazda (or Ormuzd), the Supreme Creator, was believed to be engaged in a perpetual battle against the Evil God, Angra Mainyu (Ahriman). Their struggle is told in the Avesta, the Zoroastrian holy book.

Anahita (the Unspotted) was the Persian fertility goddess.

Artaxerxes III gained the throne by murdering his brother's family and continued a reign of terror until his death. His strong rule prolonged the life of the Persian empire. Finally, he was poisoned.

B **Bactrians** lived in Bactria, an eastern satrapy through which Siberian and Indian trade passed on its way to Persia. Bactria later became an independent state and annexed part of Chinese Turkestan and northern India. About 130 BC, Bactria fell to the Sakas, a nomadic tribe.

Bactrian leading camel

C **Cambyses II** was regent of Babylon before reigning 530–522 BC. He invaded Egypt in 525 BC, and defeated and executed Pharaoh Psamtik III. Arab allies provided his solders with water across Sinai. Cambyses went insane, became irrationally cruel and probably committed suicide.

Croesus, the last king of Lydia, was probably killed by CYRUS II. A Greek story tells that Cyrus, relenting, tried to stop him burning on the Persian execution pyre. Supposedly, the god Apollo quenched the flames with

Early Persian pot

Right: This magnificent silver dish shows a man, possibly a king, killing lions. It is a fine example of Sassanian art.

Left: A gold miniature model – a masterpiece of Persian metalworking art – shows the kind of chariot used in Persia shortly before the Macedonian conquest.

Mounted couriers sped the kings' orders along the Royal Road, delivering them to the remotest borders in two weeks.

Except for Persia itself (which was privileged) all satrapies paid taxes to the central government. In previous empires taxes and tribute had been paid in kind. But now MONEY — a much more convenient form of exchange — was coming into use. Learning from CROESUS, the last king of LYDIA (defeated and annexed by Cyrus), Darius I issued a gold coin — the *daric*. Soon, this passed as currency even outside the empire. Apart from monetary taxes, each satrapy continued to send goods in kind as tribute to Persia according to its ability and Persia's need. Payments in kind from all the 20 to 30 satrapies included corn, sheep, mules, horses, hunting dogs, gold dust, children, and FRANKINCENSE and MYRRH.

Apart from the payments to the Persian court, the satrap himself exacted tribute. It is said that Darius I, having been assured that the taxes he proposed to levy could be borne, halved them. He knew that the satraps would finally double the levy to give themselves as much as the king received. However, Persia's taxes were not oppressive. Darius received every year in cash alone the equivalent of over three million gold sovereigns, but this was not excessive considering the enormous size of his empire.

The religions of the Persians

The Persian kings were not bigoted and in the satrapies the conquered peoples were free to worship their own deities. But the religions of Persia were distinctly different from those of the old empires it had annexed. Three religions were practised among the Medes and Persians. These were: the kings' religion based on the one God, Ahura-Mazda, the God of gods; the people's religion centred on the god MITHRAS and the goddess ANAHITA; and the cult of the MAGI. The three religions of Persia became to some extent intermixed.

Far right: Archers, depicted here on glazed brick, formed the backbone of the Persian armies that created the world's largest empire then known.

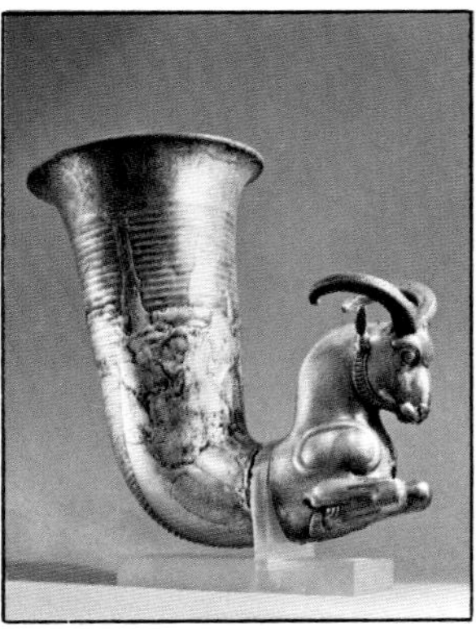

Above: A gold drinking cup of the 400s BC found at Ecbatana, one of the Persian capitals, has the decorative but highly formal design typical of ancient Persian art. Skill in depicting animals was another strong feature of Persian art.

From Ahura-Mazda, creator of heaven and earth, the Persian kings supposedly drew their authority. The god had no images but was worshipped in the form of a symbol: a bearded, upright male figure centrally placed in an open wing. The religion of Ahura-Mazda was founded by ZOROASTER (Zarathustra in Persian), who may have lived about 660-583 BC or possibly much earlier. The followers of Ahura-Mazda (called ZOROASTRIANS) were among the first peoples to acknowledge only one God. He was symbolized by a bearded man on an open wing.

Mithras, later identified with the sun, had connections with the Aryan gods of India. But Mithras was also identified as an assistant to Ahura-Mazda in his fight against evil. Anahita was the Persian goddess of fertility.

The MAGI were probably a Median tribe who provided the priests and scholars of the empire: the word 'magic' comes from their cult. They were also astrologers who drew inspiration from the Chaldeans. Their chief function was to carry out a certain ritual, the nature of which is unknown.

---

rain and Croesus became Cyrus's friend.

Cyrus II the Great (c.600-529 BC) is surrounded with legends about his birth. He died probably in present-day Pakistan and was buried at Parsagade.

D **Darius I** the Great (c.558-486 BC) was a distant cousin of CAMBYSES. He gained the throne after the murder of GAUMATA (the false Prince Smerdis). He proved a most competent general and administrator. In pursuing the Scythians he began the Greco-Persian wars.

E **Ethiopia** was traditionally founded about 1000 BC, but this cannot be confirmed. Ethiopian pharaohs ruled in Egypt's 25th dynasty (750–656 BC).

Darius I

F **Frankincense and myrrh,** used medicinally and for fumigation, came from the red gum exuded by *Burseraceaea* (incense trees). They were used by the MAGI in their mysterious ceremonies.

G **Gaumata,** a Magi, impersonated Cambyses's dead brother Smerdis (Bardiya) and usurped the throne from the mad and unpopular Cambyses. He ruled briefly in 522 BC before being assassinated. A purge of the Magi followed. Supporters of Gaumata hoped to re-establish an independent and priest-led Media.

H **Hellespont** (now Dardanelles).

Hydro-engineering projects undertaken by the Persians included the completion of a canal to link the Nile and Red Sea. They also repaired an Egyptian dam at Memphis.

I **Issus** (now Iskenderun in Turkey) was named Alexandretta in honour of Alexander the Great, conqueror of the Persians at Issus in 333 BC.

M **Magi,** the Median priests and scholars, later degenerated into tricksters. Their mysterious activities became known as

Gold armlet

Architecture, arts and language

The Achaemenians had several capitals: Susa was the main one, Pasargade another; Ecbatana was the summer capital and Babylon the winter capital. Each succeeding king tried to outdo his predecessors in architectural splendour. About 520 BC Darius I began the construction of a new capital — Parsai, known today by its Greek name, PERSEPOLIS and when it was completed some 150 years later it became one of the most impressive monuments of all time. This capital was also a shrine — the main centre for the New Year Festival (celebrated in spring). In art, the Persians borrowed freely from the peoples they had conquered.

Darius I and his court probably spoke Old Persian — an Indo-European language. Public business was quite likely conducted in Aramaic, because the Persians used local peoples for their civil servants. Perhaps it was these officials who developed from cuneiform, the 36 characters that formed the basic script of Persian writing. A few ideograms were sometimes used alongside the script. Avesta, the language of the Zoroastrian holy books was closely allied to Old Persian.

Agricultural life

The Achaemenian kings took a keen interest in forestry, agriculture and HYDRO-ENGINEERING. Once felled, trees were systematically replanted. Fruit trees from west of the Euphrates River were transplanted to the eastern empire and Persian pistachios were planted in Syria. The Persians planted rice in Mesopotamia and sesame in Egypt and experimented with viniculture. The land was worked by serfs and slaves employed on large estates. Main crops included wheat, barley and olives. The diet of rich and poor alike included meat, fish, bread, oil, wine and honey. Large estates provided for most of their own needs in clothing, furniture, and other everyday items. Under Persian government, living standards rose in most parts of the empire. The Persians kept the old waterways in good repair and constructed new ones.

Persian history

Cyrus early on faced a hostile coalition of Babylonia, Egypt, SPARTA and Lydia. With lightning speed he defeated and annexed Lydia before its allies could send aid. Then he prised Palestine

magic. The 'three wise men', stated in the Gospel of St Matthew to have visited the infant Jesus, were Magi.

Marathon, a plain 32 km north of Athens, was where the Athenians and their allies defeated the Persians in 490 BC, before the Spartans arrived.

Mithras appears as a sun god in the Indian sacred *Vedas* and as a warrior god in the Zoroastrian *Avesta.* Mithraism outlived Persia. Roman soldiers spread it throughout the Roman empire, including Britain.

Money. The first coins were minted by King CROESUS of Lydia, at Sardis in the 500s BC.

Mycale, a mountain in the coastal strip of Asia Minor, lay opposite Samos island. It is now called Mount Samsun. The Greeks defeated the Persian fleet there in 479 BC. This ended the struggle for European Greece and began the fight for Asia Minor.

P

Parthians were probably a Scythian people. Parthia lay south-east of the Caspian Sea. The Parthian empire flourished about 100 BC to AD 226. It extended from the Euphrates to the Indus, and from the Oxus to the Indian Ocean. The Parthian civilization was not outstanding culturally.

Early Persian bull

Persepolis (*City of the Persians* in Greek), stood on a 12 metre high terrace extending 450 by 300 metres. On the terrace, palaces, monuments and offices were constructed. Main buildings included the *Apadana* (audience hall of Darius I) and the Hall of 100 columns.

Persia was that part of the empire north of the present-day Persian Gulf and Gulf of Oman, and south of ancient Media.

S

Sacae (or Sakas), the nomadic Scythians of Persia's northern frontier, lived probably in the region of Chinese Sinkiang.

Salamis, an island west of Athens, was near where the

Sassanian king hunting

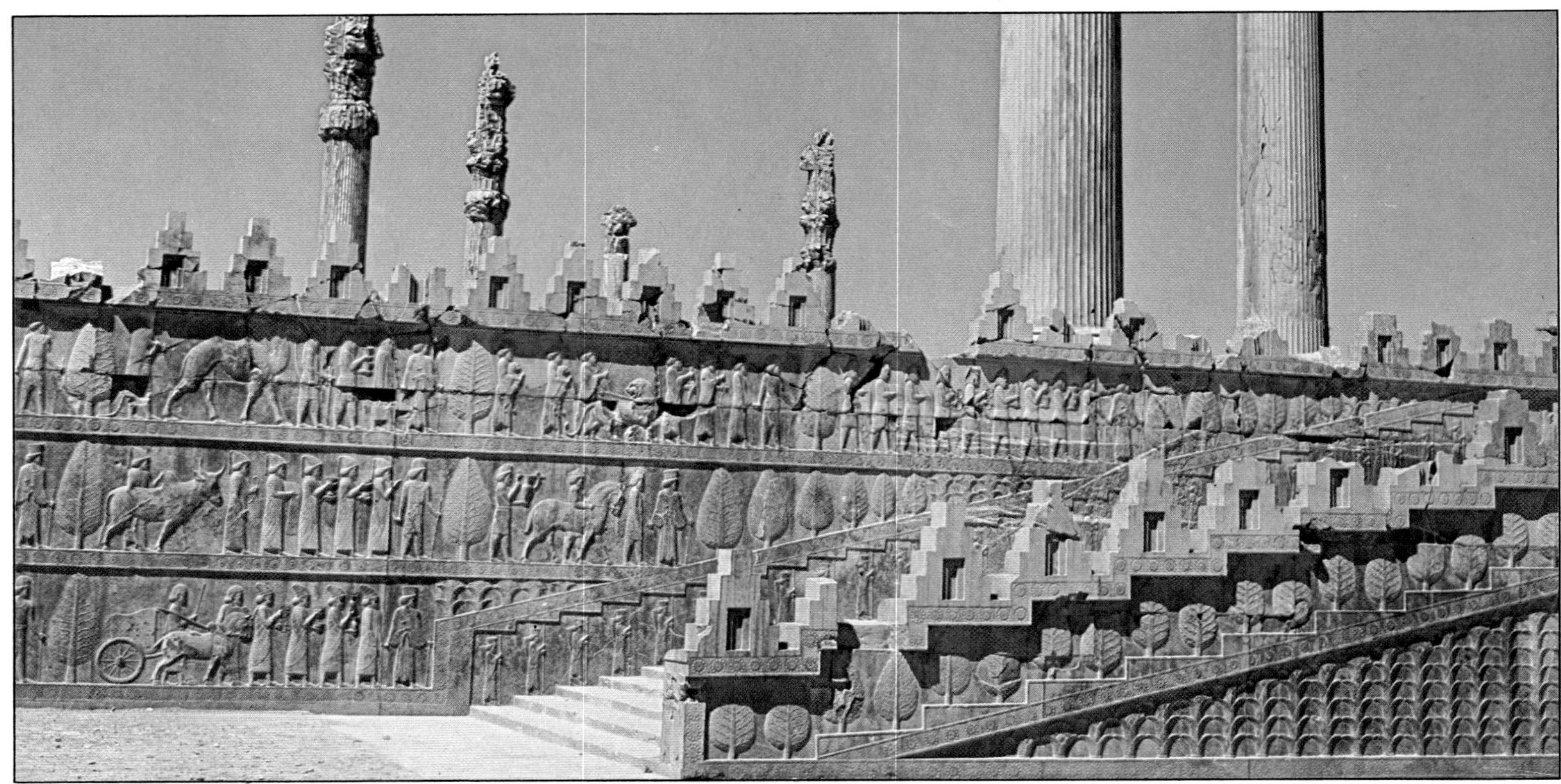

and part of Syria away from Babylonia and took Babylon itself in 539 BC. Cyrus annexed all Babylonia to the borders of Egypt. The PARTHIANS, BACTRIANS and SACAE also submitted to him.

Cyrus's son, CAMBYSES, speedily subdued and annexed Egypt in 525 BC. Several revolts then broke out against him and GAUMATA, a Magi from Media, usurped the throne. Cambyses died while hurrying back from Egypt, probably by suicide. A relative of his then killed Gaumata, crushed the rebellion, and installed himself as Darius I.

To protect the northern borders of his empire, Darius attacked the Scythian lands from east of the Caspian Sea to the Balkans west of the Black Sea. In the course of this attack, he annexed THRACE and Macedonia. Among the conquered Greeks of Asia Minor were the Ionians of the Aegean coastal strip. Ionia revolted in 499 BC, aided by Athens and this brought about a full-scale Persian attack on Greece. But the Greeks finally defeated the Persians at MARATHON in 490 BC.

XERXES I (who succeeded Darius I in 486 BC) assembled an army of 180,000 men. Using Phoenician vessels he built a double line of boats to bridge the HELLESPONT. In 480 BC his warriors advanced over it to defeat the Greeks at THERMOPYLAE. Xerxes pushed on to Athens, which he burned, but in the same year the Greeks defeated his fleet at SALAMIS. Fearful of being trapped without supplies, the main Persian force returned home. In 479 BC, the Greeks defeated the remnant of the Persian force.

Despite its victories, Greece remained weak because it was disunited, often at war within itself. The Persians kept control of Asia Minor and Cyprus by cleverly exploiting Greek divisions. However, Persia was in decline. It recovered quickly but briefly under ARTAXERXES III (reigned 358-337 BC), who retook Egypt, which had broken away.

A new power was rising in Greece. The Macedonians hammered most of Greece into a single state and invaded Asia Minor in 334 BC. In 333 BC, Alexander the Great of Macedon, defeated Darius III at the battle of ISSUS. Following further defeat in 331 BC, the Persian empire collapsed and disappeared as suddenly as it had begun.

Above: The surviving columns of Persepolis rise skyward behind the grand staircase sculptured to advertise the splendour and extent of the empire. Bringing tribute to Persia come Medes, Bactrians, Sogdians, Parthians, Elamites, Scythians, Assyrians, Thracians, Cilicians, Babylonians, Armenians, Indians, Afghans, Lydians, Cappadocians and Phoenicians. The double-headed bull capital (*below*) probably stood in front of the entrance hall of the 100-column palace.

allied Greek fleet defeated the Persian fleet in 480 BC.

Sardis, leading city of Asia Minor 650-546 BC, was the capital of Lydia.

Satrapies were originally 23 in number. In a clockwise direction from Fars (the Persian homeland) they were: Fars; Elam; Chaldea; Assyria; Arabaya (Mesopotamia, Syria, Phoenicia, Palestine combined); Egypt; Peoples of the Sea; Ionia; Lydia and Mysia; Media; Armenia; Cappadocia; Parthia and Hyrcania; Zarangia; Aria; Chorasmia; Bactria; Sogdiana; Gandhara; Sacae; Thatagus; Arachosia; Makas. Eight were added later.

Sparta, capital of the Greek state of Laconia (better known as Sparta), was created by Dorian invaders. Sparta became the most warlike state in Greece. After 600 BC, Sparta was little more than an armed camp given wholly to war pursuits. Weakling boys were killed by exposure at birth.

Figure from Persepolis

Susa, the old Elamite capital, was destroyed by the Assyrians and rebuilt by the Persians.

T Thermopylae, a narrow pass in present-day central Greece (near Lamia), was the entrance into ancient Greece from the north. Its name means 'hot gates' from the hot mineral springs near by.

Thrace was a perpetual battlefield and moved its boundaries often between 1300 BC and Roman times. Thrace was a Persian satrapy in the south-eastern-most corner of Europe (opposite the Sea of Marmara) about 512-479 BC.

X Xerxes I (c.519-465 BC) son of Darius the Great and grandson of Cyrus the Great, had several military successes. But his fleet lost the battle of SALAMIS. He was murdered in 465 BC by the captain of his own bodyguard.

Z Zoroaster (Zarathustra in Persian) may have lived 660-583 BC or earlier. Possibly he was once a MAGI. He is the reputed founder of Zoroastrianism, but there is no certainty that he lived.

Zoroastrians. Zoroastrianism is still followed by the Parsees, descendants of Persians who moved to India and now number 150,000. Fire is sacred to the Parsees; earth and water should not be polluted.

The prophet Moses, David (who fought the giant Goliath), and the fabulous King Solomon — all are part of the Hebrew religious tradition that has spread its influence throughout the world and given us both Christianity and Islam.

The Hebrews

Right: The map shows the 'promised land' of the Jews, which from about 926 BC was divided into Israel in the north and Judea in the south. Distances were small; Jerusalem to Nazareth being only about 100 km, and Jerusalem to Mount Sinai about 450 km.

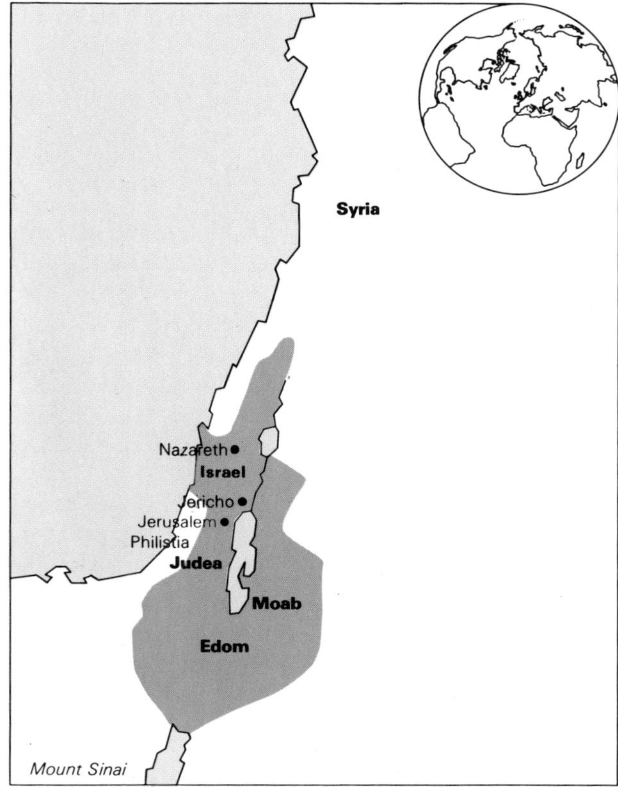

Right: The *Torah,* read by being unwound from rollers as required, contains the 5 books of the law traditionally given to Moses by God on Mount Sinai. The *Torah* is read by Christians as the first part of the Old Testament.

Most of our knowledge of the HEBREWS (or JEWS) before Roman times comes from the Jewish Bible, known by Christians as the Old Testament. But the Hebrews also appear in Egyptian records about 1200 BC. They fled from captivity in Egypt to settle in the less fertile parts of Canaan. They were then developing the worship of one supreme, invisible God (Yahweh) and despised their neighbours for worshipping idols.

The Jews were weak militarily and had little political influence. Their land was usually dominated by great powers such as Egypt, Assyria and Babylon. But their religion of Judaism, backed by its dynamic literature, became highly influential. From it stemmed two even more powerful religions, Christianity and Islam.

The covenant with God

The Hebrews did not easily accept the idea of one invisible God. When their leader, MOSES, went up to Mount Sinai to receive the TEN COMMANDMENTS from God, the people rebelled. They demanded that AARON (Moses's brother) should make them gods such as other tribes had. Yielding, he moulded them a golden calf to worship. But later the Hebrews entered into a COVENANT with Yahweh. By this they became his 'CHOSEN PEOPLE' whom he would protect and help. In return, the Hebrews promised not to follow other gods and to accept God's law.

Once in Canaan, the Hebrews were at first led by JUDGES — men and women picked for their wisdom. But the authority of the judges often depended upon whether they had the support of PROPHETS (men believed to communicate the will of God). The Hebrews called their high priests and kings messiahs. Later, the prophets foretold that an ideal king would come to lead Israel. They said he would be a direct descendant of DAVID, a Hebrew hero-king. This future ideal

Reference

A

Aaron was the brother of Moses and Miriam. Aaron represented the priesthood.

Abraham, according to the Bible, was the traditional father of the JEWS. At 75 years of age he was told by God to move to Canaan. God is also said to have promised Abraham that his descendants would inherit Canaan.

Ahaz, king of JUDEA (reigned c.735-715 BC), refused to join Israel and Syria in war against Assyria. When the 2 countries invaded Judea, Ahaz gave Assyria aid to defeat them. But he then became Assyria's vassal. Ahaz's policies were opposed by the prophet Isaiah.

Ammonites, 'sons of Ammon', were said to be descended from Lot, Abraham's nephew.

Antiochus Epiphanes seized the throne of Syria with Rome's approval. He was also ruler of Judea from about 175-164 BC. He tried to replace Judaism by the Greek religion, but failed. Judea revolted and broke away from Rome.

C

Chosen people were the Israelites (or Jews). In Judaist belief, Yahweh, or God, chose to make his covenant with them.

Covenant was a common device with nomadic peoples, among whom written documents were rare. It was a verbal agreement or bargain made in ritual circumstances, and had the force of law. A curse was believed to fall on those who broke it. Yahweh made a covenant with the Israelites that they would worship him alone.

D

David was a youthful hero who slew the Philistine giant Goliath. He fought for both Israel and Philistia. Eventually, he succeeded SAUL as king of Israel.

Sacrifice of Aaron

E

Edomites lived in Edom between the Dead Sea and the Gulf of Aqaba about 1200-700 BC. They were said to be descended from Esau, brother of Jacob.

Ezra, an expert on the law of Moses went from Babylon to Judea about 458 BC or earlier. He forced men who had married foreign wives to leave them and the children.

H

Hebrews is the earliest term for the Israelites

Left: The tents of the Israelites, referred to in the early books of the Bible, probably resembled those of present-day Bedouin.

king became known as the MESSIAH.

The Hebrew Bible was probably written between 1200 and 150 BC. It is one of the greatest literary works of all time and stories from it are known throughout the world. It is not one book, but a collection of books. The first five books, the *Torah* (Law), laid down the pattern of life to be followed by the Hebrews. After AD 200 another set of writings, the *Talmud,* was compiled as a guide to the laws and religious teachings. The Bible was almost entirely in Hebrew, which used a script derived from Aramaic. Spoken Hebrew had almost died out by 100 BC, after which most Jews probably spoke Aramaic, retaining Hebrew as the language of prayer.

Above: The Dead Sea Scrolls, discovered in 1947, are the oldest-known manuscripts of the Bible. They include parts of all the books of the Hebrew Bible except Esther. The scrolls probably formed part of a library of the Essenes, a Jewish sect flourishing about 100 BC to AD 70. A Bedouin boy found them preserved in a cave.

History of the Israelites

Traditionally, the *patriarchs* (fathers) of the Hebrews were ABRAHAM, his son ISAAC, and grandson Jacob (renamed ISRAEL). They may have lived about 1900 BC. Abraham migrated from Mesopotamia into Canaan (Palestine). Later, the Israelites (descendants of Israel) settled in Egypt. About 1300 BC they were reduced in status to slaves. According to the Bible, Moses led them out of Egypt in search of the 'promised land' of Canaan, and they journeyed 40 years through the desert.

Moses's successor, JOSHUA, led the Hebrews into Canaan probably about 1200 BC. They were forced to settle in the hills because enemies, notably the Philistines, occupied the more fertile coastal plain. Other tribes also warred with the Israelites, including the EDOMITES, MOABITES and AMMONITES.

The TWELVE TRIBES of Israel were ruled separately by judges. About 1020 BC they united and chose SAUL for their king, against the advice of the prophet Samuel. Saul was followed by David and his son SOLOMON. About 926 BC the tribes quarrelled. Ten tribes broke away to form the kingdom of Israel in the north, while the other two tribes (Benjamin and Judah) set up the kingdom of JUDEA in the south. War followed between them, but stronger powers decided their destinies.

Both Israel and Judea became tributary states of Assyria, and King AHAZ of Judea gained Assyrian aid from TIGLATH-PILESER III against invasion, by Israel and Syria. In 721 BC, the Assyrians finally destroyed Israel and dispersed its people.

The kingdom of Judea

After Babylonia had destroyed Assyria, it annexed Judea in 587 BC. Although Judea survived, its leading citizens were taken as captives to Babylon. After Cyrus the Persian conquered Babylon in 539 BC, he allowed the Judean community to return home. For a time, Judea came under the control of EZRA (a priest), and of NEHEMIAH, who acted as Persian governor. When Persia collapsed, Alexander the Great took Judea in 334 BC. He and his successors allowed the Judeans to practise their religion unhindered. When King ANTIOCHUS EPIPHANES tried to reverse this policy in 168 BC, the Judeans successfully rebelled. United under JUDAS MACCABAEUS they managed to defeat their Syrian

and also the Judeans.

Isaac, son of ABRAHAM and father of Jacob (ISRAEL).
Israel (Jacob) was the father of 10 sons from whom descended the TWELVE TRIBES of Israel.

Jesus of Nazareth was probably born in 4 BC or earlier. He was a Jew and a revolutionary thinker whose followers believed him to be the Son of God (the Christ). The Jewish priestly authorities feared that Jesus' teachings and their political consequences threatened their position. In about AD 29 he was tortured and then crucified.
Jews originally meant Judahites (members of the tribe of Judah). It has now generally replaced the earlier term HEBREWS.
Joshua, the assistant and successor of Moses, conquered part of Canaan. Traditionally, the walls of Jericho fell down at the blast of the Israelite trumpets.
Judas Maccabaeus led the resistance to ANTIOCHUS EPHIPHANES and freed Judea from Syrian domination about 168 BC.
Judea, the southern Hebrew state, existed 926 BC-70 AD. It was composed of the tribes of Benjamin and Judah, and its capital was Jerusalem.
Judges led the Israelites after they settled in Canaan and before SAUL became king. Important judges included Deborah (a prophetess); Gideon (a warrior); Samson (a giant whose strength lasted only while his hair was long) and Samuel (the first PROPHET).

Messiah in Hebrew means 'anointed one'. *Christos* or *Christ* has the same meaning in Greek. The Jews waited for the Messiah (ideal king) to lead Israel. Their priests rejected JESUS as the Messiah, and he was crucified by the Romans.

David

Moabites lived in Moab, east of the Dead Sea. They fortified their towns against the Israelites and refused them passage through Moabite territory. Moab plundered Judea after its defeat by Babylonia.
Moses, according to tradition, was found floating in a basket in the bullrushes by Pharaoh's daughter, who adopted him. (His story parallels that of Sargon of Akkad.) In the Bible, Moses had a vision and saw Yahweh in a burning bush.

overlord and won independence for nearly 100 years.

In 63 BC, the Romans took the Judean capital of Jerusalem. About 97 years later, JESUS OF NAZARETH was arrested. Some Jews thought he was the MESSIAH or 'anointed one', but the Jewish priestly leaders rejected this and urged PILATE (the Roman officer governing Judea) to have him crucified. The Judeans tried a revolt against Rome in AD 66, but in AD 70 the Romans crushed them. There was a further uprising the following century, from AD 132–135. This also failed and, during the next few hundred years, most Jews then left Judea, which disappeared from the map.

Below: Houses of poor Hebrews in Israel and Judea were single-roomed, box-like structures made of clay. Inside, the dark room lit only by small high windows, contrasted with the blazing sunlight outside. The family slept on a raised section of the floor, or on the flat roof which served as a second room, and was reached by an outside staircase. Each house had its own courtyard, within which goats and donkeys might be kept by families that could afford them. The illustration shows that dress in Biblical times differed little from the clothing still worn by many people in the Middle East. Oil lamps gave light and water had to be carried laboriously from wells, springs or rivers. The right to use a particular source of water was often disputed. While men worked outside the house, women washed and cooked in the courtyard. Roofs stood about 3.5 metres above floor level, supported by wooden beams over which brushwood, clay and straw was laid.

Yahweh told him to lead the children of Israel out of bondage in Egypt, but the Israelites rebelled against him several times. After leaving Egypt the Israelites had to spend 40 years in the desert. Few who set out reached the 'promised land'.

N

Nehemiah was the butler of King Artaxerxes of Persia, and when he took an interest in the unhappy plight of Judea about 445 BC, the king made him its governor and allowed him to rebuild its walls. His policies resembled those of EZRA.

P

Pilate, the Roman officer governing Judea, sentenced Jesus to crucifixion. He did so at the request of Caiaphas and other priests who claimed Jesus was a blasphemer because of his Messianic claims. The Romans saw in him a danger to their rule.

Elijah and the ravens

Prophets were those believed to be called by God to speak for him. They were thought to have the powers of *seers* (those who can foretell events). Consequently, they held influence over judges and kings. Leading prophets included Elijah (about 850 BC), Elisha, Isaiah, Jeremiah and Ezekiel. The prophets stressed the ideals of social justice and morality.

S

Saul, first king of Israel, had to fight against the iron spears of the Philistines. Defeated and wounded, he died by falling on his sword.

Solomon, son of DAVID, became Israel's third king, but his extravagant and un-Jewish way of life led to revolts. After his death, the Kingdom divided.

T

Ten commandments were that the Hebrews should: have no other gods but the one God; not make idols; not take God's name in vain; keep the sabbath day holy; honour their parents; not kill; not commit adultery; not steal; not lie; not covet anything belonging to others.

Twelve tribes of Israel were: Reuben, Simeon, Judah, Dan, Naphtali, Gad, Asher, Issachar, Zebulun, Benjamin (Jacob's sons), Ephraim and Manasseh (Jacob's grandsons).

The ancient Chinese were a great nation of traders who exported silk and spices, bronze and jade to the far corners of the known world. With their iron tools they built the Great Wall of China, the only man-made edifice to be seen from the moon.

The Early Chinese

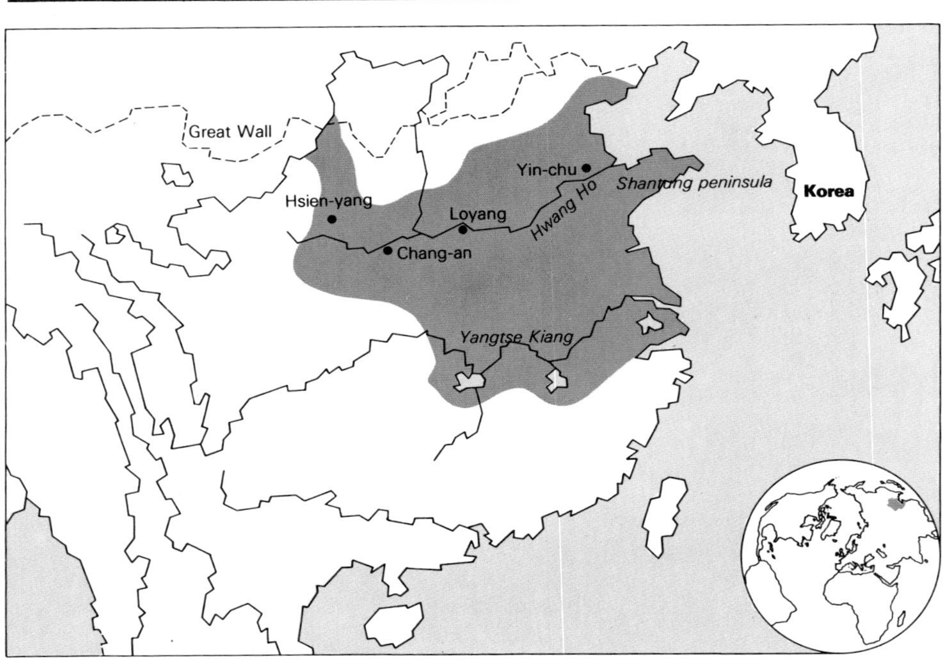

Above: Han China expanded to encompass an empire bigger than that of any other dynasty for the next 1500 years.

It was between the time of Hammurabi of Babylon and the fall of Crete that Chinese civilization began to emerge about 1600 BC. Its centre was due east of Persia beyond the mountain barriers of Central Asia in the valley of the HWANG HO (Yellow River) where settlers cultivated the fertile soil and kept cattle and sheep. From the 1500s to about 1028 BC this settlement was ruled by the SHANG DYNASTY. This was followed by the CHOU DYNASTY (1027–221 BC); the CHIN DYNASTY (221–206 BC); and the HAN DYNASTY (206 BC to AD 220).

Floods and barbarians: the twin dangers

The life-giving Hwang Ho was the Chinese people's source of food, but in times of flood the river became their most dangerous enemy and flood control was one of the two basic tasks of every emperor. The other great task was to protect the northern frontier of the civilization against invasion by nomadic Mongol tribes. Under the Chou dynasty the country was split into several vassal kingdoms, each of which built a defensive wall against the BARBARIANS. When the state of Chin hammered the other kingdoms into one unified country, it linked all the walls into the GREAT WALL OF CHINA. Inside this wall, the Chinese, sometimes united, sometimes divided, developed a single culture that has existed for an unbroken period of over 3,500 years.

Above: This bronze wine vessel shaped like an owl was used in ceremonies 3,000 years ago.

Early Chinese society

China's first important dynasty, the Shang, had a feudal structure with the court and nobles ruling over peasants and slaves. In the country the slaves worked the land, while in large towns such as YIN-CHU (Anyang), the last Shang capital, they were employed in workshops.

Shang dynasty cities and villages were walled and their buildings were of wood, with large rectangular halls raised on earthen platforms. By 1,000 BC, the total Shang population probably exceeded four millions, occupying an area about the size of modern Spain or the ancient Assyrian empire. The Shang rulers needed more labour and carried out slave-raiding expeditions on the fringes of their empire. A nomadic people, called the Chou, eventually retaliated. They fought with deadly crossbows and new, efficient CHARIOTS and finally caused the downfall of the Shang. The vassal kings of the Chou then took over most of the Hwang Ho and Yangtse Kiang basins.

Working the land

Chou rulers set up a string of village communes known as the CHING TIEN SYSTEM, whereby each family in the commune was allotted a piece of land, but was bound to co-operate with the others in farming the whole area as efficiently as possible. Each Chou commune was largely self-

Reference

B **Barbarians,** to the Chinese, were any peoples not inside their own borders. To the Shang, the Chou were barbarians.
Bone was a useful material in ancient China. Some of the earliest surviving pictographs are found on human skulls and are known as oracle bone characters.

C **Calendar.** In Shang China the year was divided into 12 months of 29 or 30 days (reckoned to be the full cycle of the moon). An extra month was added every few years.
Ceramics were made in China from prehistoric times. The scarcity of metals probably encouraged the Chinese to concentrate on developing their techniques with pottery. Partial glazing was used from the 200s BC. Han ceramics may have been influenced by ideas which came from Rome via the silk route.
Chang-an was the capital of the Western Han (202 BC to AD 25) and some later dynasties. Chang Chiao, founder of a religious cult, led the YELLOW TURBANS in revolt against the Eastern Han in AD 184.

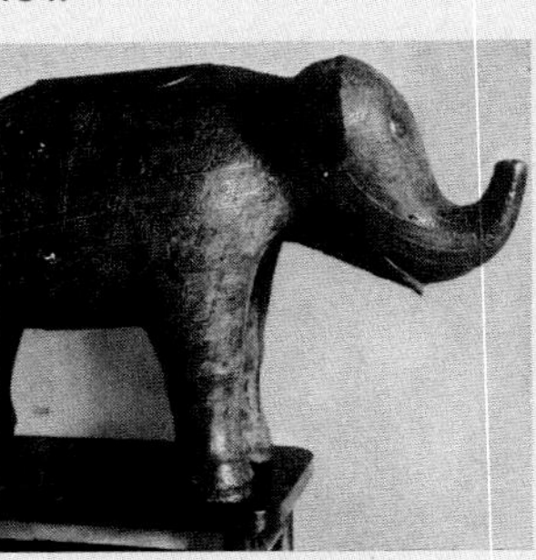

Sacrificial vessel: early Chou

Chariots came into use with horse-breeding and riding. Shang 2-wheeled chariots carried 3 men and may have been a version of the Hittite chariot taken into China by Mongol Turks.
Chin dynasty was officially founded in 221 BC, but the Chou emperor abdicated power to the king of Chin in 256 BC. The Chin united the country and named it China.
Ching tien system was so called because land was divided into plots shaped like the character 'ching'. From time to time, land allotted to families was reallocated to ensure that everyone had a share of good land and bad.
Chou dynasty was divided into Western Chou (c.1028-771 BC) and Eastern Chou (770-221 BC). Unable to hold back the Mongol tribes, Emperor Ping abandoned his western territories in 771 BC. He set up the Eastern Chou capital at Loyang in 770 BC. The Chou emperors gradually lost power to vassal kings.
Coins, or coin-like objects, circulated widely in China before 400 BC. They were bronze replicas of spades, billhooks, knives and other tools. Cowrie shells passed

sufficient, and quite highly developed.

The land was tilled with animal-drawn ploughs and manure was worked into the ground. Every so often the fields were left fallow to 'rest' them. Two-pronged wooden hoes were used to plant rice, wheat and millet, and crops were harvested with sickles of stone and shell. BONE was also used to make weapons, tools and writing materials. Animal farming included cattle, pigs, sheep, dogs and chickens, and wild animals were also hunted for their meat, sometimes from horseback. To the Chou, horses were a prized possession and used for pulling royal carts and war chariots.

Silk was produced in southern China from prehistoric times and the silk industry prospered particularly under the Shang and Chou dynasties who used advanced weaving techniques. Silk was worn by the rich; the less well-off wore clothing of skins, furs, flax or leather.

Iron and trade

Iron ploughs and tools came into general use by 700 BC. These, and advanced techniques, improved the productivity of farming and increased its scale. As capital and expenditure grew, the ching tien system died out. Land came under the control of nobles and rich peasants and disputes between states became so frequent that 475–221 BC is called the WARRING STATES PERIOD.

The demand for iron in agriculture brought a mining boom. Smelting works and metal working factories employed hundreds of workers making, amongst other things, spades. These iron spades had a direct influence on the expansion of trade, for they enabled more canals to be dug. The rising state of Chin cut a 150-kilometre canal which transformed 250,000 hectares of wasteland into farmland, besides forming an important trade route. Another waterway linked the Yangtse Kiang and other rivers into an integrated transport system, along which many new cities developed. By 400 BC, perhaps 25 million Chou people occupied an area twice as large as the old Shang territory.

Prosperity reached a high peak under Emperor WU of the Han dynasty (reigned 141-86 BC). While fighting the HSIUNG NU (Mongol Huns) he discovered that a secret and profitable trade was being carried along the 'silk route' between China and south-western Asia. Realizing its potential, he brought the trade under government control, providing protection for the caravans against the Hsiung Nu and other robbers. Chinese bronzes, jades, lacquer-wares, CERAMICS and, above all, silks travelled westwards to Damascus, Rome, Spain and even distant Britain. Eastwards into China went rugs and carpets, frankincense, camphor, coral, plants, birds, HORSES and other animals.

Above: Human skull bones provided a writing material for some of the earliest-known Chinese characters.

Above: Early Chinese characters showed things in 'matchstick' form (*top*). These later developed into present-day characters (*bottom*). Both forms are shown for a tree (*left*) and a goat (*right*).

Left: Rice has been an important crop of China since earliest known times, especially in the south. It was not, however, the main food until after Han times. In Chou China people ate much beef and mutton; in Chin and Han times people ate reduced quantities of meat and switched to pork and dog meat because pigs and dogs required less land. Wheat was then the main crop, but rice replaced it in southern China in AD 300–600. In northern China, the rich ate rice; the poor, wheat.

---

as small change. Round coins with a hole in the centre (called cash) came into use about 250 BC and are still used today. The first Chin emperor superseded all coins by new round ones with a hole.

Confucius (c.551-c.479 BC) is the Latinized name of Kung Fu-tzu. He was a philosopher concerned above all with morality and right behaviour which were embodied in tradition.

G

Great Wall of China was built by a Chin emperor who conscripted some 30% of the male population of China to link earlier walls into a 2,400 km-long towered frontier barrier. The importance of the wall lay in

Chü-Yang Gate: Great Wall

the watchmen who patrolled it and who lit beacon fires to alert mobile troops against approaching invaders. It is the only man-made object that can be seen from the moon.

H

Han dynasty was founded by LIU PANG in 206 BC. After the civil war, the Han capital of Chang-an was captured by the HSIUNG NU. LIU HSIN then set up the Eastern Han dynasty (AD 25-220) with its capital at the old Eastern Chou capital, Loyang.

Horses were rare and valuable in China. The Han emperor Wu sent 100,000 soldiers into Ferghana (near the old Persian empire's border) to seize horses refused him by Ferghana's king. Wu got his horses, but 40,000 soldiers perished from thirst, hunger, disease or exposure in the bleak lands of central Asia.

Hsia dynasty (2000s to 1500s BC) is known only in legend. Its supposed earliest chief was Huang Ti (Yellow Emperor), and its earliest legend concerns flood control on the Yellow River.

Hsiung Nu were nomadic tribes pushed northward by the first Chin emperor. Having lost their best pasture land to China, they founded the tribal federation

Model horses: Han

The Emperor Wu benefited personally from the prosperity of his people. He laid out the Imperial park of the Han emperors in Chang-an, vast ornamental gardens bounded by a wall over 160 kilometres long, where Indian rhinoceroses roamed with other exotic animals in a setting of groves, lakes and springs.

Religion and philosophy

The twin religions of China are TAOISM and Confucianism, the teachings of CONFUCIUS. Both originated in the 500s BC and can be considered as PHILOSOPHIES rather than religions. They have also played an important part in forming the Chinese character.

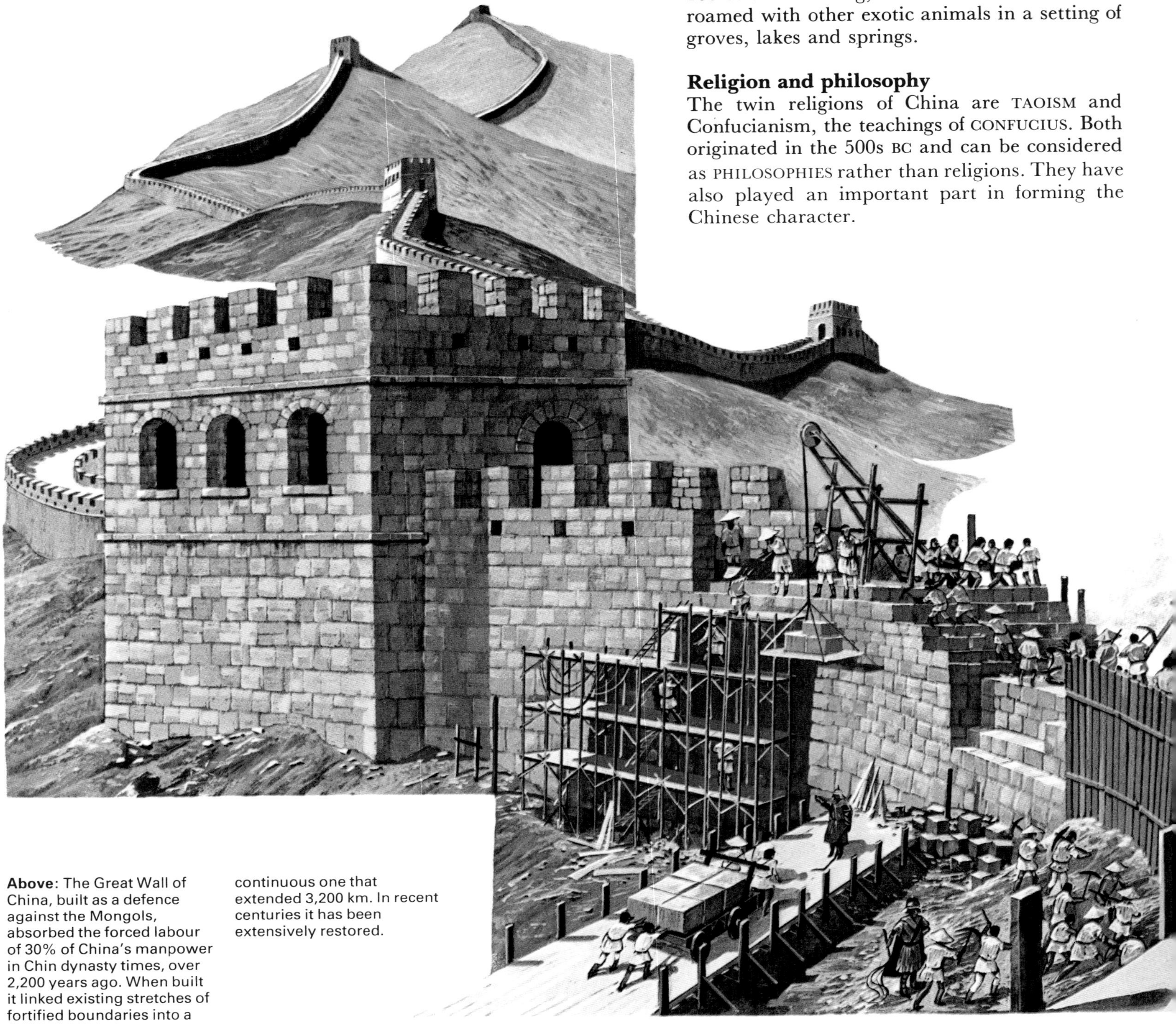

Above: The Great Wall of China, built as a defence against the Mongols, absorbed the forced labour of 30% of China's manpower in Chin dynasty times, over 2,200 years ago. When built it linked existing stretches of fortified boundaries into a continuous one that extended 3,200 km. In recent centuries it has been extensively restored.

known as the Hsiung Nu. Their first chief was Touman and during Han times they may have numbered over 2 million. They attacked China's border for 500 years.

Hwang Ho. A river that rises in Tibet and flows mainly eastwards across northern China. Following a flood in AD 1852, its course shifted 400 km to the north so that it entered the sea north, instead of south, of the Shantung peninsula. It was long known to the Chinese as 'China's sorrow' or 'Scourge of the Sons of Han' because of its severe flooding. The name Hwang Ho (Yellow River) comes from the *loess* (yellow earth) which is carried along in its waters.

J **Jade** was from ancient times used in religious ceremonies and made into jewellery. Carved into the shape of a man and worn as an amulet, it was believed to ward off disease and evil spirits. The bodies of a Han prince and his wife, clothed in pieces of jade sewn together with gold thread, were excavated in AD 1968.

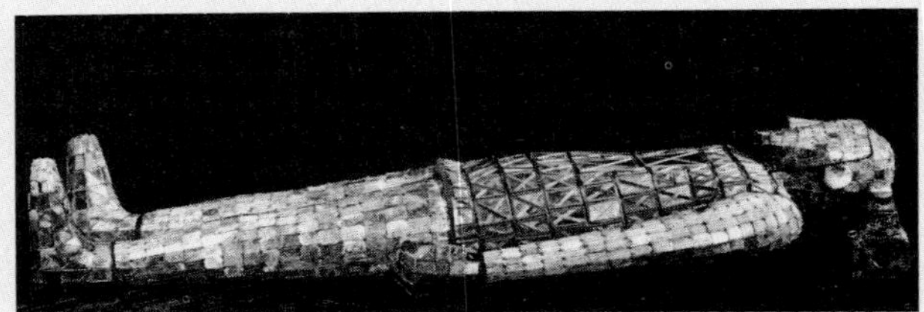

Jade funeral suit of Princess Ton Wan

L **Language** of China has no alphabet and each Chinese character conveys one complete idea. The early Chinese characters were pictures, but in time, characters became more abstract. Learning to read and write in Chinese is more difficult than in alphabetical languages, and nowadays about 3,000 characters must be learned to be able to read a newspaper, but the communication of ideas is quicker.

Liu Hsiu reigned AD 25-57 as Kuang-wu, first emperor of the Eastern Han dynasty.

Liu Pang, a minor official from a peasant family, was one of many leaders who

Bronze leopard: Han

Confucianism teaches loyalty to the family, ancestor worship, and obedience to the laws of society. It puts the accent on ceremonies, order, and the 'proper' ways of doing things. Taoism, summed up in the *Tao Te Ching* ('The Way and its Power'), ridicules Confucianist ceremonies and rules of behaviour. It says that men should always work in harmony with nature, never against it. Taoism incorporates many deities which have been worshipped from earliest times and are organized like the earthly royal court. Below the Jade emperor, the chief god, were the Moon goddess, the Rain, Wind and Thunder gods, the gods of Wealth, Happiness, Walls and Ditches, the Kitchen, and so on. The god of Examinations was probably inspired by the Confucians, who imposed on China a strict examination system for those who wanted to become MANDARINS (senior civil servants).

Arts, language and science

Developments in arts and language in ancient China were related to the demands of religion and trade. Bronze urns, often in animal shapes, were used for making sacrifices, preparing food and exporting, as were lacquerware, ceramics and JADE, which was regarded as a product of heaven. Chinese pictographic LANGUAGE was developed to record early works of literature, poetry set to music, the works of Confucianist tradition and rival philosophies, and mythology. Contact with the 'barbarians' introduced war songs, dances and MONGOL DRAMA into China.

Consistent with the Chinese character, science was regarded as of little value unless it could be directly related to practical purposes, such as hydro-engineering, agriculture, metallurgy, the CALENDAR, and weights and measures, which were especially important in trade and taxation. The early Chinese also studied mathematics, astronomy and engineering and exchanged philosophical and scientific ideas with Persia.

History

The Shang dynasty was established in the 1500s BC when a tribal chief named Tang overthrew

Above: The wrestlers, a bronze of late Chou times, shows 2 identical men poised in opposite directions with their hands joined.

Below: Confucius, the great Chinese teacher of 2,500 years ago, is seen surrounded by his pupils in this silk painting.

defeated the Chin. He then crushed several rivals to become the first Han emperor.

Loyang, capital of Eastern Chou, was later made the capital of Eastern Han.

M **Mandarins** were the public officials of China. Mandarin is also the Chinese language as spoken in Peking and most of inland China. It is now the national language.

Mongol drama came into early Han China as a result of contact with Mongol tribes. When China annexed Mongol territory it absorbed Mongol peoples. Besides dancing, Mongol drama included conjuring, tight-rope walking, weightlifting, sword and fire swallowing, and acrobatics. Some of the entertainers wore fierce masks.

P **Paper** was invented by Tsai Lun, a Han official, in AD 105. A cheap and light material to work on was needed because many people could by then read and write. Before AD 105, bamboo and silk were the usual writing materials, replacing shells, bones, stone and bronze.

Philosophies flourishing alongside Confucianism and TAOISM included that of Mo Ti, who advocated brotherly love as the basis of human relationships. Some people, known as the 'legalists', wanted to impose a severe legal code to ensure a strong government, and the Chin emperors used their code.

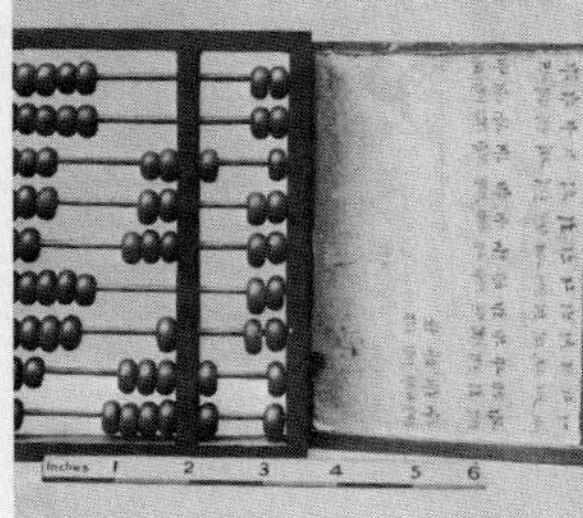

Abacus, 500s BC

Population of China possibly reached about 4 to 5 millions in Shang times, rose to 25 millions in Eastern Chou times, and probably exceeded 50 millions in Han times.

S **Shang dynasty** (c.1500–c.1028 BC) followed the HSIA DYNASTY.

T **Taoism** is believed to have been founded by Lao Tzu in the 500s BC, but some scholars think that it is much older, and that Lao Tzu

Han clay figurines

Above: A bronze flying horse of the Eastern Han dynasty symbolizes the horses imported from Ferghana and Sogdiana. The 'gallop' was shown more accurately than in any European paintings before AD 1700.

Above right: This pottery model of a Han house was entombed with a dead man to provide him with a house in the next world.

Chieh, the last ruler of the legendary Hsia dynasty. About 1028 BC, King Wu of the Chou defeated the last Shang emperor at Muyeh, near his capital, and set up the Western Chou dynasty. Many small vassal kingdoms came into being, owing allegiance to the Chou emperors. In 771 BC, the Western Chou were overwhelmed by the Yen Yun and Jung tribes. The defeated Chou emperor, Ping, moved his capital eastwards to LOYANG and began the Eastern Han empire in 770 BC. Five hundred years of border and internal wars followed and in 256 BC the last Chou emperor abdicated power to the king of Chin.

Chin systematically crushed each neighbour, Han, Wei, Chu, Chi, Chao and Yen, and annexed them. In 221 BC (when Rome was preparing for its second war against Carthage), the king of Chin took the title of Shi Huang Ti (First Emperor). In his new role he pressed millions of unwilling peasants into forced labour for ambitious building projects.

During the reign of the Second Emperor, 900 army conscripts found themselves unable to reach their frontier position on time because of floods. To arrive late would mean certain death, so they killed their commander and became outlaws. Their revolt sparked off a revolution and soon, the Chin capital of Hsien-yang fell to the peasant armies, led by LIU PANG. After defeating his rivals in 202 BC, Liu Pang became Eminent Emperor, first ruler of the Han dynasty. Once established, he managed to buy off a threatened attack by 300,000 Hsiung Nu horsemen. But under the rule of Wu, they returned again to attack the Han capital, CHANG-AN, and Wu drove them back in three bloody wars (127, 122, and 119 BC).

Wang Mang, a regent, usurped the throne in AD 8 and introduced reforms. Civil war followed, and in AD 25, LIU HSIU (a deposed Han prince) set up the Eastern Han dynasty at Loyang. Western Han territory (including the silk route) was lost to the Hsiung Nu. In AD 184, Chang Chiao led the rebellion of a million yellow-turbanned peasants. The imperial army crushed the YELLOW TURBANS, and swept away the last Han ruler. As a result of this revolt the Han empire disintegrated in 220 AD.

never existed. Legend has it that he once met CONFUCIUS and advised him to discard all his ideas, and many people believe that he wrote the *Tao Te Ching*, the chief book of Taoism. Taoism deplores human striving and encourages submission to nature. It has never sought converts.

W **Warring States period** (475-221 BC) was in the later half of Eastern Chou times. As the dynasty weakened, 7 kingdoms (Chi, Chu, Yen, Chin, Han, Chao and Wei) grew stronger and warred with one another, mainly for territory. Eventually, Chin won.

Wu, emperor of Western Han, reigned for 55 years. He

Taoist mountain symbol

was the hammer of the HSIUNG NU and also conquered western Turkestan, western Korea and southern China. Wu promoted trade with the west and sent emmissaries to the Romans. Han China prospered under him, but social and economic problems remained unsolved and in time destroyed the dynasty.

Y **Yellow Turbans** were a rebel peasant army so known because of the headdresses they wore when they rose against the Eastern Han dynasty in 184 BC. The official Han priests and the ceremonies and sacrifices they laid down were unpopular with the peasants and uprisings were common. A previous revolt against Wang Mang had been fought by the Red Eyebrows, a peasant army who had no uniforms and so dyed their eyebrows as a mark of recognition. The leader of the Yellow Turbans was Chang Chiao, founder of a religious cult known as 'Taiping Tao', who won their confidence by curing diseases.

Yin-chu, the sixth and final Shang capital, stood on the site of Anyang. The Shang capital had to be changed 5 times because of the flooding of the Hwang Ho.

Han painting

The rigid social structure imposed on the Indian sub-continent by the Aryans still exists today. Social and political life was greatly influenced by the three religions, Hinduism, Jainism and Buddhism.

The Early Indians

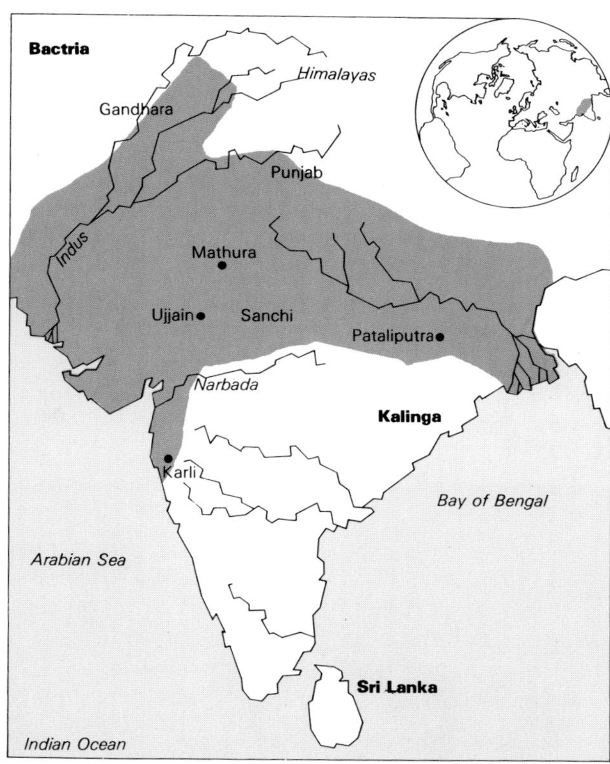

Above: The map shows Maurya India at the height of its influence under the Buddhist King Asoka, about 250 BC.

The triangular subcontinent of India is hemmed in by the snow-capped Himalayas to the north, and by other mountains to the north-east. These mountains and the surrounding seas form a natural 'Great Wall of India' and only the north-west, the area which is now Pakistan, is accessible by land. Through this north-western frontier came many invaders. The most important were the Aryans who fought their way into India about 1500 BC, shortly after Shang China began. It took the Aryans about 1200 years to conquer most of the subcontinent, but at its height under King ASOKA the Aryan empire equalled that of Chin China in area. This unified area of India broke up, however, just at the moment when China achieved unity under the Chin.

Caste and religion in early India

The Aryans imposed a rigid social order based on CASTE. From birth, people were classified as either *Brahmins* (priests and scholars); *Kshatriyas* (rulers and warriors): *Vaisyas* (merchants, craftsmen and peasants); or *Sudras* (unskilled labourers). There were hundreds of sub-castes based on hereditary occupations, while at the very bottom were OUTCASTES. The Aryans brought a vast number of DEITIES into India and in time, Aryan and DRAVIDIAN gods fused to form an inter-related hierarchy of one religion — HINDUISM.

The only way out of the CASTE SYSTEM was to adopt JAINISM or BUDDHISM — two alternative religions. Jains held all life sacred and revered 24 saints or *Jainas.* Buddhism was founded by Siddhartha Gautama, a north Indian kshatriya, later known as Buddha. He taught the way to 'Enlightenment' which can be reached only when a man secures release from perpetual rebirth. Buddha taught that the way to end rebirth and suffering is to end the selfish desire that causes it. This was a difficult concept for people to

Left: This finely carved sandstone figure from Lahore presents the Buddha in the pose of a Yogi ascetic: the soles of his feet up, his hands positioned for turning the Wheel of the Law.

Reference

A **Aryan languages** of northern India that are now official languages include Hindi, Punjabi, Kashmiri, Gujarati, Marathi, Bengali, Assamese and Oriya. The scripts of all these languages derive from *Brahmi* – the script in which Asoka's laws were written.

Asoka, the warrior king who turned Buddhist, was the grandson of CHANDRAGUPTA. A 4 lion capital from an Asokan pillar is the emblem of modern India. Such pillars had writing carved on them stating Asoka's Buddhist beliefs and principles of government.

B **Bindusara,** son of CHANDRAGUPTA, extended the Maurya empire south into Dravidian India.

Buddhism is both a philosophy and a religion. Buddhists believe that the universe functions according to principles that cannot be altered by men or gods. Buddha (born Siddhartha Gautama) advised men to end suffering, which all endured, by following the *Noble Eightfold Path* of right views, right aims or motive, right speech, right acts, right livelihood, right effort, right concentration, and right contemplation. Buddha also advised following the *Middle Way,* avoiding extremes of hardship or luxury. After his death in c.483 BC, devotees made him a god and saints and other deities were soon worshipped alongside him. Buddhism spread and Asoka's son and daughter took it into Sri Lanka. Buddhism flourished in China from AD 400, and later in Korea, Tibet, Japan, Mongolia and south-eastern Asia.

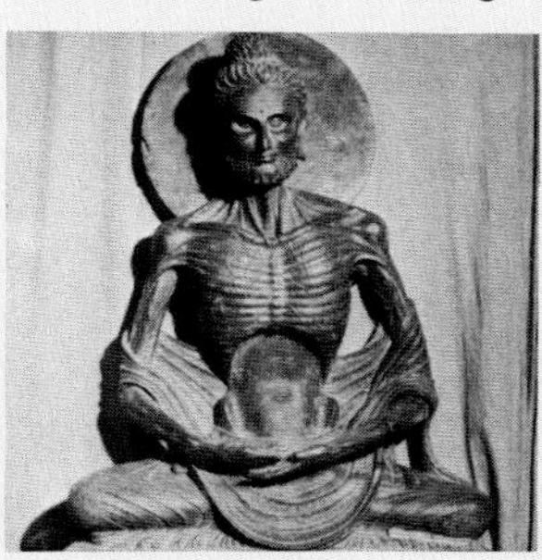

Starving Buddha, Lahore

C **Caste system** in India was 2-fold. Brahmins, Kshatriyas, Vaisyas and Sudras can be thought of as hereditary classes. About 1000 BC, other caste divisions emerged, based on occupa-

A follower of Vishnu

Left: The *Jataka Tales*, legends of Buddha's former lives on earth, are illustrated in this carving on a stone pillar at Sanchi, India. Ordinary people, unlearned in Buddhist holy books, took their ideas of Buddhist principles from these fascinating stories.

understand and as a result Buddhism soon gathered its own collection of popular deities.

The main dynasty in early India was the Maurya. Maurya India was a land of villages closely supervised by the central government at Pataliputra, the capital. The Maurya emperors stockpiled food against possible famine, and built new villages so as to distribute the population more evenly. Although rice was the main crop and diet, MEAT was more commonly eaten in Maurya India than in later times.

Government activities

The government kept harbours, sanitation and water supply in good repair and engineers built roads and canals and kept them well maintained. Censuses were conducted and records of business transactions kept. People were compelled to take precautions against fire, and were fined for littering the city streets. Mining, tree felling and other activities connected with land were strictly controlled. Gambling was permitted, and taxed at five per cent, but the government's main income came from taxing farmers. The Mauryas also kept a large standing army.

The brain behind the government of CHANDRA-

Below: Krishna, dark-skinned and most popular of Indian deities, was a fun-loving god, yet finally perished as a warrior in war.

Below: Lakshmi, golden-skinned wife of Vishnu, emerged from a milk ocean. She is revered especially by merchants as the goddess of fortune.

Below: The 4-armed god Vishnu is the preserver of the universe. His 10 incarnations are said to include Krishna and Buddha.

Below: Varaha, the boar and third incarnation of Vishnu. After killing a demon, Varaha raised the earth on his tusk out of the universal ocean.

Below: Brahma, once supreme god of the Hindus, has long been replaced by the more popular gods, Siva and Vishnu. His 4 heads denote wisdom.

tions. The caste system still functions in India, but discrimination on caste grounds is illegal.

Cave temples were cut from solid rock by Buddhists, Jains and Hindus. One of the most impressive is at Karli (near Bombay). Buddhists cut this temple 38 metres into the rock during the first century AD.

Chandragupta, supposedly once a prisoner of Alexander the Great, founded the Maurya empire (324-313 BC).

D

Deities of Hinduism supposedly number 330 million and differ from village to village. Today about 100 deities are of prime importance, the key ones being Siva (the creator and destroyer) and Vishnu (the preserver). Old gods, such as Indra and Brahma, are now seldom worshipped.

A Jain temple, Mount Abu

Dravidian languages of southern India (now official) are Tamil, Telegu, Kannada (Canarese) and Malayalam.

Dravidian sailors crossed the Indian Ocean to Burma and Malaya. Their routes were part of a larger trading system linking the Mediterranean to the East Indies. Possibly the Indians set sail to search for gold and silver after nomadic tribes cut the supply routes through central Asia in the 200s BC. The Indians planted their Hindu–Buddhist culture in Thailand, Cambodia and Indonesia, especially Bali.

Dravidians were the pre-Aryan, darker-skinned people of India who were pushed southwards.

G

Gandhara, a region in north-western India, came under Persian control before falling to Alexander the Great. It became part of Maurya India, then fell to Indo-Greeks, Sakas and Parthians. By AD 100 it had become the centre of a Buddhist-Greek style of sculpture and architecture. Muslims swept away its art style about AD 700.

Gandharan sculptured head

GUPTA (first Maurya emperor) was KAUTILYA. This minister wrote the *Arthasastra* ('Manual of Politics') advising kings how to hold on to power. No one should oppress the people except the king himself, ruled Kautilya. This principle was applied in the law courts and yet Chandragupta ruled as a despot, setting spies on his officials and executing or maiming those who opposed him. Kautilya confessed that he knew no way of controlling corruption among officials.

Arts and languages

Chandragupta's palace is said to have rivalled those of the Persian kings in splendour. But, because it was built of wood (like almost all early Indian buildings), nothing survives of it. When the Buddhists came to build STUPAS, their stone gateways and balustrades were shaped in the fashion of earlier wooden buildings.

While Hindu sculpture was full of lively movement, Buddhist sculpture was serene. At first, Buddha was portrayed only by symbols, such as alms bowls. Later, superb Buddhas were carved and CAVE TEMPLES were cut out of solid rock. Art usually followed either the GANDHARA or MATHURA styles. Hindu, Jain and Buddhist LITERATURE was vast in volume. The Hindu epic RAMAYANA is the fount of much Hindu legend and culture. India's ARYAN LANGUAGES derived from Sanskrit. In the south, DRAVIDIAN LANGUAGES were spoken.

DRAVIDIAN SAILORS from southern India braved the Indian Ocean to trade with south-

Above: The huge Buddhist stupa constructed at Sanchi in western India soon after the death of the Buddha, contains relics of him. It almost certainly comprises the oldest surviving Indian buildings. The stone balustrade resembles earlier wooden ones.

Below: Siva, god of both destruction and creation, ensures the regeneration of all things. He is often shown as Lord of the Dance in a ring of fire.

Below: Parvati, wife of Siva and mother of Ganesha, is known as 'the mountaineer', being the daughter of a Himalayan god.

Below: Ganesha, round-bellied with 4 arms and an elephant's head, is the god of wisdom, revered as the remover of obstacles.

Below: Manasa, a serpent goddess, is worshipped especially in Bengal. Snakes often appeared in Hindu myths, probably because they were feared.

Below: Hanuman, the monkey god (or sometimes merely the monkey king) was one of the heroes of the epic *Ramayana*.

H **Hinduism** is older than history and has no known founder. The central theme in Hinduism is the belief in a Supreme Spirit, *Brahman*. Hindus worship vast numbers of deities and many animals and plants are sacred to them. The *Vedas* (Hindu sacred writings) carry more authority than the deities.

J **Jainism** is claimed to be immensely old. But in its present form it dates from the 500s BC when Mahavira formulated it. Jains believe Mahavira to be the latest of 24 tirthankaras (Jainas, or saints). According to mythology Rishabha, first tirthankara, lived for 8,400,000 years and stood 500 bows high.

Jain follower

Earthly beings are believed to be reborn a million times; deities, 400,000 times. There is clearly a marked emphasis on numbers in Jain mythology. Forbidden most occupations by their religion, they dealt in precious metals and stones and many became very wealthy. Jains wear white and take great care to avoid killing any living thing.

K **Kajula Kadphises,** one of 5 chieftains among whom Bactria was divided, founded the Kushan dynasty. This extended from northern India into central Asia. He is known only from Chinese records.

Kalinga was conquered by ASOKA. In Asoka's own words, '150,000 were taken, 100,000 were killed, many more died'. Asoka went on to say that if one-thousandth part of the sufferings of Kalinga were to happen again, it would be 'pitiful and grievous' to him.

Kautilya, Chandragupta's brilliant minister, wrote the *Arthasastra* ('Manual of Politics') which advised how a king should keep his power. In order to do so Kautilya justified the use of kindness, cruelty, justice, injustice, or any other means. Some scholars think that the Italian political philosopher Machiavelli (lived about AD

Buddhist monastery, Pakistan

eastern Asia, where they planted their Hindu-Buddhist culture which still survives in Thailand, Cambodia and Indonesia (especially Bali).

Aryan peoples from central Asia advanced through the mountain passes of the Himalaya into north-western India about 1500 BC, where they may have destroyed the Indus Valley civilization. They found India inhabited by darker-skinned Dravidians who they conquered or pushed southwards. Little is known about the next 1200 years.

The Macedonians and the Mauryas

Alexander the Great conquered Persia and then occupied the Indus Valley region briefly in 326–325 BC. The departure of the last Macedonian governor a few years later, left a power vacuum. Into this gap stepped Chandragupta Maurya, a low-caste adventurer who is said to have once gained Alexander's favour. Chandragupta quickly occupied northern India eastwards to Pataliputra and southwards to the Narbada River. In 305 BC he defeated another invasion by a large force of Macedonians.

Right: The Shwe Dagon, Burma's ancient pagoda, was first constructed shortly after Indian missionaries took Buddhism to the country more than 2,000 years ago. Its massive conical stupa, which devotees have plated thick with gold, rises nearly 100 metres above the main temple platform. Some 64 smaller stupas surround it. Thousands of precious stones stud its topmost *hti* (umbrella).

Left: A capital from one of Asoka's pillars carries the lion that now symbolizes India. Asoka, a conqueror who renounced war, had the Buddhist principles of his rule engraved on 25 pillars and rocks throughout his Indian empire.

The Aryan-Dravidian religion of Hinduism was increasingly challenged by Jainism and Buddhism. Chandragupta became a Jain. His son, BINDUSARA, extended the Maurya kingdom southwards. About 272 BC, Chandragupta's grandson Asoka became king. In conquering the state of KALINGA (eastern India) Asoka caused the death of 250,000 Kalingans. In remorse, he renounced aggressive war, turned Buddhist, and encouraged the spread of Buddhism throughout the Indian subcontinent. Until Asoka died in 232 BC, India enjoyed a golden age of Buddhist rule, but about 183 BC, an army general called PUSYAMITRA SUNGA seized power from the last Maurya king and tried to restore Hinduism.

Mongol rule over northern India

The armies of Han China continued their pressure on the HSIUNG NU *(see page 57)* who in turn threatened another Mongol people, the YUEH-CHIH. These nomads pushed the Scythian Sakas through the Greek-occupied, ex-Persian satrapy of Bactria, into the PUNJAB. The Sakas ruled the Punjab from about 80 BC. The Yueh-chih pushed on. About AD 80 a Yueh-chih chieftain, KUJULA KADPHISES, became ruler of a kingdom that extended from central Asia into northern India. This was known as the KUSHAN KINGDOM. Buddhism was taken from Kushan by Yueh-chih missionaries into China. Little is known about the Kushan kingdom, or about the history of India during the following 200 years.

1500) modelled his book *The Prince* on Kautilya's book.
Kushan kingdom, established by KAJULA KADPHISES in AD 76 or later, lasted 200 years.

L **Literature** of ancient India was vast. The sacred *Vedas* included the *Brahmanas, Upanishads,* and the 2 epics: MAHABHARATA and RAMAYANA. Buddhist works (in the Pali language) included *Tripitaka* ('Three Baskets') and the *Suttas* ('Sermons') which contained the highly readable *Jataka Tales.*

M **Mahabharata** tells of a colossal war fought between 2 royal families. Gods and heroes took sides. The war probably symbolized the Aryan–Dravidian struggle.

Stone elephant, Delhi

Mathura was the centre of a style of art rivalling Gandhara. It dated from about AD 100 and was Buddhist–Jain. It showed less Greco–Roman influence than the Gandhara style.
Meat eating was normal in Chandragupta's India, although higher castes did not eat the meat of horned cattle. Asoka encouraged vegetarianism. By AD 400 higher castes had given up meat.

O **Outcastes** were divided into 2 groups: Hindus who had no caste, and non-Hindus, such as Jains, Buddhists and foreigners. Outcastes (probably descended from enslaved prisoners-of-war) were until recently treated badly.

P **Punjab** was ruled by the Sakas, a Scythian dynasty, from about 80 BC to AD 388.
Pusyamitra Sunga, a brahmin general of the last Maurya king, usurped the throne.

R **Ramayana** is a wealth of legends, myths and historical facts woven into a fascinating epic. The story concerns Rama (a dispossessed prince) and the abduction of his wife Sita.

S **Stupas** were huge dome-shaped burial mounds built to hold relics of the Buddha and saints. They were the forerunners of Sri Lankan dagobas and Chinese, Japanese and Burmese pagodas.

Y **Yueh-chih** were Indo-Scythians who ruled Bactria and part of northern India about 128 BC – AD 450.

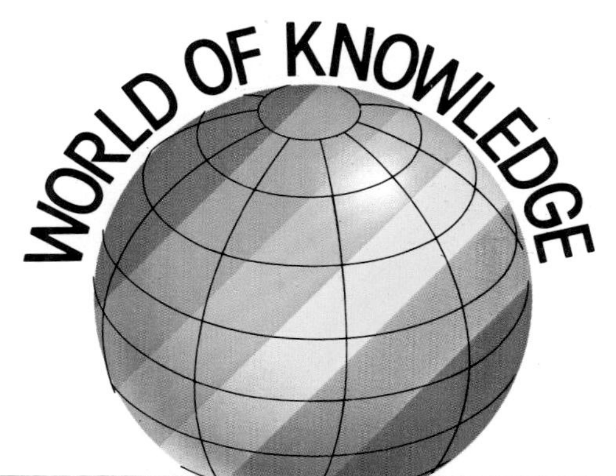

The Spread of Civilization

Ron Carter

Introduction

The Spread of Civilization covers world history from the height of Greek culture and 'the glory that was Rome' to around the start of the Age of Exploration in the 1400s. It shows how indebted Europeans are to Greece and Rome but, after the fall of Rome, the focus of world history often shifts away from Europe and **The Spread of Civilization** sheds light on important developments elsewhere. For example, during Europe's so-called 'Dark Ages', it was the Arabs of the Middle East and North Africa who preserved classical learning and it was Arab scholarship which provided much of the inspiration for the European explorers of the 1400s. By taking a global view, we can better appreciate the inter-action between human cultures and understand the shifting patterns of greatness and decadence, achieving a balanced view of man's constant quest for knowledge and progress.

The culture of the ancient Greeks forms the cornerstone of Western civilization. In philosophy and art the Greeks remain largely unsurpassed to this day. Even in science and medicine they led the field until modern times.

The Greeks

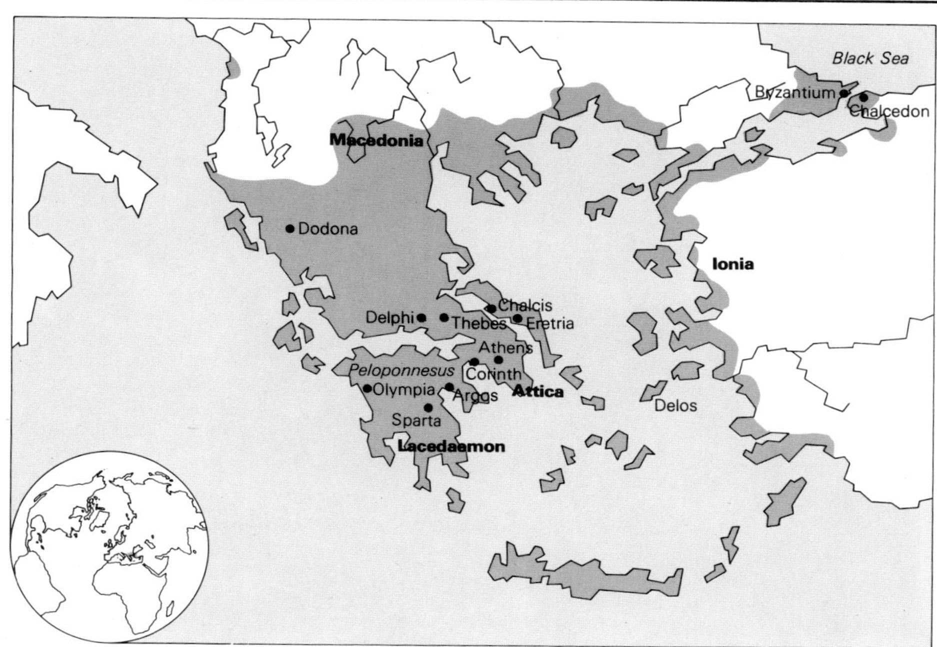

Above: Cities in the craggy peninsula of ancient Greece seldom stood far from the sea, which heavily influenced Greek history. Greeks early on founded colonies along the coastlands of Asia Minor, then spread throughout the Mediterranean and Black Seas.

Right: The head of Pericles wearing his warrior's helmet symbolizes the great age of Athenian democracy which he established in 462–454 BC. Under Pericles all citizens became eligible to hold the highest government posts, but citizenship was limited to men having both parents of Athenian birth.

The Greek civilization was a small one compared with the empires of the Persians, Chinese and Indians, occupying the southern part of present-day Greece, an area no larger than Sri Lanka or a single Persian satrapy (province). Only 25 per cent of this territory could be cultivated and so even at the height of its civilization Greece never exceeded a population of two millions, barely 10 per cent that of Chou China during the same period. The lives of the people of the Greek city-states were dominated by the surrounding sea and the Greeks became enterprising colonists although they never founded empires.

Greek achievements

Greek culture forms the basis of our present-day western civilization and was centred on Athens, which was already in political decline when at its cultural height in the 400s BC. The Greeks were great experimenters and innovators in many areas such as government, philosophy and architecture, and many consider that in the arts, and more especially in sculpture, they remain largely unsurpassed to this day. Their theories in science and medicine, though often wrong were accepted by western Europe until only a few hundred years ago. Many western European languages owe the origin of their vocabularies to the Greek language; western drama had its beginnings in Greek theatre; and Greek mythology has left the West a treasure trove of stories still told today. As for sports, every leap year the world commemorates the Olympic Games held in Greece for over 1,000 years.

Despite their advanced culture, the Greeks were in some ways as barbarian as any other ancient people. Their civilization was founded on a slave society and women were no more highly regarded than they were by any of their contemporary societies. Surplus girl children and weaklings unlikely to be able to survive unsup-

Reference

A **Acropolis** was the fortified hill of a Greek city which often contained the main temple and other sacred buildings. The most famous acropolis is that of Athens, on which the PARTHENON stands.

Aeschylus (525–456 BC) wrote about 80 plays in which he analyzed the relationship between man and God in history. Only 7 survive, including *Agamemnon* (part of a trilogy). His plays always involved 2 actors, whereas earlier plays had used only 1.

Amphorae are egg-shaped, 2-handled jars with narrow necks and there are 2 distinct kinds. Plain ones held corn, honey, oil or wine and usually had pointed bases for lodging in the earth. Decorated amphorae were given as prizes in games and the government of Athens encouraged their production in 'cottage industries' to promote export.

Apollo, god of light and purity, was the son of Zeus. He was believed to reveal the future to people through his oracles at Delphi. Supposedly skilled in poetry, music, archery and medicine, Apollo was regarded as the ideal of manly beauty.

Amphora: Ajax and Achilles

Architecture in Greece from the 600s BC onwards is called *classical* and had 3 orders set by the style of the fluted columns. *Doric* columns were the oldest and simplest; *Ionic* columns were more slender, graceful and decorated, and *Corinthian* columns, variations on the Ionic, were even more ornamental. These orders and their variations are still used by architects.

Aristophanes (c.445–c.385 BC) wrote 44 comedies, 11 of which survive. The most noted of these are *Lysistrata* and the *Frogs*. He satirized people, institutions and events of his times with a penetrating shrewdness and

Temple of Athena Nike

Right: The temple of Athena at Delphi, built about 320 BC, stood near the site of the oracle where a priestess answered crucial questions. Her pronouncements were often ambiguous, as when she said : 'If Croesus should make war on the Persians he would destroy a mighty empire.'

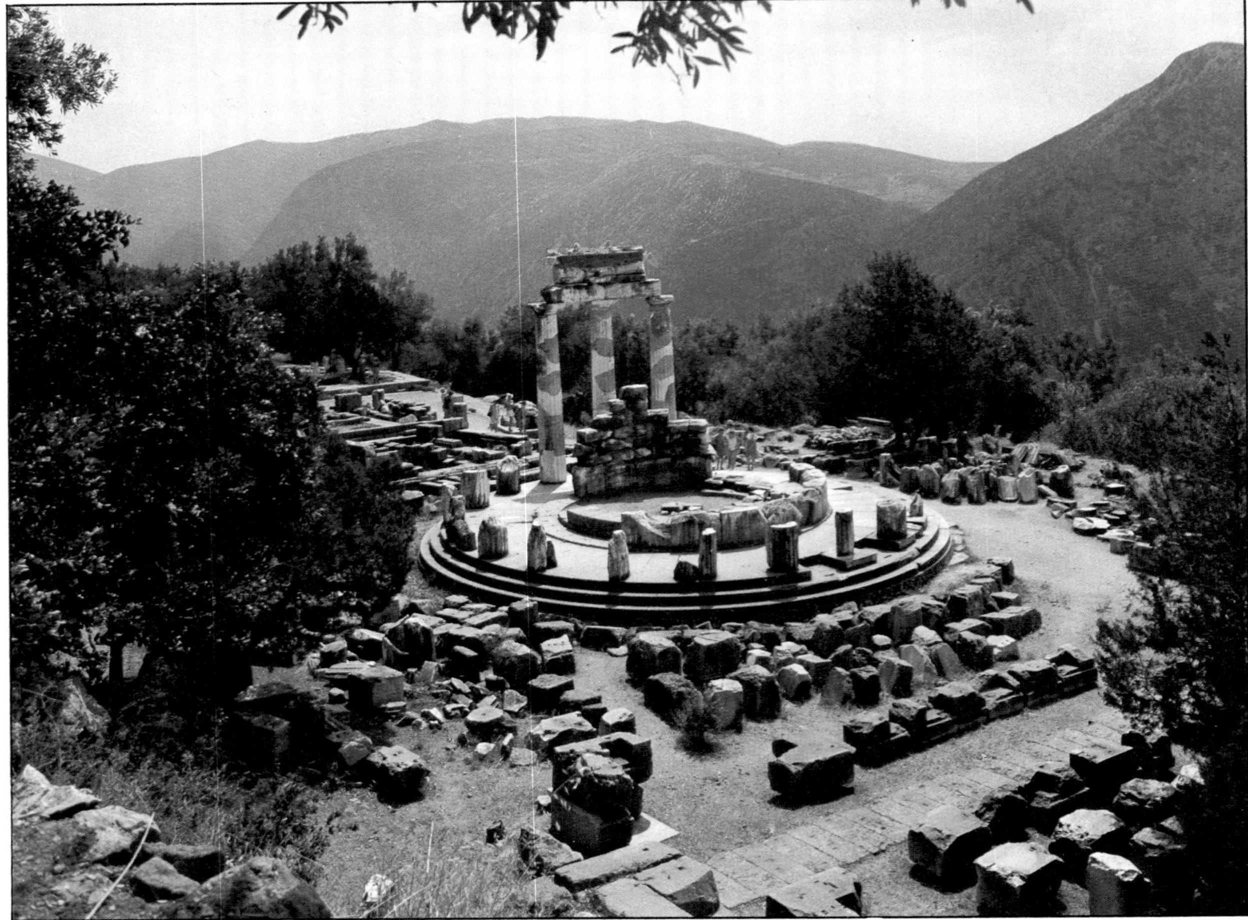

Below: The three main Greek orders of columns show an increase in elegance and decoration from the earliest Doric to the Corinthian.

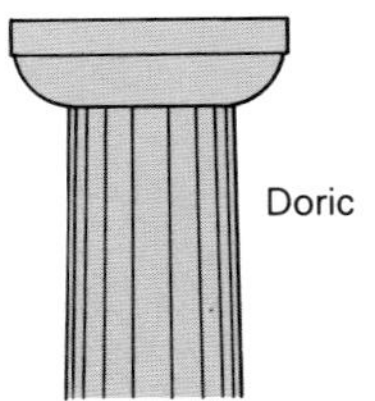

Doric

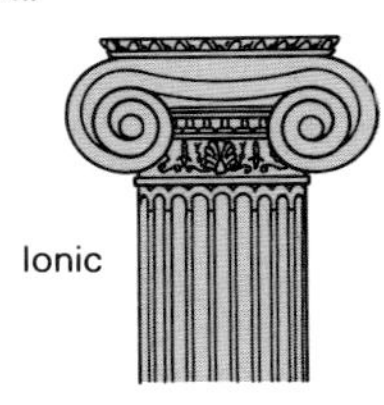

Ionic

Corinthian

ported were taken to the waste lands to die of exposure. Greek city-states were more often at war with each other than in alliance, and it was their compulsive rivalry and greed that eventually brought about the downfall of the Greek civilization.

Government, philosophy and law

About 1000 BC groups of Greek-speaking invaders, the Dorians, began pouring into Greece from the Balkans and they ruled the city-states until about 600 BC. They brought with them iron weapons, tools and implements, the advent of which resulted in greater food production and a consequent rise in population. Dorian nobles kept the best land for themselves, sustained an autocracy, and dispensed justice as they thought fit. But as population outgrew food supply, emigration increased and rebellions broke out in several states replacing the Dorians by popular leaders. The Greeks called these popular leaders tyrants (meaning 'lords'), but they soon became as self-seeking as the old rulers and the word tyrant came to mean 'oppressor'. In the 500s BC there was a new wave of rebellions and states toppled their tyrants and found new rulers.

The new governments formed differed throughout the city-states. Attica (of which Athens was the capital) set up a limited DEMOCRACY and Corinth came to be governed by an OLIGARCHY (government of leading families). SPARTA remained unchanged, and was still ruled by a military caste of Dorians who imposed an iron discipline on their subjects. Their harsh, comfortless way of life has given us our present-day meaning of the word 'spartan'.

About 450–320 BC Greece was a melting pot for ideas on government and all other aspects of life. Philosophers and schools of philosophy became fashionable. One of the most famous was run by

---

the underlying truth of his humorous criticism is as relevant today as it was in ancient Greece.

Aristotle (384–322 BC) was one of the greatest thinkers of all time, but he differed on several matters with his tutor, PLATO. Aristotle had more interest in law and science, and created the thought system of logic. His theories on astronomy, the nature of the atom and the origins of life, were slavishly followed into medieval times in Europe, and only much later did scientists prove them wrong.

Autocracy is rule by an autocrat, one who rules by his own power and without reference to others.

Aristotle

B

Byzantium, founded by the city-state of Megara in 667 BC, later came under Roman rule. It became the capital of the Byzantine empire.

C

Citizenship in Athens was restricted to those having 2 Athenian parents from 451 BC.

Cynics were philosophers in the 300s BC who believed that virtue was better than pleasure, wealth or honours. Their school was founded by Antisthenes, a disciple of SOCRATES. Diogenes was an example of an extreme cynic who ate the coarsest bread and slept in a tub. The word cynic has come to mean one who has little faith in human goodness.

D

Delian League was a naval alliance which Athens made to her great advantage with many Ionian states who were not always allied with each other. Athens decided how many ships or how much money each state should contribute. Her own contribution was 200 triremes. In the allied attack on the Persians in 466 BC, the Athenian ships carried 5,000 hoplites and were supported by 100 Ionian ships carrying marines and archers. Under PERICLES, Athens came to treat the

Demeter

Right: Theatrical masks were first used by Greek actors, who took the idea from religious practices. On the stage, masks became complex headpieces made of leather or painted canvas. Comic masks were often grotesque, having grimacing mouths and beards.

Right: Odysseus (Ulysses), one of the great heroes of Homer's works, became incorporated into the Greek mythology. Determined not to succumb to the sirens whose singing lured sailors to their doom on a barren island, Odysseus plugged the ears of his seamen. His men then bound him so that he could listen in safety.

Above: Greek theatres were considered the most remarkable of their time for their symmetry and beauty, but also for their striking acoustics. Even a whisper from the round orchestra or the stage could be heard by the seated audience.

SOCRATES, an open-air teacher who taught by question and answer, and wrote nothing. PLATO was one of his pupils, and the author of the *Republic,* which examined the place of the just man in the ideal society. This work is still studied today. In his turn, Plato tutored ARISTOTLE, who wrote *Politics,* a more scientific study of government, and was the teacher of the boy destined to become Alexander the Great.

Apart from these outstanding figures, there were two groups of philosophers: the CYNICS, who strove for virtue rather than learning and pleasure; and STOICS, who recommended men to follow pure reason free from passion.

The law of Athens was unwritten until DRACO set down a code in 621 BC. Some of his punishments were so severe that the word 'draconian' has come to mean excessively harsh. The laws of SOLON, an Athenian lawgiver, were more enlightened, as he laid down a single code for rich and poor alike. By giving votes to all those who had CITIZENSHIP, Solon also laid the basis of Athenian democracy, which enjoyed a 'golden age' about 458–445 BC under the leadership of PERICLES.

Greek religion and mythology

GREEK RELIGION, like Hindu, developed over the ages and involved the worship of deities who had the forms and characters of humans. The first wave of Aryan Greeks brought deities like Zeus, Poseidon, APOLLO, DEMETER and HERMES and later absorbed Mycenaean and Cretan deities.

The Greeks had no sacred books such as the *Avesta,* Bible, *Vedas* or *Suttas.* Instead they had works of literature by poets such as Homer and HESIOD which portrayed the deities in human situations. Most Greeks believed in pacifying their deities with prayers and sacrifices and asking their advice by consulting ORACLES.

Arts and language

Greek architecture pioneered a new style, the outstanding examples of which were the PARTHENON and other buildings set on the ACROPOLIS at Athens. Unlike the Babylonians, the Greeks did not use the arch in their architecture and Greek sculpture centred especially on the quest for perfection in the human form, which was often portrayed naked. Greek artists also developed a lively two-dimensional art, much of which has survived on vases and AMPHORAE.

Greek playwrights were the first to present drama in the modern sense. ARISTOPHANES wrote comedies; AESCHYLUS, SOPHOCLES and EURIPIDES produced tragedies; poetry continued in the high standard set by Homer, and HERODOTUS, THUCYDIDES and XENOPHON wrote histories. It was an age of great orators. Isocrates set up a school of oratory and rhetoric to rival Plato's Academy and Demosthenes spoke vigorously against

---

lonian states as colonies rather than allies.

Demeter was goddess of corn and agriculture.

Democracy is rule by the whole people, although some of the people are always excluded (for example, children). Athenian democracy excluded slaves, women and metics. Direct democracy, in which people actually vote for or against policies, could be possible only in the small city-state. Large modern states are only democracies in the sense that people elect representatives.

Draco introduced the first written code of laws in Athens in 621 BC. It sought to end blood feuds between families and satisfy people who wanted to be answerable to a written code rather than be subject to the whims of aristocratic judges.

E

Euripides (480–406 BC) wrote over 90 short plays, each about 1,500 lines of blank verse. Only 19 have survived, including the *Bacchae* and *Trojan Women.* Euripides tackled political, ethical and psychological problems recognizable in our own times. His works include myths about the deities updated to suit the temper of his own times.

Euripedes

G

Greek civilization was the parent of the present western civilization. It holds a special interest for western people because most aspects of Greek culture can be linked to present-day society; even the psychology of the West is nearer to Greece than to other early civilizations.

Greek religion taught that the universe was a sphere. The upper half was said to have light and fresh air; the lower half to be dark and dank. The earth was believed to be a flat disc midway between the 2 halves which floated on the waters of the underworld. Deities, it was believed, came after, and not before, creation. Each city-state had its special deity, such as Athena, goddess of Athens, who competed for the position against Poseidon, and won.

H

Hermes was the herald-god of his father, Zeus, and sometimes escorted people to Hades. He was also god of peaceful commerce, prudence, cunning, theft, weights and measures, astronomy, olive culture,

Above: The Parthenon, built on the acropolis of Athens in honour of the goddess Athena, still dominates the city. It is a supreme example of the Doric style of architecture.

boxing and gymnastics. He wore a traveller's hat, wings, and winged sandles.

Herodotus (c.484–c.424 BC), called the 'father of history', wrote the history of the world up to his own time. His anecdotal accounts are highly entertaining but sometimes of doubtful accuracy. He travelled widely in the eastern Mediterranean in search of material for his writings, studying people and places.

Hesiod (700s BC) was the first great Greek poet after Homer. His *Works and Days* gave instructions on farming and advice on work to be done on specific days. It also contained the story of *Pandora's Box.* (Pandora, the first woman, disobeyed the gods by opening her gift box, so releasing all the troubles that have since plagued mankind.) In his *Theogony* Hesiod tried to reconcile conflicting stories about the deities.

Hoplites were heavily armed soldiers whose function was to fight in close formation. Their introduction marked a basic change in tactical warfare and the decline of chariots and cavalry. They wore metal helmets, breast-plates, *greaves* (armour below the knees), and shields, and carried spears and swords. The hoplite phalanx (*see* INFANTRY *page 79*) was normally 8 ranks deep. Greek hoplites were valued abroad as mercenaries, while at home, their power strengthened the middle class and speeded the end of the old aristocracy.

Hoplites

M **Mathematics** was advanced considerably by the work of Greek mathematicians and philosophers, who favoured it for its theoretical rather than practical nature. Pythagoras (c.580-500 BC) studied numbers and especially geometry. He discovered that in a right-angled triangle, the square of the hypotenuse is equal to the sum of the squares of the other two sides. Euclid (300s BC), the 'father of geometry', wrote *The Elements*, a series of 13 books still used as the basis of geometry. Archimedes (c.287-212 BC), who discovered formulae for curves, spheres and spirals, was among the greatest mathematicians of all time. He probably invented the Archimedean screw, a device to draw water.

Medicine was pioneered by Hippocrates of Cos (469-399

Philip II of Macedonia.

The ancient Greek language was related to Hittite, although its present alphabet, founded about 1000 BC, derived from the Phoenician. Being isolated from one another, the Greek city-states spoke different dialects, but Attic, spoken in Athens, came to be the most important language of Greek literature. From 300 BC, Greek became the international language of cultured people.

Social structure

The class structure of ancient Greece varied from state to state. In Attica, citizens were the most numerous class, followed by slaves and *metics* (resident foreigners). In Lacedaemon (of which Sparta was the capital), *helots* (serfs) formed the largest class, followed by Spartiates (citizens descended from Dorians), and *perioeci* (non-citizens). Slaves usually belonged to private owners, but some governments used them as miners. Serfs could own personal property, but could not leave their place of birth. Metics and *perioeci* had freedom, but neither they nor any women had political rights.

Athenian citizens

Solon established four classes of citizens in Attica, based on the wealth of the land they farmed. The top class *(pentacosiomedimnoi)* were those who produced at least 750 bushels of wheat or 20,000 litres of wine or oil a year. The next class (known as *horsemen*) were those whose land provided 60 per cent of that amount. The third rank of citizens (known as HOPLITES) had to produce 40 per cent of the product of the top class. All citizens below this level of production were *thetes* (day labourers). As their names suggest, the second and third classes became cavalry soldiers and infantry (hoplites) in war time, while the poverty-stricken *thetes* probably handled an oar on the triremes during naval battles.

All adult male citizens, of whom there may have been 80,000, could vote in the Assembly, sit as jurors, and become candidates for certain offices according to rank. Travel to the Assembly was not difficult, because the whole of Attica was smaller than Greater London – or half the size of Rhode Island. But poorer men often declined to attend because even after payment for public service was introduced, they could not afford to leave their farms.

Above: The picture on the amphora shows workers knocking down olives from a tree. Olives and other fruit were sold in the *agora.* Amphorae were often produced in state workshops in Athens as part of 'job creation schemes' to provide employment.

Left: The temple of Hephaestus, set on the hill Colonus Agoraeus, dominated the *agora* (market place) of Athens. In the foreground, a trader offers 2 fair-skinned slaves for sale. Earthen vessels, sandals, fish and other goods are laid out for sale to the left. 2 scholars, members perhaps of one of the many schools in the city, enjoy an argument to the right. The agora provided a general meeting place for the Athenians.

Metics and slaves in Attica

Metics were traders not from choice, but because, as foreigners, they were not permitted to own land. Nevertheless, they seldom grew rich because Attica was a poor state with few exports, apart from the occasional surplus of olives or some other crop. Exports might also have included the products of the potters who were set to work by the state to produce luxury vases and amphorae for trade purposes.

Industry did not exist on a large scale, and the largest workshop probably belonged to Cephalus, a metic from Syracuse, who kept 120 slaves making shields. Few others employed more than 20 or 30. Slaves were used to non-agricultural manual work, but most of the 80,000 of them in Greece worked on farms or as domestic servants. According to the comedies of Aristophanes, they seem to have been given rough treatment and regular beatings by their owners.

Daily life in Greece

Most Greeks lived simply in town houses built of stone or sun-dried brick, whose windowless walls backed onto narrow alleyways. Each room had a

---

BC), who set up medical schools in Athens and elsewhere. He tried to separate medicine from superstition. Hippocrates is called the 'father of medicine' but it is probable that he borrowed heavily from the *Ayurvedic* system of medicine laid down in the sacred Hindu *Vedas.* Greek doctors were respected in the ancient world. They were less superstitious than Roman doctors.

O

Oligarchy is rule by a small exclusive class – sometimes a group of families or a caste.

Olympic Games were held at Olympia in honour of Zeus. In addition to sports, they included competitions in art, drama, gymnastics, literature, music and rhetoric. They continued (with intervals) from 776 BC to AD 394 and were reintroduced in 1896.

Oracles were supposed responses by deities to questions put to them. Usually they were uttered by priests or priestesses, who were also called oracles. Leading oracles were those of Zeus at Dodona and Apollo at Delphi.

P

Parthenon, the temple sacred to Athena, was built 444-432 BC under PERICLES and is often considered to be the greatest achievement of Greek architecture. Its architects were Ictinus and Callicrates, and Phidias supervised the sculptures.

Apollo and Artemis

Peloponnesian League, or Spartan Alliance, was formed about 550 BC. States adjoining Sparta received its protection, in return agreeing to serve under Spartan command in war, and to assist Sparta against possible risings of the helots. By 510 BC, almost all the Peloponnesian states except Argos had joined. The League fought the first Peloponnesian war against the Athenian-led DELIAN LEAGUE in 460–445 BC, and the second Peloponnesian war in 431–404 BC.

Pericles (c.490–429 BC), an aristocrat, was the champion

Plato

Below: Hoplites, the heavily armoured infantrymen of ancient Greece, fought in close formation. They came from the middle class. Their military success ended the dominance of the cavalry and chariots in war, and of the old feudal aristocracy in society. Greek hoplites fought with thrusting spears instead of the throwing spears of earlier soldiers. Hoplite phalanxes smashed through enemy ranks to throw the line into disorder.

door leading to an inner courtyard and country houses, farms and yards were enclosed by stone walls. Charcoal was burned to give warmth in the cold winters.

Most people ate two meals a day. The mid-morning meal might be a bowl of peas or beans with a raw onion or cooked turnip, while evening meals often included bread, cheese, olives, figs and occasionally meat or fish. Honey sweetened the food, and olive oil was used for cooking as well as a kind of soap. The Greeks drank either water or wine. Milk, they thought, was only for 'barbarians' (all non-Greeks).

Men and women alike wore a *chiton* – a gown that dropped to the knees or ankles. Chitons were commonly of wool, but rich people had them made of cotton or linen. Cloaks or capes were worn as overgarments.

Colonization

There were two great colonizing nations in the ancient world: the Greeks and the Phoenicians, who were the first to colonize on a major scale. (They founded Carthage 80 years before the Greeks did Syracuse in 734 BC, although by the 300s BC Syracuse had outstripped Corinth in population and then numbered 250,000 inhabitants.) The two major powers shared Cyprus amicably, but clashed during the 500s BC in Sicily.

Beginning about 750 BC, groups of landless Greek peasants set sail from mainland and island ports. Those from the Ionian states of Chalcis and Eretria founded colonies at Cumae and Aenaria in western Italy, and in Sicily; Spartans settled at Tarentum in southern Italy; Corinth founded Syracuse in Sicily; Megara colonized BYZANTIUM and Chalcedon, and Thera established Cyrene. More colonies were planted along the coasts of present-day Spain, France, Corsica, Sardinia, Yugoslavia and Egypt.

While Greek colonists appeared to have no ambitions to found empires, they sought, and usually gained, the co-operation of the peoples of the lands in which they settled. Colonization was accompanied by a strengthening of Greek sea power and the harbours of overseas settlements were soon bustling with the activities of Greek trading ships. Trading opportunities encouraged further emigration and the Greeks of Asia Minor colonized the coastlands of the Black Sea.

---

of Athenian democracy. He dominated Athens 460–430 BC, a period known as the 'Age of Pericles'. He fought a series of naval wars against Persia and Sparta and died of the plague when Athens, her power broken by war, finally submitted to Sparta.

Philosophy flourished in Greece 450–320 BC. The great philosophers made original contributions to human thought, although their subject matter had little to do directly with the serious problems of their times. To some extent, the intellectual concerns of the philosophers were a form of escape from reality, and the Athenian philosophers were at their most eloquent when Athens was dying because of its political errors.

Plato (c.427–c.347 BC), pupil of SOCRATES and tutor of ARISTOTLE, founded the Academy to teach philosophy and mathematics. He presented much of his writings in the form of conversations and letters, and the *Republic* was his greatest work.

S **Science** in Greece was pursued for intellectual rather than practical purposes, and few scientists actually put their theories to the test. Early Greek philosophers who concerned themselves with scientific matters included Thales (624–565 BC); Anaximander (611–547 BC); and Anaximenes (570–? BC). Democritus (c.470–400 BC) came uncannily close to the truth in his theory of atomic energy, and ARISTOTLE propounded theories on astronomy, atomic structure and the nature of life which, though misguided, were accepted until modern times.

Socrates (469–399 BC) concerned himself with the right choice between good and bad. Goodness, he believed, stemmed from wisdom;

Socrates

badness from ignorance. He encouraged discussion about all aspects of human relationships and taught by question and answer. Socrates thought nothing should be exempted from intellectual scrutiny. The Athenian government convicted him of heresy and corruption of youth. He was condemned to death and died by drinking hemlock in prison.

Solon (c.638–c.559 BC), an Athenian lawgiver, cancelled debts owed by the farmers of Attica. He freed those enslaved for debt and estab-

The Persian and first Peloponnesian war

Under the Persian empire, the Greeks of Asia Minor could run their own affairs so long as they did not oppose Persian interests. When the Ionian city-states revolted against Persia in 499 BC, they had at least the moral support of their fellow Greeks in mainland Greece. Although Sparta refused direct aid, Athens sent the Ionians 20 ships and Eretria sent five. So began the Greco-Persian wars which ended in Greek victory over the Persians and their Phoenician mercenary fleets at Salamis (480 BC) and at Plataea and Mycale (479 BC).

Although the Persians lost, the Greeks expected them to strike again. Sparta feared that Ionia could not be held, and advised the Greeks there to emigrate, while Athens held that Ionia could be defended by sea – especially if the Athenian fleet kept the Phoenicians out of the Aegean. In fact both states had ulterior motives for their advice. Sparta feared that its helots would revolt if its army went overseas and Athens saw the chance to increase its own influence.

In 478–477 BC Athens, with several small Ionian city-states, entered into a naval alliance known as the DELIAN LEAGUE. Athens and its 200 triremes took the command in battle and received half of all the booty won. The Athenians also became custodians of the Delian League's funds which were kept at Delos, an island between Greece and Asia Minor. The Delian League successfully attacked the Persians in Europe and in Asia Minor, which led their Spartan rivals to suspect them of planning to create a Greek empire.

Flushed with success, Athens led the allied navy into a war on two fronts in 460 BC. It defeated the navy of the Spartan-led PELOPONNESIAN LEAGUE, then sailed up the Nile and laid siege to the Persian garrisons in Egypt. But the Persians cleverly diverted the waters of the Nile, trapped and captured one Athenian-led navy, and destroyed another sent to relieve it. Its naval power temporarily crippled, Athens prudently sought a truce with Sparta. This was granted only in 445 BC, after five years of negotiation.

Above: These 2 coins show the front of a Hellenistic galley c.300 BC (*above*) and the front of a Carthaginian galley c.200 BC (*below*).

The second Peloponnesian war

In 431 BC, following Athenian provocation, Sparta led Corinth and other states of the Peloponnesian League into war against the Delian League. Athens, with its port of Piraeus, stood secure behind its walls, but the Spartans reduced the surrounding territory to wasteland and then a plague broke out in the city, claiming Pericles as one of its victims. Plague and war killed off over 30 per cent of the Athenian population. Several of Athens' allies defected, and some joined Sparta. Civil wars, guerrilla warfare, atrocities and disease carried misery throughout all Greece.

Peace came in 421 BC, but only briefly, as the war resumed in 413 BC when Sparta gained Persian aid at the price of abandoning the Greek settlements in Asia Minor. Eventually, in 406 BC Lysander, the Spartan admiral, defeated the Athenians and starved them into submission. From 404 BC Sparta led Greece, but its severe rule brought rebellion. In 371 BC, Thebes defeated Sparta and took the leadership. Exhausted and leaderless, Greece slipped into anarchy. Finally in 338 BC, Philip II of Macedon crushed a last desperate alliance of Greek states. Soon after this the whole of European Greece was absorbed into the Macedonian empire.

Below: Surrounded by the sea, the Greeks rivalled the Phoenicians as traders and outdid them as colonists. Greek warships were either *biremes* having 2 banks of oars (like the one shown) or *triremes* with 3 banks of oars.

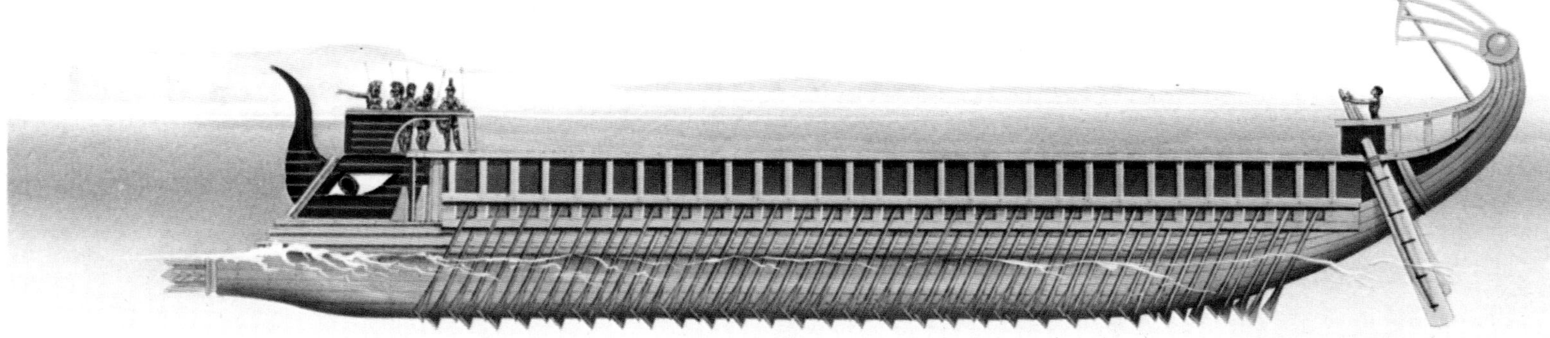

lished 4 classes of citizens.

Sophocles (496–406 BC) wrote over 100 plays, mostly tragedies, only 7 of which including *Antigone, Electra* and *Oedipus Rex,* survive. His themes included relationships between man and the city-state, and the struggle of strong individuals against fate. His characters are more down-to-earth than those in AESCHYLUS. Sophocles introduced a third actor and fixed the chorus at 15.

Sparta was the capital of Lacedaemon (or Laconia), to which it has given its name. It was perhaps the most completely military state in history. True Spartans scorned easy living and accepted harsh discipline. Strong abroad, Sparta was vulnerable at home: 25,000 *Spartiates* (Dorian-descended citizens) held as many as 50,000 helots in serfdom, and the helots often rebelled when the Spartan army went away to war. Spartan boys trained for war from the age of 7 and book learning was considered unnecessary. A Spartan finally retired from the army – if he lived – at 60. Spartan women had more freedom than other Greek women.

Spartan soldier

Stoics (300s BC) believed that the proper use of knowledge was to help men find their proper place in nature. No matter what good or evil befell a man, he should remain calm and unruffled. If a stoic thought he had control over a situation he should do as he wished. If not, there was no point in trying to alter the situation. Nowadays, we would say that he accepted the position 'stoically'.

T Thucydides (c.460–c.400 BC), an Athenian naval commander, wrote the precise but unfinished *History of the Peloponnesian War,* from which most of our information on this period comes.

X Xenophon (c.430–c.355 BC), a Greek mercenary soldier, became commander of 10,000 Greek mercenaries stranded in Persia. He wrote the history of their retreat.

The Etruscans are set in history between the great cultures of the Greeks and the Romans. They learned much from the former and passed on much to the latter, yet their civilization was unique.

The Etruscans

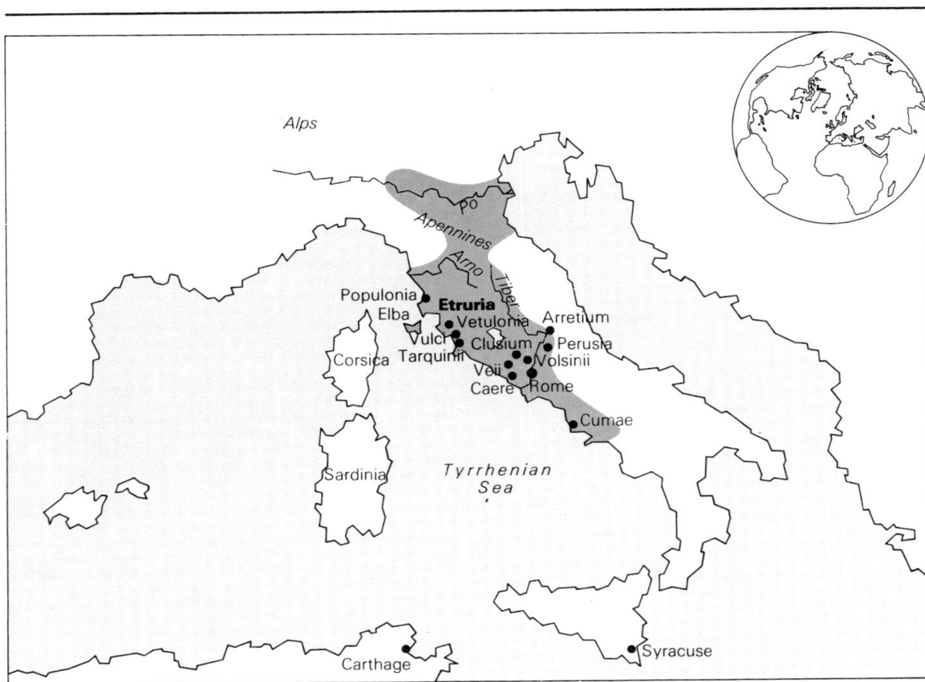

Above: The city states of Etruria occupied roughly the area of modern Tuscany southwards to Rome, but the Etruscan frontiers later extended to the Po Valley.

Left: An Etruscan couple recline together in a manner suggesting equality of status between them – a concept rarely found in the ancient world. The clay sculpture forms part of a sarcophagus dating from the 500s BC.

The Etruscan civilization flourished from about the 700s BC to the 200s BC and formed the basis for the later civilization of the Romans. It began in Etruria, the region of Italy now known as Tuscany, and extended northwards from the Tiber River to the Arno and later to the valley of the Po, and eastwards from the TYRRHENIAN SEA to the Apennine Mountains. No one knows for sure where the ETRUSCANS came from. Quite possibly they always lived in Italy, though Herodotus thought that they migrated from Lydia in the 1200s BC at about the time of the Trojan war.

Social structure

The Etruscans developed TWELVE CITY-STATES, each of which was governed by an aristocratic ruling caste formed of either priest-kings or magistrates. Cultural bonds linked the city-states, and although they had no permanent political union or military alliance, their representatives met annually at the sanctuary of the god VOLTUMNA, where they discussed religious, political and military matters.

A closely knit family system, where women had a great deal of freedom and near equality with men, formed the basis of Etruscan society. Between the nobles at the top of the social scale and the slaves at the bottom were freemen and probably a class of serfs, who worked as farm labourers, cooks, actors, musicians and dancers. From funerary inscriptions we know that the average life span was about 40 years. On average, Etruscan men were only 1.64 metres tall and Etruscan women, 1.55 metres.

Religion, arts and language

The Etruscans believed that the DEITIES who governed the universe had set rules for human conduct and decided in advance the destiny of Etruria. They were greatly concerned with life

Reference

C **Celts** were an Aryan warrior race who appeared in south-western Germany about 500 BC. Armed with iron weapons they swept on throughout western Europe, and for hundreds of years clashed with the Romans, who finally conquered them.

Colonies were established by the Etruscans in the Balearic Islands, Corsica, Elba, Sardinia and mainland Spain.

D **Deities** of the Etruscans can be equated with those of the Greeks, notably Tin (Zeus), Nethunes (Poseidon), and Apula (Apollo).

E **Engineering** projects carried out by the Etruscans included roadbuilding, hydraulic engineering, and the construction of aqueducts, bridges and sewers. They passed these skills on to the Romans.

Etruscans, claimed by Herodotus to have come from an area in ancient Asia Minor called Lydia, were said by later scholars to have been native to Italy, or to have migrated from north of the Alps. A history of the Etruscans was written by the Roman Emperor CLAUDIUS (*see page 82*).

Side panel of an urn

G **Gauls** were Celts who occupied present-day France, Belgium, and parts of Germany, Switzerland and the Netherlands.

H **Haruspicy** was the examination by *haruspices* (soothsayers or tellers of future events) of certain organs of sacrificial animals, especially the liver. It also included the interpretation of natural phenomena such as thunder, the pattern of lightning, the flights of birds, and the behaviour of animals. Haruspices worked according to rules laid down in sacred writings and had to be learned in science and technology.

Human figures were often elongated by Etruscan artists. During the present century, the Italian sculptor, Alberto Giacometti (1901–66) carried this Etruscan art mode to greater extremes.

M **Marius,** a poor-born Roman political general, fought a civil war against his opponent, SULLA. Etruria allied itself with Marius, but

after death and practised HARUSPICY to find out what had been decreed.

The art of the Etruscans was based on that of the Greeks, but they developed one unique feature: their HUMAN FIGURES were elongated and thinned, portrayed in lively movement and often with smiles or other recognizable expressions on their faces. These figures adorned tomb frescoes showing how the dead had enjoyed themselves during their lifetimes. Death was the major preoccupation of Etruscan artists and they cut elaborate funerary memorials from stone or volcanic lava and embellished them with bronze or clay effigies of their dead. In architecture, they used the arch, the dome and the vault long before the Romans.

The Etruscan alphabet was of Greek origin and the sounds of its letters are known, although its vocabulary has been lost. Most of its surviving writings deal with funerary practices.

Economic and social life

The Etruscans excelled at ENGINEERING, and there was plenty of scope to exercise their talent because Etruria was rich in metals, especially iron. Metalworking, along with piracy, provided the main base of Etruscan wealth. Their exports included their goldwork which was among the best in the ancient world, and black bucchero pottery, for which they were renowned.

Right: The tomb of a wealthy Etruscan, carved from solid rock to represent a room, had bed niches in the wall. Representations of armour, weapons and tools carved on the walls were intended to aid and protect the dead person in the next world.

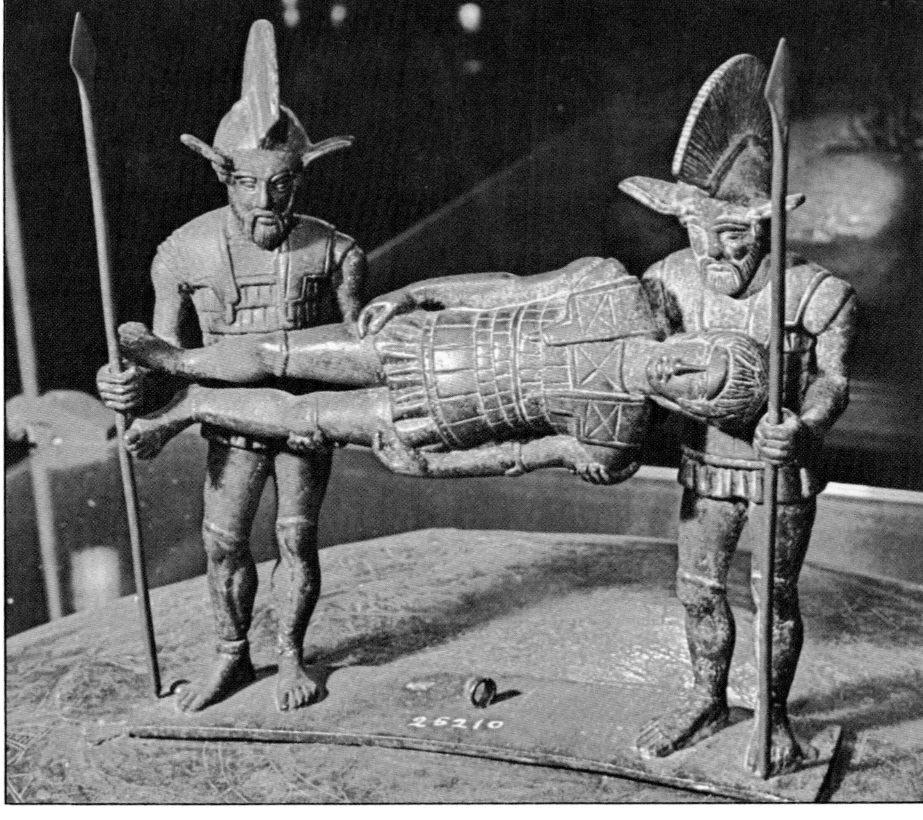

Below: Two Etruscan soldiers carrying a fallen comrade stand immortalized in bronze. Etruscan bronzesmiths gained a reputation as masters of their craft.

The rise and fall of Etruria

By the 700s BC Etruria had evolved a distinctive culture centred on its main city-states, TARQUINII, VEII and Perusia (now Perugia). In its prime Etruria was very powerful at sea and established many COLONIES, while on the mainland, in about 600 BC, the Etruscans founded Rome. When the Greeks barred their advance further southwards, the Etruscans allied themselves with the Carthaginians about 535 BC. But as it turned out, this was not a profitable move, because the terms of the alliance restricted their trade, and hastened their end as a sea power.

In 509 BC the Romans rebelled against the harsh rule of the Etruscan King Tarquinius Superbus the Proud, and declared an independent republic. This blow was followed by the crippling defeat of the Etruscan fleet by the Syracusans off Cumae in 474 BC and the fall of northern Etruria to the CELTS (whom the Romans called GAULS).

The rising power of Rome was gradually encroaching on Etruria, and the Etruscans lost Veii to the Romans about 396 BC. Civil war followed between the Etruscan city-states when some of them allied themselves with the Roman commander MARIUS against his rival, SULLA. When Sulla came to power in Rome in 86 BC, he swept away the last remnants of Etruscan independence and incorporated the city-states into the territory of Rome.

Sulla was the eventual victor.

S **Sulla** (138–78 BC), a political general and aristocrat, finally triumphed in Rome on the death of his rival MARIUS, leader of the popular party. After his success he annexed Etruria, which had been allied to Marius.

T **Tarquinii.** An Etruscan legend tells how one day, near the Marta River, a wise child rose up out of a ploughed furrow in the earth. Etruria's priest-kings ran to the spot and the child dictated to them a sacred doctrine that they wrote down. When he finished, the child died and fell back into the earth. He was said to be Tages, grandson of the chief god Tin (Zeus), and on the field where he died, the Etruscans built their first city, Tarquinii.

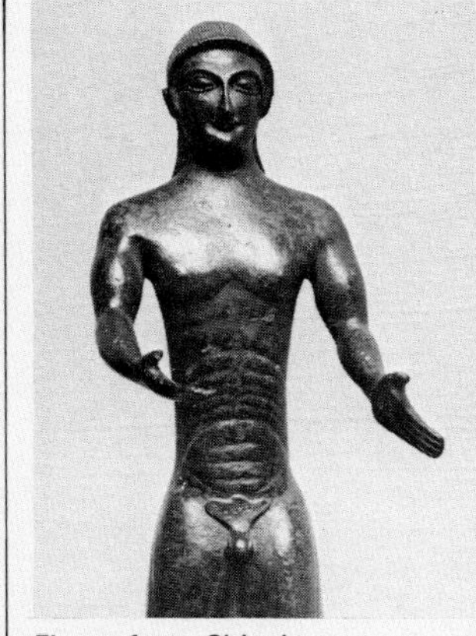

Figure from Chiusi

Twelve city-states were: Arretium, Caere, Clusium, Curtun, Perusia, Populonia, Tarquinii, Veii, Velathrii, Vetulonia, Volsinii and Vulci.

Tyrrhenian Sea is named after the *Tyrrhenoi,* the Greek word for Etruscans.

V **Veii,** one of the TWELVE CITY-STATES, stood 18 km north-west of Rome, to which it fell about 396 BC after a 10-year siege.

Voltumna was the chief deity of Etruria, but the exact location of his shrine is not known. Each year, the city-states' representatives met there, and the senior among them drove a nail into a temple wall. Etruscans believed that when the wall was covered with nails, the time-span of Etruria would be finished. When the Romans invaded the country, they carried off 2,000 bronze statues from Voltumna's shrine and melted them down to make coins to pay for the conquest of Etruria's ally, Carthage.

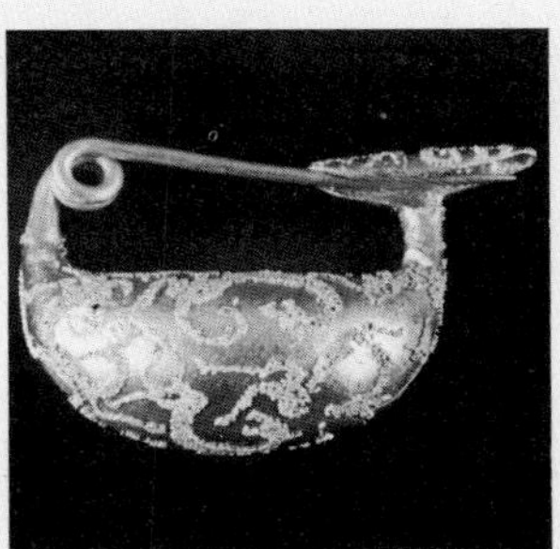

Gold pin

The beautiful bronzework of the Celts has been found in every corner of Europe – a testimonial to the extent of destruction wrought by this warrior race. Their priests, the Druids, performed mysterious rites at temples such as Stonehenge.

The Celts

It was in the 500s BC that Mediterranean traders first came into contact with the barbarous Celts, an Indo-Aryan people then centred in Switzerland and present-day south-western Germany.

The Celts later spread from central Europe, some to plunder European trade routes, others to establish a settled civilization in present-day France, Belgium, Britain and Ireland.

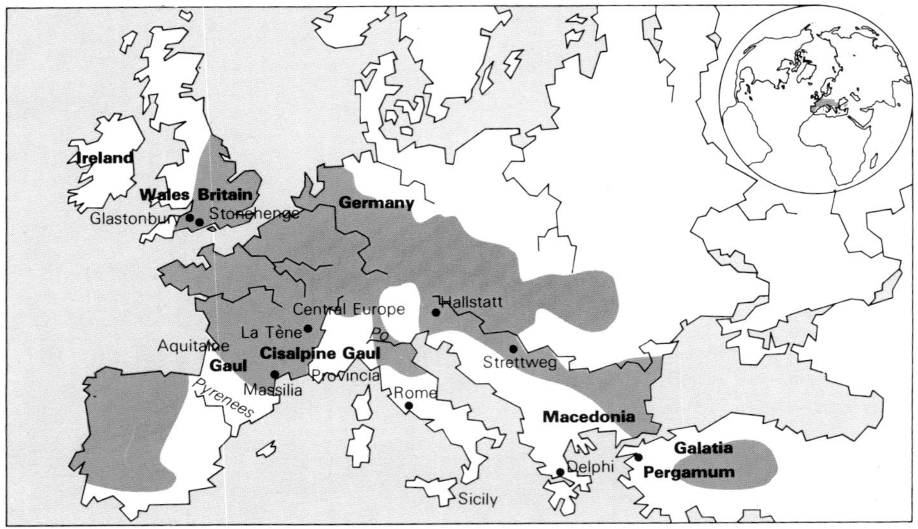

Above: The freebooting Celts, who were of unknown origin, began to migrate from central Europe about 500 BC to found settlements in what are now France, Belgium and Ireland.

Warriors, farmers and metalsmiths

Below the kings, Celtic society had an upper class of warriors, the highest rank of which were priests, called DRUIDS, and a lower class of free farmers. Large family groups of Celts lived together in stockaded farmsteads, usually within reach of a fortified hill to which the whole community could flee if attacked. Women wore long, single-piece gowns, and their status varied between settlements. Men usually wore tunics or shirts, and both sexes wore cloaks as over-garments. Trousers were introduced into western Europe by the Celts.

The Celts, who had learned metal working from nomadic tribes further east, became outstanding craftsmen and Celtic bronzework of superb quality dating from the 600s BC has been found at Strettweg in Austria. Later, Celtic chiefs from central Europe traded the masterpieces of their bronzesmiths for Greek wine-drinking vessels of bronze and pottery. HALLSTATT, in Austria, became the centre of Celtic ironworking, and from there the craft spread westwards. Celtic ART also spread from its centre in Switzerland.

Gods and Druids

Among the many deities of Celtic Ireland was the Dagda, father of all, and lord of life and death. The Dagda was an ugly, pot-bellied figure mounted on wheels, who carried a monstrous club. With one end of the club he could kill nine men; with the other end he could restore them to life. Another god, Lug, a multi-skilled craftsman, was worshipped throughout the Celtic world and Welsh deities included the Children of Don, one of whom, Govannan, was a smith and brewer.

The Druids performed secret, religious and magical rites in which noon, midnight, the full moon, the oak and its parasite the MISTLETOE, played sacred roles.

Migrants and raiders

About 400 BC, Germanic tribes began squeezing the Celts out of Germany and many of them were absorbed into the various tribes then in movement across Europe. Some, mounted on horseback and armed with iron weapons, set off to find new territory in present-day Italy, Spain and France, and crossed into Britain and Ireland.

In 390 BC, the Celts invaded Etruria, sacked Rome, and plundered southwards as far as Sicily. The Romans called them Gauls, and to northern Etruria, where some of the Celts settled, they gave the name CISALPINE GAUL (Gaul this side of the Alps). The Celts continued their ravages and

Reference

A **Aquitani,** one of the peoples of Gaul, inhabited Aquitaine – a province created by Julius Caesar and later disputed over by England and France.

Art of La Tène, a Celtic settlement on Lake Neuchatel, Switzerland, stemmed from Greek, Etruscan and Scythian motifs. The Celts combined and modified them into highly abstract designs on metal, pottery and wood. The Celts took the La Tène culture into the lands where they settled and it is found especially in a Celtic lake dwelling at Glastonbury, England.

B **Beaker people** were Bronze Age invaders who conquered Britain's New Stone Age farmers in 2000–1600 BC. Their name comes from their custom of making decorated pots shaped like beakers.

Belgae, the northern tribe of Gaul, gave its name to Belgium in AD 1830, when it gained independence from the Netherlands.

C **Cisalpine Gaul** (Gaul this side of the Alps) was the Roman name for the Celtic province of northern Italy. It was divided into Cispadane Gaul (on this side of the Po River) and Transpadane Gaul.

Sacrifice on silver cauldron

D **Deities** of the Celts were often superhuman heroes, many being chieftain gods, some with silver hands to replace their own hands lost in battle. Celtic deities, like Celtic people, lived in a world dominated by war, craftsmanship and agriculture. Later Greek and Roman gods were integrated into the Celtic pantheon.

Druids were judges, teachers, priests and keepers of the unwritten folk lore of the Celts. They taught that at death the soul passed to another body, which lessened the fear of their warriors in battle.

G **Galatians** were Gauls or Celts who migrated to Asia Minor and settled around present-day Ankara. Their territory, Galatia, comprised parts of Phrygia and Cappadocia.

H **Hallstatt,** now a small village in Austria, is the site of prehistoric remains found in the AD 1800s. They

Below: Celts lived in large family groups in farmsteads which they defended with stockades. These farmsteads stood within reach of hill forts to which all the families in an area would flee if attacked.

in 335 BC they faced Alexander the Great in Macedonia. About 279 BC they had moved as far as Delphi, where they desecrated the sacred oracle. They then crossed into Asia Minor where they became known as the GALATIANS and were finally quelled by King Attalus of PERGAMUM.

Rome strikes back

By 192 BC the Roman army had grown in strength and marched through the old Etruscan territories to conquer Cisalpine Gaul. Then they crossed the Alps into TRANSALPINE GAUL, which extended from the Pyrenees beyond modern Belgium and was inhabited by three peoples: AQUITANI, BELGAE and Celtae (Celts) – all of whom the Romans called Gauls. During the 100s BC, the Romans took the Mediterranean coastal strip of Gaul, which they named PROVINCIA, and Julius Caesar (100–44 BC) annexed the rest of Gaul in 58–49 BC.

Before this (about 75 BC) the Belgae had invaded Britain, where earlier Celtic migrants had established Iron Age settlements. Aware of cross-channel aid between the Belgae, Julius Caesar landed briefly in Britain in 55 BC, returning again a year later.

Left: The Celts practised mixed farming, especially cereal growing and cattle raising. Although men normally wore belted tunics, Celtic horse-riders introduced trousers into Europe about 300 BC.

showed that an ironworking centre was flourishing in this Celtic territory in the 300s BC.

Human sacrifice was once practically universal, and was especially practised by the Celts in times of trouble. Julius Caesar reported sacrifices by burning, but other writers report seeing blood-stained altars. Human heads were also offered to the gods.

M

Mistletoe, a parasite of many trees, was especially sacred to the Celts in association with the oak tree. Druids distributed pieces of mistletoe as charms. The Christian custom of kissing under the mistletoe at Christmas is a variation of this pre-Christian custom.

P

Pergamum became a brilliant centre of Greek civilization under the Attalid dynasty about 300 BC. It was anti-Macedonian and pro-Roman, and the last king of Pergamum, Attalus III, bequeathed his kingdom to Rome in 133 BC.

Provincia (or 'the province'), the Mediterranean coastal strip of Gaul, was given this name by the Romans. It later became the French province of Provence.

Hallstattersee

S

Stonehenge, on Salisbury Plain, England, is one of several major monuments in the area. The main section of the monument comprises 30 vertical rough-hewn stones standing in a circle. Lying across the top of these are 30 horizontal, touching stones. Unknown builders began constructing Stonehenge about 2600 BC.

T

Transalpine Gaul became known to the Greco-Roman world about 600 BC, when the Greeks settled at Massilia (Marseilles). Rome defended Massilia against attacks by Gauls in the 100s BC.

The short life of the boy-king Alexander the Great is a dramatic adventure. At its height his empire was the largest known to the ancient world, covering over 5,000,000 square kilometres.

The Macedonians

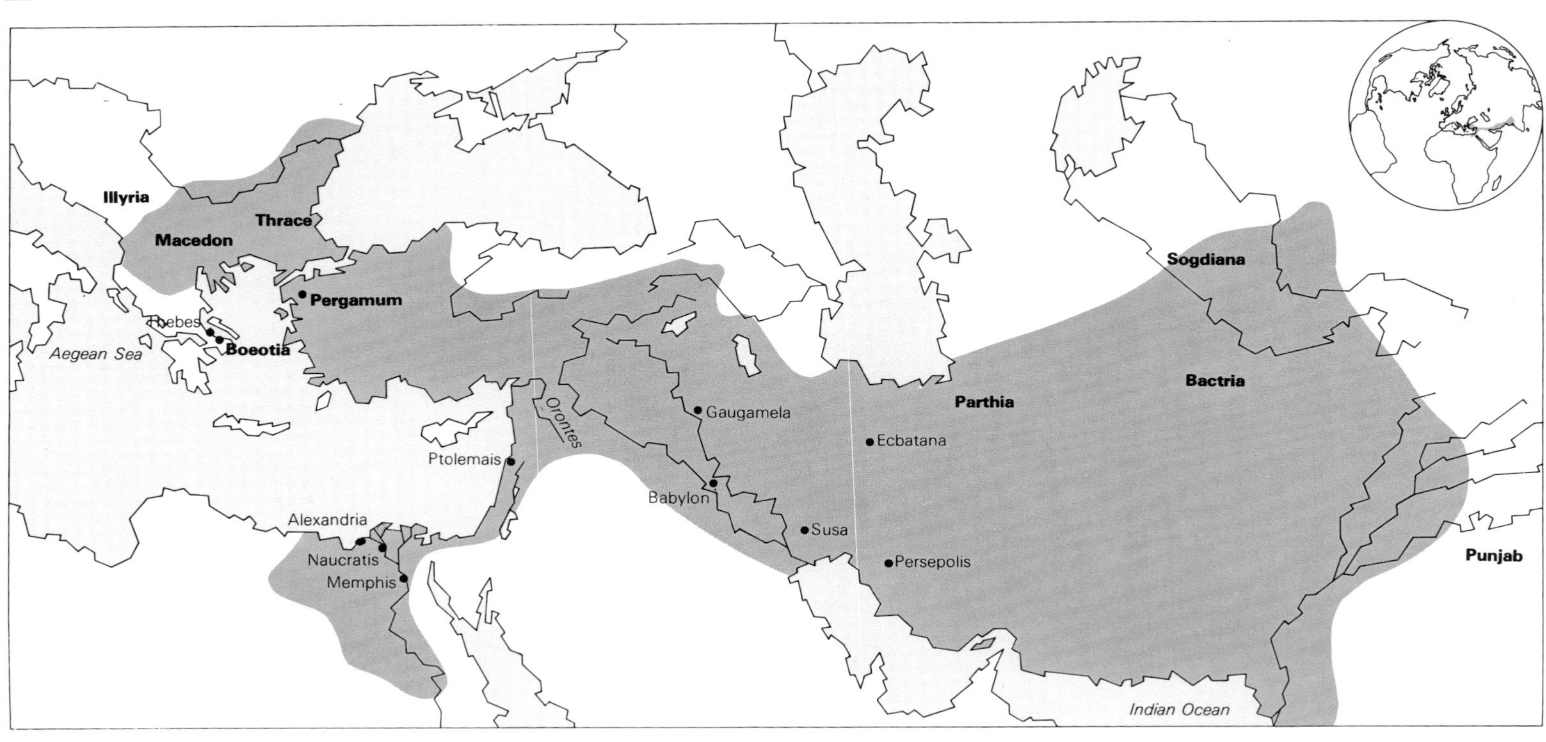

Bordering the north-western corner of the Aegean Sea was the mountainous, semi-Greek kingdom of MACEDON. The orator, Demosthenes, who died in 322 BC, represented the general Greek view of the Macedonians when he described them as useless barbarians – unable to shine even as slaves. He jibed that feuding nobles kept Macedon weak. But all this changed when PHILIP II became king of Macedon in 359 BC.

Philip II

Philip was a great general, and an accomplished politician who roused Macedonian nationalism by pursuing an aggressive foreign policy. Sure of their superiority, the Greeks did not take Philip's challenge seriously and this gave him time to hammer his recruits into a disciplined INFANTRY.

Above: The Macedonian empire begun by King Philip II of Macedon was expanded by his son Alexander into the biggest empire that the world had ever seen. The Macedonians absorbed the Persian empire and extended it into Libya, the Balkans, central Asia and India.

Right: Alexander, a fervent internationalist, forced his officers to marry foreign wives. This onyx cameo shows the heads of Alexander and Roxane, his Persian princess-wife. Rivals murdered Roxane and her son after Alexander's death.

Reference

A

Alexander's ideals included the evolution of a multi-racial Greco-Persian empire. In order to achieve this, he persuaded or forced his generals and thousands of his troops to marry women in the Persian empire. In 327 BC he himself married Roxane, daughter of a Bactrian baron. She and her son, born after Alexander's death, were both murdered in the struggle for power that followed, although Roxane managed first to kill another of Alexander's wives, the daughter of DARIUS III.

Alexandria, apart from being a centre of learning, contained one of the '7 wonders of the world'. This was the *Pharos,* or lighthouse, built by Ptolemy II about 280 BC.

Athens came under Macedonian control in 322 BC, and thereafter diminished in importance.

C

Chaeronea, in Boeotia, was the site of a battle in 338 BC, between the allied Athenians and Thebans, against the Macedonians, who won.

Court intrigues surrounded the assassination of PHILIP II. The king was killed by Pausanias, a bodyguard, in revenge for being ill-treated by the friends of Philip's new wife. Philip had 7 wives simultaneously, and the senior, Olympias (mother of Alexander), was wrongly accused of murdering the king out of jealousy. Several relatives and courtiers made the most of the confused period before Alexander was confirmed as king. The assassin was probably executed according to Greek custom: 5 iron clamps secured the neck and limbs of the murderer to a wooden board, while he starved to death in public.

Incense burner

D

Darius III fled to Bactria when he lost the vital battle of GAUGAMELA to Alexander the Great. There the satrap murdered him and later a Macedonian officer found his body in an abandoned waggon. Alexander wrapped his own cloak around Darius's corpse and had it taken to PERSEPOLIS for royal burial.

F

Fever that killed Alexander may have been malaria, although some ac-

Above: In the Macedonian phalanx, soldiers kept the enemy at bay by using their very long thrusting spears. This allowed the cavalry to charge at a weak spot in the enemy line, so breaking his ranks.

Left: The Macedonian soldier, disciplined in the new tactics of Philip of Macedon, proved superior to the soldiers of Greek states to the south. Under Alexander, the Macedonian army humbled the mighty Persian army.

Below: This mosaic from Pompeii shows Darius and his Persian army in full battle. Alexander routed the Persians at Issus and Darius fled.

In 342 BC, Philip conquered THRACE, so ATHENS and THEBES hastily formed an alliance to protect themselves. But Philip routed their armies at the battle of CHAERONEA in 338 BC. Instead of punishing the defeated Greeks, Philip forced them into an alliance called the League of Corinth, which he controlled. Then, with League support, he prepared the invasion of Persia in 336 BC, but before this took place Philip was murdered by one of his own bodyguards. Despite COURT INTRIGUES, the succession passed to Philip's power-hungry son, Alexander, who speedily put down risings in Thrace, ILLYRIA and Thebes.

Alexander the Great

Alexander the Great (356–323 BC) was soon to develop the greatest empire known to the ancient world. His campaigns began when in 334 BC, he crossed the Hellespont (on the Bosphorus) with 32,000 infantry and 5,000 cavalry troops. The Persian force was quickly defeated and Alexander then marched across Asia Minor. Although the Persian king, (DARIUS III) took Alexander by surprise, he was decisively beaten and Persia began to collapse quicker than Alexander could advance. Having taken Syria and Phoenicia, Alexander entered Egypt to be acclaimed as a god. In 331 BC, he defeated Darius at GAUGAMELA, then pressed on to take the Persian capitals of Babylon, Susa, PERSEPOLIS and Ecbatana.

Alexander then turned explorer. He enticed his armies on to remote Parthia, Bactria, SOGDIANA and the Punjab. Possibly he would have gone on to China, but his weary troops forced him to follow the Indus River south to Pattala, near the Indian Ocean. There, his army divided. Part of it put to sea and sailed up the Persian Gulf, while the main body, led by its king, made the dreary march back to Persia. The two forces linked near Susa and marched on to

---

counts given after his death suggest that he died of drunkenness. Other scholars think Alexander may have been poisoned by those intent on succeeding to his power. According to usual custom, the army was purified from the pollution of the king's death by marching between the 2 halves of a dog that had been disembowelled. It was generally believed that at death Alexander had ascended to heaven.

G **Gaugamela** was the scene of the final battle that defeated Darius III in 331 BC. Alexander had 40,000 infantry and 7,000 cavalry while the Persian army was said to number as many as a million.

Alexander on a lion hunt

H **Herophilus,** a physician known as the 'father of scientific anatomy', studied the brain structure, distinguished between motor and sensory nerves, and took the pulse with a water clock.

I **Illyria,** a western coast state of the Balkans, was located northwards from present-day central Albania. Illyrians were mixed with Celts. They were a warlike people, prone to piracy, and no one fully conquered them before the Romans.

Infantry of Macedon were organized into *phalanxes,* a concept invented in Sparta, developed in Thebes, and perfected in Macedon. Soldiers were formed in rows to make a solid block, their task being to hold the enemy infantry by thrusting with long spears. This done, the Macedonian cavalry would charge at some spot in the enemy line, so breaking their ranks. Usually, these tactics routed Macedon's foes.

L **Legend of Alexander.** After his death, Alexander's body was set in spices in a gold coffin and placed on an ornamented chariot like the one the god Mithras was said to use. It was believed that the body would confer status on its possessor and so it was

Babylon, where in 323 BC, worn out perhaps by his effort, Alexander died of FEVER at the age of 33. The MACEDONIAN EMPIRE, the largest then known, was left leaderless.

Alexander's death brought an immediate struggle for power between his generals and relatives and half a century of foreign and civil wars followed. One general, Ptolemy, resorted to stealing the general's corpse with the hope that the LEGEND OF ALEXANDER would help to make him master of Egypt. However, most of the Indian conquests were lost to Chandragupta I and the Mauryas and Macedon and Greece slipped into anarchy, while Babylonia fell to Seleucus I. The rise and fall of Macedon had been so swift that it had almost no culture to spread abroad, although the Macedonian generals did carry aspects of Greek civilization into the lands they conquered.

Ptolemaic Egypt

It took Ptolemy 18 years to secure his position in Egypt and make himself pharaoh, although he reigned 304–282 BC and his dynasty was to last 274 years. Ptolemy founded only one new city, Ptolemais, so avoided the danger of independent city-states emerging. Everything in Egypt was methodically governed and taxed by an army of Greco-Macedonian officials and as a result the Ptolemies became the richest of Alexander's heirs. Much of their wealth was lavished on ALEXANDRIA, their capital, and this 'island' of Greek culture became for several centuries the leading city of the West after Rome.

The Ptolemies patronized Greek science and scholarship in Alexandria where they founded a museum for the study of the 'muses' – nine goddesses of the arts. They also built up two vast libraries which together held about 500,000 different rolls of papyrus books. A university was founded with several leading SCHOLARS in attendance and HEROPHILUS, a physician, founded a medical school. But outside Alexandria, Ptolemais and Naucratis, a trading centre, Egypt continued largely as before. It had merely replaced its Egyptian, Assyrian and Persian pharaohs for Macedonian pharaohs.

The Seleucids

Seleucus (321–280 BC) was the founder of a dynasty which lasted 237 years. A less prominent general than Ptolemy, he nevertheless gained the biggest share of Alexander's empire and more than any attempted to recreate the empire according to ALEXANDER'S IDEALS. Winning Babylon by 312 BC, he fought perpetual wars to extend his territory to the borders of Macedon and India.

Seleucus continued the Persian system of government. He also founded several colonies which included Antioch on the Orontes River, his capital, which became second only to Alexandria. Seleucus was assassinated in 280 BC, just as he was about to seize the vacant throne of Macedon.

Pergamum

Pergamum, a Greek city-state, managed to break away from Seleucid control and at a time of Seleucid weakness, it seized western and central Asia Minor. Pergamum's empire reached its height about the 190s BC, and Pergamum itself became a brilliant centre of Greek civilization.

Pergamum avoided being attacked by the Macedonians and the Seleucids through its friendship with Rome and when King Attalus III died in 133 BC, he bequeathed Pergamum to the Romans. By then, Macedon had already fallen to them (168 BC). The Seleucid kingdom fell in 84 BC; Ptolemaic Egypt in AD 30.

Right: A Ptolemaic queen wearing the headdress of the vulture goddess Mut. This was the royal insignia of all Egyptian queens down to Cleopatra VII, the Cleopatra who committed suicide in 30 BC.

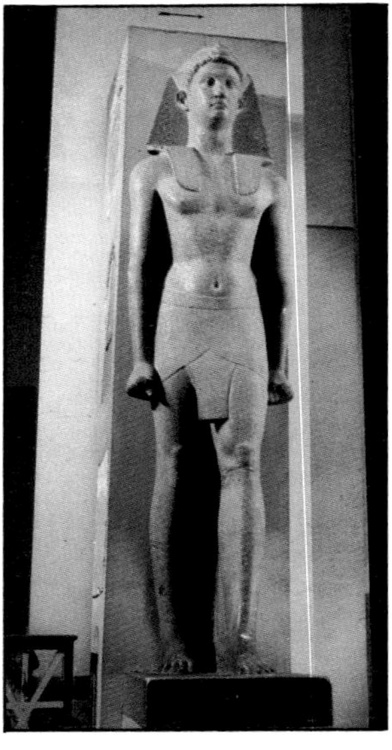

Below: This statue found in Thebes is of Alexander the Great.

kidnapped by Ptolemy, taken to Egypt and buried at Memphis. Ptolemy's son later took it to ALEXANDRIA. There, the Roman emperor Augustus saw it 300 years later.

M

Macedon had a population of perhaps 500,000 people. Although Greek-speaking, the population was Greco-Illyrian-Thracian. It never recovered from the loss of men who went abroad with the army and did not return.

Macedonian empire. Up to Alexander's time this was the largest empire. It covered over 5 million sq km – 200 times the area of all the Greek city-states.

P

Parchment, the prepared skins of animals (especially of calf, goat and sheep) began to replace papyrus as a writing material in the 100s BC. The name parchment is a misuse of 'Pergamum', where parchment was in early use.

Persepolis, one of the Persian capitals, was set afire by Alexander supposedly as an act of revenge for the earlier Persian burning of Athens. It is also said the soldiers wanted revenge because they had found some mutilated corpses of Macedonian soldiers.

Philip II, once hostage in Thebes, later introduced into the Macedonian army the phalanxes he saw there. Philip's remains were found in Macedon in AD 1977.

S

Scholars at Alexandria included Aristarchus of Samothrace (collator of Homer's writings); Euclid the geometrician; and (about AD 127–141) Ptolemy, the mathematician, astronomer and geographer.

Sogdiana, on the fringes of Persia's empire in central Asia, was the location of the later cities of Bukhara and Samarkand. It formed a buffer state between Persia and the Mongols.

Thracian leg armour

T

Thebes, the chief city of Boeotia, consistently opposed Athens. It finally joined with Athens in defence against Macedon, but Philip II conquered it.

Thrace, a land of petty kingdoms, had no Greek culture, but was famed for its music and poetry. PHILIP II seized the partly-Persian state in order to bring his armies to the Persian border. Greek states imported silver, gold, and mercenaries from Thrace.

The glory that was Rome – this city was the jewel of Roman culture. Much still remains of the Romans' work in Italy and the rest of Europe for they were skilled engineers and builders. However, for 1,000 years they were nearly always at war.

The Romans

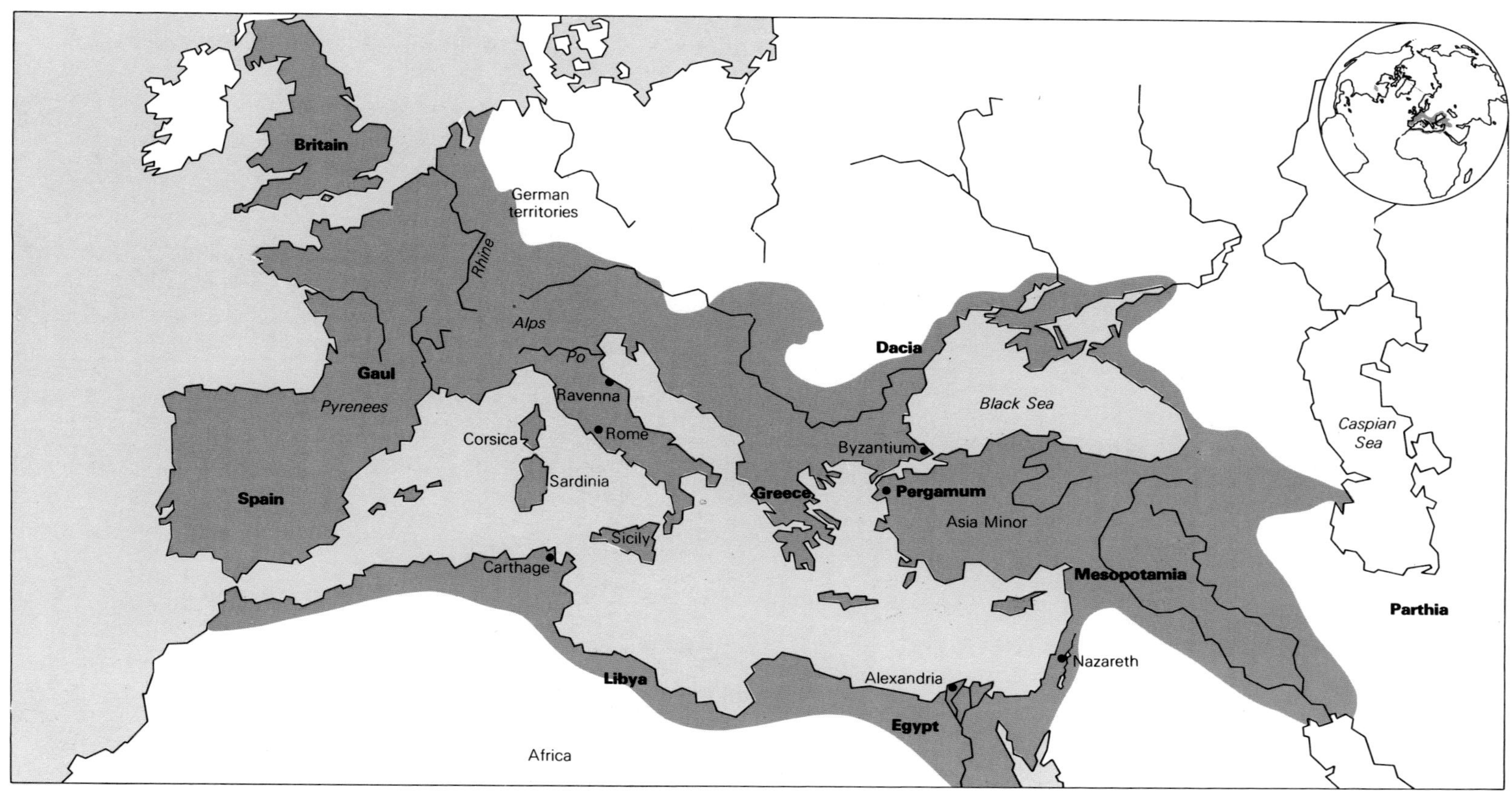

The Romans established their independence from Etruria in 509 BC, but it took them 300 years to conquer Italy. Then they spent another 300 years building up the empire to its greatest extent. Under Emperor TRAJAN it covered about 6,500,000 square kilometres in three continents and contained perhaps 60 million people. From this peak it declined for nearly 400 years. These 1,000 years of Rome were spent in almost perpetual warfare. After the city of Rome fell to BARBARIANS, the empire had another 1,000 years of life in the east. This later Roman empire, founded upon Byzantium (modern Istanbul) ended little more than 500 years ago in 1453.

Above: The Roman empire reached its greatest extent under Trajan in AD 117.

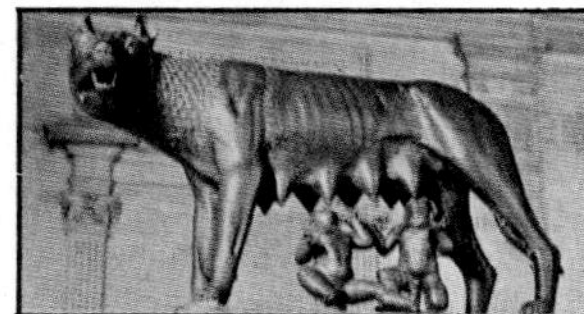

Above: In legend, a she-wolf suckled Remus and his brother Romulus, supposed founder of Rome in 753 BC. But the bronze shown was cast by Etruscans who in fact founded the city about 600 BC.

WESTERN ROME was a republic for the first half of its life and an empire for the second half. Julius CAESAR and his successor, Augustus, marked the transition at a time when the new religion of Christianity was emerging. From then the affairs of empire and church were to become closely inter-dependent.

While Roman culture borrowed heavily from Greek, the Romans were a much more practical people, excelling in government and engineering. The Macedonians took Greek civilization eastwards, but the Romans spread it in modified form throughout western Europe and the Mediterranean.

Reference

A

Angles, Saxons and Jutes began to invade southern Britain in the AD 400s. This was the result of an invitation in 449 from Vortigern, a Celtic chief, to 2 Anglo-Saxon chieftains, Hengest and Horsa, to help him fight the Picts of northern Britain. The Anglo-Saxons and the Jutes were Germanic peoples who came from the present Danish-German border area and the mouth of the Rhine.

Animals kept for their products or for transport included cattle, goats, donkeys, horses, mules, pigs, poultry and sheep. Camels bred in Syria and northern Africa were often used as pack animals.

Arians were a Christian sect who followed the heresy taught by the Libyan, Arias (AD c. 256–336). He was a parish priest in Alexandria, who said that God created his Son, who was the first living creature, but that the Son was neither equal to the Father, nor eternal, but a demi-god.

Attila's Huns forced payment of tribute from the Roman emperors until AD 450, when payment was refused by Eastern Emperor Marcian and Western Emperor Valentinian III. Attila (c. 406–453) lost his campaign in Gaul in 451 and invaded Italy (452), but plague and shortage of supplies drove him back. He was called 'the Scourge of God' yet kept Roman scholars at his court and was less destructive than most BARBARIANS.

B

Barbarians were to the Romans any peoples not having Roman citizenship. However, like the Chinese, the Romans constantly admitted 'barbarians' into the empire. This was either when they became acceptable culturally, or when they became too strong to defeat.

Cast of dog, Pompeii

Barley provided fodder for farm animals, and in Egypt it was used to make beer. In the Mediterranean countries, wine, not beer, was drunk by all classes.

Burgundians moved from the Germanic territories into eastern Gaul and established a kingdom there about AD 480.

C

Caesar, Gaius Julius (100–44 BC) was a Roman general and statesman. Elected praetor in 62 BC

In the early days of the republic, citizens were divided into upper-class patricians and lower-class plebeians. For 200 years, TRIBUNES (spokesmen of the plebeians) demanded an equal share in government and in 287 BC, the plebeians at last won the right to become senators and CONSULS. But in practice this was barely possible because, as politicians were unpaid, no plebeians could afford to take on the job and senators and consuls continued to be mostly rich landowners.

The power struggle in republican Rome

Perpetual wars made the rich richer and the poor poorer. Landowners ceased to hire freemen when they could use prisoners-of-war for nothing and poverty-stricken, out-of-work peasants either crowded into the city of Rome looking for jobs, or emigrated.

When, in 133 BC the popular tribune Tiberius GRACCHUS demanded that land should be seized and given to the landless poor, he was murdered. Rome then began 100 years of riots, rebellions and civil wars, during which time the strongest men ruled. MARIUS and SULLA *(see pages 74-5)* were followed by other military dictators and in 54 BC, Julius Caesar seized Rome to control the whole Roman world.

The emperors

Julius Caesar was murdered because the Romans feared that he would make himself their emperor, but ironically his death in 44 BC marked the beginning of the reign of about 80 emperors. The first, Augustus, was appointed by the Senate in 29 BC. Roman politics were alive with intrigue and an emperor needed either a great deal of wisdom or a great deal of cunning and an efficient network of spies to stay in power for long. Often their lives came to a violent end at the hands of their enemies, whether by poison or a dagger, and one of the most nerve-racking jobs in the court must have been that of official food-taster to the emperor.

Amongst those who ruled the Romans well was CLAUDIUS, a gentle and wise man and a strong emperor despite the fact that he stammered and was lame. At the other end of the scale were the reigns of cruelty and terror of CALIGULA and NERO, who murdered both his mother and his wife and began the persecution of the Christians.

Below: As the empire expanded the Romans built a vast network of roads to travel along safely and quickly. Where possible they took the direct line between towns, sometimes opening up dense forests as seen below. The roads were levelled, and had foundations of sand mixed with gravel or lime and were surfaced with stone slabs. They were sometimes cambered and had drainage ditches on either side.

The city of Rome

Over five centuries Rome changed from an Etruscan border town to the capital of the West, and OCTAVIAN, or Augustus as he was more commonly known, claimed that he had turned a city of brick into one of marble. No doubt though he was thinking of the luxurious villas and ornamental gardens of the wealthy rather than the squalid slums which sheltered the poor.

Rome's unemployment situation was desperate, and those who could not get work often mobbed together to protest. The most likely area

he rose to absolute power in Rome. Although he denied any ambition for kingship he accepted the dictatorship for life. He was finally assassinated in a bid to save the republic.

Caligula (Little Boot) was the nickname of Gaius Julius Caesar Germanicus (reigned AD 37–41) because he wore a pair of soldier's boots as a boy. As an emperor, he was mentally unbalanced and cruel, and his guard officers eventually killed him out of fear.

Cicero (106–43BC) set a style in Latin prose that is still regarded as a model for the language. He was an orator and a statesman who tried to save the Roman republic from decline and was killed for his idealism.

Claudius (reigned AD 41–54) was forced to become emperor by the PRAETORIAN GUARD after the murder of CALIGULA. People who had mocked him for his limp and his stammer and thought him weak-minded were proved wrong, for he became one of Rome's strongest and most capable emperors.

Colosseum. Rome's oval shaped amphitheatre was the scene of its biggest gladitorial shows and the killings of Christians and others by wild beasts. It entertained an audience of up to 50,000 people. The Colosseum was designed by Emperor Vespasian. Construction began in AD 72.

Interior of Colosseum

Consuls were chosen in pairs to rule the republic, preside over the Senate and lead the army into battle after Rome deposed its king in 509 BC. Both consuls could be replaced annually, which restricted their power. After the institution of the empire, 'consul' became an honorary title.

D **Deities of Rome** began as nature spirits and included Janus, an ancient god native to Italy who was the guardian of doors

Above: At Bath in England, the Romans built a great bath fed by hot mineral springs rich in radium. Public baths became for the Romans important social centres.

Left: Cold-seated public lavatories provided by the government in Rome's port of Ostia date from 1,900 years ago.

Below: Emperor Claudius built the *Aqua Claudia,* a 12 km long aqueduct, to ensure that Rome had an adequate water supply.

of employment lay in building the new Rome as more and more temples, public baths, government buildings and private houses rose skywards. Allied with the building trade was the transporting of stone and marble into Rome, which became a major industry. The vast COLOSSEUM took over 200,000 tonnes of stone for facing alone. As Rome expanded to house a million people, it outgrew its port of Ostia, and Claudius enlarged it, building a new harbour and extensive warehouses.

Science and technology

Although the Romans shone as engineers, they had little interest in science, except perhaps MEDICINE. Much of their technology was a by-product of militarism, like their roads and bridges, which were built by the conquering Roman army, and their aqueducts, which carried water into garrison towns. Ingenious battering rams and slings were built to attack enemy cities, and solid fortifications to defend their own. Although the Romans devised such machines as water-powered mills using gears, they were not shy of cruelty and mainly used the labour of slaves. These slaves made it possible to keep up to 750,000 men in arms, and maintain a small ruling class living in luxury.

Arts and entertainment

Roman sculpture lacked the lithe movement of the Greek and Indian, and their massive architecture was impressive rather than beautiful. Their magnificent amphitheatres were used mainly for martial sports, as befitted a war-centred civilization, and not for drama, although the Romans produced some fine dramatists, amongst whom were LIVIUS, ENNIUS and Plautus. They likewise used Greek inspiration for their themes. The Romans had an even finer array of poets, including OVID, VIRGIL, LUCRETIUS and HORACE. Other outstanding writers were historians such as LIVY, SUETONIUS, TACITUS, Pliny the Elder and his nephew, and the master of Roman prose, CICERO.

In the market places, fortune tellers, jugglers, conjurors and musicians competed for the approval of the crown, but circuses were the most popular entertainment of all, and everyone from the emperor down went to watch horse and chariot racing, wrestling and games.

---

and gates and was portrayed with 2 faces looking in opposite directions. Later on, other important gods were borrowed from the Greeks. Jupiter, chief god; Juno; his wife and the queen of heaven; Mars, god of war, and Minerva, goddess of war, arts and crafts, correspond to the Greek deities Zeus, Hera, Aries and Athena.

Diocletian (reigned AD 284–305) was made emperor by the army and thus ended half a century of anarchy. Faced with the emergency of a German attack, he divided the empire with Maximian in 286, and with Constantine and Galerius in 293. These subordinate rulers took the title of Caesar.

E

Egypt was ruled by the Ptolemies, the last of whom, Queen Cleopatra (69–30BC), cleverly kept her kingdom from Roman rule by her personal relationships with Julius CAESAR and his heir, Mark Antony (c. 83–30 BC), but OCTAVIAN refused her attentions and annexed Egypt in 30 BC.

Ennius (239–c.169BC), 'father of Latin poets', also wrote tragedies, comedies and satire. His epic history of Rome to 171 BC was written in the style of the Greek poet Homer.

External trade, though slight, was fully controlled by the state. The export of iron, bronze, arms and armour was forbidden for security reasons, but traders found ways of smuggling them out.

G

Gladiators who were both freemen and slaves, fought with weapons to entertain the Roman crowds. The shows started to become popular in 264 BC and were put on either at public expense or for political or social reasons by the rich. The winner of the fight was well rewarded, and the loser's fate, if he was not already dead, was decided by the emperor. He either gave a 'thumbs-up' sign, which meant the loser should be allowed to live or a 'thumbs-down', which meant death. In 73–71 BC Spartacus, a Roman slave and gladiator, led other slaves into revolt. But Spartacus was killed and 6,000 of his followers were crucified.

Gladiators

Gracchus, Tiberius (163–133 BC) demanded that public lands which had been taken by the rich should be seized and redistributed to the poor. At that time (133

Above: The Roman army, a citizen militia, was raised when needed by recruiting men of property or money aged 17–60. Each legion had some 5,000 infantrymen and 300 cavalry. Through safe country a legion marched in a long column, headed by a vanguard of auxiliary troops (*above left*). These took the brunt of any sudden attack, sparing the crack troops.

Above: A hand-picked body of *equites* (cavalry) and heavily armoured pikemen with long shields came next, forming an escort for the legion or army commanders.

Above: Following the elite troops came the 'pioneer corps' and the surveyors. These carried tools for felling trees, clearing the route and pitching camp.

Above: The legion commander, usually a Senator, had a Senior Tribune as assistant. Third in the chain of command came the Camp Prefect. Picked infantry guarded them.

Economy and law

The Romans did not achieve any important advances in agricultural techniques, but kept the usual ANIMALS for their products and for transport and cultivated WHEAT, BARLEY, vegetables, olives, papyrus and flax.

For most things, the Roman empire was self-sufficient, forming its own 'common market' with private craftsmen supplying local needs. The most important EXTERNAL TRADE, which was government controlled, was in slaves, who came from the Germanic lands to the north and from the old Persian empire; and silk and spices were imported from China, incense from Yemen and pepper from India. Trading with other countries was a lengthy business, as land transport was slow and seafaring risky, so inland waterways were always used where possible.

The Roman emperors were continuously issuing new edicts. A great body of law existed but clever lawyers were nevertheless often able to baffle less-knowledgeable judges, because the law was never codified until after Rome had collapsed in the West, when the job was undertaken by JUSTINIAN.

The coming of Christianity

The first DEITIES OF ROME were nature spirits, especially of woods, waterways and wells, but the Romans later adopted new gods from Greece, from Egypt (Isis and Osiris), and from Persia (Mithras). Religion of all kinds was tolerated by the state, as was witchcraft, as long as it did not challenge authority.

Above: This Roman broadsword with its decorated scabbard, was found in Germany. The cross section of a curved shield (*above right*) shows that it was made of laminated strips of wood covered with sheep's felt. The shield's edge is double-stitched.

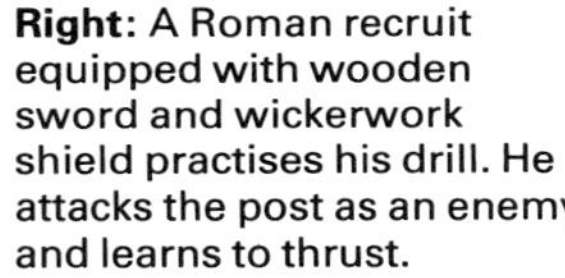

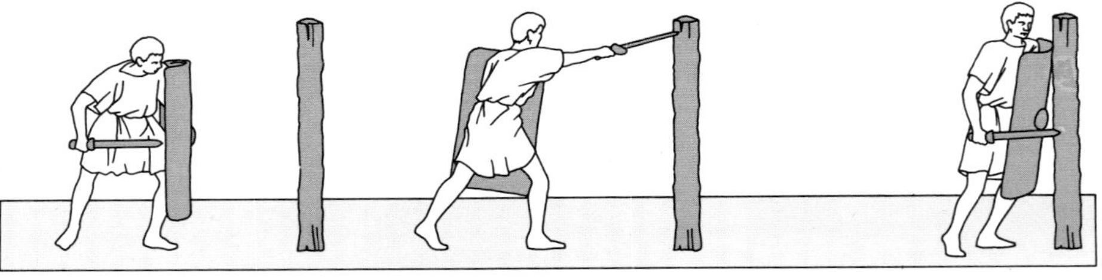

Right: A Roman recruit equipped with wooden sword and wickerwork shield practises his drill. He attacks the post as an enemy and learns to thrust.

BC), the king of Pergamum died and bequeathed his country and property to the Roman people. Tiberius demanded that the property be sold to provide capital for those who should settle in the seized lands. When Tiberius was killed in a riot, his brother Gaius (153–121 BC) took up the struggle. But in 121 BC he too was killed in an election riot. Within 10 years the work of the Gracci brothers was undone.

H

Hannibal (247–183 BC) was a Carthaginian leader who crossed the Pyrenees and Alps to invade Italy in the Second Punic War. He reached the Po Valley with a force that included 26,000 troops, 6,000 horses, and a herd of elephants, which he planned to use like tanks. In Italy Hannibal recruited a further 10,000 troops from the Gauls. The Romans lost 3 battles to the Carthaginians, yet won eventually by invading Spain and Africa.

Horace (68–8 BC), a penniless ex-soldier, wrote philosophical poetry and prose. His works are still widely read today.

J

Jesus of Nazareth was probably born in 4 BC or earlier. He was a Jew and a revolutionary thinker whose followers believed him to be the Son of God (the Christ). The Jewish priestly authorities feared that Jesus' teachings and their political consequences threatened their position. In about AD 29 he was tortured and then crucified.

Hannibal

Justinian I (reigned AD 527–565) spent 20 years fighting the VANDALS, Huns and Franks and ruled the Eastern empire from Byzantium. He codified existing Roman law into a *Body of Civil Law*, which is still the basis of law in many western European countries.

L

Latin is one of the Indo-European languages. At first, only the people of Latium, Rome and its neighbours, spoke Latin, but later it spread throughout the Roman empire and eventually became the parent language of Italian, French, Spanish and Portuguese.

Livius (c.284–204 BC) produced translations of Greek tragedies and comedies, and a Latin version of Homer's *Odyssey*.

Livy (59 BC–AD 17) was a historian recognized as a good source on Roman times. He nevertheless in-

Above: Following the commanders came the *aquilifer* (bearer of the eagle-topped standard) wearing an animal skin. Other bearers carried standards for each *century* (company).

Above: The baggage train, comprising pack mules and ox carts, carried the army's food, equipment, tools heavy weapons, siege equipment and machinery.

Above: The main infantry column, armed with shields, pikes, broadswords and daggers, marched 6 abreast. They carried their personal equipment wedged in wooden forks.

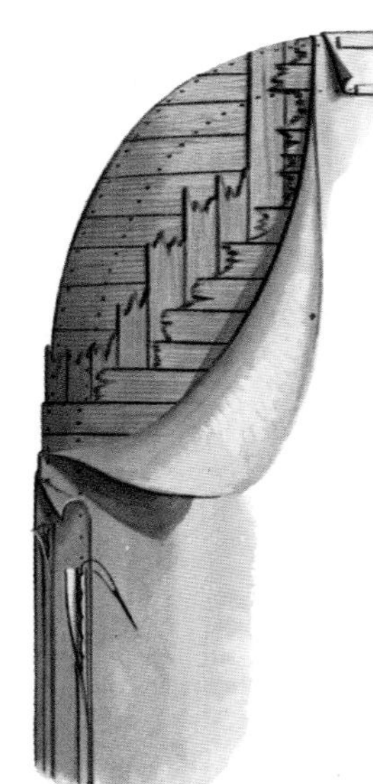

The Christians, however, had a chequered history of persecution and tolerance under the Romans. At the time of the crucifixion of JESUS OF NAZARETH in AD 30, they were insignificant in numbers, but rapidly grew as PAUL spread his teachings to Asia Minor, Greece and Italy. They first made themselves felt as a group in Rome at the time of Claudius who complained in AD 49 that their gatherings caused uproars, but they were not persecuted until Nero unjustly accused them of setting fire to Rome in AD 64.

For the next 300 years, the Christians were mostly left in peace until the reign of Diocletian (284–305), but four years after his death Galerius and Constantine I (reigned 306–337) restored their freedom of worship. As conditions improved, so the number of converts rose until Theodosius I (reigned 379–395) made Christianity the official religion in the hope of unifying his people.

The rise of the Roman empire

Legend has it that ROMULUS, the son of Mars, founded Rome in 753 BC, but in fact it was probably founded by the Etruscans about 600 BC. After its independence in 509 BC, Rome had to fight for survival against neighbouring tribes, and in 390 BC drove off an attack by the Gauls, and then another from the nearby Samnites and the Greeks of the south.

Having built up and tested its military strength and forced off its attackers, Rome then went into the attack itself. It took the granary of Sicily from Carthage in the First Punic War

Right: A legionary goes into attack. First he throws his light javelin, then his heavier one. He then draws his sword and moves in to attack at close quarters.

cluded many legendary and miraculous happenings in his works.

Lucretius (94–55 BC) was a philosopher poet who had no belief in the gods, which made his works unpopular in his own times.

M **Marcus Aurelius** (reigned AD 161–180) was a Stoic philosopher and a soldier who won several battles in Parthia, but his armies brought the plague back to the Roman empire. He spent most of his reign defending the empire from BARBARIAN attack.

Medicine was the science that interested the Romans most, and the importance of 2 of their doctors was crucial to medical history for centuries. Celsus (AD 14–37) wrote medical books that were not valued until long after the Roman empire had gone. Galen (AD 129–199), who was born in Pergamum and studied medicine at Alexandria, is regarded as the 'father of experimental physiology'.

Marcus Aurelius

N **Nero** was emperor from AD 54–68, but for much of that time Rome was governed by SENECA, his teacher. Nero is noted for his cruelty and he began the persecution of the Christians after a great fire which destroyed half of Rome. Nero held them responsible for the fire and had to rebuild Rome. Early victims of his persecution were said to have been St Peter and St PAUL, but in the end Nero's thirst for blood grew so great that his army rebelled and he was driven to suicide.

O **Octavian** (63 BC–AD 14) grandnephew of Julius CAESAR, took the title Augustus shortly after becoming emperor.

Odoacer (AD c.434–493), a German leader, overthrew the last Roman emperor in 476. In 493 he surrendered to another German, Theodoric the Great (c.454–526) king of the OSTROGOTHS, who executed him.

Ostrogoths settled by the Black Sea in the AD 300s, from where they were pushed westwards by the Huns. Under their king, Theodoric the Great, they became allies of Byzantium, whose emperor, Zeno, sent them to fight his rival ODOACER and recapture Italy from him in 493. Theodoric succeeded in conquering Italy, but instead of surrendering it to Zeno he kept it

Left: Pompeii, a Greek city in Italy that came under Roman rule, was destroyed by the eruption of Mount Vesuvius in AD 79. The volcanic lava engulfed people, animals, artefacts and buildings, so preserving some of them for nearly 1,700 years until excavations began.

(264–241 BC), later adding Sardinia and Corsica to its conquests. The Carthaginian victory over Spain, heralded the beginning of the Second Punic War (218–201 BC) when the Carthaginian commander, HANNIBAL, was followed by his brother Hasdrubal across the Pyrenees and the Alps to invade Italy. But the Romans outwitted the Carthaginians by daringly counter-attacking Africa and Spain, which they conquered. In the Third Punic War (149–146 BC), Rome renewed its attack on Africa and cruelly razed Carthage to the ground.

Meanwhile, the Romans were gaining firm footholds in other parts of the world. When the Greeks appealed to Rome to free them from Macedonian rule, its troops intervened and eventually annexed all Macedonia, and 133 BC saw the addition of Pergamum to the empire, which gave the Romans a stronghold in Asia. Julius Caesar conquered Gaul; EGYPT was annexed by Octavian, who began 200 years of the PAX ROMANA, and in AD 43 Claudius annexed Britain. Interestingly enough, the Romans neglected easier conquests closer to home and it was not until 87 BC that they had most of Italy under their control.

The empire reached its height under TRAJAN in AD 117 when it occupied a vast rectangle of land networked with Roman roads with its four corners in Britain, the Caspian Sea, Egypt and Spain. Most of this territory was still held when Theodosius died in 395, but by then Rome's power was declining fast.

Division and collapse

In 395 the Roman empire was divided by agreement into West and East. The Western empire was internally weak and its borderlands were soon invaded by attackers, who were pushed further into the more prosperous Eastern empire by stronger Asian nomads. The empire fell as its strongholds and treasures were relinquished to looters. Rome was looted by the VISIGOTHS under ALARIC in 410, and finally sacked by VANDALS in 455. ATTILA'S HUNS invaded Italy in 452 but were driven back from the Po River by famine and disease. Other attackers were more successful, and included the ANGLES, SAXONS, JUTES, Franks, BURGUNDIANS and OSTROGOTHS. The onslaught culminated in 476 with the deposition of the last Western Roman emperor by the German chief ODOACER.

Above right: This artist's reconstruction of a villa in Pompeii, shows a noble's house richly decorated with frescoes, marble columns and mosaics. The ground and first floors on the left are shops rented out by the owner. In the centre is the main living room or *atrium* with a hole in the ceiling and a pool in the middle. Bedrooms lead off it. To the right of the atrium is a *tablinium* or reception room. The colonnaded area is an open courtyard containing the family shrine (*lararium*) surrounded by a covered passage or *peristyle.* Below this is (*left*) the kitchen and (*right*) the dining room (*triclinium*). Diners reclined on couches and were waited on by slaves.

for himself and set up an Ostrogothic kingdom centred on Ravenna. After Theodoric's death in 526, his kingdom was crushed by JUSTINIAN.

Ovid (43 BC–AD 17) is famous for his *Metamorphoses,* a collection of myths written in hexametres. He wrote mainly about love, a topic which incurred the displeasure of Augustus (OCTAVIAN), who banished him from Rome.

P

Paul, earlier known as Saul, began about AD 47 to spread Christianity to Asia Minor, Greece, and eventually Rome. It is believed that he was among those beheaded about AD 67 in NERO'S persecution.

Pax Romana (Roman Peace) lasted 27 BC–AD 180, during which time Rome allowed no other powers to make war, although it fought many wars itself.

Praetorian Guard was the personal bodyguard of the emperors until it was disbanded in AD 312.

R

Romulus and his brother Remus, said to be sons of the god Mars, were supposedly set adrift in baskets on the Tiber. They were then rescued and reared by a she-wolf. In the legend, Romulus later killed Remus and founded Rome in 753 BC. He then populated Rome with male fugitives and stole wives for them from the nearby Sabines. Romulus is said to have disappeared in a thunderstorm, after which he became the god Quirinus.

Nero

S

Seneca (c. 4 BC–AD 65) a Stoic philosopher, playwrite and statesman, became teacher to NERO and later governed the empire for him. In AD 65 Nero ordered him to commit suicide.

Suetonius (c. AD 69–140) wrote biographies of Julius CAESAR and other emperors.

T

Tacitus (c. AD 55–c.120) wrote many histories. In one of these, *Germania,* he gave the first written account of the Germanic peoples.

Trajan (AD 98–117) added Dacia and Mesopotamia to the empire. He sent so many Roman colonists into Dacia that it is still inhabited by a mainly Latin people, which explains its modern name: Romania.

Tribunes were originally officers of the Roman army

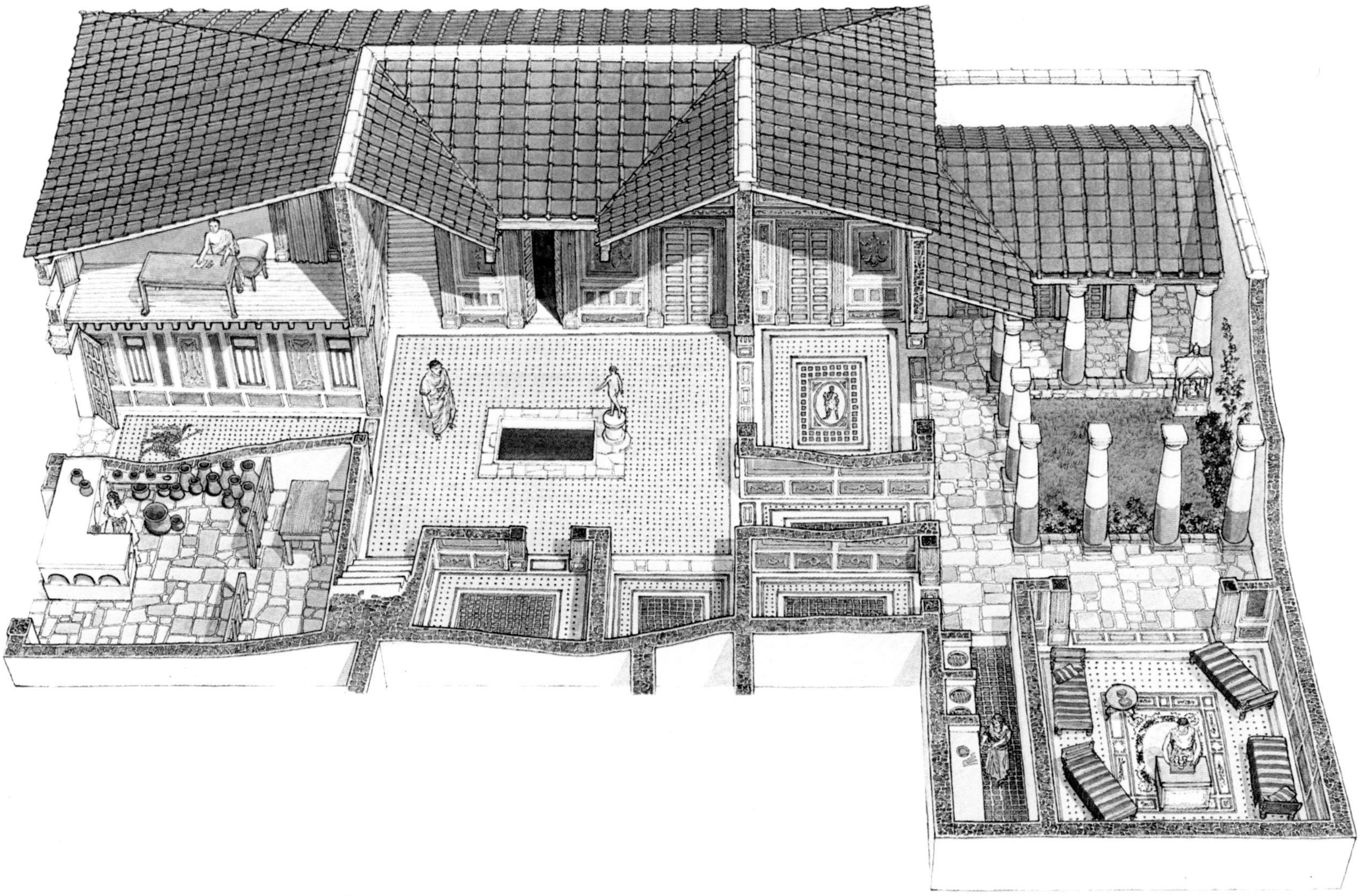

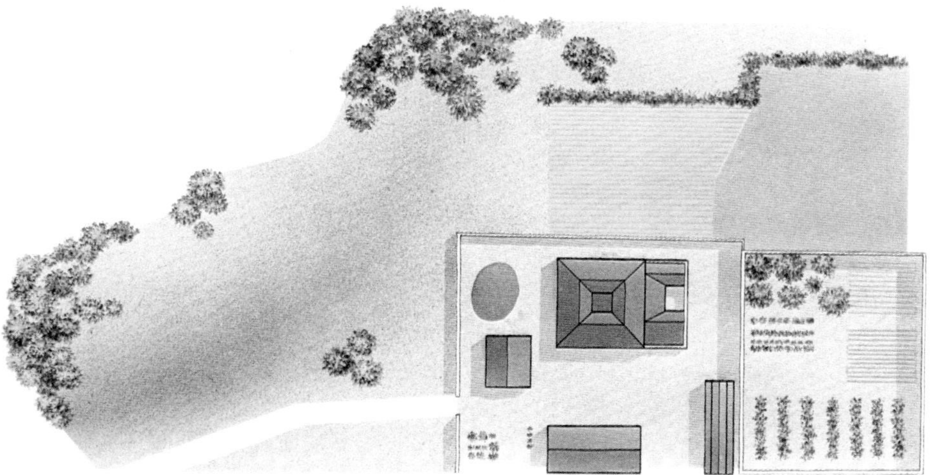

Left: A wealthy Roman's country estate was generally self-supporting. As well as the main villa there were workshops, barns and granaries. To the right is a kitchen garden and beyond the wall are cornfields, vineyards and olive groves. The owner employed both free men and slaves as workers and a bailiff (villieus) to run the farm in his absence.

legions given the power of consuls. Later, they were men elected to an Assembly of plebeians, and by the time of Tiberius GRACCHUS they held enough power to make an emperor uncomfortable. The obvious solution was for the emperor to add the office of tribune to his other functions.

V **Valens** was appointed emperor in the East from AD 364–378 by his brother VALENTINIAN I. He admitted the VISIGOTHS into the Eastern empire, but was later killed by them when they attacked the Eastern Roman army and destroyed 40 per cent of it.

Valentinian I (reigned AD 364–375) appointed his brother VALENS his co-emperor in the East. Although an Orthodox Christian, he allowed religious freedom to people of other religions.

Vandals were a Germanic people from present-day Denmark, Christians from the ARIAN sect that disagreed with the Orthodox Church about the nature of the Holy Trinity. They invaded Gaul, Spain and Africa, and by AD 455 their fleet controlled the Mediterranean, so they sacked Rome and took the emperor hostage. After this triumph, the Vandals warred with Byzantium, but in 533 JUSTINIAN captured their base at Carthage and they disappeared from history. Because of their sack of Rome, the word 'vandal' now means a person who mindlessly destroys.

Virgil (c. 70–19 BC) was one of Rome's greatest poets, and was greatly influenced by Homer. He wrote the *Aeneid*, Rome's national epic.

Visigoths. In AD 395 Theodosius I died and the Visigoths, who had been in his service, gave their allegiance to one of their own number, Alaric, who led them until his own death in 410. Under him the Visigoths sacked Rome in 410, but Alaric spared Roman temples and Christian churches.

Bacchus, god of wine

W **Western Rome** began when the Roman empire was split by agreement in AD 395 into West and East. The division ran vertically, north to south through present-day Albania and Libya. The West was by that time near its end, although the East was still flourishing.

Byzantium was the eastern capital of the Roman empire. It prospered, while Rome declined, to become the seat of the world's first Christian empire and one of the greatest centres of learning the world has ever known.

The Byzantines

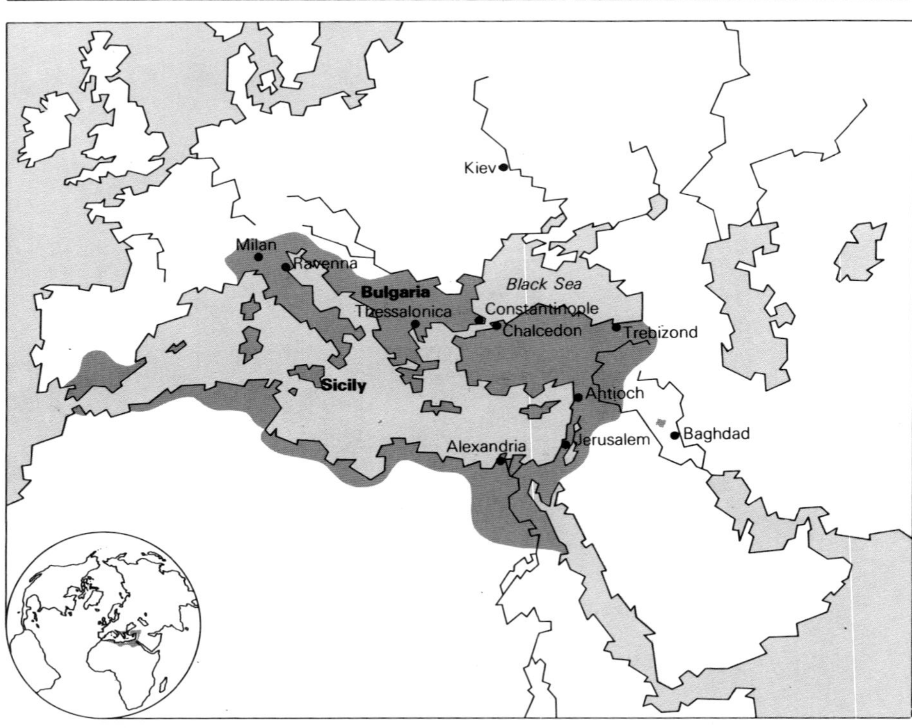

Above: Under Justinian the Byzantine empire expanded into territories belonging to imperial Rome.

When Constantine (c.280–337) became emperor of all the Roman empire, he spent the years AD 324–30 building a new city on the site of Byzantium. This city, CONSTANTINOPLE, named after its founder, grew bigger and richer than Rome. When the empire was split into West and East in 395, it became the CAPITAL of the Eastern or Byzantine empire (often called Byzantium), and one of the world's greatest seats of learning.

Rome and Constantinople

While Constantinople flourished, Rome declined. Open to BARBARIAN attack (*see page 81*), it frequently lost even its status as the Western capital and battle-weary emperors set up temporary capitals at RAVENNA, Milan or TRIER, according to the needs of war. In religious importance, Rome's heyday had also passed because it was steeped in the cult of the old gods whose power over men's minds had gone. Christianity, the new official religion of the empire, found a safer, more sympathetic base in Constantinople, which provided the ideal capital for the world's first Christian empire.

Above: Justinian's head dominated the gold coins of Byzantium which became the most stable currency from Western Europe to China.

Emperor Justinian I

Theodosius II (reigned 402–50) greatly expanded Constantinople and built a double line of defensive walls against attackers such as ATTILA, but the city reached the height of its splendour under JUSTINIAN I (*see page 84*). Justinian replaced Latin by Greek, and took to wearing a jewelled crown and silk robes in oriental style. Visitors, forced to bow or prostrate themselves before him, were overawed by the various mechanical novelties which surrounded him, including a device that hauled his golden throne ceiling-high. To promote Orthodox Christianity, Justinian punished heretics and closed the Athenian schools of philosophy.

Justinian's most lasting achievement was the codification of Roman law, which improved the status of women.

The Christian Church divides

Byzantium was obsessed with matters of religious doctrine and in 325, Constantine pronounced the Niocene Creed, defining Christianity. But Syria and Egypt disagreed, and at the Council of Chalcedon in 451, broke away to form the separate Coptic Church. Byzantium abounded in ICONS (images) of Jesus, the Virgin Mary and various saints, but neither Church nor State approved, and in 726, Emperor Leo III (717–41) banned icons, calling them idols.

In the West, Christianity survived the empire to become the religion of its barbarian successors, and was held together by the patriarchs (or popes) in Rome. As their power grew, they

Reference

A **Attila** the Hun (c. 406–53) turned back from attacking Constantinople in 447, when the rumblings of an earthquake frightened his army. Some 3 tonnes of gold eventually bought him off.

B **Byzantine missionaries** included Cyril, inventor of the Cyrillic alphabet (861), which is still used in Russia, Yugoslavia and Bulgaria.

C **Capital.** DIOCLETIAN (*see page 83*) ruled the Eastern empire from Nicomedia, (near Byzantium), but in 324–30 Constantine moved the capital to Constantinople. He thought that Rome was too attached to the old religion to become the capital of a Christian empire.
Charlemagne (reigned 768–814) became sole ruler of the Franks in 771. Two years later he supported Adrian I (pope 772–95) against the Lombards, whose Italian territories he annexed, and from then on he fought perpetual wars. In 800, he hurried to Rome to prevent Pope Leo III from being deposed. There, the pope crowned him emperor.

Hagia Sophia interior

Constantinople became rich by imposing a 10% tax on goods passing through its territory, and its gold coinage became a world currency, changing hands between Africa and China. The city held art treasures looted from many lands, and Constantine provided the rich with Roman-style houses and the poor with free bread and circuses. Constantinople boasted a Senate, hippodrome and baths, and the only cities to rival it were Thessalonica and Trebizond.

E **Eastern Orthodox Churches.** The 3 original patriarchates, or seats of patriarchs, which were later joined by Jerusalem, were Rome, Alexandria and Antioch. The last 2 objected to Constantinople becoming a patriarchate at the Council of Chalcedon in 451, and when Constantinople was given precedence over them, Alexandria and Antioch broke away to form the Coptic Church. This later developed a 'daughter Church' in Ethiopia and in time, other independent churches, such as the Nestorian (Assyrian),

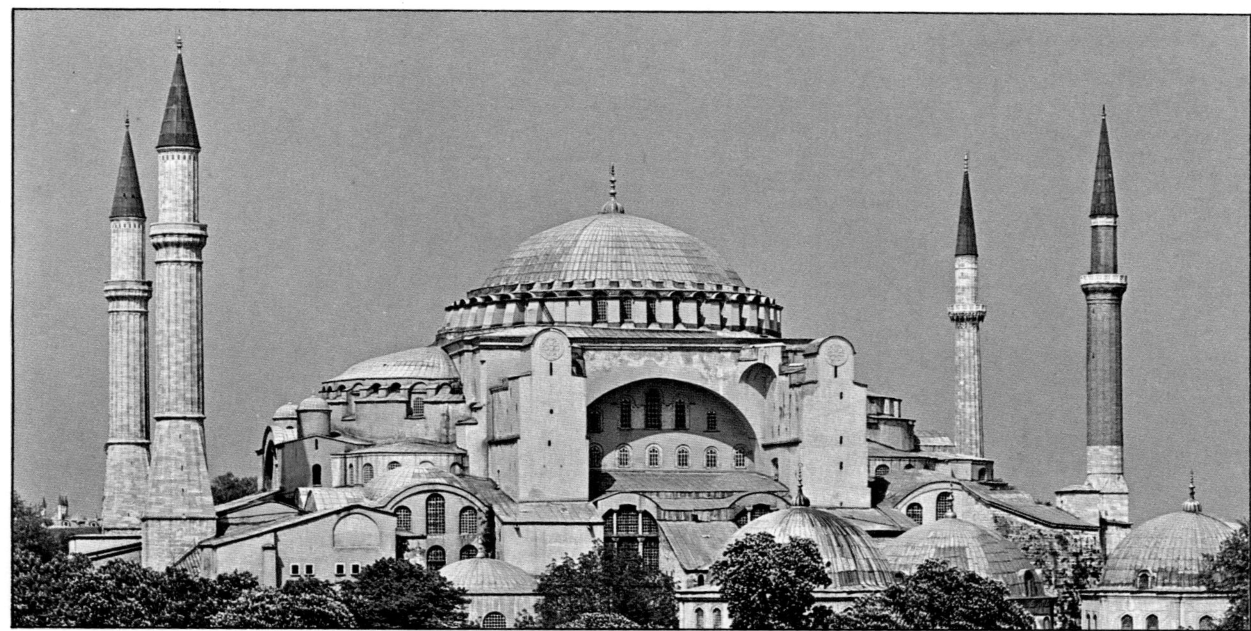

Left: The construction of the magnificent Hagia Sophia (Church of the Holy Wisdom) was built by Justinian I to announce to the world that he had become head of the Church. It fell to the Muslims in 1453 and became a mosque.

resented the claim of the Byzantine emperors to be heads of the Church, and on Christmas Day 800, in a bid to make his own position more secure, Pope Leo III placed a crown on the head of CHARLEMAGNE the Frank and declared him emperor in the West.

Understandably, Pope Leo's action worsened relations between Rome and Constantinople. The final break, or Great Schism, came in 1054 when the pope of Rome and the patriarch of Constantinople excommunicated each other.

The varying fortunes of Byzantium

The Byzantine empire reached its height under Justinian, whose generals seized Italy from the OSTROGOTHS and Roman Africa from the VANDALS (*see page 87*). Besides holding Greece, Asia Minor and Egypt, Justinian dreamed of recreating the old Roman empire, but his own empire began to crumble only three years after his death, when the Lombards began a 200 year struggle to wrench Italy from the Byzantines. Eventually, both lost to Charlemagne.

The Arabs also attacked Byzantium, fired with enthusiasm by their new religion of Islam. Emperor Heraclius (reigned 610–41) used GREEK FIRE to repel their attacks on Constantinople, but Syria, Palestine, Persia and Egypt fell to them. Under the MACEDONIAN DYNASTY (867–1056), Byzantium's frontiers expanded to the Euphrates and into Bulgaria. Bulgar and Serb attacks in the north ceased when BYZANTINE MISSIONARIES converted these SLAV PEOPLES to Christianity. Russia too, was won for the Orthodox Church when a sister of Basil II (960–1025) married Prince Vladimir of KIEV in 989.

The end of the empire

In 1071, Seljuk TURKS from central Asia chased the Byzantines back across Asia Minor, and when the NORMANS took southern Italy and Sicily by 1130, Byzantium shrank to Greece and western Asia Minor. The most cruel blow came in 1204, when fellow Christians from the West interrupted their journey to fight Muslims in Palestine, and seized and looted Byzantium instead. Although the dying empire tottered on for another 250 years, it was reduced to less than 1,000 square kilometres. Church and state struggled for supremacy over an 'empire' whose population had fallen to only 60,000.

Across the narrow waters of the Golden Horn, the Ottoman Turks had replaced the Seljuks, and their leader, Sultan Mehmet II (1431–81) saw Constantinople as a 'monstrous head without a body'. In 1453, 100,000 Turks laid siege to the city for six weeks. Finally, they attacked across the Golden Horn, and the last Byzantine emperor died bravely defending Constantinople as it fell.

Below: The halo surrounding the head of Justinian proclaims his semi-divine status as Byzantine emperor. Churchmen and officials flank the emperor on this magnificent mosaic from the Byzantine city of Ravenna.

Chaldean Catholic, and Armenian.

Greek fire, a mixture of naphtha, quicklime, saltpetre and sulphur, was used in flame-throwers by the Byzantines. This 'secret weapon' was later adopted by the Arabs.

Iconoclasts (image-breakers) were active in Byzantium 726–843 with government encouragement. The anti-icon movement probably took inspiration from the Arabs.

Icons, images painted or carved as objects of worship, developed from mosaics and frescoes. Few surviving icons predate 900.

Kiev, earliest state of the eastern Slavs, flourished 900s–1200s occupying most of modern Ukraine and Byelorussia.

Macedonian dynasty began when Michael III (reigned 842–67), known as the Drunkard, was murdered by a former stable-boy of his, a Macedonian, who usurped the throne to become Basil I in 867. The dynasty's greatest warrior was Basil II (the Bulgar Slayer) who reigned 976–1025.

Normans were originally Scandinavian Vikings and land-hungry Norman warrior-nobles. They set up the kingdom of Sicily in 1130.

Ravenna became the capital of the Western empire in 402. It was also the capital of ODOACER (*see page 85*) and Theodoric (c. 454–526) and the governors of Byzantine Italy.

Slav peoples lived between the east bank of the Elbe River and Constantinople in the 500s–700s, and are believed to have originated in Polish Galicia.

Trier, capital of Belgica (Roman northern Gaul), occasionally became the capital of the Western emperors in the 290s–400s.

Turks, about AD 500, lived between Mongolia and the Black Sea. The Seljuk Turks were converted to Islam and took Baghdad in 1055, then advanced to the Mediterranean, so sparking off the Crusades. Otterman (Osmanli) Turks took over the Seljuk empire in the 1300s.

Constantine

The 'golden age' of the Tang and Sung dynasties saw an expansion of trade and the flowering of art and literature, crafts and technology. Chang-an was then the world's largest city with a population of well over 1,000,000 people.

The Later Chinese

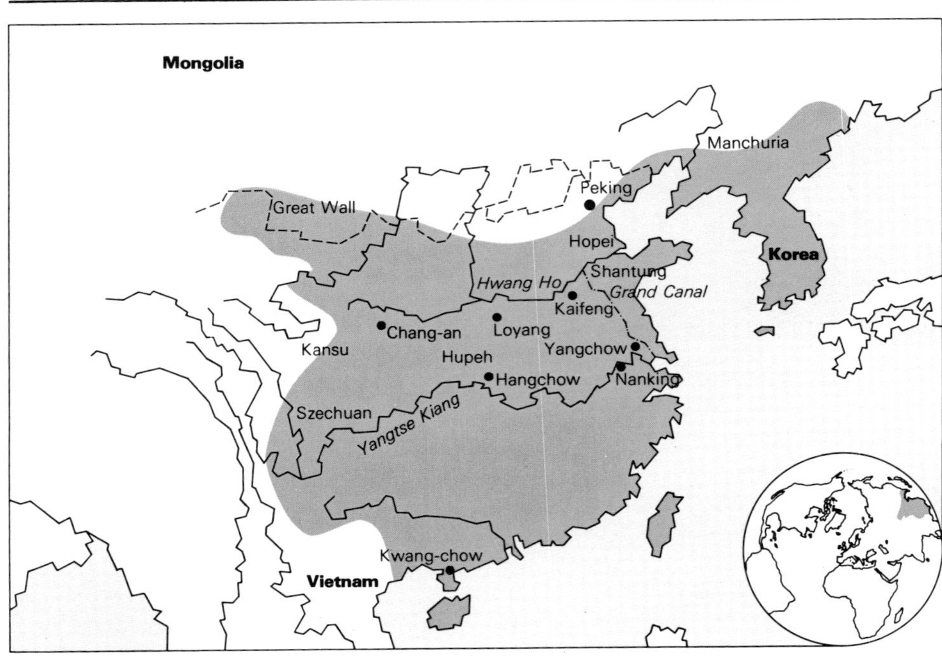

Above: Tang China, although smaller than the Han empire, had as its capital the then largest city in the world, Chang-an.

After the Han dynasty fell in AD 220, China remained disunited until the nobly-born YANG CHIEN established the Sui dynasty (581–618). He began an ambitious reconstruction drive, pressing millions of peasants into forced labour. Nearly half of the labourers conscripted to rebuild LOYANG (the eastern capital) were worked to death, and in consequence, the peasants became bitterly hostile to the regime. Yang Chien's son murdered him to inherit the throne, but lost prestige when he tried and failed to conquer Manchuria and Korea. The peasants took to arms and Sui soldiers deserted the dynasty. Then LI YUAN, a Sui army officer, seized Chang-an and became the first Tang emperor.

Tang and Sung dynasties

Tang armies conquered Manchuria, Korea, Mongolia, Tibet and Turkestan to build an empire that extended from the Caspian Sea to Korea and Vietnam. But by the mid-700s most of the border regions were lost and discontent again brought peasant revolts that weakened the dynasty. When CHU WEN, warlord of the Hwang Ho region, usurped the throne in 907, China disintegrated.

The empire became reunited (with reduced territory) under the Northern Sung (960–1127), who set up their capital at KAIFENG, near the Hwang Ho in north central China. But it suffered perpetual attacks from the north, especially from the NUCHEN of Manchuria, who founded the KIN KINGDOM in 1115. When the Kin took northern China in 1127, the survivors of the Sung family fled south to establish the Southern Sung dynasty (1127–1279). Its capital, at first at Shangchiu, was later moved to HANGCHOW.

The plundering Kin massacred or enslaved the Chinese, and when the Mongols invaded China in 1211, the northern Chinese welcomed them as liberators. Southern Sung unwisely allied itself with the conquering Mongols to destroy the Kin, on condition that they would reoccupy Kin territory south of the Hwang Ho. But the Mongols cheated them out of the fruits of victory, and when Sung troops made for Loyang, their Mongol 'allies' treacherously opened the dykes of the Hwang Ho and drowned them. Then the Mongols advanced into Southern Sung China and established the Yuan (Mongol) dynasty.

Above: This Tang figure is typical of the finer pieces of ceramic ware of the period.

Social and economic life in Tang China

With the Tang dynasty (618–907), China entered a 'golden age' and its capital, CHANG-AN, became the world's biggest city. Learning from mistakes made by their predecessors in the short-lived Sui dynasty of 581–618, the early Tang emperors tried to improve the lot of the peasants without antagonizing their powerful landlords. The peasants were demanding a redistribution of land, and to appease both factions the emperors

Reference

C **Chang-an** (now Sian), capital of Tang China, was then the world's biggest city with well over 1,000,000 people. Like other major Chinese cities, it attracted thousands of foreign merchants. The square-walled city was built on the grid pattern.

Cheng Ho. Several reasons have been suggested for the ending of Admiral Cheng Ho's trading missions. 1) They cost too much. 2) Shortly after the death of Timur the Lame (1406) interruptions to the central Asian trade routes ceased. 3) Having 'shown the flag' in the Indian Ocean, China's need for political prestige was satisfied. 4) Japanese piracy became a threat.

Chu Wen, most powerful warlord of the Hwang Ho region, deposed the last Tang emperor in 907. But he failed to keep China unified and until the rise of Northern Sung in 960, it was split into 5 dynasties: Later Liang, Later Tang, Later Tsin, Later Han, Later Chou.

Chu Yuan-chang (1328–98) a peasant's son orphaned by plague, became a monk and conspired with the White Lotus secret society to form the Red Turbans, a band which sought to overthrow the rich. But his wealthy enemies persuaded him to join them in an all-Chinese attack on the Mongol overlords and in several battles between 1355 and 1368 he beat the Mongol armies and took Peking without opposition. The Mongols fled back to Mongolia and in 1368 Chu Yuan-chang became the first Ming emperor.

Copper coins changed hands in 'strings' for large amounts. One tonne of copper made about 300 strings. Each string held 1,000 of the round coins with a square hole, called *cash*.

F **Fire guns** were long bamboo tubes filled with gunpowder.

G **Gunpowder,** invented in Tang China, was at first used only for firework

Sampan on Yangtse Kiang

gave them the territory that had gone to waste during the Sui civil wars. They kept rents and taxes within reasonable limits and avoided taking men for forced labour during busy periods of the farming year. Even so, they managed to cut new irrigation canals, improve the quality of livestock, grain and textiles, and wipe out crop-destroying locusts. They developed water transport to bring trade directly into the new towns that sprang up along the river banks.

Foreign trade also expanded. Nomads from the north brought furs and skins strapped on horses or camels to the border towns, and caravans from central Asia and further west carried jade, carpets and other commodities into Tang China. Arab and Persian ships sailed to the ports of southern China loaded with drugs, gems, pearls, spices, and other luxuries. The foreign ships carried away bronze mirrors, ironware, PORCELAIN, silk and tea. Trade stimulated the demand for MONEY, and each year, the Tang government put into circulation another thousand tonnes of COPPER COINS.

Town planning was a feature of Tang China. From Chang-an, good roads led to Hopei, Hupeh, Kansu, Shantung and Szechuan provinces. Loyang stood at the hub of the Grand Canal, and the great trading city of Yangchow stood at its confluence with the YANGTSE KIANG. Kwang-chow (Canton) became the leading seaport.

Right: This large blue and white bowl is characteristic of ceramic ware of the Ming dynasty. Contrasting sharply with the finer but plainer Sung ware, Ming 'blue and white' was widely copied in Japan, Persia and south-eastern Asia. Shipped to the Netherlands it inspired the Delft porcelain of Holland.

Below: The picture shows part of the Rainbow Bridge from Chan Tse-tuan's silk scroll painting *The Ching Ming Festival on the River*. It is fairly representative of the Sung dynasty style.

Technology under the Sung

The Sung dynasty (960–1279) heralded China's 'silver age'. Sung China was a weak military power compared with Tang China, but to compensate, it became the world leader in military technology, and one of its achievements was the development of the use of GUNPOWDER, which had been discovered by the Tang.

Yuan and Ming dynasties

The greatest of the Yuan emperors was KUBLAI KHAN, who moved the Chinese capital to Peking. Marco POLO, the Italian traveller, visited him there and returned to Europe with stories that made him a legendary figure in the West. Although Kublai Khan admired Chinese culture and ruled well, later Yuan emperors were less able. Agriculture declined as waterways fell into disrepair, and resistance to the Mongols increased.

The Chinese rebels were eventually united under the leadership of the Red Turbans, who defeated several Yuan armies. In 1368, despairing of holding China, the Mongol army withdrew north of the Great Wall and the Yuan dynasty crumbled away.

CHU YUAN-CHANG, a poor peasant-monk turned rebel commander, took Nanking and made himself the first Ming dynasty emperor. The Ming soon restored prosperity, but eventually, they too came up against the irrepressible power of the peasants. A 17-years' PEASANTS' WAR (1627–44) against the Ming dynasty whittled away China's internal strength, while from abroad, the Japanese raided shipping and battled with China for control of Korea.

---

displays. Sung China used it to produce bombs, rockets, flame throwers, and the power for FIRE GUNS.

H

Hangchow, capital and hub of Southern Sung's commerce, became one of the richest and largest cities in the world. There, life was easier than in the cold, wind-swept Hwang Ho region. With the move to the south in 1127, the Sung way of life changed. Marco POLO claimed that the Southern Sung fell to the Mongols because they were too busy paying attention to women to be warriors. Hangchow offered luxury international shops, popular entertainment, fashionable restaurants, and tea houses with 'sing-song girls'.

K

Kaifeng, the Northern Sung capital, was also called Pienching, Pien-liang, and Yeh. A colony of Jews built a synagogue there in mid-Sung times.

Kin kingdom was established by the NUCHEN in 1115.

Kublai Khan (1216–94) grandson of Temujin (1162–1227) who was known as Genghiz Khan, nominally ruled the whole Mongol empire from eastern Europe to China. His actual rule was confined to China and Mongolia. Kublai did not interfere with Chinese culture, which he admired. He was followed by 7 less effective Yuan emperors.

Chinese fresco, AD 700s

L

Li Po (701–762) is often considered to be China's greatest poet. His poems, frequently written when drunk, reflect the freshness of the passing moment.

Li Yuan, first Tang emperor, reigned 618–627. He was appointed by his son, who overthrew the Sui dynasty with the help of Mongol Turks.

Loyang, capital of the Eastern Chou and Eastern Han, became a subsidiary capital of Tang China.

M

Malacca, founded by a fugitive Malay king

Ante-room of tomb, Loyang

The economies of Yuan and Ming China

When the Mongols conquered China they made little impact on its cultural tradition apart from introducing NORTHERN DRAMA, and soon adopted Chinese ways.

The Mongols did nothing to further the Chinese economy, and when the Ming emperors succeeded them, this was their first task. Vast 'factories' were set up to mass-produce porcelain, which became China's export, and the Ming sent large trading fleets under Admiral CHENG HO off to Vietnam, India, Persia, Arabia, and eastern Africa. But these voyages stopped abruptly when foreign traders proved willing to exchange their products with the Chinese in the Malayan port of MALACCA. A constant hazard for Chinese coastal settlements and shipping came from Japanese pirates, and the Portuguese seizure of Malacca in 1511 convinced the Ming emperor that European traders were no better than the Japanese pirates.

Such was the fame of Chinese porcelain in the European markets that it became highly prized and a number of potteries tried to copy it – the Chinese fashion of decoration on pottery became very popular. For some wealthy people, landowners and noblemen in England, copies were not good enough for them. They sent orders direct to China for complete dinner services and other pieces of the marvellous porcelain. They even went to the lengths of sending engravings, such as bookplates, or miniature paintings of their family coats of arms and mottos to be placed on their custom-ordered porcelain. It took nearly two years for these heraldic orders to be completed and the porcelain delivered. When the drawings supplied to the Chinese were not sufficiently clear some curious heraldry resulted – they copied what they thought they saw, even at times down to the instructions on the drawings, which appeared on the final porcelain.

Religion and the arts

Indian Buddhism had reached China during mid-Han times, but did not become popular until the introduction in 520 of Chan (Zen), a more practical kind of Buddhism, which spread rapidly throughout the land. Buddhism did not replace Confucianism and Taoism; it coexisted with them and the Chinese combined all three religions, together with the cult of their ancient deities, into one integrated system of worship.

Above: The world's oldest printed book, the Buddhist *Diamond Sutra*, was block printed in China in AD 868. Moveable type printing, experimented with by the Chinese, was accomplished by the Koreans in the 1300s.

Right: Mongol horsemen under Kublai Khan swept down upon China during the closing years of the enfeebled Sung dynasty. Although Kublai showed little mercy in conquering China, he respected Chinese culture and governed the country well.

about 1403, quickly became rich from foreign trade. Chinese junks sailed there to sell their wares and return to China with Indian, Persian, Arab and European goods. Through Malacca, Islam became part of the Malay culture. The Portuguese took the port in 1511.

Manchus was the later name of the NUCHEN.

Money. As more money circulated in Tang China, reflecting increased prosperity, the weight and bulk of strings of copper cash made them difficult and risky to transport. To avoid the problem, merchants issued 'deposit certificates'. These passed instead of money. Later Tang governments issued their own certificates. The Sung took the system one stage further, issuing paper money.

N **Northern drama** developed during Yuan times, when over 500 plays were written. Typical Yuan plays had a prologue, 4 acts, and an epilogue. Most were tragedies. Male actors portrayed set characters of both sexes.

Nuchen (also known as Jurchen, and later as Manchus), a Manchurian tribe, founded the KIN (or Chin) kingdom in 1115. They were then hunters and fishers, just settling to a semi-farming way of life. Having seized northern China from the Sung, they were conquered by the Mongols. Later (as the Manchus) they seized Ming China and ruled from 1644-1911.

Women making silk: Sung

P **Peasants' war** (1627–44) against the last Ming emperor was the biggest internal upheaval in Chinese history. The peasants fought under the slogan 'Equal distribution of the land among rich and poor'. The peasants toppled the dynasty, but it was the MANCHUS who profited by its collapse.

Peking (Cambaluc) was the Yuan capital (1279–1368). After a brief break it became the Ming capital in 1421, and has remained the capital of China except for brief periods during the Japanese and civil wars of the present century.

Polo, Marco (c. 1254–1324) became the most famous traveller to take the silk route to China. He travelled over much of Asia in the service of KUBLAI KHAN. His book, a marvellous mixture of fact and fancy, was written later, when a prisoner-of-war in Italy. To sell the book, he

Tang architects built Buddhist temples on a palatial scale and their literature concentrated on romantic tales and religious or supernatural themes. The dynasty produced China's two greatest poets: LI PO and TU FU. In Sung times, village groups gathered to hear priests read Buddhist tales known as Pien-wen. This began the tradition of story-telling to provide popular entertainment.

Kuan-yin (goddess of mercy) and Buddhist saints caught the imagination of Chinese Taoist–Buddhist artists, who reached their peak in the Sung dynasty with the mountain and water landscapes that still symbolize China today. Chinese porcelain also reached unsurpassed standards with SUNG CERAMIC ware and potters used coloured glazes and often took their shapes and decorative motifs from Persian metalwork and Greek designs.

The end of the Chinese dynasties

During the long period of Ming China's internal collapse, the Nuchen again threatened the north-eastern border. As the MANCHUS (taking their name from Manchuria) they fought the Ming for 30 years. Finally, they took PEKING and founded the Manchu dynasty (1644–1911). The Chinese hated and despised their conquerors, and the Manchu retaliated by making them wear Manchurian clothing and tie their hair into pigtails as a badge of servitude. Chinese civilization stood still under the Manchus and China slowly degenerated into a backward area, sheltered only by the illusion of a cultural and technological superiority that had actually been lost to western Europe.

inserted many untruths into his story. By chance he wrote accurate accounts about aspects of Asia which were at that time unknown,

Chinese likeness of Marco Polo

but he also described unicorns, dog-headed men, wizards and giant rubies. Medieval Europeans rejected much of what was actually true, preferring to believe the fantasies.

Porcelain, mass produced in vast quantities in Ming China, went mainly for export. In one year (1643), China shipped some 130,000 pieces to the Netherlands alone, where it inspired the creation of Delft china. Ming white-glazed porcelain with blue decoration was imitated in Japan, south-eastern Asia and Persia.

Printing. Forms of block printing in China probably go back to the 200s BC and true printed pieces date from very early Tang times. Moveable type printing, experimented with by Pi Sheng in China, was successfully accomplished by the Koreans, who set up a type foundry in the 1300s. There was probably no feedback between East and West in this area and when Johann Gutenberg began to print with moveable type in Germany about 1440, it was most likely an independent development.

R

Red Turbans, see CHU YUAN-CHANG.

S

Sung ceramic ware was valued outside China for its shape and colouring. Arab rulers favoured the leaf or bluish green *celadon* ware, which they believed cracked or changed colour if poison touched it. This supposedly enabled them to escape assassins.

T

Tu Fu (712–70) a poverty-stricken Tang poet, wrote about human suffering. His poems are longer and deeper than LI PO'S, but lack their freshness.

Y

Yang Chien, first Sui emperor, tried to keep people contented by providing public spectacles much as the Romans had done. He is said to have kept 30,000 performers and built special sites for public audiences.

Yangtse Kiang, according to Marco POLO, carried 200,000 craft upstream every year – 'more wealth and merchandise than all the rivers and seas of Christendom put together'.

The philosophical teachings of Hinduism and Buddhism created an atmosphere in which art, literature and science flourished. The Ajanta cave paintings, the *Kama Sutra*, Angkor Wat and the introduction of yoga all date from this period.

The Later Indians

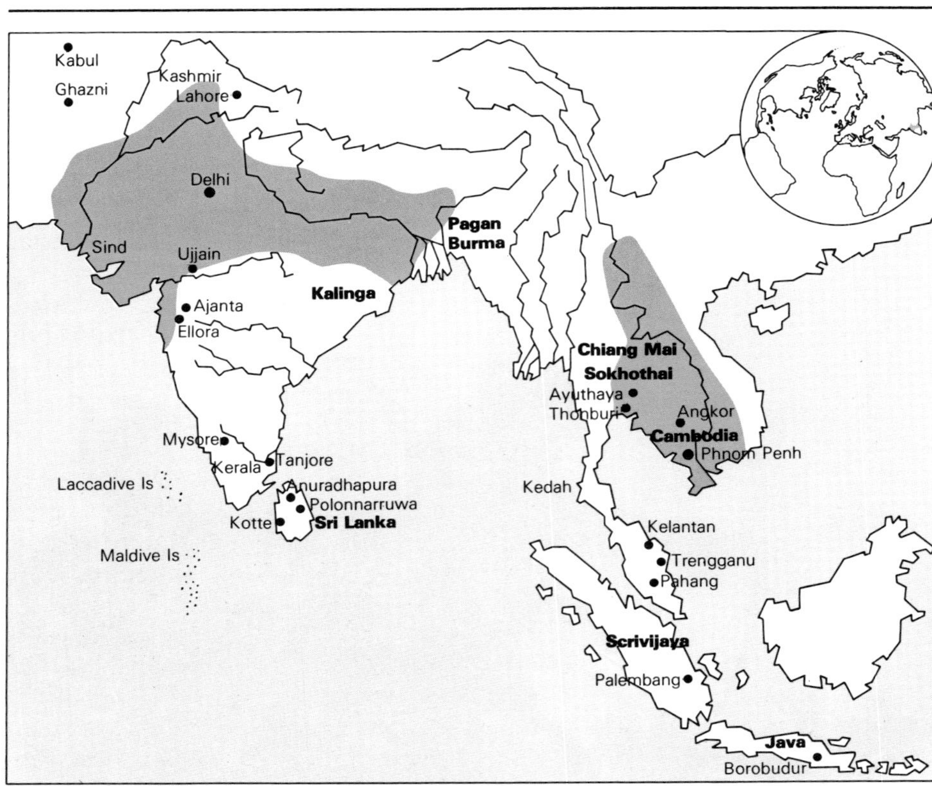

Above left: The map shows the Gupta empire about 400 with its leading city of Ujjain, and the Indianized civilizations that flourished in Sri Lanka, Cambodia Malaya and Indonesia during the next 1,000 years.

Above right: A sari-clad woman weaves on a simple loom. The sari, a single length of unsewn material dyed in pleasing colours and patterns, symbolizes India's unchanging cultural pattern.

Northern India entered a new era of civilization under the Hindu GUPTA DYNASTY (AD 320–c.500). Chandragupta II (reigned 375–415) brought many small states into a confederation that extended from coast to coast. Gupta India saw the revival of Hinduism on a higher philosophical plane. With greater knowledge of anatomy, yoga developed, its disciples seeking to achieve physical, mental and spiritual harmony. Art, literature and science flourished. Indian achievements in mathematics made possible the later scientific revolution of the Europeans.

Religion and art in Gupta India

With the introduction of iron axes into Gupta India, vast areas of forest land were cleared and new villages sprang up. The peasants who settled there were converted by Hindu priests who brought them iron ploughs and scientific farming knowledge as well as the supposed magical power to protect the village. Buddhist monks had become too comfort-loving to serve these poverty-stricken rural areas which could not afford the costly temples and monasteries they deemed necessary.

The Gupta period produced a wealth of outstanding literature. Sudraka, an early Gupta dramatist, described in *Mricchakatika* ('Clay Toy Cart') the pleasures of middle class people in the leading Gupta city of Ujjain. He caricatured the racy underworld life of thieves, gamblers, courtesans and political rebels. In the *Kama Sutra* of

Reference

A **Ajanta and Ellora.** In the first 700 years AD Buddhist monks at Ajanta adapted 28 natural caves into monasteries of outstanding Buddhist art. More caves were cut by Buddhists and Hindus at nearby Ellora, including the huge Kailasa temple, with its sculpted figures, passages and chambers. The Kailasa temple was cut 30 metres downwards out of solid rock.

Angkor was the jungle site of several Cambodian capitals, the earliest dating from 802. It reached its peak under Jayavarman VII (reigned 1181-c.1219) who built the vast city of Angkor Thom. The city was surrounded by 13 km of walls and moats, with 5 gated avenues leading to the Bayon, its central temple. Here the head of the god Lokeswara surmounted each gateway. Angkor's population of a million was self-sufficient in rice because of the advanced irrigation system constructed by the Khmers. In 1431 the city was sacked by the Thais, and the Khmers moved their capital to Phnom Penh.

Ajanta

Aryabhata, a Hindu astronomer mathematician, was reasonably accurate in his theories concerning the earth's shape, rotation and revolution. Other Indian astronomers were able to forecast eclipses correctly.

B **Borobudur,** in central Java, is a vast stupa-temple built in the 800s on a natural mound. It represents in stone the Buddhist concept of the cosmological system. It has 6 square terraces in diminishing tiers, topped by 3 circular terraces. Several small bell-shaped stupas cap the huge structure.

C **Cholas** established a small kingdom around Tanjore (Thanjavur) in southern India about 800. Rajaraja I (985-1012) and his

Buddha statue: Borobudur

Above: A village barber shaves his customer, who inspects the result in a mirror. The barber's trade was highly esteemed in the village, where he traditionally acted as matchmaker in marriages.

Vatsyayana, love was dealt with in an innovatory way and became both an art and a science. KALIDASA reflected the typical preoccupation of the Gupta dynasty writers in his *Shakuntula* where he told a story of royalty, hermits, dense forests and the intervention of gods and demons into human affairs.

Although most of the treasures of early India have been lost, several of the Buddhist-Jain-Hindu cave temples of AJANTA AND ELLORA, which were constructed during Gupta times, contain colourful wall-paintings which have miraculously escaped decay. These portray the lively Gupta court life with dancers, musicians, actors, acrobats and magicians in attendance. The vigour and prosperity of Gupta India was recorded about 405 by the visiting Chinese Buddhist monk, FA-HSIEN.

Scientific achievements

Indian mathematicians had clear concepts of abstract numbers. They developed algebra and trigonometry and devised the system of numbers now used by the whole world (the system of nine digits and a zero). This numeral system found its way to Alexandria in the 500s, but it took another 1,000 years for it to reach northern Europe and gain acceptance there.

The Iron Pillar of Delhi, a seven-metres length of rustless iron cast about 400, is a tribute to Indian metallurgical skill. The rustlessness of the pillar is due to the great purity of the metal, which could not have been achieved outside India until the mid-1800s.

The astronomer Aryabhata also made a great step forward for science when his studies led him to the conclusion that the earth was a rotating sphere moving around the sun.

The end of the Guptas

Gupta India fell into decline by 500, when Hunas, or WHITE HUNS invaded from central Asia. Although the Guptas eventually pushed them back into Kashmir and the north-west, their efforts heralded the end of the dying dynasty. North Indian civilization achieved a brief rebirth under HARSHA (reigned 606–647), who patronized Sanskrit literature though he favoured Buddhism. This divided loyalty cost him his life when jealous brahmins (priests and scholars) egged on his own soldiers to kill him. His death brought about the final disintegration of northern India.

One thousand years of Muslim domination

In the early 700s the Arabs took Sind, the first Indian stronghold to fall in the Muslims' gradual but persistent infiltration into India. This was typified by the determination of Mahmud of Ghazni, ruler of Persia-Afghanistan (997-1030), a fanatical Muslim known as the Idol-Breaker who raided India year after year until his death. He was followed by Qutb ud-din Aibak, a former slave from Turkistan, whose conquests led to the setting up of the SULTANATE OF DELHI (1211–1526). After this most of India passed under the rule of the MUGHALS (Mongol Mus-

---

son Rajendra (1012-44) extended the kingdom into an empire that included Kerala, Mysore and Kalinga. The Cholas attacked the SAILENDRA in SRIVIJAYA, and conquered the Laccadive and Maldive islands and parts of Burma and SRI LANKA. They built magnificent temples which are still standing at Tanjore.

F **Fa-hsien** (c.399-414) was one of several Chinese Buddhist travellers whose writings provide records of events in the Indianized world. During Chandragupta II's time, he travelled to India in search of authentic copies of the Buddhist scriptures. He reported that most Indians had become vegetarians and that travellers could move throughout India unhindered by bandits or bureaucrats. He also commented that northern India had a just and tolerant government.

G **Gupta dynasty** established itself in Magadha, the centre of the earlier Maurya empire by 319, but its power had ebbed away by about 500-600.

H **Harsha,** who ruled 606-647, befriended Hsuan Tsang, a Chinese Buddhist pilgrim whose writings provided much of our present knowledge about the king and his times.

Gateway at Angkor Thom

K **Kalidasa,** greatest of Sanskrit dramatists, is generally supposed to have lived about 400, in the time of Chandragupta II. In addition to his greatest play, *Shankuntula,* he composed epics and poems.

M **Mughals** formed a Mongol Muslim dynasty in India. They were established by Baber (a descendant of Genghiz Khan). He became king of Ferghana in 1495, fought the Uzbeks, and in 1504 took Kabul. In 1526 he invaded India, ended the SULTANATE OF DELHI, and replaced it by the Mughal dynasty.

P **Parakrama Bahu I** (reigned c.1153), a great Sri Lankan builder of temples and palaces, also restored its ancient irrigation system. He is quoted as saying 'None of the water that comes from rain must flow into the ocean without being made useful to men.' He ruled a flourishing Buddhist civilization from Polonnaruwa, but his fore-

Left: A Buddha sits serenely in a niche in the vast brick-built monument of Borobudur in central Java. Built about 800 by the Sailendra dynasty, Borobudur began as a natural earth mound around which the monument was constructed. The terrace walls are carved with scenes depicting the lives of the Buddha and Buddhist saints. Borobudur represents in stone, the Mahayana idea of the universe.

lims) for 200 years, but even they did not fully conquer the south, where several independent kingdoms flourished, notably the CHOLAS.

The Cambodian empire of the Khmers

Cambodia came under the influence of the Indians about AD 100, when the kingdom of Funan was founded by Kaundinya, a brahmin known as King of the Mountain. Funan was the basis for the Buddhist-Hindu empire of the Khmers, whose capital was built at Angkor in 802 and reached a population of a million.

Below: Ritual bathing in the holy Ganges River at Benares has been practised by Hindus for perhaps 2,000 years or more. Bathing begins before dawn and is over by early morning. Hindus hope that after death their cremated remains will be finally thrown into the Ganges.

At the height of its achievement, the empire was ruled by Jayavarman VII (reigned 1181–c.1219), who was famous for his highly sculptured temples and palaces. The Bayon was his most extravagant temple dedicated to the god Lokeswara, who combined four personalities: Siva, Vishnu, Buddha, and Jayavarman himself. The god was represented 200 times on the temple.

The king's architectural excesses exhausted the Khmers and they eventually fell to the newly emerged Thai kingdom. Encouraged by KUBLAI KHAN *(see page 91)* the Thais constantly attacked Angkor, and sacked it in 1431. The Khmers retreated and abandoned their fabulous capital to the jungle.

Malaya and Indonesia

Several Indianized kingdoms grew up in Malaya and Indonesia, especially the empire of SRIVIJAYA. This spread from Palembang in southern Sumatra in the 600s to control most of Malaya by 775. Java too was Indianized by the SAILENDRA dynasty, who in the late 700s built Borobudur, a huge Buddhist stupa, or monument, in central Java. When the Sailendra lost Java, they took over Srivijaya, but their power waned by the 1000s, and their empire disintegrated. Nearer the mother country, the Indian Tamil Chola kings invaded Buddhist SRI LANKA where they introduced Hinduism.

ign wars exhausted SRI LANKA'S energies. After his reign had ended northern Sri Lanka was invaded by the Tamils and its capital was moved further and further south to reach Kotte (near Colombo) in the 1500s.

S **Sailendra** (Kings of the Mountain), the Javanese dynasty that built BOROBUDUR, lost Java but took over SRIVIJAYA by the mid-800s.

Sri Lanka, an island off the coast of India which used to be called Ceylon, was a flourishing Buddhist civilization centred on the northern capital of Anuradhapura. About 1001-04 the Chola King Rajaraja I invaded from India and brought Hinduism with him. The Sri Lankans then moved their capital south to Polonnaruwa until King Parakrama Bahu I drove out the Cholas. He also restored the irrigation system that had been built by Mahasen, a heretical king reigning in the 300s.

Srivijaya, based on Palembang, southern Sumatra, profited in the 600s from Arab-Chinese trade. By 775 it controlled the waters around Sumatra and had annexed Kedah, Kelantan, Pahang and Trengganu in Malaya. But by the mid-800s, a SAILENDRA king from Java had taken over Srivijaya. The empire went into slow decline after several Chola attacks began from southern India in 1031.

Sultanate of Delhi (1211-1526) was set up following the conquests of Qutb ud-din Aibak in the 1190s. Qutb assumed power in Lahore in 1206, but was killed playing *chaugan* (a game similar to polo) in 1210, a year before the Sultanate came into being.

T **Thai** people had lived near the Yangtse Kiang for 600 years before they began to muster their forces around AD 100. Then they moved south to form the kingdoms of Sukhothai (about 1238), Chiang Mai (later 1200s), Laos and Siam (by about 1350). When the Burmese kingdom of Pagan collapsed in 1287, the Thai were encouraged to expand further by KUBLAI KHAN (*see page 91*). In 1431 they sacked ANGKOR, and set up their capital at Ayuthaya.

Iron Pillar of Delhi

W **White Huns** may have been a fair-skinned branch of the Yueh-chih who set up the Kushan kingdom in India about AD 80.

Muhammad's teachings and the *Arabian Nights* of the Caliph of Baghdad lie at opposite ends of the Islamic cultural spectrum. What is often forgotten is the great Arab contribution to medicine, the physical sciences and literature.

The Arabs

The outside world knew little about the Arabs until the 600s, when, fired with the fervour of their new religion of Islam, they swept out of the sand deserts of Arabia into the more fertile regions of Asia, Africa and Europe. Within a century, they conquered and converted to Islam an area larger than the old Roman empire. They absorbed the learning of the ancient world, and later passed it on to the Europeans. They evolved unique styles of ART and for several centuries led the Western world in cultural attainment. The Arab-Islamic civilization began dramatically in 622 as the result of a single incident in the life of one man - Muhammad (570–632).

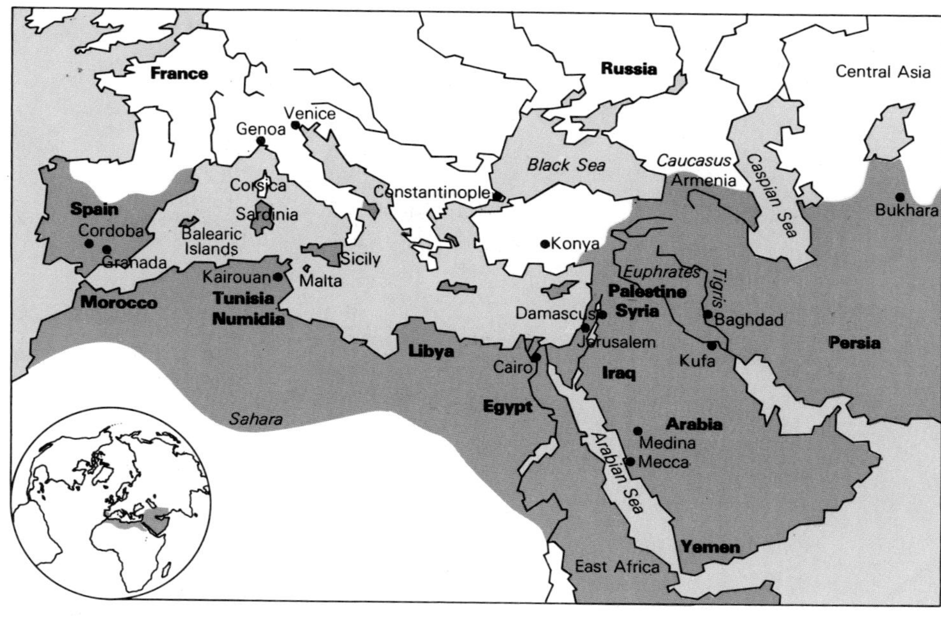

Above: Emerging from the Arabian desert in AD 632, the Muslims won a great empire. The map shows the empire's extent in 945.

Muhammad – a prophet from the desert

Muhammad, an orphan, was brought up by his relatives in Mecca, a wealthy town standing at the crossroads of the Arabian trade routes, and a centre of religious pilgrimage. The Arabs of that time worshipped the moon, many idols, and certain stones. The most sacred of these was the Black Stone, housed in the Kaaba, a large, cube-shaped building in Mecca. But not all visitors to Mecca worshipped the Black Stone. Some were Jews, Christians or MANDAEANS and the many religious arguments that Muhammad heard made a deep impression on him.

At the age of 25, Muhammad took employment as caravan manager to Khadija, a wealthy widow of 40 whom he later married. Muhammad began to have visions in which he claimed that Allah spoke to him, and gradually he evolved a new faith, *Islam* (Submission). Its demands were simple: give up the worship of idols and stones and submit to the one God, Allah.

Few supported Muhammad beyond close relatives, some slaves, and a merchant named Abu Bakr, because most Meccans saw their profits bound up with the continuance of the pilgrimages to the Kaaba. They believed that Muhammad's activities threatened their livelihood, and one night civic leaders sent soldiers to arrest him. Muhammad escaped in the darkness accompanied by Abu Bakr. The Meccans put a price of 100 camels on Muhammad's head, but did not catch him. His flight from Mecca – the Hegira (622) – is the most important event in Islam's history. From it dates the MUSLIM ERA.

Above: The bustling spice market in Cairo still retains the character of the past.

A triumphal return to Mecca

Muhammad and Abu Bakr first hid in a cave, then travelled on camel-back 300 kilometres north to the rival trading town of Medina. Word had gone before and the Medinans accepted Muhammad's new religion and made him their ruler. In 630, Muhammad rode back in triumph to Mecca at the head of an army. He smashed the idols in the Kaaba but, by sparing the Black Stone, won the Meccans for Islam.

When Muhammad died in 632, most of Arabia

Reference

A Abbasid family descended from Abbas, uncle of Muhammad. In 750 the head of the family, Abu-L-Abbas, became the first of 37 Abbasid caliphs ruling mainly from Baghdad.

Abd al-Rahman (731-88), a boy of 20 when the Abbasids murdered his UMMAYAD relatives, swam the Euphrates to escape the killers. His brother turned back, and was murdered. Destitute, Abd al-Rahman wandered for 5 years as a fugitive before reaching Spain, where he re-founded the Umayyad dynasty.

Alcohol, strictly forbidden by Muhammad and the Arabian caliphs, was illegally enjoyed by the easier-going citizens of Damascus and Baghdad. Jews and Christians became the 'bootleggers' of the times.

Ali (c. 600–61) expected to become caliph at the death of Muhammad (his father-in-law), but Umar arranged the accession of Abu Bakr instead. Ali eventually became fourth caliph in 656, but was assassinated by the Kaharijites, an extreme Muslim sect. His death divided Islam.

Al-Kindi (c.800s), primarily a philosopher who interpreted Aristotle, wrote some 265 works on an immense number of topics. He attacked alchemy and miracles.

Gardens of Alhambra palace

Arab travellers included Ibn Batuta, who left Morocco on the HAJJ to Mecca in 1325. Travel so inspired him that he went on for another 120,000 km into Yemen, East Africa, Persia, India, Sri Lanka, Sumatra, China, central Asia and Siberia. Later, he crossed the Sahara into the kingdoms of Mali and Songhai. His accounts reveal otherwise unknown aspects of history.

Arabian Nights, originally a collection of tales from several countries, especially India, were 'arabized' in Baghdad and set amid the

Below: The *mihrab*, a niche in the mosque wall, must be accurately positioned. By facing it when they pray, Muslims can be sure that they are also facing Mecca. The *mihrab* shown is in the solidly-constructed Hassan mosque built in Cairo by the Mamluke rulers of Egypt in the mid-1300s.

Right: Beautifully-illustrated Korans became one of the main features of Arab art. Because Muhammed disapproved of portraying humans and animals, Muslim artists set their talents to devising pleasing geometrical designs and superb calligraphy, such as is shown on this double page from a Koran.

had been conquered for Islam. Mecca became the main religious centre, while Medina remained the hub of political affairs.

The caliphs of Mecca

At Muhammad's death, the faithful Abu Bakr was elected caliph (successor). Humble as ever, he continued to sell his cloth in the market place of Medina, while his army commanders began a *jihad* (holy war) in his name against the Byzantines in Syria. Abu Bakr outlived Muhammad by only two years. Umar, an early convert who had at one time persecuted Muhammad, succeeded him (634–44), and was in turn followed by Uthman, Muhammad's elderly son-in-law (644–56). Both men met death at the hands of assassins.

Uthman's killers appointed ALI, also a son-in-law of Muhammad, as fourth caliph (651–61), but many took up arms against him, including AYESHA, one of Muhammad's widows. Eventually, Ali took her captive on a battlefield where more than 12,000 Muslims lay dead. After five years as caliph, Ali too, was assassinated. The caliphate at first passed to his son HASAN, but Ali's sworn enemy, Muawiya, forced him to abdicate and founded the UMAYYAD dynasty, which ruled from Damascus 661–750.

The Umayyads in Damascus

Damascus had been a Roman-Byzantine city for 700 years, and in Muawiya's time it took on a lively character that remained largely unchanged into the present century. Baggy-trousered turbanned merchants jostled in the narrow market streets with loose-gowned Bedouin from Arabia.

court of Harun al-Rashid (c.764–809).

Architecture of merit barely existed in Muhammad's time. In spirit, the Arabs lived as tent-dwelling nomads. Their conquests changed this, and they took over the temples and churches of conquered peoples and turned them into mosques. Their own buildings usually followed local architectural styles and they had no desire to compete with the Byzantine grandeur. They thought rather that mosques should be simple houses of prayer. When churches or Zoroastrian fire temples became mosques, structural changes had to be made. Christians faced eastwards to the altar; Muslims southwards to Mecca. In newly built towns, early mosques were extremely simple, and at Kufa, in Iraq, the Muslims merely enclosed a square of land by a ditch. Then they built a *zulla*, or covered colonnade, from the marble of ruined buildings along the side nearest to Mecca to protect worshippers from the burning sun. Within half a century, Islam lost its simplicity and the Dome of the Rock in Jerusalem (built 687–91) and the Umayyad mosque in Damascus (completed 715) borrowed much from the Byzantine style. The Muslims also built great citadels which influenced castle architecture in Europe by way of the CRUSADES.

Golden Friday mosque, Baghdad

Art in the Arab world centres mainly around the mosque. It includes glassmaking, metal working, ceramic tilework, plasterwork, textiles, wood carving, carpet and rug making, book illustration, book binding and calligraphy. Muhammad banned idols and images, which led to an absence of sculpture and of the representation of humans and animals in paintings.

Assassins belonged to the Ismaili sect. The name came from *hashish*, the drug under whose influence they carried out sacred murders.

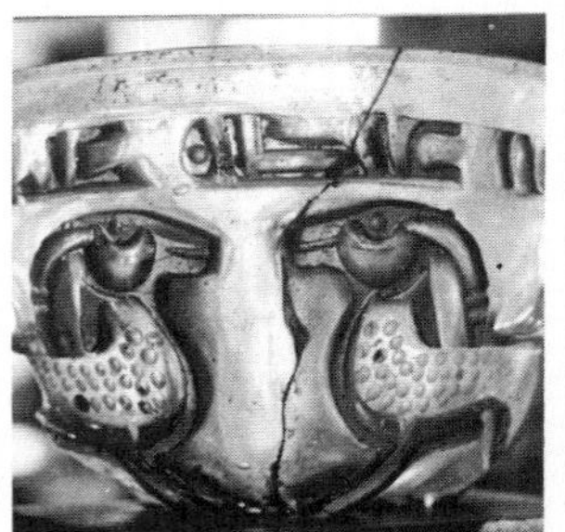

Early Arabic glass

Veiled women peeped through high latticed windows into the traffic below where sherbert and sweetmeat vendors called their wares above the din. Harassed men whipped donkeys and camels into the bazaars, rich with the smell of spices, perfumes and foodstuffs. The rooms of private houses surrounded courtyards in which stood fountains connected to the city's water supply.

Class structure

Below the caliph and his household were four classes: the Arabian Muslims; newly-converted Muslims; *dhimmis* (Jews, Christians and Mandaeans); and SLAVES. The converts included mainly Jews, Byzantines, Syrians, Persians and Egyptians, who quickly adopted Arab ways, but had a higher cultural level than the true Arabs. They eagerly married Arabs, served in the government, and became the most fanatical Muslims. The dhimmis enjoyed considerably more freedom than the slaves, who came mostly from Spain, Africa and central Asia.

The converts led the way in Arab medicine, philosophy, mathematics, science, art, literature and even language. Because of their origins, they borrowed heavily from higher civilizations. Converts rebuilt the Christian Basilica of St John in Damascus (originally a temple to Jupiter), which became the magnificent Umayyad mosque.

The caliphs of Damascus and Baghdad

In Damascus, the stark puritanism of the desert Muslims seemed out of place. The easy-going Caliph Muawiya married a Christian, appointed non-Muslims to government posts, and honoured poets, a group abhorred and banned by Muhammad. The Umayyad court enjoyed music, song, gambling and drinking. Successive caliphs became more and more worldly, and Hisham (reigned 724–43) neglected the empire for horseracing. His nephew Walid, who inherited an empire extending from Morocco to Mongolia, was atheistic, proud and talented, but incompetent. The Damascus mob cut off his head in 744, and paraded it through the streets on a spear.

The Umayyads tottered on for another six years, until the rival ABBASID FAMILY mustered a large army in Persia, where people still mourned the murder of Ali. They attacked in alliance with a breakaway sect called the SHI'ITES. In remembrance of Ali, the Abbasids and Shi'ites draped their soldiers, horses and camels in black, and

Above: The black-draped Kaaba in Mecca, the holiest shrine in Islam, was a centre of worship long before the time of Muhammad. It houses the sacred Black Stone. Muslims from every part of the world are expected to visit the Kaaba once in their lifetime. They are then respected as *hajjis* or pilgrims.

Left: Oases were the settled homes of the early Arabs and the halting places for desert traders and nomads. The essential thing that an oasis must have is water. The picture shows Nefta, an oasis of south-western Tunisia that grew into a town. Islam spread through the desert from oasis to oasis before it was established in the cities of the Mediterranean hinterland.

Hasan Sabbah founded the order of Assassins about 1090, from a mountain top south of the Caspian Sea.
Astrolabes, used to measure altitudes, positions and movements of heavenly bodies, became the main instrument of navigation until the invention of the sextant in the 1700s.
Avicenna or Ibn Sina (980–1037) was a converted Arab physician-philosopher born near Bukhara. His views led the field in world medicine 1100-1500.
Ayesha (died 678), daughter of Abu Bakr, married Muhammad when she was 9 and he was 52. About the same time, Muhammad's 15-year-old daughter, Fatima, married ALI. Ayesha opposed Ali's appointment as caliph in 656, raised Iraq to revolt and fought him until he captured her.

B **Baghdad,** on the Tigris, was founded by Mansur, second ABBASID caliph, in 762 and its population reached 2 million. It was destroyed by Mongols in 1258 and 1400, and again by Persians in 1524.
Berbers have lived in north-western Africa since prehistory, and their culture has been traced back to 2400 BC. Many were Jews or Christians before they became Muslims.

C **Circassians** came from the Black Sea-Caucasus area (now south-western USSR).
Crusades. The First Crusade (1096–99) began at the urging of Pope Urban II (c.1042–99), who responded to an appeal from the emperor of Constantinople to free Palestine from the Seljuk Turks. The Crusaders (mainly Franks) took Jerusalem in 1099. The Second Crusade (1147–49), led by Franks and Germans, ended in a Muslim victory.

Arab tilework

The Third Crusade (1189–92), led by the French, German and English kings, failed to recapture Jerusalem from SALADIN. In the Fourth Crusade (1202–04) penniless Crusaders stranded in Venice struck a bargain with the Venetians to ship them to the eastern Mediterranean. In return they joined forces and plundered wealthy Constantinople. They deposed the Byzantine emperor and installed Baldwin of Flanders as first of the Latin emperors who ruled from Constantinople 1204–61. A Children's

Left: Granada, one of the showpieces of the Arab world, was the last part of Spain to be lost by the Arabs. The splendid Court of Lions in the dream-like Alhambra palace in Granada city, incorporates the finest features of Arab architecture. It took 200 years to build and was completed shortly before all Spain was lost to the Christians.

flew black banners. West of the Tigris they defeated the Umayyads in a terrible nine-days' battle and swept into Damascus. Then, by a trick, they murdered almost the entire Umayyad family and set up the Abbasid caliphate in the SUNNITE tradition. The second Abbasid caliph transferred the capital to the new city of BAGHDAD, and for the next 500 years nearby PERSIA dominated the character of Islam.

By the reign of Harun al-Rashid, fabled caliph of the ARABIAN NIGHTS, Baghdad became one of the world's most splendid cities and the caliph's luxurious palace, rising to a height of 40 metres over the audience chamber, boasted the costliest furnishings in Asia. Harun's cousin-wife, Zubaydal, studded her shoes with gems. Musicians, poets, and other worldly guests of the royal pair ate sumptuous food from gold and silver containers ornamented with jewels. The wealthy merchants of Baghdad took to drinking ALCOHOL, and spent much of their time at the public baths or at sports meetings.

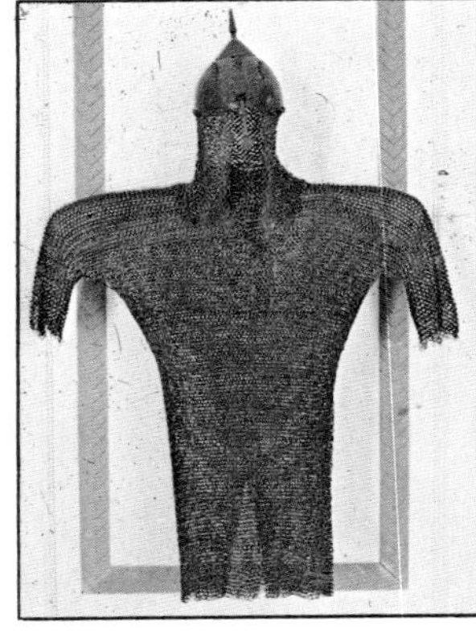

Above: A Mamluke soldier wore this coat of mail in the early 1300s. The Mamlukes twice halted foreign invaders when all other Arab resistance had failed.

Trade and translation

The Muslims first turned to seafaring in Muawiya's time and under the Abbasids, Arab and Persian ships laden with drugs, gems, pearls and spices sailed to Tang dynasty China and brought back bronze mirrors, ironware, porcelain, silks and tea. The wharves of Baghdad's port on the Tigris extended for several kilometres, and their warehouses held a hundred imports from Arabia, Egypt, Africa, Syria, Persia, central Asia, India, Malaya, China, Russia and Scandinavia. The Arabs traded along overland camel routes. Their Arab ships did not use the square sail of the Europeans, but the *lateen*, a tall triangular sail that caught the wind on either side, yet kept the same edge forward. Diplomacy followed in the wake of trade. But an Arab envoy to the court of China ruffled court etiquette by refusing to kowtow to the Tang emperor, saying that he bowed only to Allah.

The Abbasids grew hungry for learning and promoted translations into Arabic from Greek, Persian, Sanskrit and Syrian works of science and philosophy. Gradually, Arabic became the language of all learned people from Spain to central Asia. While the Frank emperor Charlemagne *(see page 88)* could just write his name, Harun al-Rashid studied translations of complex works. Through Arab scholars, the forgotten learning of the ancient world eventually found its way into the Latin books of medieval Europe.

Culture and science in Baghdad

By 850, Arab scholarship flourished in its own right. Textbooks on medicine were written by RHAZES and AVICENNA, and AL-KINDI wrote some 265 works on subjects ranging from optics to music. The Arabs were interested in more than the theory of medicine, and established pharmacies, hospitals and rural clinics.

Learning from India, Arab astronomers made regular observations with accurate instruments by the 900s and built observatories near Baghdad and Damascus. Using the ASTROLABE, dial, globe and quadrant, the caliph's astronomer measured the length of a degree of the

---

Crusade (1212) resulted in the death or enslavement of 50,000 children before they left Europe. There were several further Crusades, lasting into the 1400s, but these were not of great importance.

E **Emir,** a title given to Arab chieftains, is especially connected with the supposed descendants of Muhammad's daughter, FATIMA.

F **Fatima** (606–32) daughter of Muhammad and Khadija, married ALI.

Fatimite (or Fatimid) dynasty claimed descent from Fatima. Between the 900s and the 1100s, they occupied at various times, Tunisia, Sicily, Algeria, Libya, Malta, Sardinia, Corsica, Balearic Islands, Genoa, Egypt, Palestine and Syria. The Fatimite dynasty ended when SALADIN took Egypt in 1170.

G **Granada** became capital city of the kingdom of Granada, the last Spanish region held by the Moors, in 1238. It fell to the Christians in 1492. The city contains the Alhambra, the Moorish citadel and palace.

H **Hajj** (pilgrimage to Mecca) is commanded by the Koran, and millions make the journey every year. Hajji walk 7 times around the Kaaba and kiss the sacred Black Stone while wearing only unsewn clothes. They usually also visit the Muhammad mosque at Medina and the pilgrimage ends with Id al-Adha, a feast at which healthy sheep, goats or camels are sacrificed, and their meat given to the poor.

Hasan, son of ALI and grandson of Muhammad, abdicated as fifth caliph in 661 under pressure from the UMAYYADS. The SHI'ITES believed that the Umayyads poisoned Hasan. He and Ali are the two chief Shi'ite martyrs.

Masyaf Castle, near Hama, Syria

I **Iberians** settled in Spain before 600 BC, probably coming from Africa.

Iman is the faith in Allah and in his prophet, Muhammad, that all Muslims must have. It is also the name given to the priest of a mosque.

J **Jerusalem,** already sacred to Jews and Christians, was also favoured by the early Muslims. They believed that

earth's circumference to within one per cent of accuracy. One of the astronomer-mathematicians about 1100 was UMAR KHAYYAM better known in his role as the free-thinking Persian poet.

The Arabs also pioneered alchemy and chemistry, using the experimental method rather than the inadequate philosophical approach of the Greeks. Arab research proved fairly accurate, and was based on the patient collection and analysis of fact. Their weakness lay in failing to project hypotheses from which they could draw scientifically-based conclusions.

Arab geography and Muslim law

The religious obligation for Muslims to make the HAJJ (pilgrimage) to Mecca, and to position the MIHRAB in mosques so that worshippers faced Mecca, inspired the study of geography. Al-Masudi, one of many intrepid ARAB TRAVELLERS, visited places as far apart as Madagascar, Sri Lanka and China, questioning peoples of different religions and recording his findings.

Astrology also promoted geography, because astrologers needed to determine latitudes and longitudes. Using a translation of PTOLEMY'S GEOGRAPHY, some 70 scholars, led by a mathematician called Khwarizmi (780–c.850), constructed a vast map of the earth and sky. But although Muslim merchants found their way into Africa, China and Russia, they feared to venture into the 'Sea of Darkness': the Atlantic.

Below: A Crusader knight engages in a fight to the death with his Saracen counterpart in one of the many bloody battles for possession of the 'Holy Land' of Palestine and Syria. 'Saracen' became the general term for all those Muslims who fought the Crusaders.

Muhammad ascended to heaven from there, at the spot where a rock now protrudes through the Dome of the Rock. Muhammad at first prayed towards Jerusalem; only later towards the Kaaba in Mecca. The city is still sacred to the 3 religions.

M

Mamlukes (in Arabic, *slaves*), were originally Turks, Mongols and CIRCASSIANS enslaved by the Arabs. The caliphs of Egypt used them as soldiers, but they came to dominate their 'masters' and from 1250 became sultans of Egypt. Ottoman Turks ended their dynasty in 1517, but the Mamlukes kept most of their power until 1811.

Mandaeans (or Sabians), a sect from Persia, held beliefs similar to the Zoroastrians, Magi, and Babylonian astrologers. They honoured St John the Baptist because they believed in ritual bathing, although they baptized long before St John's time. Mandaeans still practise their religion in Iran and Iraq, and their holy book is the *Ginza Rba*.

Marrakesh, the south-western centre of Muslim trade and culture, was the Moroccan capital 1062–1259.

Mihrab, a niche in the mosque wall, is the place where an IMAN leads the Muslims in prayer. Because they must face Mecca when praying, the positioning of the *mihrab* is crucial.

Mosque in Tinerhir, Morocco

Muslim era dates from the Hegira, Muhammad's flight from Mecca to Medina in 622. AH is used before Muslim years, just as AD is used in front of Christian years. Following the moon rather than the sun, the Arabs had 12 months alternately of 29 or 30 days in length, giving a 354-day year. The Muslim year is therefore 11.25 days short of the solar year of the Christians.

Muslim law (Sharia) is a combined and complex system of civil and criminal law and social and religious behaviour, still used by Islamic countries. It is based on the *Revelations*, words of God revealed to Muhammad and recorded in the Koran, and *Hadith* (tradition). *Hadith* is the teachings of Muhammad not directly revealed by God and not included in the Koran.

Muslim-Christian clashes encouraged the Christians to consider an alliance with the

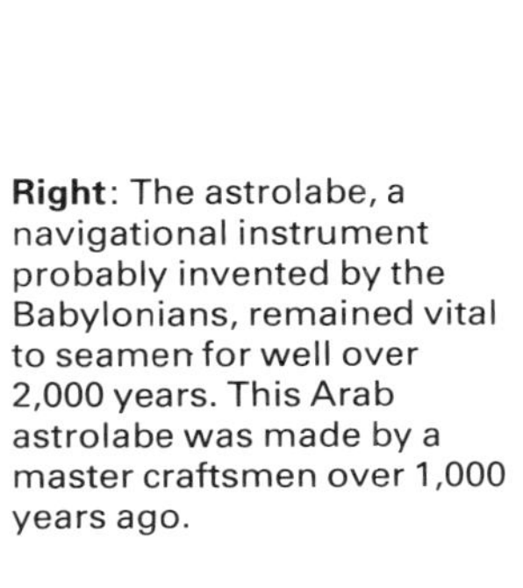

Left: Arab trading boats such as the one shown became a familiar sight in the Mediterranean and Arabian seas from the time of the Umayyad caliphate onwards. Later, Arab seamen sailed eastwards to India and China.

Right: The astrolabe, a navigational instrument probably invented by the Babylonians, remained vital to seamen for well over 2,000 years. This Arab astrolabe was made by a master craftsmen over 1,000 years ago.

A complex system of MUSLIM LAW derived from the Muslim holy book, the Koran, and from *Hadith*, which laid down the rules for political, social and religious behaviour. A Muslim's duties were contained in the 'five pillars of Islam': hajj (pilgrimage); IMAN (faith); SALAT (prayer); SAUM (fasting); and ZAKAT (almsgiving).

Umayyad Spain

Not all the Umayyads died in 750. One, ABD AL-RAHMAN, fled westwards and became EMIR of Spain (756–88). He transformed Spain into a land of spacious cities laid out with gardens and strove hard to weld the various peoples of the country, Arabs, BERBERS, Goths, IBERIANS, NUMIDIANS and Syrians, into one nation.

Abd al-Rahman chose for his capital the ancient city of Cordoba, where he built a palace with gardens and the Great Mosque, all in the Syrian style. He also built hundreds of smaller mosques, baths, and an aqueduct to supply the city with pure water. Cordoba soon grew to a city of 500,000 surpassed in culture only by Constantinople and Baghdad. In 929, Abd al-Rahman III (891–961) took the title caliph in opposition to the ABBASID FAMILY.

Industry and trade boomed in Umayyad Spain. The cordwainers (leather workers) especially, were world-famed. The country also excelled in agricultural science, especially fruit-growing. The 'hard currency' coinage of Umayyad Spain passed freely throughout the Christian countries to the north. Cordoba became the centre of learning, and its university, founded in the 900s, was known all over the world. The caliph Al-Harun is said to have accumulated 400,000 books, more than 20 times as many books as then existed in Christian Europe.

North Africa

All North Africa fell to the Arabs in the 600s. At first, the Egyptians remained Coptic Christians, but later most converted to Islam to secure social and financial advantages. Arab migration into Egypt played an important part in forming the country's culture and religion.

Kairouan in Tunisia, founded as a sacred city in 670, became the capital of the Arab FATIMITE dynasty in 909. This dynasty, founded by Ubaidullah, claimed descent from Muhammad's daughter, FATIMA. From Tunisia, the Fatimites took Libya and Egypt, founded Cairo in 969 and the Al-Azhar mosque and university in 970. Their dynasty lasted 200 years before falling to SALADIN in 1171.

Mongols, and in 1245 the pope sent a Franciscan friar to the Great Khan in Mongolia. Louis IX of France followed suit and sent a Flemish missionary in 1253, but nothing came of either of these contacts.

N

Numidians came from Numidia, roughly present-day Algeria.

P

Persia destroyed by Alexander the Great, rose again in 226 under the dynasty of the Sassanids, who restored the Zoroastrian religion. In 260 the Sassanid emperor Shapur I (241–72) defeated the Roman emperor Valerian, who died in captivity. The Sassanids built an empire that at times extended into Syria, Armenia and Egypt. Sassanid Persia finally fell to the Arabs in 641–42, and replaced Zoroastrianism with Islam.

Ptolemy's Geography remained a standard work for 1,400 years after the Greco-Egyptian scientist produced it in about 127-41. The work had many errors because Ptolemy underestimated the earth's circumference.

R

Rhazes (c.860–c.925), chief physician at the Baghdad hospital, produced several textbooks on medicine. In one of these he distinguished between smallpox and measles. Europeans printed his textbooks in Latin translation 500 years after his death.

S

Saladin (or Salah-al-Din, 1138–93), a Kurd, took Egypt for the ABBASIDS, but in 1170 proclaimed himself sultan, so beginning the Ayyubite dynasty. He extended his territory into Tunisia, Yemen, Damascus and Jerusalem. A brilliant general who fought the Crusaders, Saladin was also a man of considerable culture.

Inscriptions in plaster, Alhambra

Salat (Muslim prayers) must be recited 5 times a day: at dawn, noon, afternoon, evening and nightfall. Desert Muslims prayed facing Mecca after washing in water; if there was none, they used sand.

Saum (fasting) is prescribed during Ramadan, the ninth month of the Muslim year, when Muslims may not eat, drink or smoke between sunrise and sunset. Travellers, sick people, nursing mothers, and soldiers on active service are exempt. Ramadan ends with the feast of Id al-Fitr.

In the 1000s the Almoravides (Muslim Berbers) seized Morocco for the Arabs, then took over Umayyad Spain. Another Berber dynasty, the Almohades, took over in Morocco and Spain in the 1170s.

Seljuks and Crusaders

Although the Abbasids never held Spain, and lost North Africa and Syria-Palestine to the Fatimites, the period 750-1055 proved to be a 'golden age'. This was followed by a series of troubles, beginning when the Seljuk Turks attacked from central Asia. In 1055, the Seljuk leader Tughril swept unopposed into Baghdad. Although he allowed the Abbasids to remain caliphs, Tughril dominated their empire as sultan. Further west, the tougher Fatimites successfully resisted the Seljuks, who set up their capital at Konya in Asia Minor, but in 1092 after the death of their strong sultan, Malik Shah, they split into factions.

By the late 1000s, several strong Christian kingdoms had been established which resented the Muslim occupation of Spain and Syria-Palestine, and consequently MUSLIM-CHRISTIAN CLASHES became frequent. The most important were the CRUSADES, fought about 1096-1291. The Crusaders took JERUSALEM in 1099, but SALADIN retook it for the Abbasids in 1187.

Mongols and Spanish Christians

The Abbasids' most terrible and final peril came when Genghiz Khan began the great Mongol expansion. Having conquered northern China, he and his successors rode westwards into Russia and central Europe. In 1258, Hulagu, grandson of Genghiz Khan, led the final assault that breached the walls of Baghdad. The Mongols poured into the starving city, murdered the caliph, his family and officials, massacred more than half of Baghdad's two million people, and razed the city to the ground. Plague inevitably broke out. Once again, effective resistance came from Egypt, since 1254 under the control of the MAMLUKES.

In Spain, the Christians pushed the declining Muslims ever southwards, and by 1276, only GRANADA remained Muslim. Although the great days of the Arabs were over, the Islamic religion continued to expand under foreign leadership.

Below: Baghdad's chequered history reached its climax in 1258, when Hulagu, grandson of Genghiz Khan, laid siege to the city with stone-slinging machines and flame throwers. The Mongols destroyed the city after its surrender, killed half of its 2 million inhabitants, and beat the caliph to death. Here Mongols and Arabs are seen in full battle.

Shi'ites (or Shiahs), supporters of ALI and his descendants, belong to the smaller of the 2 main divisions of Islam. Shi'ite sects include Ismailis, and their sub-sect ASSASSINS, FATIMITES and SUFIS.

Slaves of the Arabs numbered several millions of captives from different nations. Muslims could not enslave other Muslims, but slaves who converted to Islam remained slaves. Several slaves gained their freedom and attained high positions – even the caliphate. In Egypt slaves founded the successful MAMLUKE dynasty.

Sufis added ideas from Plato, Buddhism and Christianity to their SHI'ITE beliefs. UMAR KHAYYAM was one of several Sufi poets.

Gateway in Marrakesh

Sunnites are members of 4 Islamic sects (Hanifite, Malikite, Shafi'ite or Hanbalite) that follow the main tradition of Islam. 90 per cent of all Muslims are Sunnite. Apart from SHI'ITES, other sects include Ikwan (Wahabis) and Kharijites.

U

Umar Khayyam (1000s), a Persian poet and scientist, became the outstanding mathematician of his time. His RUBAIYAT contains the famous lines (in translation) 'The Moving Finger writes, and having writ moves on . . .'

Umayyads, a family at first hostile to Muhammad, provided the third caliph, Uthman, Muhammad's son-in-law. The sixth caliph, Muawiya, made the caliphate hereditary, and was followed in Damascus by 13 other Umayyad caliphs.

Z

Zakat (almsgiving) is both compulsory and voluntary for Muslims, who had to give some 2 per cent of the wealth they had held for a year. They were also expected to give alms beyond this amount.

Sand dunes in the Sahara

Charlemagne was the first of the Holy Roman emperors, crowned by Pope Leo III. In return for papal backing, he promoted church affairs and education. Many of the great European monasteries and monastic orders were founded by the Franks.

The Franks

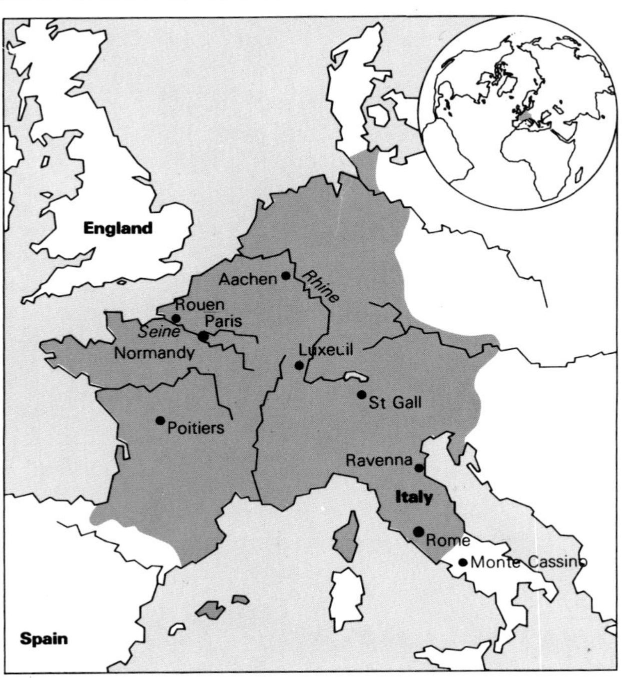

Left: Under Charlemagne, the kingdom of the Franks emerged as the successor to the Roman empire in the West. But culturally it proved no match for Byzantium, and its unity disappeared soon after Charlemagne's death.

The collapse of Rome signalled the rise to power of the Germanic Franks. Between 481 and 800 they built up a star-shaped empire with its 'points' in modern Spain, Normandy, Denmark, Hungary and Italy. It became the first truly European Christian empire and one of its important legacies was the establishment of many great MONASTERIES, centres of learning and art. Under Charlemagne (*see page 88*) the empire reached its peak and challenged Byzantium as heir to Rome.

The tribal empire

The Franks were the northernmost of the GERMANIC TRIBES attacking the old Roman frontiers, and by the 200s they had settled along the middle and lower Rhine River. The northern Franks allied themselves to Rome and moved southwards into Gaul. When the northern leader, CLOVIS I, united all the Franks into an orderly Christian empire, the pope readily supported him. Clovis established the Merovingian dynasty and reigned 481-511.

Frankish arts

The period of the Frankish empire before Charlemagne is often called the 'Dark Ages', but the arts flourished in north-west Europe. Information about them comes mainly from finds made in graves of the period; much jewellery as well as normal grave goods were based on Roman originals.

Frankish jewellery is very distinctive, the early forms copying late Roman belt buckles. Massive gold brooches are typical, often heavily set with garnets, ornamented with gold or silver filigree, and sometimes using late Roman gold coins as pendants. Particularly rich Frankish graves have been found at various places such as Cologne and outside Paris.

Right: This magnificent gold reliquary set with precious jewels is a fine example of the superior quality of Frankish art.

Reference

A **Aachen** (Aix-la-Chapelle), probable birthplace of Charlemagne, became his main capital, where he built his palace and a splendid cathedral that houses his tomb. The cathedral was largely rebuilt in the 900s after NORSEMEN destroyed it.

Administrators. Charlemagne ruled as an autocrat aided by his favourites and religious and secular officials. Dukes or 'margraves' ruled groups of counties in border areas, and from 200–250 interior counties each came under the control of a count. Each bishop's diocese normally covered the same area as a county. From 802 the counties were gathered in groups of 6–10, each of which became a district inspected annually by Charlemagne's envoys. He also visited each district in turn himself until ill health prevented him from travelling.

Architecture and art of the Carolingians was a combination of Roman, Byzantine and German styles reflected particularly in the illustrated manuscripts and ivory and enamel work of the Frankish monks. Charlemagne's round palace church at Aachen was embellished by columns, mosaics and marble which Charlemagne ordered to be brought from Italy.

C **Capet,** Hugh (reigned 987–96), fought the last Carolingian king to possess the French crown and found the Capetian dynasty.

Church affairs became a special interest of Charlemagne's. He arranged for the clergy to be educated, intervened in the appointment of bishops, and arbitrated in religious disputes.

Carolingian ivory plaque

Clovis I (465–511) a tribal chieftain, murdered his way to the leadership of the Salian (northern) Franks by 481. In 486 he finally ended Roman control over Gaul, and became a Christian in gratitude for victory over the Alemanni in 496.

E **Education** was encouraged by Charlemagne, who set up schools to teach and train the clergy. His own palace was a centre of intellectual activity.

F **France** as a kingdom dates from the signing of

the Short (reigned 751–68) deposed the last Merovingian king in 751, Pope Zacharias hastened to crown him first king of the Carolingian dynasty.

Charlemagne

Pepin's son, Charlemagne, expanded the empire to its greatest extent. On Christmas Day 800, Pope LEO III crowned him emperor of the West. Until Charlemagne, the Franks had lived in small self-sufficient communities which had existed since pre-Roman times, where money had virtually no value because little trade existed beyond barter. Charlemagne reimposed a centralized government from his capital at AACHEN in the north and gave land to nobles who worked as judges, ADMINISTRATORS and army commanders, instead of paying rent. Poorer people had to provide food for the court and labour for government projects. Charlemagne promoted the interests of the CHURCH, EDUCATION, ARCHITECTURE and ART.

In 843, Charlemagne's three grandsons split the empire between them. The western part, the kingdom of FRANCE, soon fell prey to the NORSEMEN whose raids were concentrated around the present day Normandy area. In 987, France fell to Hugh CAPET, whose descendants ruled the kingdom for 800 years, although when Capet took over it had shrunk to little more than the area around PARIS.

The Merovingians

The Franks conquered several other Germanic tribes, and by the 700s their empire covered much of western Europe, but it was disunited into several kingdoms with shifting borders. Its main kingdoms were Neustria (roughly modern France); Austrasia (roughly Netherlands to southern Germany); and Burgundy (roughly eastern France to Switzerland). After 639, the Merovingians became known as 'the idle kings' because real power had passed to the mayors of the palace.

The popes continued to support the Franks, seeing through their power the best hope for the Church's survival through dangerous times. Their wisdom was confirmed in 732 when the energetic mayor Charles Martel (c.689-741) decisively defeated an invading Arab Muslim force near Poitiers. When Charles's son, Pepin

Above: While in Rome to act as judge over Pope Leo III's trial, Charlemagne was tricked by him. The pope put an emperor's crown on the unsuspecting king's head. In crowning him emperor of the West, the pope sought to enhance his own power and status.

Right: The power of the Frankish empire lay in Charlemagne's own military leadership. At his death there was little left to sustain its strength.

---

the Treaty of Verdun in 843, when Charles II became king of the western Franks.

Germanic tribes who were conquered by the Franks and had their lands annexed, included Alemanni, Bavarians, Burgundians, Lombards, Saxons and Thuringians.

Leo III (pope 795–816) crowned Charlemagne emperor in 800 after he had restored Rome to the pope after a revolt. This gave a sacred seal to Charlemagne's position as emperor, initiating the idea of the divine right of kings bestowed by the pope.

Monasteries existed before Christianity among the Buddhists and Jains. St Benedict (c.480–c.543) founder of the Benedictine order, probably founded European monasticism when he established the Monte Cassino monastery in about 529. He drew up rules apportioning a monk's day between worship, meditation, study and manual labour. Early Frankish monasteries were established in the 500s at Luxeuil and St Gall.

Norsemen (Norwegian and Danish Vikings) became a serious threat to the Franks and Charlemagne built a fleet to stop them. However, his successors let the fleet fall into a state of disrepair, and from about 843 the Norsemen sailed up the Seine River to loot Rouen and Paris. They encamped at the mouth of the river, preventing trade, and thus seriously threatening the future of Western civilization until in 911 they moved into their own territory. This land had been ceded to the Norse leader Rollo (c.860–c.931) by the French king, Charles the Simple (879–929). As their land expanded, it became the duchy of Normandy and the Norsemen adopted the French language and laws, were converted to Christianity, and came to call themselves Normans.

Vezelay Abbey, France

Paris became the capital of CLOVIS I and several other Merovingian kings, after which it suffered looting and famine from Norse attacks. It recovered only after Hugh CAPET made it his capital.

The history of England from the collapse of the Roman empire to AD 1100 is one of invasion. First came the Jutes, Angles and Saxons, then the Vikings, and finally the Normans under William the Conqueror.

The English

Among the Germanic peoples set in movement by the collapse of the Roman empire were the JUTES, SAXONS AND ANGLES. They left their crowded homeland near the present-day Danish-German border, crossed the North Sea, and invaded southern Britain in about 450–550. Many of the native Britons fled to the west, where they preserved their Christian religion. By 827, the invaders had established the first permanent nation-state, which survived conquest by the Danes in 1013 and by the Normans in 1066.

Germanic invasions of Celtic Britain

Roman civilization soon fell into decay after 407 and organized government gave way to control by local Celtic chieftains. One, called Vortigern, is said to have invited two Jutish leaders, HENGEST AND HORSA, to land in Kent in 449 because he needed an ally against marauding Picts from the north.

The invaders avoided the crumbling towns and moved along river valleys or Roman roads. They settled in forest clearings off the main routes to avoid attack by the next wave of immigrants, and by 613, almost all present-day England was under their rule. The three tribes lost their separate identities and eventually became known as the Anglo-Saxons.

Northern and western Britain

In the 500s, the Angles extended their kingdom of Northumbria northwards to the Firth of Forth. To the west of them, refugee Britons set up the independent kingdom of Strathclyde. Then SCOTS crossed from Ireland to establish their own kingdom of Dalriada, north of Strathclyde, bringing with them their own form of Christianity. North of Northumbria, the warlike Picts had already established a southern kingdom and a northern kingdom and by the mid-700s they also dominated Dalriada and Strathclyde. However it was the culture of the Scots that survived in Dalriada and spread with the small groups who constantly migrated eastwards into the more fertile lands of the Picts and Angles, where their Gaelic language eventually replaced Pictish.

Some Britons became slaves of the Anglo-Saxons, while others integrated with them, often by marriage. Those who fled, set up kingdoms in

Right: Having united their 7 kingdoms into a loose confederation (the Heptarchy), the English later had to share England with the Danes. To the north of England (present-day Scotland), several kingdoms emerged.

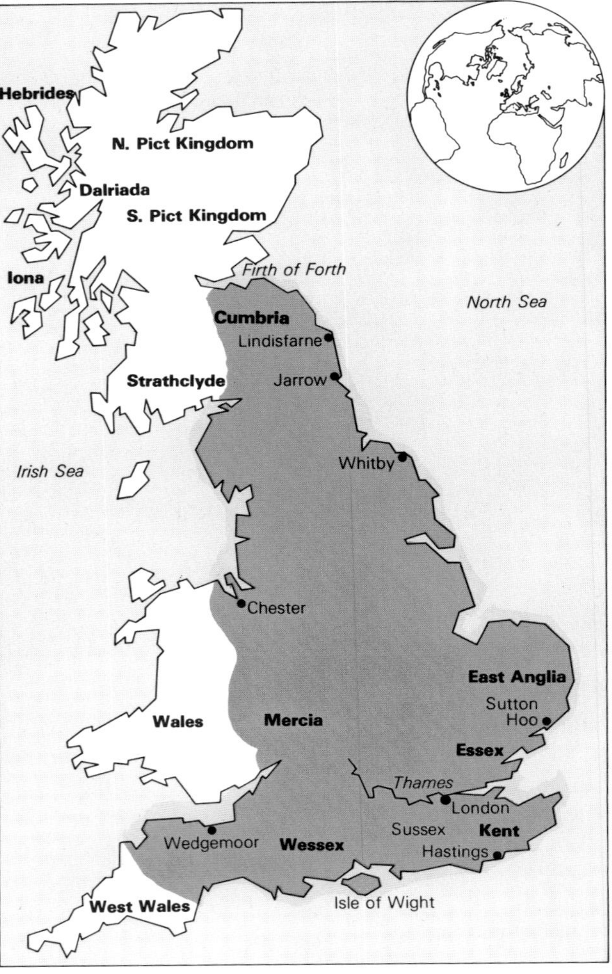

Above: Alfred's jewel, bearing an inscription reading 'Alfred ordered me to be made', includes an enamel portrait of the king holding 2 sceptres.

Reference

A **Alfred** the Great, king of Wessex 871–99, had to divide England with the Danes. He revived English scholarship, and was himself a scholar.

Anglo-Saxon Chronicle recorded English history from early times to the 1100s.

Arthur (c.500s) traditionally lived in the west country. Although legend depicts him as a chivalrous king, records from a Welsh monastery of his own day, establish him not as a king but as a great British warrior.

Augustine, St. (c.600s) led missionaries from Rome into Kent in 597, where its Jutish king, Ethelbert, accepted Christianity and made Augustine the first Archbishop of Canterbury.

B **Beowulf** is the epic story of a warrior-king who fought dragons and monsters, eventually losing his life to protect his people.

C **Caedmon,** author of the *Hymn,* probably composed several other religious poems and influenced other poets.

Celtic Christians. St Ninian, a Briton appointed bishop by the pope, preached Christianity to the Southern Picts before 400, and St Patrick came from Rome to convert Ireland in 432. In 563, St Columba of Ireland founded a monastery on the island of Iona, and converted the Northern Picts. In turn, St Aidan and others from Iona founded a monastery at Lindisfarne, the Holy Island, in Northumbria. From there they converted kingdoms southwards to Mercia.

Tintagel – King Arthur's castle

Cumbria, a Briton territory, lay south of and joined Strathclyde.

D **Danelaw** was roughly the land north-east of a line from London to Chester, extending almost to the present Scottish border. The Norman conquest brought about its end.

H **Harold II** (c.1022–66) ruled for only 9 months in 1066 and was defeated and killed at the battle of Hastings.

Hengist and Horsa (according to Bede) quarrelled with and defeated Vortigern about 455, when Horsa was killed and Hengist formed the kingdom of Kent.

Below: Anglo-Saxon warriors, displaced by the collapse of the 'Pax Romana', put to sea from the region of north Germany and Denmark and easily took southern Britain from the Romanized Celts. As Anglo-Saxon civilization developed, it came under increasing attack from the last warrior-migrants – the Vikings.

Right: High quality Anglo-Saxon metalworking came to light in 1939, when a great treasure, mostly gold, was found at Sutton Hoo, Suffolk, England. The objects found in a 25-metre longship in an East Anglian king's burial mound included the helmet and shoulder clasp shown. Many other objects were of gold, or were jewelled.

CUMBRIA, WALES, and WEST WALES. A semi-legendary British warrior, ARTHUR, is said to have fought against the Anglo-Saxons in the 500s.

Seven Anglo-Saxon kingdoms developed by 600: East Anglia, Essex, Kent, Sussex, Mercia, Northumbria and Wessex. The last three soon came to dominate the whole country, and fought each other for supremacy for two hundred years.

Religion and the arts

The Anglo-Saxons brought the old Germanic NATURE GODS with them into Britain, especially Odin (Woden) and Thor, and destroyed Christianity wherever they settled. However, the CELTIC CHRISTIANS spread their religion throughout present-day Ireland, Scotland and northern England. In 597, Saint AUGUSTINE of Rome landed in Kent and converted its people to Christianity. From there, Roman monks converted East Anglia, Sussex and Wessex. For a while, the Celtic and Roman forms of Christianity competed, but at the Synod of Whitby in 664, the Celtic Christians accepted the authority of Rome.

Early Anglo-Saxon literature included the *Hymn* of CAEDMON, composed in the 600s. About 100 years later, an unknown author composed the epic BEOWULF. At Jarrow, the VENERABLE BEDE (673–735) wrote the *Ecclesiastical History of the English People.*

The unification of England

While the Anglo-Saxon kings warred against each other, Viking attacks began, but by 828 King Egbert of Wessex (c.775–839) claimed to be king of all England. Welsh unity came about the same time, but did not last. In 850–70, Danish VIKINGS conquered all England except Wessex. King ALFRED of Wessex fought them constantly, but in 886 he signed the Treaty of Wedgemore with Guthrum the Danish leader. The Danes accepted Christianity and agreed to live in a vast area called the DANELAW. In 1016–35, King Canute of Denmark (c.994–1035) ruled all England, but his Anglo-Scandinavian empire collapsed at his death. The last Vikings to arrive landed from Normandy. The Normans defeated the last Saxon king, HAROLD II, at Hastings and brought all England under the iron rule of WILLIAM THE CONQUEROR in 1066.

Jutes, Angles and Saxons occupied southern Britain by 613. The Jutes took Kent, the Isle of Wight, and the mainland opposite to it. The Saxons settled around the Thames River and pushed westwards to the Irish Sea. The Angles settled in central southern Britain and the eastern coastlands.

Nature gods of the Anglo-Saxons included the sun and moon and Odin (Woden) and Thor, after whom Wednesday and Thursday are named.

Offa's Dyke was an earthwork built on the Welsh border by King Offa of Mercia (757–96).

Scots. King Kenneth MacAlpin of Dalriada (c.800s) claimed all the mainland north of the Firth of Forth as his kingdom of Scotland by 843. By 1034, Duncan I (c.1000s) ruled all Scotland.

Three field system meant that 1 field was kept fallow, another sown to wheat or some other cereal, and a third was allocated to barley. In Anglo-Saxon villages they were cut into equal-sized strips and each family had strips distributed over the three fields.

Venerable Bede, a great scholar, compiled an accurate history which influenced all western Europe.

Vikings from Denmark raided southern Britain, and those from Norway attacked northern Britain and Ireland. They pillaged isolated coasts and took slaves, settling in the Hebrides, Orkneys and Shetlands.

Wales, never conquered by the Anglo-Saxons, was bordered by OFFA'S DYKE. The Welsh became semi-nomadic, keeping their own Celtic law, language and form of Christianity.

West Wales was the name for Cornwall and part of Devon.

William the Conqueror (1027–87) married Matilda, Duke of Flanders' daughter, a descendant of King ALFRED. He was promised the throne of England by HAROLD II while the latter was still a duke, and invaded when Harold pronounced himself king, defeating him at Hastings in 1066.

William on the Bayeux tapestry

The Vikings were expert sailors who used their seafaring skill to become pirates and coastal raiders. A Norwegian explorer, Leif Ericsson, may well have been the first European to discover America.

The Vikings

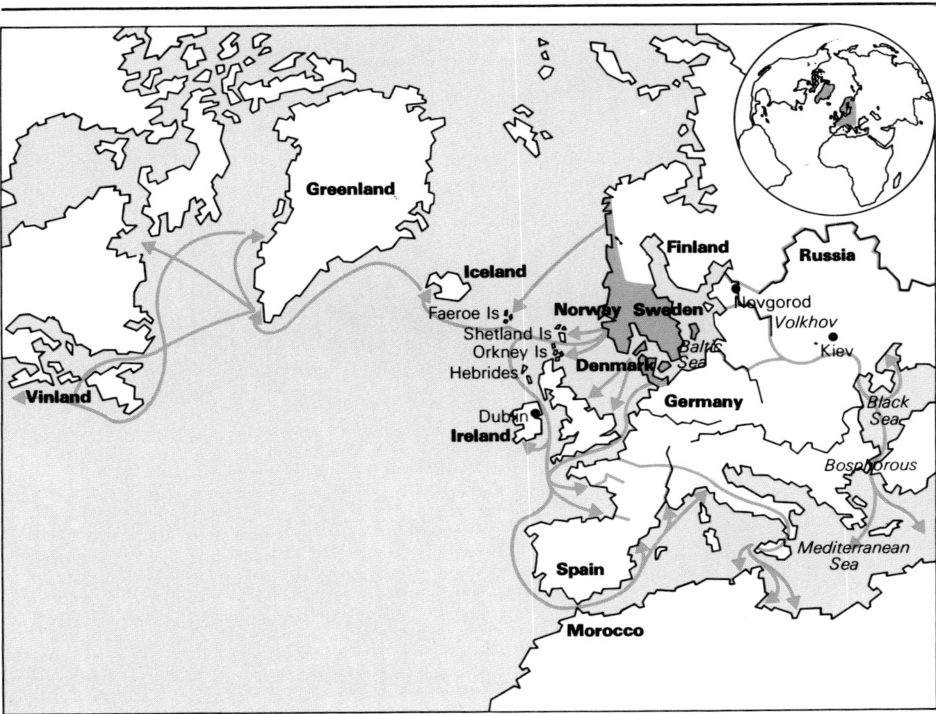

Above: The Vikings put to sea first as pirates, later as settlers. Danes raided England, France and the Mediterranean; Swedes invaded Germany and Russia down to Constantinople; Norwegians braved the bleak Atlantic westwards to Iceland, Greenland and the coast of America.

The Norsemen lived in Denmark and other colder lands of Norway and Sweden. Their own name for themselves was Vikings (men of the *viks* or creeks). They took to the sea in the 700s, seeking wealth through piracy and coastal raiding. They were probably forced to set sail because the climate in their homelands worsened, so reducing the productivity of their land. By contrast, the countries they raided seemed more attractive for settlement. Expert at shipbuilding, they became the most daring seamen Europe had ever known. Viking LONGSHIPS penetrated the seas and waterways of Europe and pioneered the route to North America.

The Vikings at home and abroad

Viking voyages were seasonal. At home, they planted crops in the spring before beginning their expeditions, and returned in summer to harvest them. Then they put to sea again, to return in winter before the sea became too dangerous. Ashore, they processed salt, tar and fish and made tools and weapons.

The Vikings built their long, shallow ships, sometimes as long as 100 metres, but typically 20 metres in length by five metres in width. These carried about 90 men. Oarsmen rowed the ships until they were out at sea, when they hoisted a single square sail. Using a steering oar (the early form of a rudder) they boldly set course to destinations mostly unknown to earlier seamen.

At sea, the Vikings were unbeatable, but they avoided battles on land, landing instead in force at lonely points to steal harvests, plunder rich monasteries, and seize monks and nuns as slaves. They struck silently and speedily after hiding their boats and those who survived their raids often starved to death.

The Vikings gained an evil reputation for needlessly killing, burning and destroying, but with more experience on land they proved highly adaptable to different circumstances. For example, if they landed where horses were to be found, they soon learned to ride them skilfully. Becoming bolder, they attacked and captured walled towns, improved their fortifications, then used them as bases from which to found permanent settlements. Once settled they prepared to repel the next wave of Vikings. Like the Anglo-Saxons before them, they gradually abandoned Odin and THOR, forgot their MYTHS, and accepted Christianity. In general, the Danes advanced to the south; the Swedes to the south-east; and the Norwegians to the far west.

The Danes and the Swedes

The main Danish attacks were made against the Franks and the English, and their efforts led to

Reference

B **Brian Boru** became king of Munster (southern Ireland) about 976, and High King of Ireland 1002–14. His reign marked an Irish 'golden age' and in 1014 he finally defeated the Danes at Clontarf (now part of Dublin) but he was killed in the battle.

D **Dublin** was built by Irish settlers in the 800s as a market centre from which they could exchange slaves and furs for silver and luxuries from the European mainland.

G **Germany** became a confederation in 962, when the pope crowned the duke of Saxony, Otto the Great, first Holy Roman Emperor. His crowning in Aachen signified that he was the 'new Charlemagne'. The Holy Roman emperors ruled until 1806.

Greenland, known to the Irish, was discovered by Eric the Red, a Norwegian banished from Iceland, about 982. He gave the barren land its attractive name to encourage colonists and about 986, he managed to settle 500 people there. The colony may have survived 400–500 years.

I **Iceland,** possibly visited by Irish monks, became a Viking settlement about 850–75. In 930 Icelandic settlers set up *Althing*, the world's oldest parliament. Norway imposed its rule upon Iceland in the 1200s and Denmark took it over in 1380–1944.

Icelandic sagas describe the colonization of Greenland and also tell how Bjarni Herjolfsson, a merchant blown off course from Norway to Greenland, first sighted the coast of North America about 985. The story continues with the subsequent voyages of his passenger, Leif Ericsson (Leif the Lucky) to VINLAND about 18 years later. Another story in the sagas tells how, in Greenland, Leif's sister Freydis treacherously persuaded her husband to kill some seamen from Iceland. When he would not kill their 5 wives, Freydis had them tied, then killed them herself with an axe.

Carved post from burial ship

L **Longships** had high sterns and prows decorated with figures of monstr-

Below right: The Vikings became expert shipbuilders and the most skilled seamen that Europe knew until 500 years ago. Viking *longships*, shallow and narrow in the beam, rose to a high point at prow and stern. The prow often had a dragon-like beast carved on it. Vessels with 20 oars carried about 90 men in all, and had a steering oar on the starboard side. They were easily manoeuvred in narrow creeks or shallow bays.

the complete but temporary conquest of England. In the Frankish empire they pursued more limited aims, but their conquest of Normandy was permanent. The Danes also attacked the Muslims in Spain and Morocco, and raided along the Mediterranean coasts.

Swedish Vikings traded and plundered along the inland waterways of GERMANY, but their reputation was never as bad as that of the Danes. As fierce merchant-warriors called the Varangians they settled the coastlands and lakesides of the Baltic Sea and Finland, and a group of them called the Rus daringly penetrated the rivers of the vast land which was later to be called Russia after them.

The Slav people of NOVGOROD (New City) on the Volkhov River are said to have invited the Rus leader, Rurik, to rule their city, hoping that his strong presence would bring peace and stability. Rurik founded a dynasty there in 862 which lasted over 500 years. His successor, Oleg, moved the Russian capital to Kiev about 873. Other Varangians sailed on to reach the Black Sea and the Bosphorous, raiding Constantinople in the 900s, until the Byzantine emperor bought them off, employing some to serve him as his Varangian Guard.

The Norwegians

Norwegian Vikings first seized and settled in the Hebrides, Orkney, Shetland and Faeroe islands. Their influence extended to Ireland, where they founded DUBLIN in 840 and held it until the Irish King BRIAN BORU defeated them in 1014. But the most daring Viking exploits were the Norwegian voyages to ICELAND, GREENLAND, and VINLAND (possibly modern Massachusetts). Leif Ericsson led this North American landing about 1003 and his settlement probably lasted about 12 years before being abandoned by the Norwegians. Several ICELANDIC SAGAS describe these courageous explorations into the icy north.

Before 1000, the Vikings had ceased to raid their neighbours and established stable kingdoms in Denmark, Sweden and Norway, and permanent settlements in Iceland and Greenland. Elsewhere, they integrated with the local peoples. Even the Normans evolved into the French and English, becoming staunch upholders of Roman Christianity.

ous animals. The single sail had vertical stripes of different colours, and round shields hung on the sides of the ships. They commonly had crews of 90 including 30 oarsmen.

M **Myths** of the Vikings are preserved in the Icelandic *Eddas*, composed 800–1300. The *Eddas* describe how, before the earth was formed, there was a northern land of clouds and darkness and a southern land of fire. Warm winds from southland melted the ice of northland, and from it stepped a human giant named Ymir. Also from melted ice, came Audumla, a cow, to provide milk for the giants. She nourished herself by licking salt from the ice, and as she licked, it melted to release another being, Buri. His son married Ymir's daughter, and their children became the gods Odin, Vili and Ve, who killed Ymir, and from his body made the earth, sea and sky. Then they made the sun, moon and stars. Odin, chief god, lived in splendour in his palace at Valhalla. His enemy was Loki, a powerful demon, who led other demons and giants in war against the gods. In the terrible destruction, gods, demons and giants died as Valhalla collapsed.

Thor, god of thunder

N **Novgorod** (south of modern Leningrad) probably began as a Slovane city before Rurik's time (c.860s). It remained the main centre for foreign trade after Kiev became the capital. Novgorod gained independence from Kiev in 1136, and held all northern Russia west of the Urals until 1748.

T **Thor,** warrior god of thunder, struck down giants and monsters by throwing his hammer, Mjolnir, at them. Thursday (Thor's day) is named after him.

V **Vinland** may have been the area around Cape Cod, or possibly Newfoundland. Leif Ericsson so named it because he found grapes growing there (together with self-sown wheat). A map drawn in Switzerland about 1440 has Vinland marked on it, and this may have helped later explorers of the Atlantic.

The feudal system of western Europe provided the basis of stability from which the Renaissance blossomed. Non-landowning serfs were at the base of this social pyramid, with freeholders and land-owners above them.

The Feudal Europeans

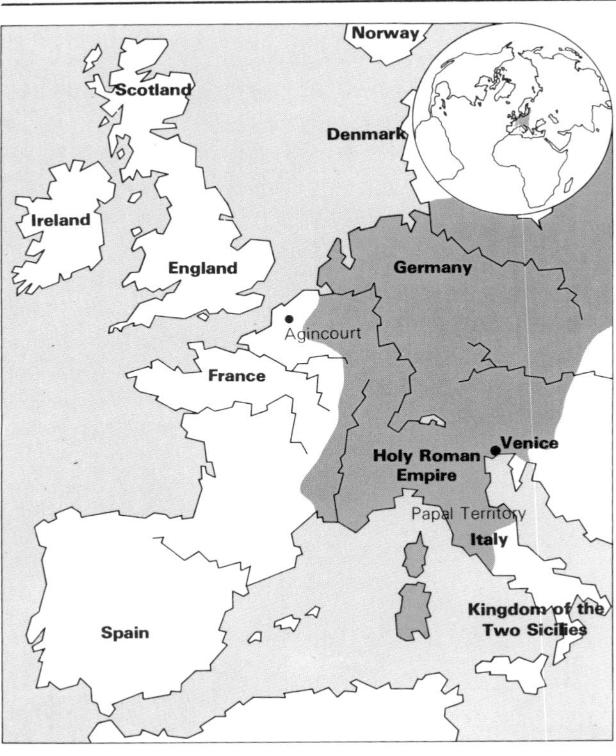

Left: Large areas of western Europe found stability in the feudal system which flourished about 1100–1300. Feudal kingdoms extended from Scandinavia to Christian Spain. The Holy Roman Empire straddled central Europe.

By about 1000, Viking raids and 'barbarian' invasions ceased in western Europe. Several kingdoms emerged, but heads of strong families sometimes held more power than the kings. These powerful lords kept private armies to fight wars both at home and abroad. Apart from the soldiers, most people worked as farmers or craftsmen in the village of their birth. They lived under the protection of the lord who owned their village, but were bound to him as SERFS. This was the basis of the feudal system, under which land was leased in exchange for services.

FEUDALISM reached its height about 1100–1300 in France, ENGLAND, GERMANY, Scandinavia, Italy and northern (Christian) Spain. Despite many shortcomings, feudalism provided the basis of stability from which the brilliant civilization of RENAISSANCE Europe later developed.

Above: Sheep became highly important as medieval Europeans exchanged their skins and furs for woollen clothes. Spain and England were noted suppliers of raw wool, but by 1400 the English processed their own wool and sold it as finished cloth.

Land tenure and class structure

In theory, all land belonged to the king, but he leased most of it to his lords. In exchange for their estates, they had to swear loyalty to him and to provide certain services, notably support in war. In England, a feudal estate constituted a manor, roughly a self-sufficient village, usually with its own castle and church. Such an estate was known as a *seigneurie* in France, a *señoria* in Spain, and a *signoria* in Italy.

Each lord possessed several estates according to his status. He had a duty to his king to protect his estates, to dispense the king's justice, and to ensure that the land was cultivated according to traditional methods. In fact, the lord seldom visited a manor, but in his absence a steward acted for him.

The lord kept much of the land on the estate as his own DESMESNE, and let out some to FREEHOLDERS in exchange for money rents. Freeholders could quit the estate at will. But most of the land was farmed by bound serfs who had to give part of their produce to the lord. They also had to provide 'week work' two or more days a week on his desmesne, and 'boon work' at harvest time. Villagers also had to pay in kind for the use of the lord's mill and oven.

Land outside the THREE FIELD SYSTEM *(see page 107)* was common. There anyone could feed cattle, poultry and sheep. Firewood could be gathered from the surrounding forest, where pigs were let loose to eat acorns. But the forests were were largely reserved as HUNTING grounds for the king and his lords and poachers, when caught, received speedy execution. Farmers slaughtered most of their animals in late autumn, and salted the meat for food throughout the winter. Only a few animals could be kept and fed for breeding in spring.

Reference

A **Alchemy** (an Arab word) was the non-scientific use of chemistry in an age of superstition. Alchemists sought mainly the 'philosopher's stone' which could turn cheap metal into gold; and the 'elixir of life', a drug to restore youth.

B **Black Death,** a virus carried by fleas that lived on rats, came from China about 1330 to reach Europe in 1348–49. Research suggests that up to 35% of Europe's people perished. In places, crops rotted unharvested in the fields through lack of labour.

C **Changes in warfare** brought the need for smaller, better trained professional armies. This became clear at the battle of Agincourt fought between England and France in 1415. Some 13,000 English cavalry, crossbowmen and pikemen routed 50,000 French soldiers who still used traditional tactics and techniques. Crossbows and cannon (both developed in China-Mongolia) came to dominate warfare in Europe during the 1300s. With cannon, kings could demolish castles of rebel lords and these changes made feudal armies obsolete.

Allegory of Black Death

Church, between 664 and 1521, meant in western Europe the Roman Catholic Church headed by the pope in Rome.

D **Desmesne,** the lord's land, often comprised half the manor. Like serfs' land, the desmesne was in the form of STRIPS scattered throughout the 3 fields.

E **England** was surveyed for taxation purposes by 1086 under WILLIAM THE CONQUEROR *(see page 107)*. The information gathered and incorporated into the *Domesday Book,* provides a clear account of FEUDALISM in England. The king's tenants-in-chief numbered some 1,500 lords and churchmen. These subdivided their estates under 8,000 second-tenants, mainly knights.

F **Feudalism** derived from the medieval Latin word *feudum,* and meant a piece of land awarded in return for services.

Freeholders sometimes had to give military services

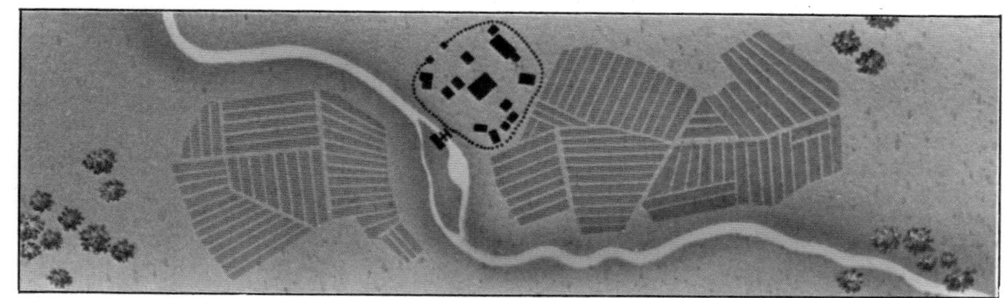

Left: Crop land was divided into 3 huge fields, usually rotated as wheat, barley or fallow fields on a 3-year system. Every household held a number of strips of about 1 acre scattered throughout the 3 fields. Meadow, common and heath – or wasteland – provided grazing land and firewood.

Below: Lords of the manor held their land from the king to whom they had to swear allegiance. They also had to run their estates efficiently, dispense justice, and maintain adequate military forces for defence or war. In practice, stewards usually ran the estates for the lords.

The Church

In all the feudal kingdoms, the CHURCH wielded great economic, political and psychological power. Bishops and other churchmen held land in their own right as feudal lords. Church lands tended to increase, because guilt-ridden nobles often willed land to the Church at death, hoping thereby to expiate their sins.

The popes insisted that, as God's representatives, they held power of appointment or dismissal of kings. They threatened kings and other rebels against their authority with excommunication, which would cut them off from God in this life and the next. The Church's ultimate weapon, was the authority to excommunicate a whole nation. Few kings dared to flout the power that the Church held over the minds of their subjects. On the other hand, the popes often needed the military power of strong kings to keep their own positions.

Many serious disputes occurred between Church and Crown. In 1075 Pope Gregory VII and the German emperor Henry IV began a bitter quarrel about which of them should appoint bishops. The dispute outlived them both, to be settled by their successors in 1122. Soon after, the papal lands around Rome were threatened by the massive HOLY ROMAN EMPIRE under Frederick Barbarossa (Redbeard) in the north, and the Kingdom of the Two Sicilies (ruled by Frederick's nephew) in the south. The pope broke this domination only in 1266, when he reached a deal with the French monarchy, in which a French prince annexed the Two Sicilies with papal blessing. When Pope Innocent III placed England under an interdict (1208–13), its king, John, had to submit. On the other hand, Frederick II, who between 1196 and 1229 was successively crowned ruler of Germany, Sicily, Italy, the Holy Roman Empire, and Jerusalem, flourished despite excommunication.

Below: Serfs formed the lowest rank of society after slavery died out. But changing times brought freedom and relative prosperity to some serfs by the 1300s.

Above: Freeholders formed a class between serfs and lords, able to leave the estate when they chose. Wealthier freeholders often employed serfs on their own account.

in exchange for their land. They also had to give boon work, but never week work. It is not fully known why a few farmers remained free

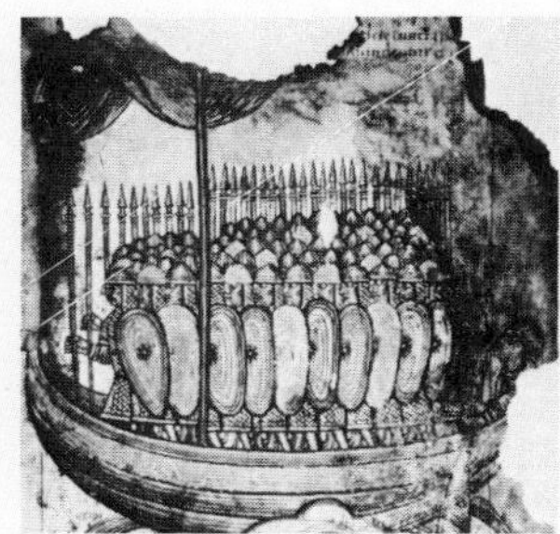

The Norman fleet lands

when most were bound in serfdom, but towards the end of feudalism, many serfs commuted (had their 'rent' changed from services to money), and so became freemen.

Germany in feudal times was divided into hundreds of states, all within the Holy Roman Empire.

Holy Roman Empire extended into present-day Netherlands, Denmark, Poland, Hungary, Italy and France. Otto the Great was crowned Roman emperor in 962 and the empire continued until 1806.

Hunting, mainly of deer and wild boar, was the sport of the upper class who kept vast forestlands for pleasure. Lords often drove people from their homes to turn the land back into hunting forests. The resentment of underprivileged people to such treatment has been expressed in many stories, such as the Robin Hood legends.

Jousting took place at tournaments where mounted knights in armour charged each other with lances, often in front of the king. Such contests were governed by the code of chivalry.

Jousting

Measurements became standardized in England by the 1300s, due to the demands of trade. They included: 1 foot (length of a shoe sole); 1 yard (width of cloth); 1 rod, pole (of an ox team); 1 furlong (furrow length); 1 acre (area of 1 strip). To end disputes, Henry I of England (reigned 1100–35) decreed that the yard should be fixed as the distance from the tip of his nose to the end of the thumb of his outstretched arm.

Renaissance (rebirth of learning), the liberation

The feudal lord was primarily a warrior. At home, he joined alliances for or against the ruling king. Abroad, he fought alongside his king or, draped in the cross, campaigned in the CRUSADES *(see page 99)*. He was supposed to observe the rules of chivalry – a moral and religious code that governed conduct in peace and war. Knights, originally a class of untitled warriors, supported their lords in battle and were recruited from squires, who began their military training as pages from about the age of seven. Knighthood became almost a cult, backed by its own traditions such as JOUSTING.

The break-up of the feudal system

By the 1300s, cracks appeared in the feudal system. CHANGES IN WARFARE rendered the barons' armies less efficient and when more money came into circulation, many lords found it convenient to receive money rents instead of services. Labour became scarce, and therefore expensive, and rents, traditionally fixed, could not be raised. Many lords rented out their desmesnes or turned to sheep farming.

The decline of feudalism was speeded by the BLACK DEATH, a deadly plague that killed off a large proportion of Europe's people in 1348–49. Meanwhile, new ideas from Italy shook old beliefs. In England, feudalism had largely died out by 1400 but it lasted until 1789 in France, and 1867 in Russia.

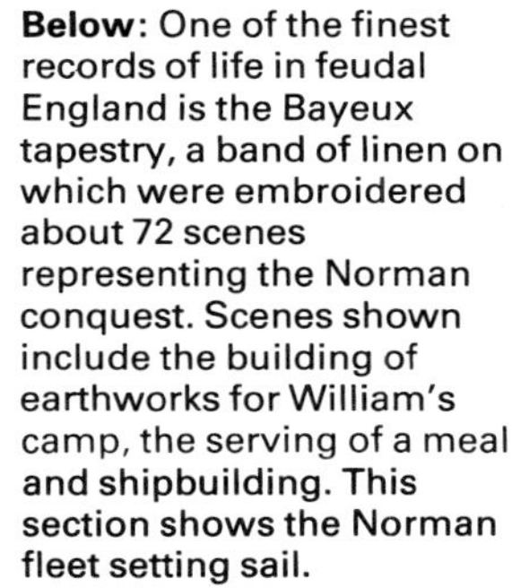

Right: Much of life in Europe of the 1400s revolved around the streets rather than behind walls. Craftsmen made their products where they sold them. Drapers, bakers and candlestick-makers plied their trades in public. Guilds imposed strict rules.

Towns and trade

The growth of towns and TRADE also speeded the end of feudalism. Towns flourished first in Italy, then north of the Alps, located where rivers provided fresh water and transport. In northern Europe the Hanseatic League, an early 'common market' of some hundred towns linking England to Russia, dominated international trade. The economic power of wealthy merchants undermined the feudal authority of kings, lords and Church.

Below: One of the finest records of life in feudal England is the Bayeux tapestry, a band of linen on which were embroidered about 72 scenes representing the Norman conquest. Scenes shown include the building of earthworks for William's camp, the serving of a meal and shipbuilding. This section shows the Norman fleet setting sail.

of ideas after the Dark Ages, began in Italy in the 1300s. It spread throughout western Europe in the next 200 years. It sparked off advances in religion, SCIENCE, art, exploration, technology, and economic, political and social life.

S **Science** found little scope in feudal Europe beyond ALCHEMY. However, Roger Bacon (c.1214–92) an English friar, wrote *Opus Majus* ('Greater Work') which covered a variety of sciences. Bacon understood and believed in the value of observation and experiment, the beginnings of scientific method. Although Pope Clement IV befriended him, Bacon suffered imprisonment by the Church for the 'dangerous ideas' in his works.

Serfs comprised over 90 per cent of Europe's population. Generally, the more land a serf held the more work was required of him. Consequently, richer serfs farming perhaps 30 or more STRIPS, often employed poorer serfs to work for them. A poor serf, holding perhaps 3 to 5 strips, might work either on the richer serf's own land, or give services direct to the lord on his wealthier neighbour's behalf. This variation of serfdom speeded the end of feudalism. In England, serfs who fled from their lords to towns, became free by custom if not caught within a 'year and a day'. In England, the small number of slaves had disappeared, probably to become serfs, by 1100.

Battle of Crécy (1346)

Strips varied in size but generally comprised as much land as could be ploughed in a single day. In England, a strip usually measured 1 furlong (furrow long) by 1 chain. Basic MEASUREMENTS came from farming and crafts.

T **Trade** on the lords' estates barely existed beyond imports of salt, iron, and luxuries for the lord. Within towns, craftsmen produced goods on the premises where they were sold. Standards of quality, training, employment and trading, were strictly laid down by the various guilds to which merchants, masters, craftsmen and apprentices belonged.

The African cultures that developed south of the Sahara were based on trade in gold, slaves and nature crafts to the Arabs. Native arts reached a peak in the magnificent Benin bronze sculptured heads.

The Africans

While the Arabs developed their civilization in northern Africa, African cultures developed south of the Sahara, especially in GHANA, MALI and Songhai. The scanty knowledge we have about these empires comes from Arab sources, especially the writings of the Arab geographer AL-BAKRI and the great Arab traveller Ibn Batuta (1304-77). However, distinct styles of African sculpture have survived to influence modern artists and traditional African music has greatly influenced the jazz and popular music of the 20th century.

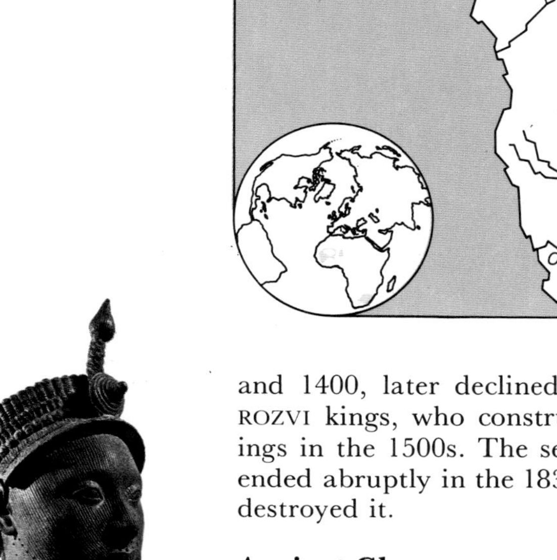

Right: Except in the Arab north, Africa for a long time lay outside the mainstream of civilization. Then came African civilizations in Ghana, Mali and Songhai. Other centres of civilization included the Hausa states, Kanem-Bornu, Axum, Ethiopia and Zimbabwe.

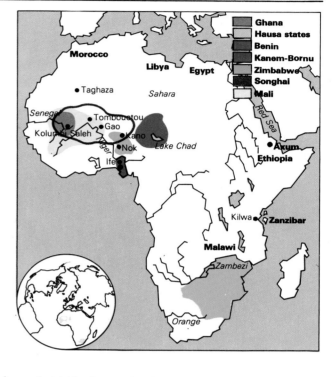

Eastern Africa

The most ancient of black African states, the kingdom of KUSH (which had once ruled Egypt) fell to King Ezana of Axum in the AD 300s. Axum (in Ethiopia) prospered by controlling much of the world's ivory supply. Ezana, persuaded by St Frumentius (a Syrian apostle to the Abyssinians) Christianized his country in 333, developed a written language, constructed palaces and churches, and spread its culture throughout Ethiopia. After northern Africa and the Red Sea coasts fell to Islam, Ethiopia remained an isolated Christian state, whose Christian culture has continued up to present times. The Europeans knew it only in legend as the 'land of PRESTER JOHN'.

Further south, along the coast north and south of ZANZIBAR, Muslim traders from the Persian Gulf and southern Arabia founded several city-states. The prosperity of these states attracted African migrants from the interior, who developed the distinct language and culture of SWAHILI. Ibn Batuta, who visited the island city-state of KILWA, wrote that it was a flourishing crossroads of trade between south-eastern Africa and countries as far east as China.

The mainstay of Kilwa's trade was gold, which came from the region of Zimbabwe. The fortified settlement of Zimbabwe, first built between 1000 and 1400, later declined but revived under its ROZVI kings, who constructed its largest buildings in the 1500s. The settlement declined, and ended abruptly in the 1830s when Zulu warriors destroyed it.

Above: This head of an *Oni* (king) of Ife, Nigeria, cast in brass in the 1200s, represents a high peak in African art. Facial features, including scarring, are finely rendered. Beads decorate the crown.

Ancient Ghana

During the 300s, BERBERS from Libya migrated south-westwards across the Sahara and organized the MANDINGO-speaking people into the Ghanaian empire. According to al-Bakri, GHANA was the title given to the emperor, who ruled through chiefs subject to him. The Ghanaians later expelled their Berber overlords, to bring the empire under black rule by 700.

To the Arabs, Ghana was the 'LAND OF GOLD'. But the gold did not originate in Ghana. Simple

Reference

A **Al-Bakri** (c. 1040–94) an Arab geographer of Cordoba, compiled his *Book of Roads and Kingdoms* as a guide to Africa in the late 1000s. He collated many travellers' reports.

Ancestor figures were created in the hope that spirits of dead ancestors would come to inhabit them. If one was thought to have arrived, people treated it with great respect, for it was thought to grant favours: a good harvest, victory in war, or children to a childless woman.

B **Barter** was usual in African lands, where coins were rare or non-existent. In Mali, gold dust provided currency for objects of high value; cowrie shells for small change. Ibn Batuta carried beads, salt and spices to barter for his needs.

Berbers may have entered Africa from south-western Asia. They remained nomads, but became powerful in and around Morocco. The Berbers who founded ancient Ghana came from Libya and may have been of the Judaist religion.

Bronzes of Ife are really 'brasses' made from an alloy of copper and zinc.

Blue men – desert nomads

C **Camels,** introduced from Asia, came into widespread use for transport in Africa only during the 200s. Until then, the Sahara formed an almost impassable barrier between north and south (although oxen and horses did sometimes cross it).

G **Ghana** (ancient) lay north of the area where the Niger and Senegal rivers come near together in present-day Mali-Senegal. Ancient Ghana lay 600 km north-west of modern Ghana.

H **Hausa states** (of which Kano was the most important) were semi-independent vassal states of Kanem-Bornu. After 1513, they came under Songhai until that empire collapsed.

K **Kilwa** flourished as an island storehouse for ivory, copper, gold, slaves and other items. These were transported by camel caravans from as far south as MALAWI, northward to the coast. Small dhows took them to Kilwa. From Kilwa, ocean-going dhows left for southern Arabia and the

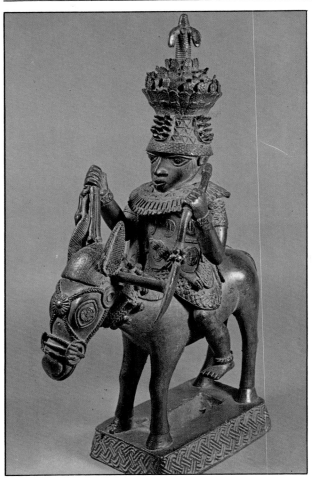

Left: The proud figure of an African king on a horse represents one of the best pieces of bronze-working in the kingdom of Benin.

traders brought it from the south to the fringes of the empire to exchange it for basic necessities such as SALT from the north. The exchange took place through a strange kind of dumb barter in which the traders themselves did not speak, and usually did not even meet. Other traders then took the gold to the Ghanaian capital. This stood at the centre of trade routes along which passed ivory, gum, ostrich feathers, KOLA NUTS and slaves. Berbers kept control of the main trade routes, along which they had earlier introduced camels.

The Moroccan Almoravid movement, a religious reform movement, which had reunited all the Berber tribes in about 1042, reconquered Ghana in 1076. However, their heavy-handed intervention destroyed the trade along with the empire and the Ghanaian capital (then Kolumbi Saleh) was finally destroyed by the Mandingo king, Sundiata, in 1240.

Mali

King Sundiata (1230-55) laid the basis for a new empire, Mali, which enhanced its status with the Arabs by adopting the Muslim religion. When Emperor Mansa Musa (1307-32) made the pilgrimage to Mecca, he distributed so much gold that the Cairo money market was thrown off balance. Tombouctou (Timbuktu) became a leading centre of Muslim learning, and together with Gao, a great trading centre. The Arab traveller Ibn Batuta remarked on the number of lawyers there and on the high standard of justice. He praised the schools, with their many books and classes in music and dancing, but had little respect for Mali's architecture. In the 1400s Mali underwent internal decline, speeded by attacks from the TUAREG and other southern peoples.

east. Luxuries such as Chinese silk and porcelain came through Kilwa into eastern Africa from about 1150.

Kola nuts, a mild narcotic, were prized by the Arabs because the Koran forbade alcohol. Islam had no prohibition against kola nuts, probably because Muhammad never knew them.

Koumbi Saleh, located about 600 km west-south-west of Tombouctou, consisted of 2 towns. A large Muslim trading town with 12 mosques stood alongside the African capital.

Kush, which ruled Egypt 750–656 BC, became rich from its gold and iron. Learning from the Assyrians (who eventually chased them out of Egypt) the Kushites made iron tools and weapons.

L

Land of gold was the Arab name for ancient Ghana. The king's horses wore gold-embroidered trappings; his attendants held gold-hilted swords; and courtiers had their hair plaited in gold.

Lost wax process was the African method of bronze casting. Sculptors shaped heads roughly in clay, then coated them in wax which they cooled and then carved with fine detail. Then another layer of soft clay was put over the wax, the inside being moulded exactly into the wax carving. The sculptor then poured molten metal between the 2 layers which melted the wax, and replaced its exact shape in the clay mould. After cooling, the sculptor broke away the clay to expose his work of art. Some heads are less than 2 mm thick.

Pendant cast by lost wax process

M

Malawi kingdom, a loose federation based on the Malawi kings' control of local trade, reached its height in the 1600s as an ally of Portugal. The kingdom disintegrated when the Yao people of Mozambique-Tanzania seized control of the trade in slaves and ivory.

Mali was visited by Ibn Batuta, who was shocked by the freedom allowed to African women in contrast to the seclusion of Arab women. He reported that the king enforced his authority by keeping on the move with a troop of cavalry.

Mandingo-Bambara group of languages are spoken in the corner of western Africa bounded by southern Senegal-Mali and the Ivory Coast.

Right: The animal hunt illustrated on this rock painting from Tassili, Algeria, shows the lively movement of prehistoric art in the Sahara. Early North African paintings portrayed a wealth of animal life. Nearby, pictures have been found of war chariots, humans and animals.

Then a subject people of Mali, the Songhai, captured Tombouctou, Djenne and Gao and established their own empire.

Under emperors Sonni Ali (reigned 1464-92) and Askia Muhammad (reigned c.1493-1528), Songhai became the strongest African power. But Islam, which had strengthened Mali, brought the downfall of Songhai as it provoked opposition from the upholders of the old tribal religions.

Above left: Iron smelting in Africa was first practised by the people of Kush, who learned it from the Assyrian conquerors of Egypt. The picture shows an iron smelting furnace and bellows still used by some tribes in Zimbabwe.

The end of Songhai

Moroccan jealousy of Songhai's control of the trade routes exploded into hatred when Songhai took the TAGHAZA salt mines. In 1590-91, the Moroccan sultan, Ahmed IV (al-Mansur) sent a small army equipped with English firearms to defeat the cavalry and bowmen of Songhai. The Moroccans took Tombouctou, Djenne and Gao. They deported Songhai's learned men to Morocco and stole or destroyed their books. The Moroccan army then refused to recross the desert, and set up a weak state of their own. Mandingos and Tuaregs attacked them and the civilization of Ghana-Mali-Songhai disintegrated.

Hausa states and Kanem-Bornu

East of Songhai, several HAUSA STATES flourished, famed for their fine leatherwork, which was exported north and known as 'Morocco leather'. Around Lake Chad the Muslim state of Kanem-Bornu drew inspiration not from Morocco but from Egypt. Kanem-Bornu lacked the economic strength of Ghana, Mali and Songhai, but it grew into a formidable power under King Idris Alooma, who used Turkish firearms and military techniques. Kanem-Bornu succumbed only to European invasion in the 1880s.

The arts of western Central Africa

Nigeria has a tradition of sculpture dating back to the NOK CULTURE of 2,000 years ago. By 1200 the city of Ife (sacred to the Yoruba tribe) produced superbly sculptured heads in terracotta and BRONZE which was cast by the LOST WAX PROCESS. By 1400 African bronze heads reached new standards of excellence in the secular court art of Benin. Almost all other African art stemmed from religion, such as ANCESTOR FIGURES.

Much of the rest of African art came from the region between Nigeria and Zaire, but little survives. Objects made of perishable materials such as wood or straw rotted in the humid climate, were eaten by ants, or burned in war. Muslims and Christians destroyed the works of art they found, damning them as false idols.

Although the number of languages spoken by the peoples of Africa was about 2,000, their music had a common pattern, bound up with drums and dancing. Essentially spontaneous, it nevertheless kept within traditional patterns of melody and rhythm. One purpose of the drum dance (especially in religious ceremonies) was to work the dancers up to a frenzy of religious zeal, so the drumming was hectic and insistent.

Religion, and mythology

African religion, like African art, had a common basis. At one level was the belief in a supreme god; at another level there was a belief in many gods and the power of the spirits of ancestors. Men had to live at peace with these powers, therefore the supposed intermediary between man and the gods was a specialist in magic known as a witch-doctor. Age-old folk myths gave explanations for every aspect of daily experience. Africans recited these tales from one generation to the next, for (outside Ethiopia) they had no written languages.

A Songhai tale told of a chief who went fishing at night and found a small sheep in the middle of the river. As he recited magic spells in fright, the sheep turned into a baby. The chief shouted for help, knowing he had seen a ZIN (water spirit). When the villagers found the chief he was dead, for the sight of a Zin meant death for mortals.

N **Nok culture.** Several finely-sculptured terra-cotta heads, dating from over 2,000 years ago have been found at Nok in Nigeria. Nok people probably used iron from about 400 BC.

P **Prester John,** a legendary Christian priest-king, was supposed to have lived in the 1100s. Marco POLO *(see page 92)* and other travellers claimed that he once ruled over a large kingdom in central Asia. Later, the Portuguese claimed that he ruled in Ethiopia. Prester John was said to have been descended from a Persian Magi.

Nok head

R **Rozvi,** a clan of the Shona tribe, constructed several stone buildings in the Zimbabwe area. Local tribes imitated these in wood, wattle and mud in villages in the Zambezi-Orange rivers region.

S **Salt,** vital to life, could not be found where it was most necessary — the humid forest land. Consequently, the forest peoples collected gold to trade for it.
Swahili means coastal people in Arabic. Swahili people are of mixed descent, mainly Afro-Arab. Swahili is also the name of their African language with Arab admixture. It is now the chief commercial language of eastern Africa.

T **Taghaza,** the salt city in northern Mali, had houses built from blocks of salt roofed with camel skins. Ibn Batuta visited it in 1352. Antonio Malfante, an Italian bank agent, reported seeing salt houses 95 years later. He visited Mali to search for the source of African gold which was then pouring into Europe.
Tuareg, a Berber people, now live mainly in the Air Mountains region of the Niger Republic. The Tuareg dialect has a writing system partly derived from ancient Berber.

Z **Zanzibar** flourished from early times as an island trading centre between Africa and Asia.
Zin, supposed water spirits, may have derived from Arab *djinn* (fire spirits). One of these was the djinn or *genie* of Aladdin's lamp.

The uniqueness of Japanese arts and crafts stems from the fact that they evolved in relative isolation from the Asian mainland. Origami, Kabuki theatre and flower arranging are just some of the new art forms that flourished.

The Japanese

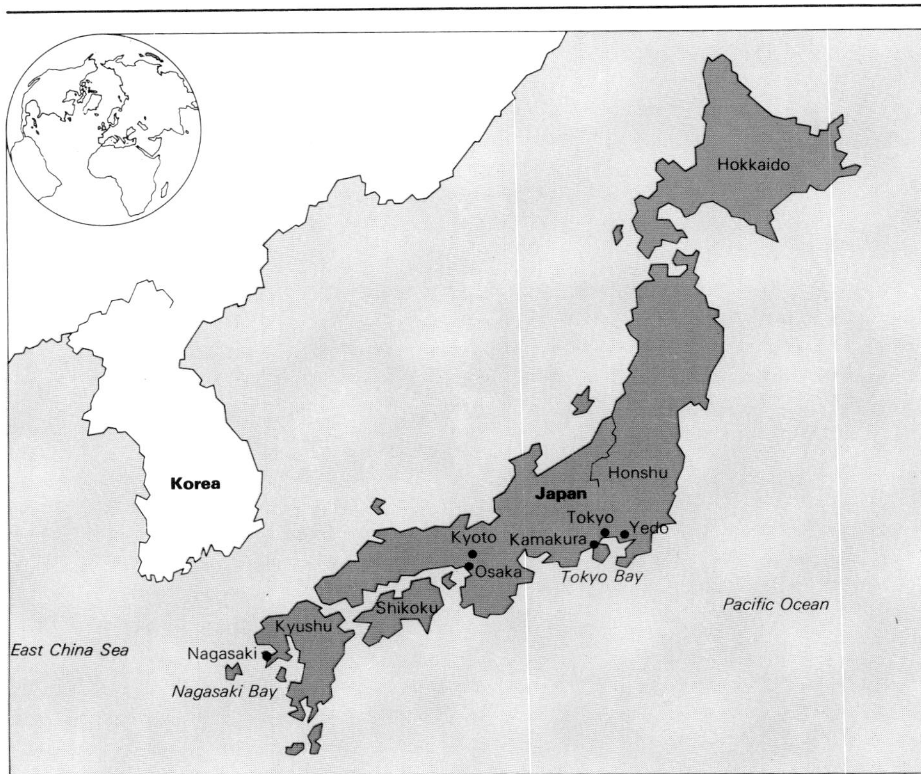

Above: Japan developed both because of its isolation and its nearness to China, from which it borrowed heavily.

Cut off by 200 kilometres of sea from the Asian mainland, Japan developed in isolation. Earthquakes, volcanic eruptions, storms and winds lashed the rocky, infertile Japanese islands, giving rise to the belief in an infinite number of *kami* nature spirits. These were thought to control every aspect of life within the religion of SHINTO. Into Japan's closed society of the mid-500s came Chinese priests bringing BUDDHISM, along with China's art and written language. From this clash of cultures emerged a new civilization, which incorporated amongst other things, several unique arts.

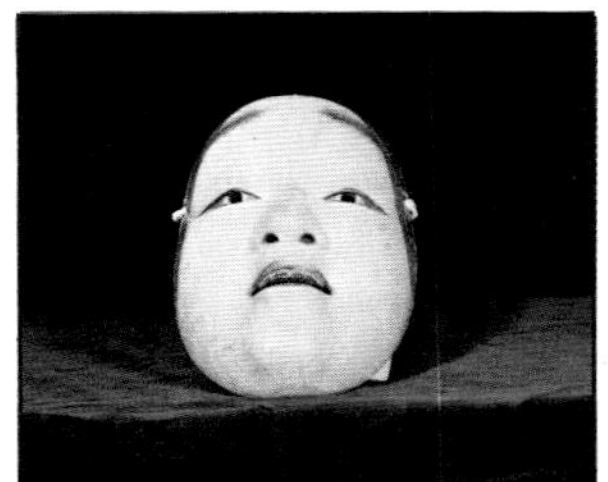

Above: Expressive masks cover the faces of all-male actors in Japan's highly stylized Nō plays.

Emperors, feudal lords, and shoguns

In 794, Emperor Kammu established his capital at Kyoto. From there, his descendants reigned as gods for over 1,000 years, although they had little authority. As in medieval Europe, the real power lay with feudal families, or *clans,* who fought unceasing civil wars. Eventually, about 858, the FUJIWARA CLAN gained power and reduced the emperors to puppet status.

The Fujiwara ruled for 300 years, but then split into two factions, one of which called in the Taira clan to fight its battles; the other faction called in the Minamoto. Both clans had ambitions to oust the Fujiwara, and the Taira finally succeeded about 1160. Once in power, they constructed harbours, dredged shipping channels, developed trade with China, and generally improved the economy. But the Minamoto overthrew the Taira in 1185.

The Minamoto set up their *bafuku* (military government) at Kamakura (near Tokyo Bay), and in 1192 persuaded the emperor to give Minamoto Yoritomo the title of SHOGUN. MINAMOTO SHOGUNS ruled from Kamakura until 1333 when Ashikaga Takauji became first of a line of Ashikaga shoguns who ruled from Kyoto.

The Ashikaga shogunate

The Ashikaga shogunate was a period of turmoil during which the power of the shoguns often sank as low as that of the emperors. Local lords increased their power but many warriors lost their status to become peasants. Meanwhile some poor people pushed their way up into a new aristocracy.

The upheaval led to certain improvements. Cultural activities flourished, encouraged by the shoguns and ZEN Buddhist monks, and metalworking, weaving, papermaking and other industries expanded. Many small market places grew into bustling towns and the new city of Osaka grew to rival Kyoto. As a result TRADE WITH CHINA boomed.

Reference

B **Buddhism** and Chinese ideas met determined resistance in Japan although they were eventually accepted. Prince Shotoku, regent 593–621 and 'founder of Japanese civilization', actively encouraged Chinese culture.

Bunraku, the Japanese form of puppet theatre, reached its height under the romantic dramatist Chikamatsu Monzaemon in the 1600s.

D **Dutch** traders were the only 'red-haired barbarians' (the Japanese name for Europeans) allowed to remain in Japan after 1636. Those who came to trade were penned in on a small man-made island in Nagasaki Bay. Chinese merchants could also trade with Japan, under strict control.

F **Fujiwara clan** gained power by constantly marrying Fujiwara girls to reigning emperors. They then reduced the emperors' activities to SHINTO duties, making them little more than puppet emperors.

K **Kabuki** is a lively form of drama still popular today that developed from dancing. It contains elements of NŌ and BUNRAKU, but is less stylized than these.

Golden Pavilion, Kyoto

M **Minamoto shoguns,** in power 1185–1219, mostly lacked the forcefulness of Minamoto Yoritomo (1147–99). From his death, his widow's family, the Hojo, totally dominated the shogunate.

Mongol attacks on Japan started in 1274. The Mongol navy first attacked the islands, where the garrisons fought to the death. Later they landed in Kyushu despite fierce resistance, and when a severe storm threatened the Mongols' ships, the Mongols fought their way into Kyushu again in 1281, but a typhoon destroyed their fleet. Shinto and Buddhist priests took credit for the *Kamikase,* or Divine Wind, that saved the country.

N **Nō plays** combine dancing, chanting and music into a slow-moving, simple drama with a simple plot.

O **'Opening-up' of Japan** began in 1853

Left: Fujin, god of the winds, carries his bag of winds slung across his shoulders. Japan's Shinto-Buddhist religion includes the belief in an infinite number of *kami* (spirits), which may vary from a volcano to a tree or even the concept of happiness.

The Japanese also built ships and put to sea in expeditions financed by feudal lords and merchants. By 1400, Japan dominated the East China Sea, which was rife with Japanese pirates.

The unique art of Japan

By 1600, Japanese artists had mastered Chinese techniques in sculpture, ceramics, woodworking, jewellery, lacquer, bronze, architecture, painting and calligraphy. They produced their own, essentially Japanese styles in an amazing variety of media and fashion, swords and sword furniture, miniature gardens and ORIGAMI became new art forms. Ladies of culture were marked by their skill in delicate flower arranging and by their peaceful and ritualistic tea ceremonies.

Literature paralleled the development of these visual arts. One of the world's greatest novels, The TALE OF GENJI, was written by a Japanese lady of court nearly 1,000 years ago. NŌ PLAYS, BUNRAKU and KABUKI developed as unique forms of drama, unrivalled in the western world.

Japan and the outer world

KUBLAI KHAN *(see page 91)* attacked Japan in 1274 and again in 1281, but with help from the weather, the Japanese beat off both MONGOL ATTACKS. The next foreigners to land in Japan, the Portuguese, brought two disrupting innovations: firearms, about 1542, and the Roman Catholic religion. Despite Buddhist opposition, the Roman Catholics claimed 300,000 converts within two generations.

In the late 1500s, a humbly-born general, Toyotomi Hideyoshi (1536–98), seized power from the crumbling Ashikaga shogunate. He invaded Korea in 1592 and 1597, but the Chinese forced him to withdraw. His successor, Ieyasu (1542–1616) founder of the Tokugawa shogunate (1603–1867) crushed Christianity in Japan and sealed its island borders. For over 200 years the threat of execution hung over Japanese trying to leave Japan, or foreigners trying to enter.

Below: The tea ceremony, performed as a ritual, is one of several uniquely-Japanese arts that combine national traditions with deep symbolic meanings.

when Commodore Perry of the US navy anchored his fleet off Japan. He demanded stores and the opportunity to open up diplomatic relations. The talks were unsuccessful but Perry returned in 1854 to impose trading relations upon Japan. Having allowed Western civilization in, the Japanese borrowed heavily from it and in 50 years they had defeated China and Russia in war and founded an empire.

Origami comes from 2 Japanese words, *ori* (fold) and *kami* (paper). Paper folding was taught from generation to generation in old Japan and Japanese books on origami appeared from the early 1700s.

S

Shinto religion has its basis in nature and ancestor worship. Shinto priests and Buddhist monks initially clashed in Japan but eventually became integrated. Buddhists tended to be more politically involved than Shintoists, who were generally dedicated to religious affairs.

Shogun, an old title for army commanders, had fallen into disuse before the MINAMOTO SHOGUNS took it. It meant 'a great general who subdued barbarians'.

Bunraku puppets

T

Tale of Genji, written by Lady Murasaki about 1008, gives an insight into the sophisticated court life of the time. Japanese courtiers wrote in classical Chinese when their European counterparts could seldom write their own names.

Trade with China boomed in Ashikaga times (1338–1568) as silks, porcelain, paintings, books and manuscripts made their way into Japan. Through China too, came goods from south-east Asia and India. Japan's exports of timber, mercury, mother-of-pearl, sulphur and gold, were supplemented by new manufactures such as swords, and decorated fans and screens. The Japanese had no money, so they imported Chinese copper cash as currency.

Z

Zen, a Buddhist creed for scholars, warriors and aristocrats, involved meditation and a rigid self-discipline. The aim was enlightenment, or an understanding of the inner-self. It influenced art, the tea ceremony, flower arrangement, and rock and sand gardens.

Genghiz Khan and his savage nomadic Mongol hordes built up the largest empire the world has ever known. But they also enabled eastern and western cultures to meet. The magnificent Taj Mahal in India was a development of Mughal art.

The Mongols

Mongol peoples drained the energies of the Chinese from the beginnings of their history by constant invasions. Tribes later called 'Huns' speeded the end of the Roman empire, and Turkish tribes seized the leadership of Islam from the Arabs. By about 1300 the MONGOLS had burst across Asia into Europe to build the largest empire that the world has ever known.

Although these savage conquerors spread terror across two continents, they also brought benefits. Through them, Chinese culture spread to Persia and beyond, and East and West came into full contact for the first time.

The nomadic way of life

Having been pushed north of the Great Wall of China by the Chin emperors (221–206 BC), the Mongols inhabited the inhospitable Gobi desert, and land westwards to central Asia. Mounted on small HORSES, they wandered this arid area in search of pasture for their sheep, cattle and goats. These provided them with their basic necessities: MILK, cheese, cheese curds, meat, furs and skins.

Mongol populations moved like large armies, with teams of oxen dragging wooden waggons that held their vast tents, or GER. In the drier regions, the Mongols harnessed Bactrian (two-humped) camels to pull their high-wheeled carts. Constant movement, meant hard work – loading pack animals, guiding wagons, hunting and defending the camps. Both men and women wore a long, sack-like garment fastened at the neck, over trousers, and in freezing weather they donned fur coats and caps.

The Mongols were SHAMANISTS, whose witch doctors claimed to mediate between humans and the world of spirits. Tengri, their supreme god, ruled over this spirit world, assisted by lesser deities. Fire was sacred as a purifying agent, and execution came to those who polluted running water.

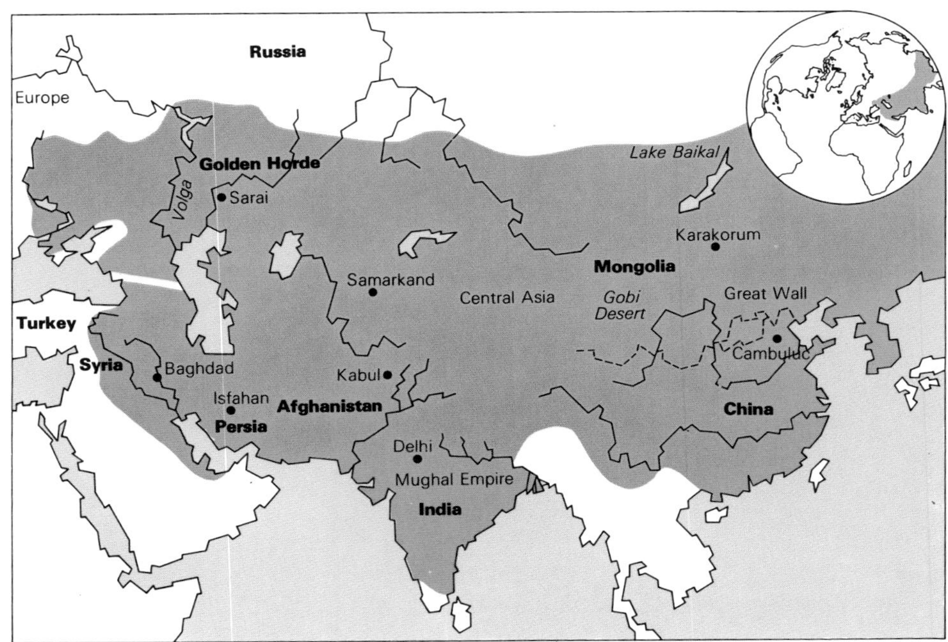

Above: Mongol conquests spread like wildfire across Eurasia in the 1200s from China into central Europe, dwarfing earlier empires.

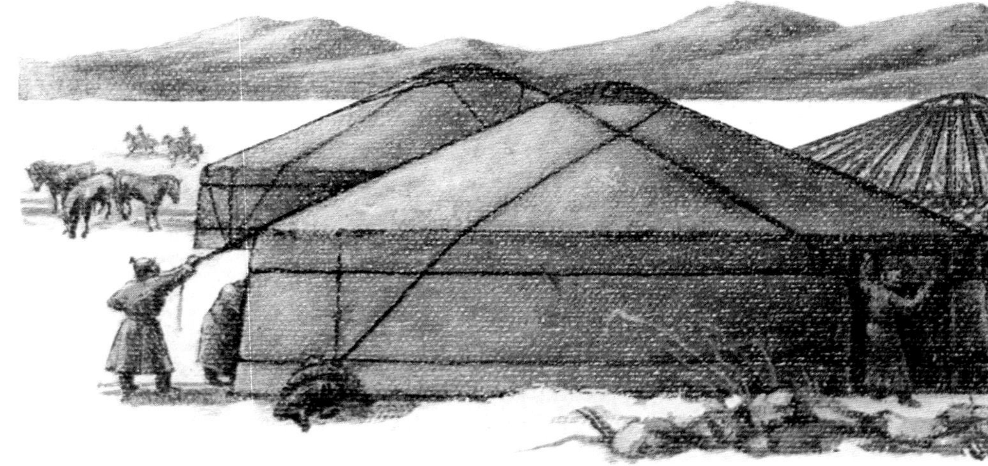

Reference

B **Baber** (1483–1530), prince of Ferghana in 1495, fought the Uzbeks to take Kabul in 1504. He took Delhi in 1526 and set up the Mughal empire that controlled most of India until the 1700s.

Batu (c. 1200s), led the 'Golden Horde'. This Mongol group, with its capital at Sarai on the Volga River, was so named because of the magnificence of Batu's camp. Later, TIMUR conquered its territory.

Bows and arrows. Lightweight arrows had a range of up to 200 metres and heavy arrows were used for shorter ranges. Some Mongol soldiers carried swords or sabres with shields, while heavy cavalry used lances, and wore head armour. Mongol armies took over the military technology of conquered countries. From Chinese firearms they developed cannon.

G **Ger,** Mongol round tents, were constructed of felt stretched over wooden frames, set in circles with the doorways facing south. The interior of a ger had 2 compartments. Women lived and cooked in the eastern compartment; men lived and entertained in the western one. The chief male of the ger had his couch by the central hearth, directly under the smoke outlet. Several idols made of felt watched over the ger's inmates. Khans and chiefs had similar ger but greater in size. They could be collapsed or transported erect in giant ox carts. The word 'yurt', often confused with 'ger', meant the homeland (Mongolia).

H **Horses,** kept in herds of up to 10,000, were carefully tended. Up to 20 spare mounts followed each rider.

Hulagu (1217–65), sent to quell a revolt in Persia, wiped out the ASSASSINS (*see page 98*) in 1256. He sacked Baghdad in 1258, took

Mongol encampment, Afghanistan

Genghiz Khan and his successors

In 1206, the Mongols united under Temujin, a military leader of genius, better known as GENGHIZ KHAN (1162–1227). He set up his capital at KARAKORUM. In 1212, filled with the idea of a heavenly mission to rule the world, Genghiz Khan began the piecemeal conquest of China. His armies swept westwards through central Asia, Persia and southern Russia, to threaten the Byzantine empire. Before his death in 1227, Genghiz nominated his shrewd, genial but drunken son Ogodei (1185–1241) to succeed him. After Ogodei's death, BATU (a grandson of Genghiz) looted and laid waste to eastern Europe, and another grandson HULAGU destroyed Baghdad in 1258, savagely killing a million people. Meanwhile, KUBLAI (a third grandson), completed the conquest of China. Ruling from Cambuluc (Peking), he became nominally Great Khan of all the Mongol empire by 1260. But Kublai had little real power outside China. Local khans warred against one another and the empire soon disintegrated.

Right: Marco Polo, his father and uncle, are presented to Kublai Khan, conqueror of China. The European artist has 'Italianized' the 4 Mongols standing at the rear, not knowing what they looked like.

Left: The giant Mongol bow hangs from one side of this horseman's belt, his quiver of arrows at the other. In the background, his comrades complete the erection of a *ger*, or portable tent. The Mongols lived, moved and went to war as one single community. Although usually outnumbered by their victims, they almost always won through superior organization.

The Timurids and the Mughals

Just as the Mongols were leaving China, the Mongol Khan TIMUR THE LAME (Tamerlane), took southern Russia in 1369 and set up his capital at Samarkand. Persia, Afghanistan, Mesopotamia, Syria and eastern Turkey soon fell to him. Timur, a brutal conqueror who built pyramids of human skulls, was nevertheless a devout, educated Muslim who encouraged art and science.

When Timur sacked Delhi (in 1398), he destroyed the Sultanate and over a century of instability followed. Then, in 1526, BABER, a descendant of Timur, established the Mughal empire from Delhi. This empire finally fell to the British in the 1700s. By then, the Mongols had become an obscure people confined to the bleak, Buddhist land of Mongolia.

Damascus and Aleppo in 1260, but was held by the Egyptian MAMLUKES (*see page 101*) in Syria. Hulagu withdrew eastwards, became a Muslim, and founded the Il-khan dynasty in Persia. It disintegrated in 1335.

I **'Isfahan** is half the world', wrote travellers of the 1600s. Shah Abbas (1557–c.1628) of the Safavid dynasty drove the Turkic tribes out of Persia but lavished Timurid styles of architecture on Isfahan. Timurid paintings inspired Persian miniatures.

K **Karakorum,** Genghiz Khan's military capital, was also a nomadic trading centre. Ogodei built a palace there which was visited by foreign ambassadors.
Kublai (1216–94), emperor of China 1279–94, was known for his tolerance of other religions and patronage of the arts. He became well-known to Europeans from the book by Marco POLO (*see page 92*).

M **Milk** products drunk by the Mongols included *kumiss,* fermented mare's milk, which was alcoholic.
Mongols probably originated south-east of Lake Baikal. They formed the nucleus of a larger group of people, including Turks and Tartars, collectively known as Mongols. On their marches, Mongols added many peoples to their army, including Chinese, Afghans, Arabs, other Muslims and Europeans. The descendants of these multi-lingual armies are now integrated into the populations of at least 20 countries.
Mughal art developed from the fusion of Timurid-Persian and native Indian styles. Its greatest achievements were the magnificent Taj Mahal and detailed Mughal miniature paintings.

S **Shamanists** believed that the visible world was dominated by invisible forces or spirits. Shamans (medicine men or witch doctors) were supposed to control these spirits in the interests of their followers. Shamans were also considered to be the wise men of the tribe, acting as priests, doctors, teachers, judges and war leaders.

T **Timur the Lame** (1336–1405) claimed descent from Genghiz Khan and seized the old territories of HULAGU. His tomb at Samarkand is like a tall GER.

Genghiz Khan in battle

Much of the history of the Maya and their neighbours remains something of a mystery. Their society was built on slavery and a popular revolt may well have brought about their downfall.

The Central Americans

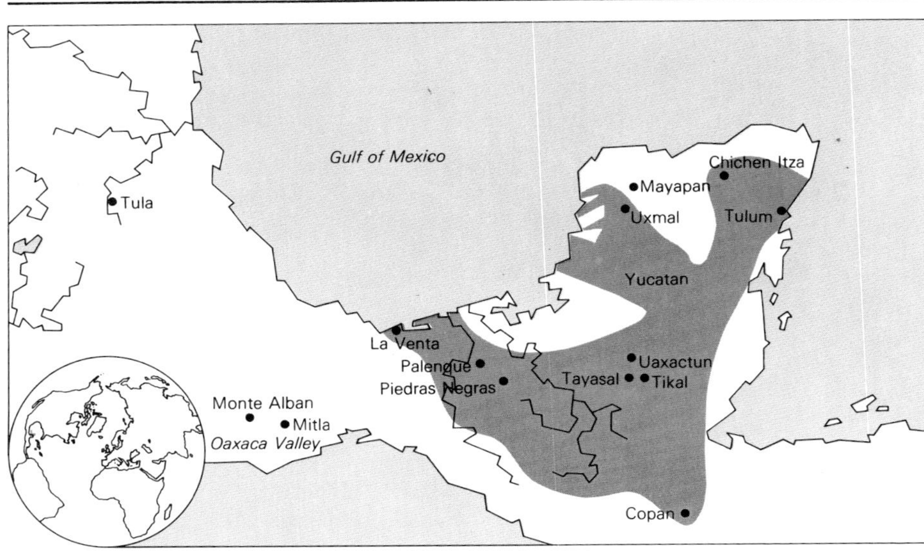

Above: The Mayan civilization stretched from Chichen Itza in the north to Copan in the south.

The humid plain of Yucatan juts riverless into the Gulf of Mexico. It is monotonously flat, with thin soil barely sufficient to support the thorny scrub found in the north. This gives way to tropical forest in the central area, which peters out as it approaches the rocky mountains to the south. This unfavoured spot and its surrounding area became the heartland of the first-known American civilizations. The Olmecs came first, a people known for carving huge STONE HEADS. A later people, the Maya, achieved spectacular success in ASTRONOMY and arithmetic and developed hieroglyphic writing. Yet they had no iron, ploughs or wheels, and no cattle, sheep, pigs, goats or horses.

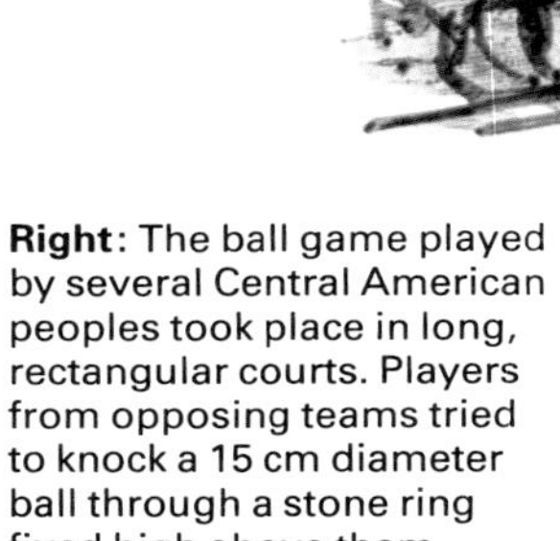

Right: The ball game played by several Central American peoples took place in long, rectangular courts. Players from opposing teams tried to knock a 15 cm diameter ball through a stone ring fixed high above them.

Early civilizations

The Olmec civilization sprang up about 1200 BC, west of Yucatan. There, north-flowing rivers deposited silt to make the coastal plain more fertile. At the island site of La Venta, the Olmecs constructed a pyramid temple characteristic of those in later cities of ancient Central America.

Reference

A Astronomy was studied by Maya priests. They had no glass or optical instruments, but recorded changes in the position of heavenly bodies by sighting them through crossed sticks in relation to fixed features on the horizon.

B Ball game (*pot-a-tok*), was played in most Maya cities, in long rectangular enclosed courts. The aim was to knock a rubber ball about 15 cm in diameter through a stone ring set high in the centre of the court. Players wore protective hip pads, belts and gloves, and could hit the ball only with their fists, elbows or buttocks. Maya pictures suggest that the game was taken very seriously. In one, a player can be seen standing over the decapitated body of another. Scholar's suggest that they represent the victorious and defeated captains.

Bar and dot system of arithmetic was jealously guarded by Maya priests, although merchants used it to some extent. Like Gupta dynasty India, the Maya used the zero. They developed not a decimal, but a *vigesimal* (based on 20s) system. The bar and dot system had only 3 signs: a dot and bar represented 1 and 5 and the zero symbol was a shell. Like the Indians, the Maya used their skill in arithmetic for religious purposes, referring to supposed dates millions of years earlier.

Stone ring in ball court

C Cacao beans were the money of Maya society and an able-bodied slave could be bought for 100 beans. Unwary people sometimes accepted counterfeit beans, the insides of which contained only sand.

Calendars became an obsession among Maya priests, who had several which they used in combination to find auspicious days. The *Haab* year had 18 months, each of 20 days and 5 'unlucky' days. The *Tzolkin*, a sacred calendar, had 20 periods of only 13 days. The *Long Count* calendar, using the *Haab* year, dated from a year corresponding to 3113 BC. Maya priests knew of 2 other calendars, one geared to the moon, the other to Venus.

Clothes for male peasants

The other main traces of Olmec civilization, the huge basalt heads, stood two to three metres high and weighed up to 40 tonnes. As the stones for these heads had to be transported from a spot over 130 kilometres inland, transportation posed problems for the central Americans. Although the Olmecs mounted their toy clay figures on wheels, neither they nor any other American peoples put the wheel to practical use. The Olmecs carved miniature figures in jade as part of their jaguar-cult religion. Yet they remained a STONE AGE people, using only flint or OBSIDIAN tools. The Olmecs also invented systems of writing and arithmetic.

About 200 kilometres south-west of the Olmec settlements, around the Oaxaca Valley, the Zapotecs built a civilization that reached its peak about 300–900. The Zapotecs believed that their ancestors (whom they worshipped) sprang from trees, rocks and jaguars. About 600 BC, the Zapotecs levelled a hill site overlooking Oaxaca Valley to construct the pyramidal buildings of their capital, Monte Alban, where many art treasures have been found in tombs.

Above: Masks modelled on skulls form a common theme of Mayan art. The mask shown, made from some 200 pieces of jade, had shells for eyes. It was found in the sarcophagus of a secret tomb at Palenque.

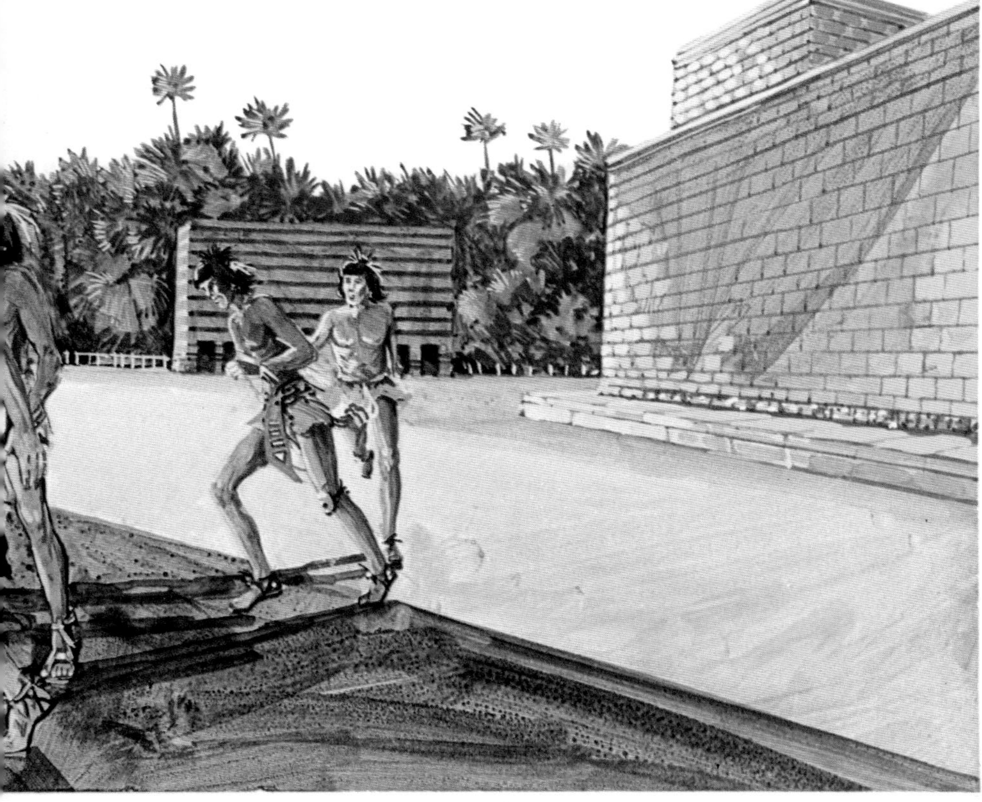

The Zapotecs reconstructed the city several times, and built a religious centre at Mitla, where they worshipped Cosijo, the rain god, and other deities. A collective priesthood ran the Zapotec kingdom, constantly organizing sport and warfare. The Zapotecs used the BAR AND DOT SYSTEM of Olmec arithmetic and this and other features of Olmec-Zapotec culture were taken over by the Maya. The beginnings of Maya civilization in Yucatan go back to before 1000 BC, but the greatest Maya period coincides with that of the Zapotecs (300–900). Much of the history of the Maya and their neighbours remains unravelled, and several mysteries remain to be solved.

The Maya and their cities

The Maya were a short, dark people. Men stood on average about 1·5 metres high and women about 1·4 metres. In the tropical heat, they wore few clothes, but two Maya customs particularly affected their appearance. In their civilization an elongated head was the sign of beauty, so they strapped boards to the head of each infant, thus flattening the front part to produce a receding forehead. Mothers even dangled beads before the eyes of their babies to make them grow up with a squint, a feature that was also considered beautiful.

Between 300 and 850, the Maya built many cities, including Copán, Palenque, Piedras Negras, Tikal, Tulum and Uaxactún. Temples, shrines, palaces, baths and other buildings were constructed as pyramids with steep staircases leading to the tops. Scholars once believed that only priests and officials lived in these cities. They thought that other people lived in clearings made in the jungle by cutting and burning the trees, and moved every two or three years as their crops exhausted the soil. However, excavations at Tikal suggest that an area of about 130 kilometres around the central square was crowded with family compounds. Each compound had a plot of farmland around its buildings, where crop rotation was probably practised. Good ROADS connected Maya cities.

The ruling hierarchy included feudal lords who, as in Europe, received produce and services from the peasants. SLAVES usually received tolerable treatment, but they could be sacrificed to the gods at any time, or, after a knock on the head, be entombed with their dead masters.

comprised little more than loincloths, sometimes with moccasins of deerskin. Women wore a *kub,* a piece of decorated cloth with holes cut for the arms and head, over a light petticoat. Both sexes kept a square of heavier cloth used alternatively as coat, blanket, or draught-excluding curtain.

D **Dancers** impersonated deities and wearing claws and masks they danced to the music of trumpets, rattles and drums. This supposedly ensured good harvests, successful hunting or other boons from the gods, to whom flowers and maize were offered.

H **Human sacrifices** included boys aged 6–12; slaves; and high-ranking prisoners-of-war. Sometimes priests skinned the corpses so that they could then dance in the skins and occasionally they ate the flesh of their victims.

Hunters used bows and arrows introduced from Mexico in the 900s. The Maya set traps and snares and shot birds with clay pellets from blowpipes. The prey were retrieved by hunting dogs.

I **Itza** rulers either went as hostages to Mayapan, once defeated, or trekked to Lake Peten Itza. There they founded Tayasal, the last independent Maya state.

Toltec stone figures

M **Maize** was shelled and cooked by Maya women, then ground into flour. From maize, women made *tortillas,* flat, unsweetened pancakes. Tortillas were rolled into pipes and served as spoons with which to scoop up other food before they too were eaten. Maize was also made into dumplings or gruel. It was the staple food, and so a god in its own right.

O **Obsidian,** a glassy volcanic rock, was made into tools. Priests used obsidian knives to cut out the hearts of HUMAN SACRIFICES.

P **Pictographic language** of the Maya was written into colour books made from the treated bark of wild fig trees. Spanish priests destroyed all the books or *codices* that they found. But 3 somehow made their way to museums in Dresden, Madrid and Paris and Russian scientists deciphered parts of them with the aid of a computer.

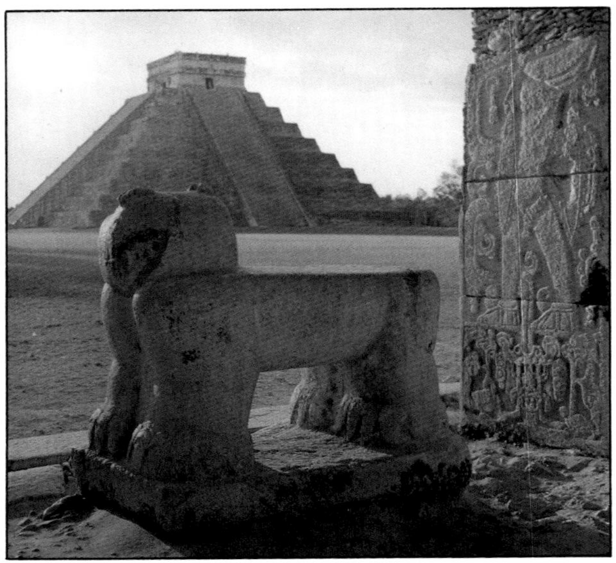

Left: Chichen Itza is a ghost city with well-preserved architecture of the pyramidal type typical of ancient America. It has the largest ball court in Central America. In the foreground stands the sacred jaguar, set by a temple dedicated to the jaguar cult.

The staple diet of the Maya included MAIZE, beans, root crops, sweet potatoes and pumpkins and several kinds of fruits and spices were grown, including melons and chillies. Doves, ducks, curassows (turkey-like birds), and a breed of hairless dogs were fattened for eating, and fish, snails, and the larvae of mud-wasps were added to the diet. Deer, wild pigs, armadillos and tapirs were hunted.

CACAO BEANS, roasted, ground, and mixed with maize flour, provided a chocolate beverage while stingless bees produced the honey to make a fermented drink. Other stimulants included cactus juice, tobacco, and the hallucinatory drug mescalin, from the peote plant. The resin of copal trees provided incense for the temples; rubber trees gave the material for making rubber balls; and from chicle trees came chewing gum. Cacao beans were prized for being more than a food: they passed as currency in a society otherwise without money.

Gods, priests and scientists

The Maya heaven had 13 layers above earth, and the Maya hell nine layers below. Beneath the supreme but remote god, Hunab Ku, lesser deities included QUETZACOATL (Feathered Serpent), a god shared with other peoples. At frequent religious ceremonies, DANCERS impersonated deities, while priests freely sacrificed birds and animals, and occasionally humans. Worshippers often drew blood to please the gods.

Below: This ceramic vessel was made by a Toltec craftsman who worked without the potter's wheel. Toltecs, from the Mexican highlands, were probably the warriors who reoccupied Chichen Itza about 930.

The partly-hereditary priesthood had many functions. Priests kept the CALENDARS and so decided when planting and harvesting should begin, buildings be constructed or WARS begin. Much concerned with time, the Maya erected stone slabs to record the end of each *katum*, or 20-year period. As keepers of horoscopes, the priests took to astrology, which led them on to astronomy and they were able to calculate accurately the solar year and predict eclipses. The priests, who kept arithmetical records, using the bar and dot system of the Zapotecs, dominated Maya art and the PICTOGRAPHIC LANGUAGE.

Even *pot-a-tok*, a strange Maya BALL GAME, had religious associations. Spectators sat in tiers watching players attempt the near-impossible task of knocking a ball through a high stone ring. Betting was heavy on popular players.

The ghost cities

For some unknown reason the Maya abandoned their cities by about 850, leaving the jungle to reclaim them. Some scholars think that a popular revolution occurred in which the peasants killed their priests and rulers. As a result people moved from one area to another, and the 'old empire' ended. The ITZA, a people who, according to their own records, had abandoned the city of Chichen Itza centuries earlier, returned to it about 930. With them came a warrior people, probably TOLTECS, whose leader was named Feathered Serpent.

The old empire people hated the newcomers, who brought with them new styles of art with stiffly-carved figures of warriors. The invaders founded new cities, including Uxmal and Mayapan and their new empire flourished for over a century, before disintegrating into civil war. Peace came in 1194, after the Itza suffered defeat by the warriors of Mayapan. The tyrannical rulers of this city dominated Maya territory until 1441, then their subjects rebelled, killed their rulers and sacked the city.

Yucatan then split into many tiny city-states fighting ceaseless civil wars. Decline was speeded by a devastating hurricane in 1464, and an unknown epidemic in 1480. In 1511 the first Spanish invaders arrived, bringing with them smallpox and ultimately, the end of Maya independence.

Q **Quetzacoatl** (Feathered Serpent), a god shared between Toltecs and other peoples, took many forms. He supposedly discovered art, science, MAIZE and the CALENDAR. He is identified with the cult hero, Kukulkan.

R **Roads,** built by peasants to a width of 4·4 metres, linked Maya cities. Tough, roughly-hewn stones formed a foundation, surfaced with gravel or limestone chippings and cities had raised, paved causeways. Only the Incas built better roads in the Americas.

S **Slaves** among the Maya came from 4 main classes. They included children sold by impoverished parents; orphans; convicts enslaved as a punishment; and low-ranking prisoners-of-war.

Stone age culture in central America was general, except that the Maya made splendid figures in gold and copper. Nothing has been found to indicate that they mixed tin with copper to make bronze.

Stone heads of the Olmecs were probably floated down river on huge rafts. They probably represent Olmec rulers.

T **Toltecs,** a warlike people, built an empire in the Mexican highlands about 750. Their leader, Topiltzin, who founded Tula in the 900s, added the name QUETZACOATL (Feathered Serpent) to his own name. In 1224, the Toltecs fled Tula after it was sacked. The warriors who reoccupied Chichen Itza about 930 were probably Toltecs.

W **Wars** were fought usually in the dry season, when agricultural tasks had finished. All men bore arms and women accompanied them to war to prepare meals. Battles ended at nightfall, when food was ready. Maya soldiers sought to capture rather than kill the enemy. Wars ended when one of the leaders was taken prisoner. He and his officers then became sacrifices. Soldiers fought with shields, clubs, daggers, lances, tridents and (from the 900s) bows and arrows. They wore padded 'armour' of cotton soaked in brine.

Olmec stone head

The Aztec god, Huitzilopochtli, needed constant nourishment in the form of human blood, in return for which he promised the tribe domination over the neighbours. The Spanish *conquistadores* put an end to their domination.

The Aztecs

While the Olmecs, Zapotecs and Maya built up civilizations in and west of Yucatan, other, inter-related cultures developed farther west. One small tribe, the Mexica (or AZTECS), grew out of obscurity to found a great empire. But the WAY OF LIFE of this talented people was tainted by their obsession with BLOOD SACRIFICE.

Teotihuácan: Zapotecs and Mixtecs

About 100 BC, an unknown people began to build Teotihuácan (Place of the Gods) – the biggest city of central America housing about 200,000 people. For some mysterious reason the city was abandoned about 750. This coincided with the decline of the Zapotecs of the Oaxaca Valley whose culture came under the domination of the Mixtecs, craftsmen who produced fine works of art in stone, metal, wood, bone and pottery. After subduing the Zapotecs in a series of long wars, the Mixtecs took over Monte Alban and Mitla. The Zapotec-Mixtec wars halted in the late 1400s when the two enemies combined to fight a new warrior people from the north: the Aztecs.

The wanderings of the Aztecs

According to their legends, the Aztecs took their name from Aztlán (White Land), the supposed place of their origin. About 1111, they began a long migration in search of a home. For a while they settled near the old ruined Toltec capital of Tula. There, they learned simple agricultural techniques, irrigating farmland and building CHINAMPAS ('floating gardens'). They entrusted their fate to their god, Huitzilopochtli (Humming-bird). This god, according to Aztec priests, needed constant nourishment in the form of human blood. In return, the priests said, Huitzilopochtli promised the Aztecs domination over their neighbours, but he ordered them to leave Tula and resume their wanderings.

Just before 1300, the Aztecs reached the city of Chapultepec in the Valley of Mexico, the centre of the Toltec civilization. After the collapse of the Toltecs and the suicide of their last king, many people had migrated to the valley. The Aztecs, being the last to arrive, met opposition. Those Aztecs who survived the ensuing massacre, threw themselves on the mercy of the city of Culhuacan, which had already sacrificed the Aztec leader to its own god. Surprisingly, the Culhua granted the Aztecs some nearby land.

Although it was only a snake-infested rocky wasteland, the Aztecs prospered. They intermarried with the higher-cultured Culhua, and proudly called themselves 'Culhua-Mexica people'. However, as allies, the Aztecs proved so fierce that, in about 1345, the Culhua tried to exterminate them. Culhua soldiers forced the Aztecs back to the edge of a swampy lagoon. Desperately, the Aztecs made rafts from javelins and spears padded with coarse grass. On these, they floated out to the safety of a small, reed-choked island in the lagoon. The Aztecs had reached their final home.

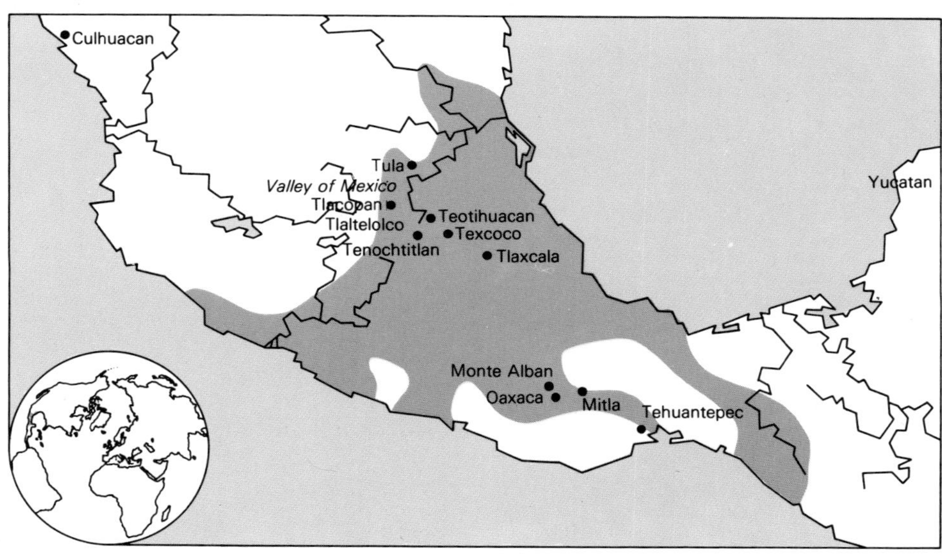

Above: The civilization of the Aztecs began with a small settlement at Tenochtitlan. This city grew to became the capital of a vast empire under Montezuma.

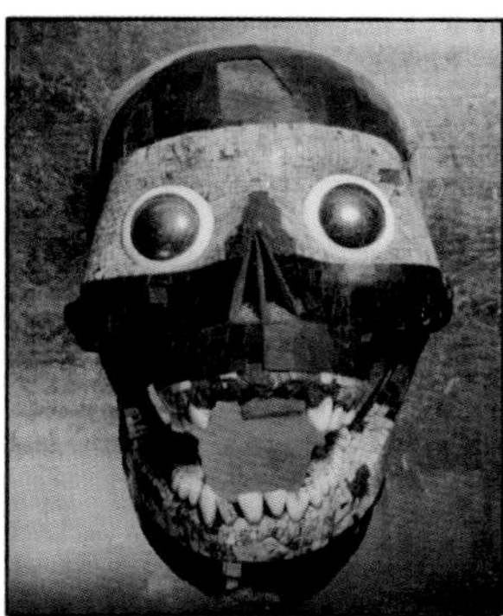

Above: A human skull was used to shape this Aztec mask – a mosaic of turquoise, sea-shell and lignum. It may represent Tezcatlipoca (Smoking Mirror) the great sky god.

Reference

A

Artefacts included the 'Aztec Calendar', really a sun stone dedicated to Tonatiuh, the sun god. His face adorns the centre of the stone, and claws are carved gripping human heads. The stone symbolizes the eternal struggle between Quetzacoatl and Tezcatlipoca (Smoking Mirror) — evil god of the night sky. These and other symbols on the stone represent the Aztec idea of the nature of the universe.

Aztecs, according to tradition, changed their name to *Mexica* or Mexicans on the orders of Huitzilopochtli, who then gave them a net, bow and arrows. After this, the Aztecs shot arrows expertly. *Mexica* came from the word *meztli* (moon) in the Nahuatl language spoken by the later Aztecs.

B

Blood sacrifice claimed over 20,000 victims a year and horrified the Spaniards. The Aztecs were equally shocked that the Spaniards burned people alive. At least sacrifice brought a quick death because priests cut out the heart with obsidian knives within seconds.

Stone calendar

C

Chinampas, misnamed 'floating gardens' were tiny island 'farms' built in shallow fresh water. In Tenochtitlan, agricultural land being scarce, the Aztecs cultivated the shallow lagoon. They made platforms from layers of mud and water plants walled in by basketwork. Intersected by canals, these formed excellent land for crops.

Codices, a term denoting manuscripts in book form, also describes the picture books of ancient Mexico painted on tree bark, deerskin, or 'paper' made from agave leaves. Aztec 'books' were either rolled up into scrolls or folded like modern maps.

Cortés, Hernando (1485-1547) sailed to Hispaniola in 1504 and Cuba in 1511. When he landed in Yucatan in 1519, Cortés recruited a shipwrecked Spanish sailor who spoke the Maya language. He also received the gift of an enslaved princess, Malinche, who knew the speech of the Maya (Putum) and the Aztecs (Nahuatl). On the march towards Tenochtitlan, Cortés recruited the Tlaxcalans as

The Aztec struggle for supremacy

Settled on the island, the Aztecs first built a simple shrine to Huitzilopochtli. Around it grew the city that became TENOCHTITLAN. Thirteen years later, the Aztecs built a second city, TLATELOLCO, on a nearby island. The peoples of Tenochtitlan were warlike; those of Tlatelolco were merchants and traders. Through trade, the Aztecs prospered, but three strong powers surrounded Tenochtitlan, ready to cut off its supplies. Unable to survive alone, the Aztecs had to choose an overlord. They therefore offered allegiance to the TEPANECS, who claimed to be the heirs of the unknown builders of Teotihuácan.

Through three generations the Aztec-Tepanec relationship changed. The Aztecs progressed from a state of humiliating subservience to junior partnership, and eventually to rivalry. To rid themselves of Tepanec domination, the Aztecs entered into a triple alliance with the anti-Tepanec state of Texcoco and with Tlacopan (a breakaway Tepanec city). After defeating the Tepanecs in 1428, the triple alliance continued, dominated by the Aztecs. Gradually, some five million people came under the rule of the Aztec empire in a 1500-kilometres-long territory from north of Tenochtitlan to Guatemala. Under MONTEZUMA (Moctezuma) II, ninth king to rule from Tenochtitlan, the promises of a great empire said to have been made by Huitzilopochtli, came to fruition.

Above: A macabre artefact from the civilization of the Mixtecs is this ornamental knife made of chalcedony. It was used to cut out the hearts of human sacrifices. Skilled in anatomy, priests killed their victims within seconds.

The Aztec way of life

Tenochtitlan, joined to Tlatelolco and several smaller islands, grew to become a city of some 165,000 people. Causeways with movable drawbridges linked it to the mainland in the north, west and south, and canals gave access to all parts of the city. Fresh water from hillside springs supplied the city through an aqueduct. Among the city's most impressive buildings was the magnificent pyramid raised to Huitzilopochtli. Lesser DEITIES had their own temples and special sacrifices.

Left: The caricature of human sacrifice by Aztec priests was painted from memory by a man who, in his youth, had been a subject of the Aztec emperor. Temple orderlies drag away the body of a victim from the foot of the temple steps. In front of the temple, a priest has just cut out the heart of a second victim, which he holds up. A second priest has held the victim's legs as he stretches backwards over a stone block awaiting the knife. The blood-smothered temple contained racks for the dead men's skulls. Priests ate the flesh of their victims at certain ceremonies.

allies. In Tenochtitlan, he took MONTEZUMA hostage and tried to govern through him. In 1520, during Cortés's absence from the city, his deputy unwisely began a fight with the Aztecs. After Cortés's return, the Aztecs besieged the Spaniards. During a battle, Montezuma stood on a battlement to try to bring peace. The Aztecs (who had already rejected him) threw stones, one of which hit his head and killed him. (Other versions of his death exist.) The Spaniards retreated to Tlaxcala, but recaptured Tenochtitlan in 1521. They annexed all Mexico, which they called 'New Spain'.

D **Deities** below Huitzilopochtli included Tlaloc, the rain god; his sister, the water goddess; Tlazolteotl, goddess of love; and Coatlicue, earth goddess and mother of Huitzilopochtli. The Aztecs also worshipped Quetzacoatl, universal god of central America. These deities had their own temples and human sacrifices. By each temple stood a huge rack holding thousands of skulls. All deities had their special sacrifices and ceremonies.

Tlaloc, god of rain

E **Evil omens** troubled MONTEZUMA before the arrival of the Spaniards. One was the accidental burning of a temple. Another was a large bird with a mirror in its head, said to have been brought to Montezuma by priests; when he looked into it he saw the stars in daylight. Looking again, the king saw many warriors who seemed to be part men, part 'deer'. (The Aztecs had never seen horses.)

M **Montezuma II** (reigned 1502-20), was the Aztec emperor at the time of the Spanish invasion under CORTÉS. He was regarded as a demi-god but was finally stoned to death by his own people who regarded him as a traitor.

O **Oaxaca** in the late 1400s was a mainly Zapotec city under Mixtec rule. Although Monte Alban had been abandoned for centuries, the Mixtecs used it for burials, and fine goldwork has been found in its tombs. Some Zapotecs had moved southwards to Tehuantepec to retain their independence.

Aztec craftsmen dyed cloth expertly, made distinctive pottery of quartz and clay, and produced fine jewellery and ARTEFACTS in stone, jade, silver and gold. The Aztecs recorded important events in 'books' of 'paper' made from agave leaves. They used a pictographic script similar to that of the Maya. In Montezuma II's time, the Aztecs produced the CODICES which recorded the organization of the empire and the payment of tribute.

All goods that did not travel by water were carried by men. Agricultural techniques remained primitive, digging sticks being the main implements. Tribute arriving in Tenochtitlan from subject tribes included rubber, feathers, cacao, and precious metals and stones. People also paid taxes to the government in the form of food, clothing, skins, silver, gold and feathers. Aztec warriors had similar equipment to Maya soldiers, except that they wielded swords made of obsidian.

The end and the beginning of time

Like the Maya, the Aztecs combined their solar and sacred calendars to find auspicious days. Time, they believed, was granted by the gods in 52 year cycles. At sunset on the final day of the cycle, people climbed to the summit of Huixachtecatl (Hill of the Star), an extinct volcano. From here they anxiously scanned the sky for a certain star.

At the exact moment when the time cycle ended, a priest kindled a fire in the open breast of a newly-killed human victim. This macabre ceremony would help to ensure that the world would go on. As the vital star passed the centre of the sky, the whole Aztec nation sent up a shout of joy, for the gods had allotted a new cycle of time for the world.

The end of the Aztecs

From the time of his accession in 1502, Montezuma fought wars of annexation around OAXACA. Nearer home, a war begun against Tlaxcala and its allies in 1504, brought no quick victory. As the conflict dragged on over 13 years, the king grew more and more haggard and depressed, and vindictive towards his priests and astrologers. Aztec accounts say that many EVIL OMENS came to trouble him. Then, in 1519, came reports of 'mountains moving in the sea'. These were Spanish ships heading for Yucatan, where the Spaniards were welcomed as RETURNING GODS.

After a brief clash, the Tlaxcalans and Spaniards joined forces. This pact sealed the Aztecs' doom. Two years later, Hernando CORTÉS, leading 1,000 Spaniards armed with guns, horses and iron weapons, captured Tenochtitlan for the second and final time, and put an end to the Aztec civilization.

Above: Aztec *tonalamatl* were the reference books of the priests. They were made from paper made from the beaten bark of the wild fig tree. Paper-makers cut them into long strips which they coated to take paint, then folded them like modern maps. Either one or both of the open pages related to affairs of a particular week. Artists drew the controlling deity of the week extra large, and other figures represented subordinate deities or symbolized objects of worship. In the remaining space, ruled-off squares contained the 13 day-names and numbers, and the deities in their various forms.

Left: This jade mosaic jewel set in gold is one of many fine examples of Mixtec artistry.

Returning gods. According to legend, Quetzacoatl vanished with the fall of the Toltec empire, and his return was expected from the sea to the east. MONTEZUMA, thinking CORTÉS was the returning god, sent envoys with presents to meet him in the old Olmec territory. They came back with Spanish presents for Montezuma, who had them buried in Quetzacoatl's temple in Tula with appropriate sacrifices.

Tenochtitlan or present-day Mexico City, was named after Tenoch, chief priest-ruler of the Aztecs when they reached their final home. He died about 20 years after the founding of the city. This would be 1325 if the traditional Aztec date is taken. But many scholars think 1345 is more likely. Estimates of the city's peak population vary between 60,000 and a million.

Tepanecs settled west of the lagoon in which Tenochtitlan was later founded, and built Azcapotzalco (Place of the Ant Heaps) as their capital. It is now a suburb of Mexico City. The Tepanecs became in turn the oppressors, tutors, partners, rivals and subjects of the AZTECS. When the Aztecs first arrived, they and the Tepanecs formed the 2 great civilizations seeking to fill the gap made by the Toltecs' collapse.

Tlatelolco developed as a city-state in its own right, set up its own dynasty and even fought a brief war against Tenochtitlan in 1473. Although the war quickly ended, Tlatelolco lost independence.

Way of life. Many people in the Aztec empire lived in remote villages, in adobe huts with thatched roofs. Men worked in the fields, while women cooked food such as tortillas and spun and wove cloth. Men wore capes and loincloths; women wore sleeveless blouses and calf-length skirts. Colourful decorations on clothes showed the wearer's position in society. Lesser chiefs wore white; priests wore black.

All that remains of Chinampas, the 'floating gardens'

The Inca emperors were supposedly descendants of the sun. They organized Inca society broadly as a welfare state at the expense of individual liberty. However, they pioneered 'pensions' for the old and work for the disabled.

The Incas

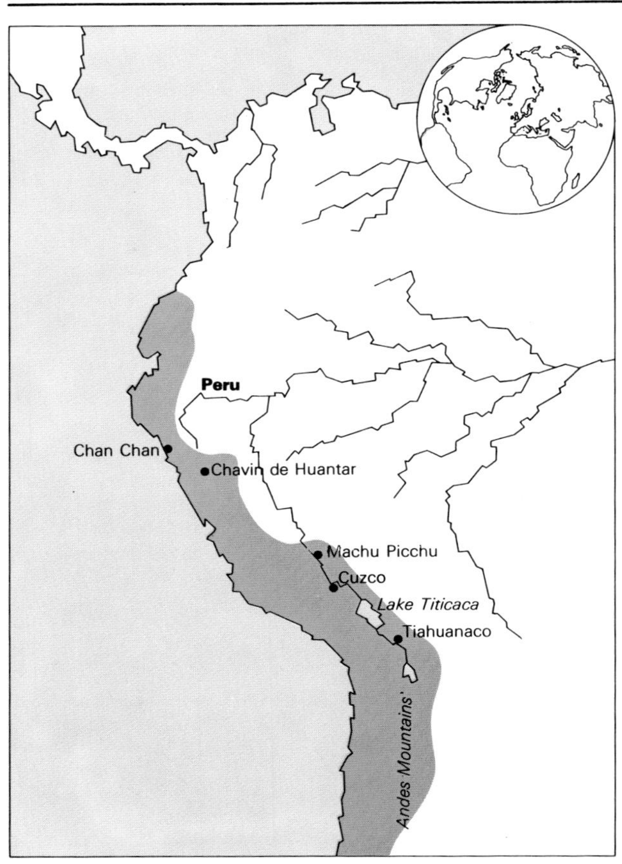

Left: The empire of the Incas extended 4,000 km north to south, straddling the Andes through what is now Ecuador, Peru, Bolivia, Chile and north-western Argentina.

Civilizations emerged along the Andes Mountains and the western seaboard of South America in about 1000 BC. Several cultures, centred on present-day Peru, rose and fell over a period of 2,500 years. Although the peoples of Peru and Yucatan (4,000 kilometres to the north-west) shared the same ORIGINS, no evidence has come to light to suggest that they were in contact. They had, however, several features in common: both civilizations constructed pyramidal buildings and had broadly similar art forms, and in religion, both had BLOOD SACRIFICE and a JAGUAR CULT. The Inca tribe set up their capital at Cuzco (300 kilometres north-west of the sacred LAKE TITICACA) in about 1200, and had incorporated most neighbouring peoples into their EMPIRE by 1476. INCA EMPERORS, supposed descendants of the sun, organized society broadly as a socialist state; used bronze tools and weapons; devised a unique system of counting; kept good ROADS; and introduced the potato to the rest of the world. However, they did not use the wheel, money or a written language.

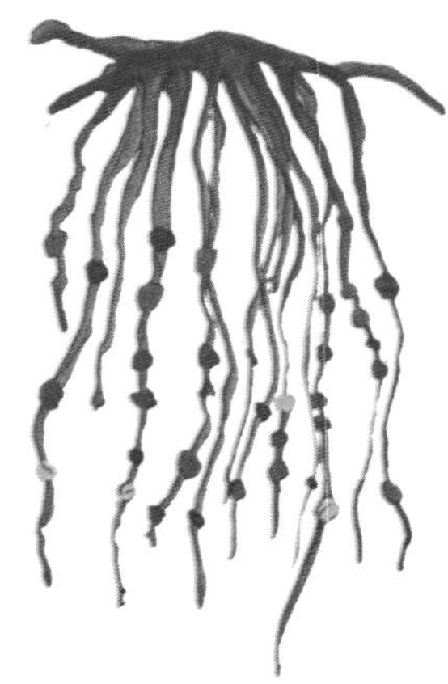

Above: The quipu, an ingenious system of recording numbers by means of coloured knotted cords, could also store coded messages. An hereditary class of quipu keepers kept and interpreted the quipus.

Early civilizations

In South, as in Central, America, the ruins of several mysterious ancient settlements still stand. The oldest-known, Chavín de Huántar, lies high in an Andean valley over 1,000 kilometres north-west of Lake Titicaca. It dates from about 700-200 BC. Chavín's large, well-built stone temples have colourful sculptures of complex symbolism. Chavín art comprises ceramic ware, textiles and goldwork. Its styles influenced the arts throughout the surrounding region.

On the southern shore of Lake Titicaca, on a plateau 4,000 metres above sea level, stood TIAHUANACO, believed to have been the religious and political capital of the AYMARA INDIANS before AD 500.

While Tiahuanaco still flourished, the Chimú culture developed around the Moche River. Its capital, Chan Chan (1,300 kilometres north-west of Lake Titicaca) covered 15 square kilometres. At its centre stood ten walled buildings, which were probably palaces. Chan Chan's tombs once contained gold and silver artefacts, jewellery, textiles and ceramic ware and scales were found for weighing precious metals and stones. Because no system of writing existed, nothing records the history of these cities beyond their material remains. However, from their artefacts, it appears that they heavily influenced the civilization built up by the Incas.

Reference

A

Adobe, mud mixed with straw, was sundried to make bricks for houses.

Aymara Indians occupied the Lake Titicaca area and probably built TIAHUANACO. Though conquered by the Incas, their descendants still live there and speak their own language.

B

Blood sacrifices among the Incas consisted mainly of llamas, guinea-pigs or birds. However, up to 200 children might be sacrificed to mark the coronation of a new emperor, or to persuade the gods to intercede in defeat, plague or famine. Victims included prisoners-of-war and children collected as 'taxes'.

C

Clothes of alpaca or llama wool were at a later stage supplemented by cotton. Men wore sleeveless tunics over breechcloths (a type of loincloth) and turbans and women wore long dresses with sashes. Both sexes had long cloaks and leather sandals.

Criminals who killed while robbing were put to torture before execution. Manslaughter was sometimes punished by exile to the emperor's coca plantations. Sabotage, bribery and corruption often carried the death penalty.

Crops included maize, root crops, peppers, peanuts, avocadoes and pineapples. Tomatoes were introduced into South America from Central America and potatoes originally grew around the Peru area, before spreading throughout the world.

E

Ear ornaments were a sign of the wearer's nobility. A noble's son had his ears pierced to show that he had become a warrior.

Empire of the Incas extended 4,000 kilometres north to south through modern Ecuador, Peru, Bolivia, Chile, and the north-western tip of Argentina.

Farming implements of the Incas surpassed those of Central America. The *taclla,* (foot plough), a 2-metres long pole with bronze or hardwood point, had a footrest and handle. Bronze-bladed hoes and stone clod-breakers were used.

H

Hunting in the Inca empire was a privilege reserved mainly for the royal

Bolivian women weaving

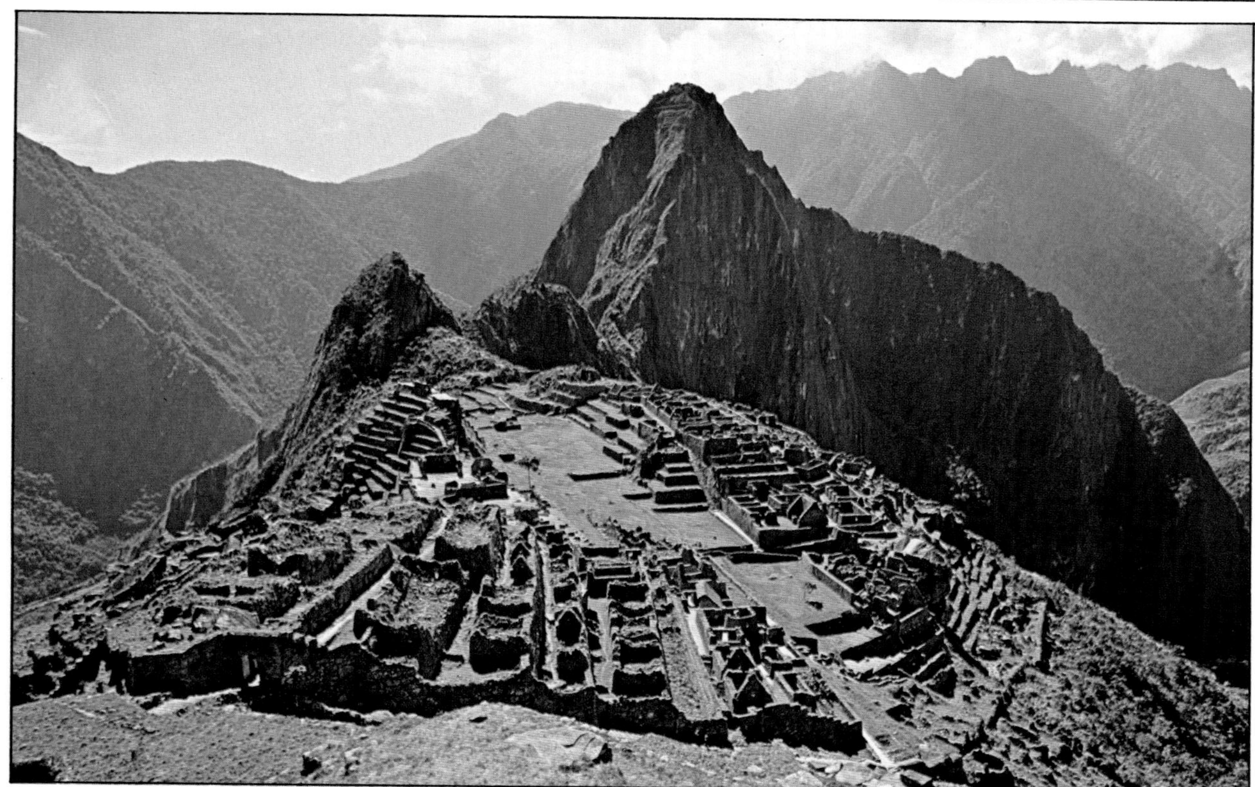

Left: Machu Picchu, lost city of the Incas found only in 1911, is perched high in the Andes near Cuzco. Surprisingly, the Spaniards never knew of its existence.

The Inca empire

Inca, the name for the emperor, the empire and the tribe, derived from the name of the ruling family. Inca legends do not go back beyond 1200, when the first Inca emperor is said to have begun his reign.

Inca history begins with the ninth emperor, Pachacutec Inca Yupanqui (reigned 1438-71) who probably built the city of Cuzco. He and his son Tupac Inca (reigned 1471-93) achieved a series of lightning conquests. Under father and son the empire expanded to cover nearly 100,000 square kilometres with perhaps eight million inhabitants, but it lasted only two generations (1476-1534).

The very existence of the Inca empire marked a triumph over geography. Most of its forts, towns and cities including Cuzco, MACHU PICCHU and Ollontaytambo stood far up in isolated mountain valleys in the Andes. Despite the absence of wheeled vehicles, good roads connected these mountain settlements with outposts of the empire, linking the hot, rainless deserts of the north to the tropical wet coastlands of the south.

The welfare state

The Inca empire was a despotism, with an absolute ruler, supported by a hereditary aristocracy, where all people had their place; the family, nobles, workers and slaves. Nevertheless the well-being of each social order was taken into account. Censuses were taken and local government was geared to units of ten. Each ten heads of family had a leader, and each 40,000 families a governor. In conquered territories, local officials were kept on to implement the Inca system. They imposed their own language, Quechua, upon the whole empire; bureaucracy thrived, and government inspectors enforced social and moral codes diligently. One of their many duties was to call from house to house checking that women were good housewives and mothers.

Begging was unknown and unnecessary in this welfare state. Officials provided 'pensions' for OLD PEOPLE in the form of food and other necessities. They also allotted suitable work to disabled people and regulated their lives: blind persons could marry only other blind persons, and dwarfs had to marry dwarfs. However, strict laws governed peoples lives. Able-bodied boys

Above: A gold knife made by a Chimu craftsman was intended for use in religious ceremonies rather than in sacrifices. The Chimu god figured on the handle was absorbed into the Incas' pantheon.

household, although it was permitted to others at certain times. Slings and clubs provided the main hunting weapons.

I **Inca emperors** supposedly date from 1200. Seven of the 13 reigned before 1400. Little is known about them except that they fought constant war against neighbouring states.

Inca temples served as living quarters for priests and attendants. The Temple of the Sun in Cuzco was plated with gold. Ceremonies often took place in the central square of Cuzco. The chief priest of the Temple of the Sun (probably a close relative of the Inca) headed the priesthood of the empire.

J **Jaguar cult** was widespread from about 850 BC and dominated the Chavín culture. The jaguar was probably the chief deity. People believed that certain men could turn themselves into jaguars at night.

L **Lake Titicaca,** sacred to the Andean people, is the subject of many legends. One tells that in pre-Inca times the Sun failed to rise. After much praying, the Sun rose from an island in the lake and at the same time, a white father figure appeared from the south working miracles like a god. People called him *Ticci Viracocha* or *Tuapaca.* Some of the teachings of his cult matched those of Jesus. This may account for the speedy Christianization of the Incas.

Inca baths

M **Machu Picchu,** most visited of the Inca cities, lies 80 km north-west of Cuzco, perched high on a rock between two mountain peaks. A 'lost city' until 1911, Machu Picchu was found largely intact. It may have belonged to the early Incas.

Mummies. Coastal people buried their dead in deep sandy graves after first wrapping them in cloth, then the skin of a sea lion or a woollen blanket. The bodies were buried in a sitting position, heads propped on knees. In the dry sand they became dessicated (dried out) and mummified.

O **Old people,** kept by the state, were expected to make themselves generally useful around the house. Officials found disabled people suitable jobs. For ex-

and girls of marriageable age lined up in front of the governor for the boys to choose wives, and the governor settled pairing disputes on the spot. Torture or death came to those who left one district for another without permission and CRIMINALS received just but severe sentences.

Agriculture

Unlike the Central Americans, the Incas had two useful animals. Alpacas provided wool for CLOTHES and llamas served as light pack animals. Although llamas did not pull ploughs, the Incas had much better FARMING IMPLEMENTS than the Central Americans. Highland PLOUGHING began in August, and farmers had to till land belonging to the government and temples first, then their own. The chief CROPS included potatoes and maize from which they made *chicha* (a rough alcohol). They also chewed the dried leaves of the coca plant as a narcotic. HUNTING was a privilege reserved for the nobility although fish were caught along the coastlands and in lakes.

Medicine, science and technology

Like the Maya, the Incas practised the strange custom of flattening babies' heads by pressing them between boards. Surgeon-priests practised TREPANNING (cutting, drilling or scraping out parts of the skull).

The Incas used pebbles in a tray as a kind of abacus and weighed with scales and stone weights, but their main device for recording numbers was the QUIPU. They measured the time of day by the position of the sun, and probably had three ten-day weeks in a month. Extra days were added occasionally.

Early Peruvians were well advanced in metallurgy. Inca bronzesmiths produced a variety of articles, ranging from axes to tweezers and ceremonial objects.

Architecture, art and religion

The Incas and their predecessors built with ADOBE and stone. Their stone WALLS interlocked exactly and needed no mortar. The Incas did not use the arch, but the roofs of earth tombs around the Moche River have a form of arching. Houses had wall vents for ventilation, but no chimneys; smoke escaped through the doorways.

INCA TEMPLES housed priests and cult objects rather than worshippers. Religious practices included offerings to Viracocha (the supreme god) and other deities; fasting, consulting oracles; 'reading' the organs of animals; omens; and blood sacrifice. At religious ceremonies people danced frenziedly and became drunk from *chicha.* At death, they looked forward to either a luxurious heaven or a comfortless hell. Myths and legends surrounding the many deities often incorporated fabulous animals. Inca religion also included nature worship, stone worship, cult heroes, the concept of a great flood, and belief in the creation of successive races of men by the deities.

Above: Boats made from reeds, called 'little sea horses' by their makers, have been used for perhaps 2,000 years on Lake Titicaca.

Above: Naturalistic scenes painted in bright colours make many Inca pots particularly distinctive.

The end of the Incas

When Tupac Inca died in about 1487, Huayna Capac succeeded him. At his death in 1525, the empire was divided between his two sons, Huascar (c.1495-1533) and Atahualpa (c.1500-33). By 1532 Atahualpa had imprisoned Huascar in a bid to win the whole empire. At this stage came invasion by some 177 Spaniards equipped with horses and firearms. Led by Francisco Pizarro (c.1470-1541), the Spaniards ambushed Atahualpa and held him hostage. Although the Incas paid an enormous ransom for Atahualpa, the Spaniards broke faith and killed him. In spite of civil war among the Incas, organized popular uprisings delayed the complete Spanish conquest until 1539. In time, Peru became part of the empire of the western Europeans.

---

ample, blind persons cleaned the seeds from cotton.

Origins. The ancestors of the peoples of ancient America almost certainly came from Asia. Probably they walked over from Russia to Alaska before the 90 km Bering Strait formed. Mongoloid features can be seen in present-day descendants of the migrants.

P **Ploughing** involved the men moving ahead in line while their womenfolk followed, breaking the clods of soil with hoes.

Q **Quipu** was a device consisting of several knotted cords attached to a main cord. The colour, length and thickness of the knots indicated different numerical values. Quipus could also record coded messages. A hereditary caste of quipu keepers kept accounts and decoded messages. They guarded their secrets jealously.

R **Roads.** Although they inherited good coastal and mountain roads from earlier peoples, the Incas did not use the wheel. They maintained and improved the roads so that armies, human porters and pack llamas could move about speedily. Messengers, running in relays, provided a communications system with relays every 2-3 km.

T **Tiahuanaco** predated AD 500. Its great gate of the sun cut from one stone block and adorned with carvings, once formed part of a ceremonial enclosure. This, and other stones weighing up to 100 tonnes, had to be transported several kilometres.

Trepanning (removal of pieces of the skull) was practised by Inca surgeon-priests. More than half of their 'patients' survived.

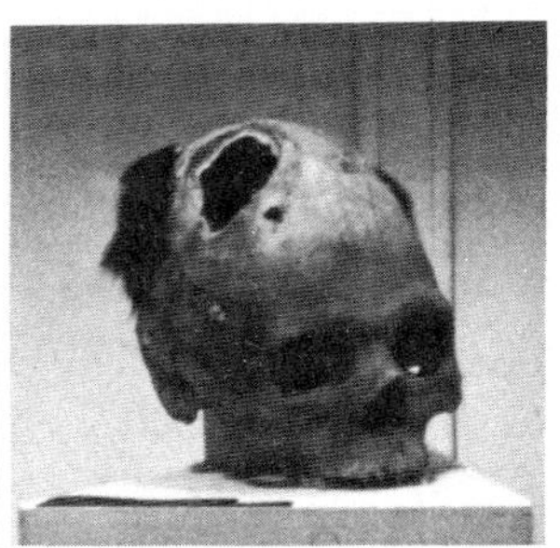

Skull showing trepanning, Peru

Possibly they treated soldiers clubbed on the head, to relieve pressure on the brain. Occasionally, gold plate was used to cover the cavity where the bone had been removed.

W **Walls** of the Andean buildings had their stones interlocking exactly. They withstood earthquakes – unlike modern buildings.

Index

Page numbers in **bold** type refer to the reference sections. Page numbers in *italics* refer to illustrations.

Acknowledgements

Contributing artists
Marion Appleton, Peter Archer, Charles Bannerman, Raymond Brown, Richard Coggan, Chris Forsey, Geoff Hunt, Ivan Lapper, Dennis Lascelles, Jim Marks, Nigel Osborne

The Publishers also wish to thank the following:
Aerofilms 10B
Ashmolean Museum, Oxford 106C
Bibliothèque Nationale, Paris 102TL
Bodleian Library, Oxford 119TR
Jean Bottin 33C, 43B, 68T, 125C
British Library 110C
British Museum 18-19T, 44C, 45C, 71TC, 111BR
J. Allan Cash 18TC
Peter Clayton 19C, 22B, 23BL, 28BR, 30CR B, 31BL BR, 42, 49BR, 70B
Colorpix 7B, 18BR, 20BR, 21BL BR, 57TR, 62TL, 63TR, 64TR, 69TL, 96C, 123C
Douglas Dickins 77B, 79B, 94BR, 97B, 99B, 101B, 102B, 103BC, 116B, 124B, 128B
Robert Estail 106B
Werner Forman Archive 35B, 38BC BR, 40BC, 41BL, 42B, 44BL, 45B, 49BC, 50C, 57BC, 59BR, 60BC, 67BR, 76B, 86B, 90B, 91BR, 93B, 96TL, 98BC, 98BR, 100B, 108B, 109B, 114B, 117B, 119BR, 121B, 122B, 123B, 125B
Fotomas Index 111BC
Richard & Sally Greenhill 57C
Sonia Halliday 31C, 32C, 53CL, 71BC, 81B, 86TL, 87B, 89TL CR, 104CR
Robert Harding Associates 6B, 8B, 9B, 29B, 33BC, 34T, 44BL, 46B, 47BC BR, 48B, 50BR, 51BC, 52T, 56B C, 57BR, 58BC BR, 59CR BC, 60CL BR, 67BC, 71BR, 73BR, 75BC BR, 91BC, 92B
Michael Holford 7TR, 9TL, 14TR, 15TR, 17TL TR, 19TR, 36TL TR, 37T, 45TR, 47TR, 48CL, 54B, 59TR, 64BL, 69TR, 74B, 82, 84B, 90C, 98CL, 99C, 100TL, 107C B, 112C, 113, 114TL, 115B, 117TL, 122TL, 123C, 127CR
Sarah King 103BR
Kunsthistorisches Museum, Vienna 77CR
William Macquitty 21TR, 25TR CR B, 50BL, 51BR, 52B, 54TL, 61CL, 94BC, 102TR
Mansell Collection 12TR, 18BL
Middle East Archive 99TR
Tony Morrison 126B, 127B
Musée du Louvre/Hubert Josse 43TL
Musées Nationaux, Paris 14TL
Oesterreichische Nationalbibliothek, Vienna 103C
Josephine Powell 24T, 26B, 28T, 30CR, 31T, 32T, 61BC BR, 62BC BR, 63BC BR, 64B, 82B, 83B, 85B, 88B, 89B, 95B, 96B, 113B
Walter Rawlings 127TR
Scala 110B
Servizio Editoriale Fotografico 75TR, 78CL
Ronald Sheridan 9TR, 11CR B, 12C B, 13C TR B, 14C B, 15TL BL B TC, 16B, 17BC BR, 19TL C B, 20R BL, 21TC, 27B, 28BC, 32B, 33BR, 34BC BR, 36B, 37B, 39B, 40TR BR, 41BR, 43CL, 48TR, 50TL TR, 53B, 55TR B BR, 67, 68BR, 69T B, 70TR, 72B, 73BC, 74CL, 75CL, 78B, 80B, 81C, 83, 88C, 98CL, 100C, 104B, 105CR B, 120B
Snark International 11CL, 36CR, 51TR, 105TL, 112TR B
Spink & Son Ltd 91TR
Mireille Vautier 116C, 121T, 128T C
ZEFA/Clive Sawyer 97C
Ziolo/R. Roland 26C